Lecture Notes in Computer Science 14636

The series Lecture Notes in Computer Science (LNCS), including its subseries Lecture Notes in Artificial Intelligence (LNAI) and Lecture Notes in Bioinformatics (LNBI), has established itself as a medium for the publication of new developments in computer science and information technology research, teaching, and education.

LNCS enjoys close cooperation with the computer science R & D community, the series counts many renowned academics among its volume editors and paper authors, and collaborates with prestigious societies. Its mission is to serve this international community by providing an invaluable service, mainly focused on the publication of conference and workshop proceedings and postproceedings. LNCS commenced publication in 1973.

Nilufar Baghaei · Raian Ali · Khin Win ·
Kiemute Oyibo
Editors

Persuasive Technology

19th International Conference, PERSUASIVE 2024
Wollongong, NSW, Australia, April 10–12, 2024
Proceedings

Springer

Editors
Nilufar Baghaei
The University of Queensland
St Lucia, QLD, Australia

Khin Win
University of Wollongong
Wollongong, NSW, Australia

Raian Ali
Hamad Bin Khalifa University
Doha, Qatar

Kiemute Oyibo
York University
Toronto, ON, Canada

ISSN 0302-9743 ISSN 1611-3349 (electronic)
Lecture Notes in Computer Science
ISBN 978-3-031-58225-7 ISBN 978-3-031-58226-4 (eBook)
https://doi.org/10.1007/978-3-031-58226-4

This Springer imprint is published by the registered company Springer Nature Switzerland AG
The registered company address is: Gewerbestrasse 11, 6330 Cham, Switzerland

Preface

Persuasive Technology (PT) is a multidisciplinary field that centers on designing, advancing, and assessing interactive technologies with the goal of influencing people's attitudes or behaviors through persuasion, without resorting to coercion or deceit. Our community seeks to enrich individuals' lives across diverse areas like health, education, safety, and the environment by empowering them to pursue personal behavior changes.

The PERSUASIVE conference series is the leading venue to meet and discuss cutting-edge theoretical, methodological, and technical perspectives and to present recent insights from research and development. The conference provides a venue for networking between researchers and practitioners from all corners of the world and has been held in previous years in different places such as Chicago, USA; Padua, Italy; Linköping, Sweden; Oulu, Finland; Sydney, Australia; Amsterdam, The Netherlands; Salzburg, Austria; Waterloo, Canada; Limassol, Cyprus; Aalborg, Denmark; Bournemouth, UK; Doha, Qatar; and Eindhoven, The Netherlands.

The 19th International Conference on Persuasive Technology (PERSUASIVE 2024) was hosted by the University of Wollongong, NSW, Australia, on 9–12 April. The Doctoral Consortium session and the Steering Committee meeting were held on the 9th. Four adjunct workshops were held on the 10th: Algorithmic Behavior Change Support (ALBECS 2024), Personalizing Persuasive Technologies Workshop (PPT 2024), Data & Design Education and Practice: Changing behavior through data-driven design (DDEP 2024), and Behavior Change Support Systems (BCSS 2024). On April 11th and 12th, the main conference took place with six single-track sessions, including oral presentations of the accepted papers. The allocation for the full papers and extended abstracts was 15+5(QA) minutes per paper and short papers had 10+5(QA). The program furthermore included two keynotes on personalised persuasion and persuasive technology for mental health, presented by Shlomo Berkovsky (Macquarie University) and Terry Fleming (Victoria University of Wellington) respectively as well as a poster session and industry demos.

This volume contains the accepted papers presented during the main conference. Seventy-one (71) submissions were made by 222 authors from 18 countries around the globe, out of which 51 were submitted to the main track. The accepted papers were grouped into four sessions in the conference and proceedings, based on their content: 1) Methods for Tailoring and Personalization, 2) Persuasive Design and Applications, 3) Persuasive Strategies, & 4) Persuasive Technologies and Ethics. The papers were reviewed by the program committee in a double-blind review process conducted in EasyChair. Overall, 57 reviewers were assigned to review the papers. Each paper received at least 3 detailed and constructive reviews, which not only provided the program chairs with significant insight concerning the individual submissions but also ensured that the authors were provided with high-quality feedback and recommendations for the final version of their paper. The final list of papers to be presented at the conference was decided after a careful assessment of the reviews. Out of the 51 submissions, 14 papers were accepted as full papers (acceptance rate of 27% for full papers) and 8 papers were accepted as short papers.

We would like to thank all the reviewers and organizers that contributed to the success of PERSUASIVE 2024. In particular, we would like to thank the authors from 18 countries (Europe: 6, Asia: 5, North America: 2, South America: 1, and Middle East: 4) who submitted their papers to the conference. We also thank the program committee for the critical role they played in the review process and for helping to promote the conference. We are also thankful to Wollongong University for the organisation and sponsoring of PERSUASIVE 2024.

February 2024

Nilufar Baghaei
Raian Ali
Khin Than Win
Kiemute Oyibo

Organization

General Chair

Khin Than Win	University of Wollongong, Australia

Program Chairs

Nilufar Baghaei	University of Queensland, Australia
Raian Ali	Hamad Bin Khalifa University, Qatar

Workshops and Tutorial Chairs

Luca Chittaro	University of Udine, Italy
Wenzhen Xu	Hitotsubashi University, Japan

Doctoral Consortium Chairs

Rita Orji	Dalhousie University, Canada
Alexander Meschtscherjakov	Paris Lodron University of Salzburg, Austria
Jaap Ham	Eindhoven University of Technology, The Netherlands

Poster Track Chairs

Alaa Al-Slaity	Dalhousie University, Canada
Vivienne Guan	University of Wollongong, Australia

Local Chair

Elena Vlahu-Gjorgievska	University of Wollongong, Australia

Proceedings Chair

Kiemute Oyibo	York University, Canada

Industrial Chair

Roberto Legaspi	KDDI Research, Inc., Japan

Web and Communication Chair

Mark Freeman	University of Wollongong, Australia

Program Committee Members

Rhodora Abadia	University of South Australia, Australia
Ifeoma Adaji	University of British Columbia, Canada
Dena Al-Thani	Hamad Bin Khalifa University, Qatar
Aftab Alam	Kyung Hee University, South Korea
Mona Alhasani	Dalhousie University, Canada
Raian Ali	Hamad Bin Khalifa University, Qatar
Sameha Ahmed Ali Alshakhsi	Hamad Bin Khalifa University, Qatar
Alaa Alslaity	Dalhousie University, Canada
Emily Arden-Close	Bournemouth University, UK
Areej Babiker	Hamad Bin Khalifa University, Qatar
Nilufar Baghaei	University of Queensland, Australia
Shlomo Berkovsky	Macquarie University, Australia
Fred Charles	Bournemouth University, UK
Luca Chittaro	University of Udine, Italy
Nelly Condori-Fernández	Universidad Santiago de Compostela, Spain
Berardina Nadja De Carolis	Università degli Studi di Bari, Italy
Boris De Ruyter	Philips Research, The Netherlands
Peter De Vries	University of Twente, The Netherlands
Alexander Felfernig	Technical University Graz, Austria
Terry Fleming	Te Herenga Waka I Victoria University of Wellington, New Zealand
Thomas Fotiadis	University of Cyprus, Cyprus
Mark Freeman	University of Wollongong, Australia
Yann Glémarec	Inria Rennes, Université de Rennes 1, France
Vivienne Guan	University of Wollongong, Australia
Jaap Ham	Eindhoven University of Technology, The Netherlands

Curtis Haugtvedt	Ohio State University, USA
Paul Salvador Inventado	California State University Fullerton, USA
Md Rafiqul Islam	Australian Institute of Higher Education, Australia
Sriram Iyengar	University of Arizona, USA
Randy Klaassen	University of Twente, The Netherlands
Roberto Legaspi	KDDI Research Inc., Japan
Magnus Liebherr	University of Duisburg-Essen, Germany
Uwe Matzat	Eindhoven University of Technology, The Netherlands
Alexander Meschtscherjakov	University of Salzburg, Austria
Christos Mettouris	University of Cyprus, Cyprus
Cees Midden	TU Eindhoven, The Netherlands
George Mikros	National and Kapodistrian University of Athens, Greece
Mohammad Naiseh	Bournemouth University, UK
Harri Oinas-Kukkonen	University of Oulu, Finland
Rita Orji	Dalhousie University, Canada
Oladapo Oyebode	Dalhousie University, Canada
Kiemute Oyibo	York University, Canada
Zelinna Pablo	Torrens University Australia, Australia
Constantina Panourgia	Bournemouth University, UK
George Angelos Papadopoulos	University of Cyprus, Cyprus
Daniel Playne	Massey University, New Zealand
Ampere Qiu	Unprovided, Japan
Peter Ruijten	Eindhoven University of Technology, The Netherlands
Stefan Schiffer	iTec|RWTH Aachen University, Germany
Hanne Spelt	Philips Research, The Netherlands
Rhia Trogo	IBM, Philippines
Robby van Delden	University of Twente, The Netherlands
Lisette van Gemert-Pijnen	University of Twente, The Netherlands
Evangelia Vanezi	University of Cyprus, Cyprus
Julita Vassileva	University of Saskatchewan, Canada
Elena Vlahu-Gjorgievska	University of Wollongong, Australia
Isaac Wiafe	University of Ghana, Ghana
Khin Than Win	University of Wollongong, Australia
Burkhard Wuensche	University of Auckland, New Zealand
Wenzhen Xu	Hitotsubashi University, Japan
Affan Yasin	Tsinghua University, China
Leah Zhang-Kennedy	University of Waterloo, Canada

Sponsoring Organizations

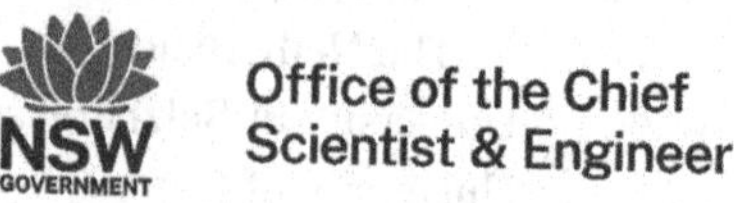

Contents

Harnessing Large Language Models for Automatic Evaluation of Mobile Health Applications Based on Persuasive System Design Principles and Mobile Application Rating Scale

Yasin Afşin[1(✉)] and Tuğba Taşkaya Temizel[2]

[1] Department of Information Systems, Middle East Technical University, Ankara, Turkey
yasin.afsin@metu.edu.tr

[2] Department of Data Informatics, Middle East Technical University, Ankara, Turkey
ttemizel@metu.edu.tr

Abstract. Mobile applications have seen a growing prevalence in the healthcare sector, yet the absence of comprehensive regulations and preliminary assessments can lead to significant frustration and time loss for users. To address this, Persuasive System Design (PSD) principles and the Mobile App Rating Scale (MARS) have emerged as popular tools for gauging application quality and user engagement. However, their manual assessment requirements hinder scalability, especially given the high volume of mobile health applications in the market. This study introduces a novel automatic evaluation approach designed to enhance the assessment of mobile health applications, leveraging PSD and MARS. The proposed method mainly relies on large language models to filter user reviews and generate sentence embeddings for classifying the PSD principles implemented in these applications. The results, calculated using performance metrics that compare the model's predictions with expert evaluations, demonstrate the feasibility of predicting the application's implementation of PSD principles based on user reviews while also highlighting the limitations of using application descriptions alone for successful prediction. Furthermore, the study augments the predicted classification probabilities of PSD principles with supplementary descriptive data, such as installation counts and user ratings, to predict MARS scores. Regression models, trained using these techniques, consistently outperform basic models, with feature importance scores showing the significant contribution of predicted classification probabilities of PSD principles to the models. In summary, this study suggests that automatic evaluation techniques can effectively assess the quality and user engagement of mobile health applications, offering a viable alternative to manual assessments.

Keywords: Persuasive System Design · Mobile Application Quality · Large Language Models

N. Baghaei et al. (Eds.): PERSUASIVE 2024, LNCS 14636, pp. 1–14, 2024.
https://doi.org/10.1007/978-3-031-58226-4_1

1 Introduction

Mobile Health Applications (MHAs) serve patients, healthcare providers, and caregivers for numerous purposes, including patient record management, health condition monitoring, and motivation for specific diseases. These applications offer cost-effective healthcare services, supported by the studies [7,26,30]. The ever-growing popularity of MHAs is evident, with approximately 41.5 thousand in Apple's App Store and 54.5 thousand in Google Play Store as of Q3 2022 [42,43]. However, research shows that low-quality MHAs, often provide inaccurate information or inappropriate responses to users [2]. As the market continues to expand with new applications, mobile application evaluations for the effectiveness and quality of MHAs are necessary.

Persuasive System Design (PSD) offers a framework for developing and assessing mobile applications' abilities to influence user behavior and attitudes [35]. Additionally, the Mobile Application Rating Scale (MARS) [44] assesses the quality of MHAs, considering various aspects such as functionality, engagement, and aesthetics. However, both methods depend on manual expert assessments, which can be time-consuming and inefficient in terms of resources. This limits their widespread use, especially when considering the vast number of mobile health apps available.

This study proposes automatic evaluation techniques as an alternative to manual assessments. Three datasets are created for evaluation purposes, with each including different feature combinations, such as application descriptions, user reviews, and application qualities. Each dataset was filtered through textual entailment-based classification using pre-trained LLMs and used for each experiment. The filtered textual data is then used to create sentence embeddings (numerical representations of sentences), combined with descriptive mobile application data. These feature sets are then used as input for supervised machine learning models to test the hypothesis of automating PSD principle predictions and MARS quality scores for MHAs. User reviews and application descriptions are hypothesised as containing the MHA's main features, functionalities, and purposes from the perspectives of users and developers, making them valuable for content analysis related to employed PSD principles. Additionally, the significance of other information such as customer ratings and installation counts, along with the predicted likelihood of PSD principles, are investigated for predicting overall MARS scores.

This study addresses two research questions:

1. How can we predict PSD principles of an expert-evaluated MHA based on user reviews and application descriptions?
2. How can we predict MHA quality on the scale of MARS using the collected descriptive MHA information? How do the PSD principles, predicted by the models, contribute to this prediction?

This study makes several significant contributions to the field of Mobile Health Applications (MHAs) evaluation. The paper's approach significantly enhances scalability by reducing the time required for evaluations once the model is built, offering a more efficient alternative to traditional manual assessments. It focuses on evaluating key Persuasive System Design (PSD) principles such as *Tailoring*, *Self-monitoring*, *Praise*, and *Reminders*, which were chosen for their relevance to MHAs and the feasibility of assessment through available data. Moreover, the study advances the understanding of MHA qualities in the context of MARS and reports the importance of various features in these regressions. Furthermore, we employ pre-trained Large Language Models (LLMs) in a manner that diverges from the Generative AI perspective, applying them to text classification and feature set generation. The experiments were mainly carried out on the dataset from the study of Geirhos et al. [12].

In this study, Sect. 2 summarizes earlier research, while Sect. 3 details the architecture and methodologies employed. Section 4 covers dataset collection, analysis, and experiment outcomes. Section 5 summarizes and extends the discussion of the results. Lastly, Sect. 6 concludes the study.

2 Related Work

2.1 Mobile Application Quality

While platforms like *Google Play Store* or *Apple's App Store* mandate rules and regulations for mobile applications, the quality of these applications can vary significantly. Metrics like user ratings, reviews, and download counts may not always provide reliable indicators of quality, especially in the case of MHAs [16]. Consequently, systematic evaluations of MHAs are essential to prevent potential adverse events [9]. The Mobile Application Rating Scale (MARS) offers a comprehensive assessment of MHA quality across four main categories: engagement, functionality, aesthetics, and information quality, using a five-point Likert scale [44]. Studies have explored the relationship between MHA quality, as measured by MARS, and application specifications using factors like application's last update date, install counts, developer affiliation, application categories, and user ratings [13,18,20]. Some studies have found a significant correlation between MARS scores and user ratings [23,39], while others have not [13,18,20]. All these studies focus on quality tools and factors that demonstrate their importance in the health application categories.

2.2 Persuasive System Design

The persuasive system design (PSD) framework [35] outlines 28 persuasive design principles categorised into primary task support, dialogue support, social support, and system credibility. These principles guide the development of persuasive mobile applications. Notably, PSD principles have been explored in mental health applications [5,19] and personal well-being applications [27], revealing their importance in these contexts. Natural language processing (NLP) and topic modelling techniques are also employed to identify PSD principles in mobile health applications [4,36], showing that these principles align with manual expert assessments. Additionally, the relationship between PSD principles and application quality scores is explored in the context of diabetes self-management MHAs [12]. The results emphasise the significance of PSD principles in enhancing user engagement with MHAs.

2.3 Natural Language Processing

NLP, mainly focusing on understanding and generating human language [29], encompasses Natural Language Understanding (NLU) and Natural Language Generation (NLG) [22]. It has evolved from rule-based approaches to statistical techniques and deep learning models. Large language models have demonstrated exceptional performance improvements in various NLP tasks, including text classification, machine translation, text generation, and question answering [46]. NLP techniques have been successfully applied to health-related data, enabling the extraction of information about symptoms, medications [24,28,40], and potential medical problems [31]. Moreover, NLP has been employed to automate expert evaluations in various fields, such as classifying stroke patients [10], detecting patients with congestive heart failure risk [11], and reviewing radiology reports [37]. NLP techniques enable comprehensive analysis, replacing manual expert evaluations, eliminating human errors, and saving time.

3 Method

This proposed methodology includes four major phases: dataset collection and preprocessing (Step 1), filtering relevant text (Step 2), PSD principles prediction (Step 3), and MARS quality score prediction (Step 4), as shown in Fig. 1.

3.1 Dataset Collection and Preprocessing

Application descriptions and user reviews were collected using the Google Play Store Scraper API [17] including user reviews in all available languages, and non-English reviews were translated using the Google Translate API [14]. To prepare the data for analysis, preprocessing is applied to both user reviews and application descriptions. This involved removing emojis, hashtags, and special characters. We also eliminated reviews containing less than two words, as longer sentences are necessary for referencing PSD principles effectively.

3.2 Textual Entailment

In this study, there are multiple user reviews and single application description for each MHA. However, not all of these texts are informative regarding PSD principles. We employed the Natural Language Inference (NLI) classification to determine their relevance to PSD principles and filtered only the related texts. NLI classifiers evaluated logical relationships between two sentences: a premise and a hypothesis. The premise is an assumed truth or condition, while

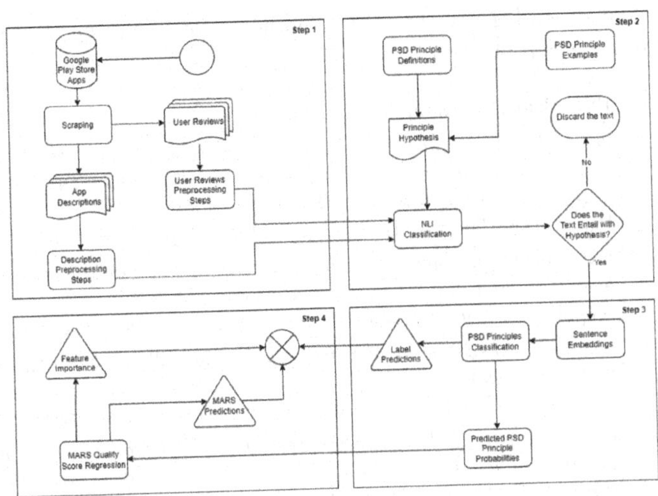

Fig. 1. Architecture diagram

the hypothesis is tested against these assumptions to determine their logical relations. NLI classifiers categorize the relationship as "entailed" (supporting), "contradicted" (opposing), or "neutral" (insufficient information).

NLI classifications were implemented for both user reviews and application descriptions to eliminate irrelevant data with PSD principles and textual data was filtered effectively. Each premise was generated from user reviews and application descriptions while hypotheses were created based on descriptions from [35] and examples provided to experts during PSD principle labeling in [12]. Each hypothesis in Table 1, was created starting with *"The text is about..."*, to establish a direct semantic relationship between the hypothesis and the input texts. The classification was performed as zero-shot due to the absence of ground truth labels. Only inputs classified as "entailed" were retained for subsequent steps, while others were discarded. The XLNET [45] NLI classifier, fine-tuned on multi-purpose datasets, was chosen for this task due to its strong performance in the Adversarial NLI benchmark [34].

3.3 PSD Principles Prediction

Filtered user reviews related to hypotheses for each MHA were concatenated to form paragraphs. Sentence embeddings were generated from these paragraphs using the ST5-large sentence transformer model [33], which excels in paragraph-based text classification tasks according to the Massive Text Embedding Benchmark (MTEB) [32]. The generated text embeddings were utilized in well-known machine learning classification models, each exhibiting different characteristics: LightGBM [21], Support Vector Machine (SVM) [15], and Elasticnet [47]. These models were chosen for their capability to handle high-dimensional data, a common challenge in text classification. SVM and Elasticnet models address overfit-

Table 1. Examples and generated NLI hypotheses for *Tailoring*, *Self-monitoring*, *Praise*, and *Reminders* principles.

Principle	PSD Principle Example and Hypothesis
Tailoring	Ex: *Adapting information according to type of diabetes* [12]. *Personal trainer Web site provides different information content for different user groups, e.g., beginners and professionals* [35]. Hypothesis: The text is about providing adaptive information for users.
Self-monitoring	Ex: *Feature for glucose tracking* [12]. *Heart rate monitor presents a user's heart rate and the duration of the exercise* [35]. Hypothesis: The text is about tracking user performances.
Praise	Ex: *Feedback/compliments on tracked data* [12]. *Mobile application uses text messages with praises to motivate teenagers* [35]. Hypothesis: The text is about motivating users with praises.
Reminders	Ex: *System-based daily pop-up messages* [12]. *Caloric balance monitoring application sends text messages to its users as daily reminders* [35]. Hypothesis: The text is about sending notifications to users.

ting and high dimensionality through regularization parameters. Although LightGBM models may overfit in small datasets, ensemble methods were employed to mitigate this issue [6,25]. To optimize the LightGBM model's hyperparameters, the Optuna framework was used [3], while grid search was employed to select hyperparameters for the SVM and Elasticnet models. Given the small dataset size, high number of folds was used, equal to the count of positive labels for PSD principles. This setup allows for more extensive training splits, with each positive-labeled data placed in a separate test fold. The trained models for each fold were saved with their data splits for predicting unseen datasets. Nested stratified k-fold cross-validation was used to train, validate, and test the models. The primary performance metric was the Matthews Correlation Coefficient (MCC), which is an effective performance metric for imbalanced datasets that considers all four confusion matrix categories [8]. Accuracy, precision, recall, and F1 scores were also reported. Moreover, this study was the first, to our knowledge, to predict employed PSD principles through automated means, so we had to employ simple baseline models to benchmark our model. The first baseline model (B1) randomly predicts labels using true label weights, while the second baseline model (B2) predicts labels as the most frequently observed label in the training dataset, serving for accuracy comparisons.

App descriptions offer a more compact corpus compared to the user reviews due to each MHA having just one description, primarily focusing on diabetes self-management. We ensured the informativeness of these descriptions through additional manual investigation and annotation based on the criteria from [12]. These criteria encompassed aspects such as tailoring information for type-1 and type-2 diabetes, features for self-monitoring of health statuses like glucose levels, reminders through notifications, and motivational praise about user health status.

3.4 MARS Quality Scores Prediction

In this step, to predict MARS quality scores various categorical and continuous features alongside the predicted classification probabilities of PSD principles were utilized. These descriptive features were gathered from the application store. Install counts were treated as ordinal categorical features, while predicted probabilities and average user ratings were treated as continuous variables. Additionally, binary categorical features, such as the presence of advertisements, published privacy policies, shared developer addresses, advertisement support, and shared developer websites, were considered. The target variable, MARS quality scores, exhibits nonparametric behavior with boundaries set by maximum and minimum values, making it challenging to fit known distributions. Given this mixed feature type and the nature of the target variable, decision tree-based LightGBM [21] and CatBoost [38] regressor models were selected, and trained using the 5-fold nested cross-validation method. CatBoost was chosen as the preferred model due to its effective handling of categorical features, which are the predominant feature types in this context. CatBoost also utilizes ordered target statistics in a different way compared to the LightGBM model. Various metrics were calculated and compared with baseline models to assess model performances. These metrics include the mean absolute error (MAE), root mean squared error (RMSE), and relative root mean squared error (Relative RMSE). Among these, Relative RMSE was chosen as the primary performance metric because it expresses the error rate as a percentage relative to the mean observed values, clearly indicating the error magnitude in terms of percentage. Feature contributions were also calculated using the LightGBM and CatBoost regression models. These feature importance functions reveal information gains in decision tree splits. By analyzing the results, the least contributing features were detected and tested with regression models that excluded them to assess if predictions improved with a reduced feature set.

4 Experiments

4.1 Datasets

PSD Principles Datasets. In the study by Geirhos et al.'s study [12], one hundred and twenty MHAs were manually assessed by domain experts for 24 of the 28 recommended PSD principles, excluding non-technical principles to focus on design features that were only provided through the technical system itself. The lists of MHAs with binary labels indicating the presence of these principles were generated for 89 Google Play Store applications. Seventy five applications were found from this list by matching application and developer names. On May 2, 2022, application descriptions and user reviews were scrapped to create the Descriptions Dataset (DD). The scraping process was conducted using open-source reviews, ensuring the exclusion of any personal information from reviewers and adhering to the terms and conditions of the website. Only reviews posted before the expert evaluation data collection date (December 2020) were included.

For balanced datasets in supervised learning, principles with ratios close to 50% are preferred to achieve a more balanced dataset that affects the training of models. *Tailoring*, *Self-monitoring*, *Praise*, and *Reminders* principles from both the Reviews Dataset (RD) and Descriptions Dataset (DD) were selected based on their ratios and their higher correlations with MARS Quality Scores and PSD categories of Primary Task Support and Dialogue Support as identified in Geirhos et al.'s study [12].

MARS Quality Score Dataset. The Mobile Health App Database (MHAD) serves as an open repository for MARS quality ratings of MHAs [41]. To obtain data from MHAD, a custom web scraper was developed using Python's Selenium library. This scraper compiled a list of 489 MHAs, including their names, webpage links, and MARS quality scores. As of May 4, 2022, 194 MHAs with user reviews were identified. Additional descriptive features for these MHAs were gathered using the Google Play Store API [17]. These collected variables were then combined with the scraped MARS scores to create the MARS Quality Scores Dataset (MD), which serves as our primary dataset.

4.2 Results

PSD Principles Prediction from User Reviews. In the textual entailment step, hypothesis-related reviews were correctly classified as "Entails", while there were occasional misclassifications for the "Neutral" and "Contradicts" labels, which were assumed as "not related" and subsequently discarded. For example, the user review *"Easy to keep up with has reminders easier for older people to use"* was incorrectly classified as *Contradicts*, even though there was no evidence contradicting the *Praise* principle's hypothesis. The misclassification between these labels does not impact the implementation in this step. Separate sets of user reviews were obtained for each PSD principle, resulting in different numbers of review paragraphs for *Tailoring*, *Self-monitoring*, *Praise*, and *Reminders*. After filtering, prediction models were trained and fine-tuned. The results of the baselines, LightGBM, SVM, and ElasticNet classifiers were presented in Table 2. The LGB-Rev model outperformed baseline and other models, demonstrating that its superior performance is not due to chance.

PSD Principles Prediction from Application Descriptions. Upon manually comparing the descriptions to the criteria, some examples revealed discrepancies between expert decisions and annotations obtained solely using application descriptions. For instance, the MHA "Diabetes World" mentioned only type-2 diabetes in its description, yet experts labeled it as having the *Tailoring* principle. Similarly, "Glucose Buddy" lacked evidence for *Reminders* and *Praise* principles, but experts identified both in the app. Conversely, the MHA "Diabetes Symptoms Causes" was labeled as not employing the *Self-monitoring* principle by experts, despite the presence of the term "self-monitoring" in the description. The annotations were then compared to the expert-decided PSD principle labels (true labels), resulting in low Matthews Correlation Coefficient

Table 2. Binary classification results for Tailoring, Self-monitoring, Praise and Reminders principles on test folds of nested cross-validation.

Principle	Model	Accuracy	Precision	Recall	F1	MCC
Tailoring	B1	0.66	0.50	0.47	0.48	0.23
	B2	0.66	NA	0	NA	0
	LGB-Rev	**0.89**	**0.86**	**0.80**	**0.83**	**0.75**
	SVC-Rev	0.87	0.80	0.80	0.80	0.70
	Elast-Rev	0.87	0.85	0.73	0.79	0.69
Self-monitoring	B1	0.48	0.33	0.28	0.30	0.11
	B2	0.55	NA	0	NA	0
	LGB-Rev	**0.92**	**0.94**	**0.88**	**0.91**	**0.84**
	SVC-Rev	0.84	0.82	0.82	0.82	0.68
	Elast-Rev	0.87	0.80	0.94	0.87	0.75
Praise	B1	0.46	0.25	0.23	0.24	0.18
	B2	0.61	NA	0	NA	0
	LGB-Rev	**0.78**	**0.77**	**0.63**	**0.69**	**0.53**
	SVC-Rev	0.71	0.64	0.56	0.60	0.37
	Elast-Rev	0.68	0.59	0.63	0.61	0.34
Reminders	B1	0.50	0.20	0.21	0.21	0.16
	B2	0.66	NA	0	NA	0
	LGB-Rev	**0.83**	**0.95**	**0.50**	**0.67**	**0.63**
	SVC-Rev	0.74	0.67	0.50	0.57	0.40
	Elast-Rev	0.69	0.53	0.75	0.62	0.38

Table 3. Annotation performance scores according to expert-evaluated true labels

	Accuracy	Precision	Recall	F1	MCC
Tailoring	0.65	0.42	0.50	0.46	0.21
Self-monitoring	0.69	0.50	0.65	0.57	0.34
Praise	0.67	0.43	0.41	0.42	0.19
Reminders	0.79	0.40	0.38	0.39	0.31

(MCC) scores, for all PSD principles, showing that using application descriptions for PSD principles' classification is uninformative and misleading.

As there was only one application description for each Mobile Health App (MHA), textual entailment was not used for data filtering. Out of the 75 application descriptions, three were found to be related to the hypotheses of the *Tailoring* principle, 14 to *Self-monitoring*, 12 to *Praise*, and 5 to *Reminders*. These counts are consistent with the results of manually comparing descriptions. Both experiments confirm that application descriptions do not provide sufficient information related to PSD principles for further Natural Language Processing-based classification experiments.

MARS Quality Score Regression. Considering the results of the PSD principle prediction step, only user reviews were used in this step. The textual entailment step (Step 2 in Fig. 1) was also applied to the MARS Quality Scores Dataset (MD) to filter user reviews. Filtered user reviews were used as input for the pre-trained PSD classification models (Step 3 in Fig. 1) from the previous experiment to obtain PSD-predicted probabilities. These probabilities, equal to the number of fold counts, were then used in LightGBM and CatBoost regressor models alongside various features, including "app score", "installs", "ads support", "having ads", "dev. website", "dev. address", "privacy pol.". Baseline models utilized mean (B3) and median (B4) MARS quality scores from the training set for performance benchmarks. Absent unsupervised models in existing literature for direct comparison, these baselines validate that the regression model outcomes are not merely random. Table 4 details the regression model results on the test folds. To compare the performances of the LightGBM and CatBoost regression models with the better-performing baseline model (B3), Wilcoxon-Bonferroni post hoc tests were conducted. The results showed that both LightGBM (RMSE = 0.37, MAE = 0.27) and CatBoost (RMSE = 0.38, MAE = 0.29) significantly outperformed the baseline model (RMSE = 0.42, MAE = 0.33), with p-values of 0.0001 for both comparisons (LightGBM - Baseline and CatBoost - Baseline).

Table 4. MARS regression models results in test folds of nested cross-validation

Model	MAE	RMSE	Relative RMSE
B3	0.33	0.42	11.2%
B4	0.33	0.43	11.3%
LG-Reg (All features)	**0.27**	**0.37**	**9.7%**
LG-Reg (8 features)	0.29	0.38	9.8%
Cat-Reg (All features)	**0.29**	**0.38**	**10.1%**
Cat-Reg	0.31	0.41	10.4%

Features Importance of MARS Quality Score Prediction. Overall feature importance values were computed for both the *LG-Reg* and *Cat-Reg* models using the same setup as their prediction performance calculations. The feature importance results, based on information gain from decision tree splits, are presented in Table 5. Both regression models indicate a significant difference in information gain between the last three features and the rest. Therefore, further experiments were conducted with LightGBM and CatBoost regression models after excluding these features. However, as shown in Table 4, the model test performances decreased despite the lower importance of these features compared to others.

Table 5. Feature importance obtained with information gain of regression models.

Feature	LG-Reg	Cat-Reg	Feature	LG-Reg	Cat-Reg
Installs	0.123	0.266	having ads	0.034	0.065
praise prob.	0.166	0.125	ads support	0.033	0.063
reminders prob.	0.173	0.106	**dev. address**	**0.023**	**0.029**
selfmonitoring prob.	0.187	0.096	**dev. website**	**0.003**	**0.005**
tailoring prob.	0.129	0.111	**privacy pol.**	**0.001**	**0.007**
app score	0.128	0.127			

5 Discussion

This study successfully leverages user reviews to enhance the understanding and prediction of PSD principles in MHAs, highlighting the potential of LLM. By using the LLM-based textual entailment process, we filtered and combined user reviews into informative paragraphs for each MHA. These paragraphs were then used to generate sentence embeddings as feature sets for binary classification models. This approach allows for more accurate predictions of principles than baseline models. Therefore, the current results suggest that user reviews are valuable for predicting PSD principles. However, it is worth noting that prediction performance can vary for each PSD principle, as seen in Table 2.

Although we achieve significantly high MCC scores for predicting the *Tailoring* and *Self-monitoring* principles, the prediction performance for the *Praise* principle falls short. This variance can be attributed to distinctions in the original definitions of PSD principles. These principles were identified during expert evaluations based on predefined features, as exemplified in Table 1. A manual examination of MHAs positively labeled for the *Praise* principle revealed that users seldom mention motivational feedback provided by the applications. In contrast, there is clear evidence supporting the existence of *Tailoring* and *Self-monitoring* principles in user reviews. User reviews, such as *"...diabetes-specific attention..."* and *"...keeps track of my blood sugar..."*, contain directly relevant keywords ("specific" and "track") aligned with the definitions of PSD principles. On the other hand, the relatively lower model performance to predict *Reminders* principle in comparison to others can be attributed to its lower representation among positively labeled MHAs in the extracted datasets. The *Reminders* principle has the lowest implementation rate among the explored principles in the training dataset. Consequently, the prediction models were trained with fewer positive labels and fewer folds in the nested stratified cross-validation ensemble approach. This reduced predictive performance for the *Reminders* principle further justifies the exclusion of other PSD principles with low implementation rates from the study.

Conversely, a low entailment ratio was found when comparing application descriptions with PSD principle definitions. To ensure accuracy, the outcomes from this comparison were manually checked and found to align with the model predictions, as detailed in Table 3. Therefore, the procedures applied to user reviews were not applied to application descriptions due to their limited ability to provide informative insights regarding PSD principles. Furthermore, the study was limited by the presence of user reviews containing misinformation, which could not be detected within the scope of this research.

The information gain scores reveal that all four predicted classification probabilities of PSD principles were among the top six most important features. Additionally, we conducted further tests by using the same models to predict mobile application qualities while excluding the three least important features (dev. address, dev. website, privacy pol.). Surprisingly, the performance of the regression models decreased when these features were excluded. This indicates that all predicted classification probabilities of PSD principles significantly contribute to the prediction of MARS quality scores.

Furthermore, ablation studies for selected NLI classification models and used NLI hypothesis were conducted to see the impact of the choice of the model. More details about these steps and additional examples of the models' results can be found in the thesis study [1].

6 Conclusion

This study introduces automated evaluation techniques for mobile health applications, using PSD principles and MARS. It involves collecting MHA descriptions and user reviews, employing large language and supervised machine learning models to predict experts' assessments of PSD principles. The predicted probabilities are then used to assess application qualities and understand the relationship between PSD principles and MARS quality scores. The research addresses a gap in the literature on how PSD principles can be used to predict mobile health application qualities, providing insights for researchers and practical implications for developers.

Acknowledgement. This work has been supported by Middle East Technical University Scientific Research Projects Coordination Unit under grant number ADEP-704-2024-11486.

References

1. Afşin, Y.: Automatic evaluation of mobile health applications according to persuasive system design principles and mobile application rating scale. Master's thesis, Middle East Technical University (2023)
2. Akbar, S., et al.: Safety concerns with consumer-facing mobile health applications. J. Am. Med. Inform. Assoc. **27**(2), 330–340 (2020)
3. Akiba, T., et al.: Optuna: a next-generation hyperparameter optimization framework. In: Proceedings of the 25th ACM SIGKDD International Conference on Knowledge Discovery & Data Mining, pp. 2623–2631 (2019)
4. Al-Ramahi, M.A., et al.: Discovering design principles for health behavioral change support systems: a text mining approach. ACM Trans. Manag. Inf. Syst. (TMIS) **8**(2–3), 1–24 (2017)

5. Alqahtani, F., et al.: Apps for mental health: an evaluation of behavior change strategies and recommendations for future development. Front. AI **2**, 30 (2019)
6. Banfield, R.E., et al.: A comparison of DT ensemble creation techniques. IEEE Trans. Pattern Anal. Mach. Intell. **29**(1), 173–180 (2006)
7. Cerea, S., et al.: Cognitive training via mobile app to reduce body dissatisfaction in high-risk young females. Body Image **42**, 297–306 (2022)
8. Chicco, D., Jurman, G.: The advantages of the MCC over F1 score and accuracy in binary classification evaluation. BMC Genomics **21**, 1–13 (2020)
9. Eng, D.S., Lee, J.M.: The promise and peril of mobile health apps for diabetes and endocrinology. Pediatr. Diabetes **14**(4), 231–238 (2013)
10. Garg, R., et al.: Automating ischemic stroke subtype classification with ML and NLP. J. Stroke Cerebrovasc. Dis. **28**(7), 2045–2051 (2019)
11. Garvin, J.H., et al.: Automating quality measures for heart failure using NLP in veterans affairs. JMIR Med. Inform. **6**(1), e9150 (2018)
12. Geirhos, A., et al.: Standardized evaluation of the quality and persuasiveness of mobile health applications for diabetes management. Sci. Rep. **12**(1), 1–10 (2022)
13. Gross, G., et al.: German mobile apps for patients with psoriatic arthritis: systematic app search and content analysis. Health Policy Technol. **11**(4), 100697 (2022)
14. Han, S.: googletrans v3.0.0. https://github.com/ssut/py-googletrans
15. Hearst, M.A., et al.: Support vector machines. IEEE Intell. Syst. Appl. **13**(4), 18–28 (1998)
16. Hood, M., et al.: Mobile applications for diabetes self-management: a review of reviews. J. Behav. Med. **39**, 981–994 (2016)
17. Jo, M.: Google play scraper v1.2.3
18. Jovičić, S., et al.: Quality evaluation of smartphone applications for laboratory medicine. Clin. Chem. Lab. Med. **57**(3), 388–397 (2019)
19. Kaasinen, E., et al.: Technology acceptance model for mobile services as a design framework. In: Human-Computer Interaction and Innovation in Handheld, Mobile and Wearable Technologies, pp. 80–107 (2011)
20. Kalhori, S.R.N., et al.: Quality evaluation of English mobile applications for gestational diabetes: app review using Mobile Application Rating Scale (MARS). Curr. Diabetes Rev. **17**(2), 161–168 (2021)
21. Ke, G., et al.: LightGBM: a highly efficient gradient boosting decision tree. In: Advances in Neural Information Processing Systems, vol. 30 (2017)
22. Khurana, D., et al.: NLP: current trends and challenges. Multimedia Tools Appl. **82**(3), 3713–3744 (2023)
23. Kim, B.Y., et al.: Consumer mobile apps for potential drug-drug interaction check: systematic review and content analysis using the Mobile App Rating Scale (MARS). JMIR Mhealth Uhealth **6**(3), e8613 (2018)
24. Koleck, T.A., et al.: NLP of symptoms in free-text narratives of e-health records. J. Am. Med. Inform. Assoc. **26**(4), 364–379 (2019)
25. Kotsiantis, S.B.: Decision trees: a recent overview. AI Rev. **39**, 261–283 (2013)
26. Kumar, S., et al.: Mobile health technology evaluation: the mHealth evidence workshop. Am. J. Prev. Med. **45**(2), 228–236 (2013)
27. Langrial, S., et al.: Native mobile applications for personal well-being: a persuasive systems design evaluation (2012)
28. Le Glaz, A., et al.: Machine learning and NLP in mental health: a systematic review. J. Med. Internet Res. **23**(5), e15708 (2021)
29. Liddy, E.D.: NLP. In: Encyclopedia of Library and Information Science (2001)

30. Linardon, J., et al.: Efficacy of app-supported smartphone interventions for mental health problems. World Psychiatry **18**(3), 325–336 (2019)
31. Meystre, S., Haug, P.J.: NLP to extract medical problems from clinical documents. J. Biomed. Inform. **39**(6), 589–599 (2006)
32. Muennighoff, N., et al.: MTEB: massive text embedding benchmark. arXiv preprint arXiv:2210.07316 (2022)
33. Ni, J., et al.: Sentence-T5: scalable sentence encoders from pre-trained text-to-text models. arXiv preprint arXiv:2108.08877 (2021)
34. Nie, Y., et al.: Adversarial NLI: a new benchmark for natural language understanding. arXiv preprint arXiv:1910.14599 (2019)
35. Oinas-Kukkonen, H., Harjumaa, M.: Persuasive systems design: key issues, process model, and system features. Commun. Assoc. Inf. Syst. **24**(1), 28 (2009)
36. Oyebode, O., Orji, R.: Deconstructing persuasive strategies in mental health apps based on user reviews using NLP. In: BCSS@ PERSUASIVE (2020)
37. Pons, E., et al.: NLP in radiology. Radiology **279**(2), 329–343 (2016)
38. Prokhorenkova, L., et al.: CatBoost: unbiased boosting with categorical features. In: Advances in Neural Information Processing Systems, vol. 31 (2018)
39. Selvaraj, S.N., et al.: The quality of Indian obesity-related mHealth apps. JMIR Mhealth Uhealth **10**(5), e15719 (2022)
40. Sezgin, E., et al.: Extracting medical information from patient-generated health data using NLP. JMIR Formative Res. **7**, e43014 (2023)
41. Stach, M., et al.: Mobile health app database-a repository for quality ratings of mHealth apps. In: 2020 IEEE 33rd International Symposium on CBMS, pp. 427–432 (2020)
42. Statista: Number of available health apps in Google play worldwide from 3rd quarter 2014 to 3rd quarter 2022 (2022). https://www.statista.com/statistics/779919/health-apps-available-google-play-worldwide/. Accessed 5 May 2023
43. Statista: Number of mHealth apps available in the Apple app store from 1st quarter 2015 to 3rd quarter 2022 (2022). https://www.statista.com/statistics/779910/health-apps-available-ios-worldwide/. Accessed 5 May 2023
44. Stoyanov, S.R., et al.: Mobile app rating scale: a new tool for assessing the quality of health mobile apps. JMIR Mhealth Uhealth **3**(1), e3422 (2015)
45. Yang, Z., et al.: XLNet: generalized autoregressive pretraining for language understanding. In: Advances in Neural Information Processing Systems, vol. 32 (2019)
46. Young, T., et al.: Recent trends in deep learning based NLP. IEEE Comput. Intell. Mag. **13**(3), 55–75 (2018)
47. Zou, H., Hastie, T.: Regularization and variable selection via the elastic net. J. Roy. Stat. Soc. **67**(2), 301–320 (2005)

Evaluating the Persuasive Potential from Software Design Specifications

Eunice Eno Yaa Frimponmaa Agyei[1(✉)], Markku Kekkonen[1,2], and Harri Oinas-Kukkonen[1]

[1] University of Oulu, Oulu, Finland
{eunice.agyei,markku.kekkonen,harri.oinas-kukkonen}@oulu.fi
[2] Oulu University of Applied Sciences, Oulu, Finland

Abstract. In the early stages of developing persuasive systems, one of the key challenges is to know whether a specified system that is yet to be programmed really can be expected to influence its users. To explore this, experts evaluated software design specifications of a behavior change support system by using the Persuasive Systems Design (PSD) model. The findings show how persuasion postulates and persuasive features can be recognized and evaluated from software design specification documents, and thus how the persuasive potential can be evaluated already at the specification phase. This will enable designers to resolve related design challenges early on, and ultimately increases effectiveness to achieve targeted behavior change.

Keywords: Software design specifications · evaluation · persuasive potential · Persuasive Systems Design · Behavior Change Support Systems

1 Introduction

Behavior Change Support Systems (BCSS) involve the use of information and communication technologies to support behavior change leading, for instance, to well-being and improvements in health outcomes [1]. BCSS have been successful in improving outcomes such as reduction of sedentary habits [2], medication adherence [3], and weight management [4].

Cardiovascular care is one area where BCSS have been deployed. The European Society of Cardiology supports the use of technology for the management and prevention of coronary heart disease (CHD) due to the potential of technologies in remote healthcare services [5]. BCSS can engage people to modify unhealthy behavior to prevent CHD and reduce morbidity and mortality resulting from CHD [6]. Such systems can be designed with persuasive features that have the potential to support self-management (of these health conditions) and improve health and well-being [7]. Persuasive design principles have been identified as the key ingredients in BCSS and associated with the effectiveness of applications [8, 9]. These principles, when implemented in software systems, can help users to complete tasks and work towards achieving their goals. However, one big challenge when making BCSS is figuring out early on how well the system can achieve

N. Baghaei et al. (Eds.): PERSUASIVE 2024, LNCS 14636, pp. 15–25, 2024.
https://doi.org/10.1007/978-3-031-58226-4_2

its persuasive potential. Doing this early helps to prevent unhappy users and saves a lot of resources in the development phase. While there exists a plethora of research that evaluates the persuasiveness of functional systems, little is known before the system is fully developed. Prior work on the evaluation of software specifications has been conducted to assess how persuasive features work together [10].

The aim of this research is to determine the potential influence of a yet-to-be-programmed system on its users in the early stages of developing persuasive systems. This is explored through expert evaluation of software design specifications for a behavior change support system, using the Persuasive Systems Design (PSD) model [11].

2 Study Setting

Persuasive Systems Design Model. The PSD model is a comprehensive framework that aids the development of information systems supporting individuals to change their behavior and attitudes [11]. The model has been used extensively in previous research for designing [12, 13] and evaluating [7, 14] persuasive systems. It advocates postulates that generally describe fundamental issues behind these persuasive systems. The design principles of the PSD model specify how to *support*: users to perform recommended activities towards the desired behavior and/or attitude (i.e. Primary task support), users to interact with the system (i.e. Dialogue support), the perceived credibility of the system (Credibility support), and social influence (i.e. Social support) [11].

System Under Investigation. The app under evaluation, known as the Patient App in the CoroPrevention research project, is part of a personalized BCSS being developed to support the prevention of CHD via lifestyle changes to improve the quality of life for patients. See Figs. 1, 2, 3, and 4 for some of the planned tools. The Patient App is made up of modules for *medication adherence*, *physical activities*, *healthy nutrition*, *smoking cessation*, and *stress-free living*. The Transtheoretical Model (TTM) [15] was adapted to structure the behavior change process in terms of three stages, *preparation*, *action*, and *maintenance* [15]. The PSD framework was used to elicit requirements and define influential features to support behavior change. This paper assesses the persuasive potential of the *physical activity* module's preparation and maintenance stages using design documents, including wireframes and specifications.

Research Method. Expert review can be used in the various phases of software development to evaluate the quality of a product based on the judgment of one or more experienced professionals (e.g. designers, developers, or usability specialists). This happens by assessing software against a set of predetermined criteria or heuristics to uncover problems in its use [16]. The optimal number of experts depends on the scope and complexity of the project, the resources available, and the experience and skills of the evaluators [17].

Expert review can be fast and cost-effective however, evaluator effect, caused by factors such as differences in the backgrounds of experts and expertise level, can affect the credibility of the findings [18]. This can be mitigated via investigator triangulation method to reduce biases [19].

In this research, the goal was to examine if the envisioned system will be able to achieve the predefined persuasion goal(s). A team consisting of three experts with 3–20 years of research experience in persuasive design undertook the assessment of the Patient App's persuasiveness, guided by the PSD model [11]. The evaluation focused on persuasive features and postulates in the app. Ratings were assigned on a 3-point scale (ordinary, more than ordinary, extraordinary) for the role (i.e. the impact a software characteristic is expected to play in supporting, *ROLE*) and level of designed persuasiveness (i.e., design effort, *DEPE*). For example, if a postulate and/or feature is found to play an important role or has a great influence, then it is rated as extraordinary, otherwise it is rated as ordinary or more than ordinary. Two experts independently reviewed specification documents and wireframes thoroughly and documented their findings. The extracted data from the documents served as evidence to support the identified persuasive design principles. The third expert planned, led and coordinated this research.

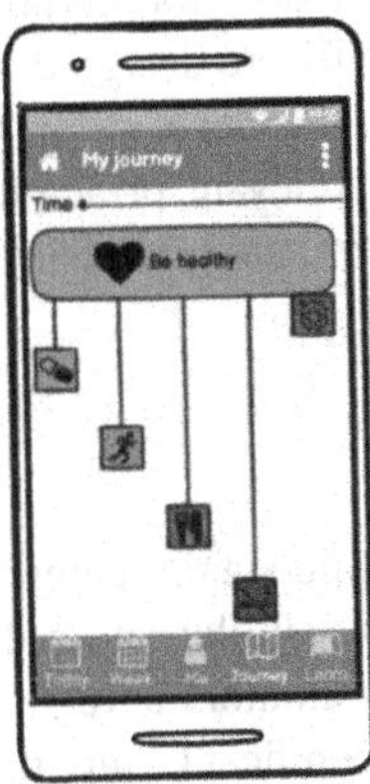

Fig. 1. The main screen of the app

Fig. 2. Step counter tool for tracking

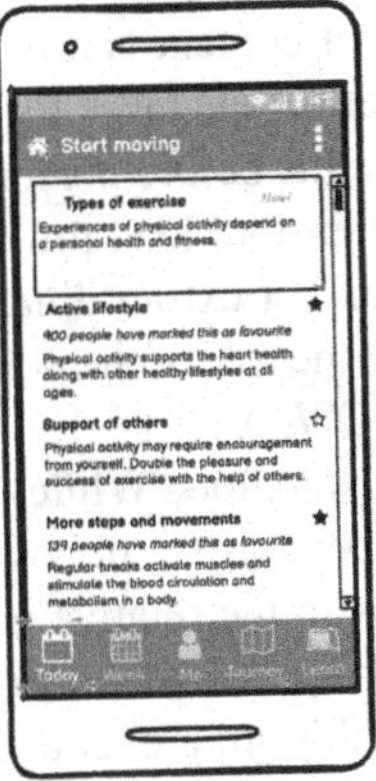

Fig. 3. Example of educational content

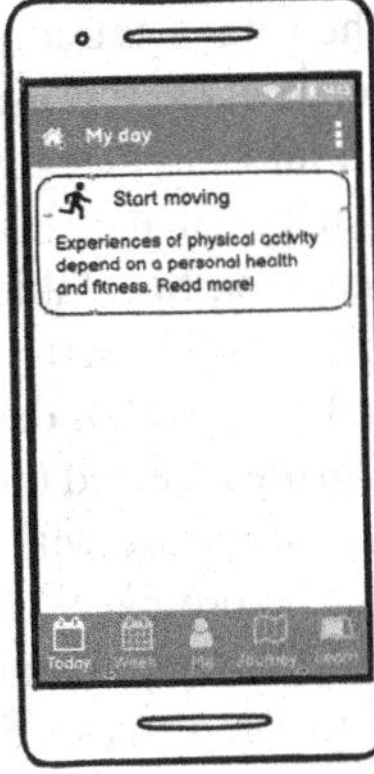

Fig. 4. Reminder to read content

3 Findings

The evaluation focused on assessing the extent to which each postulate and each software feature was integrated into the app's design and thus its persuasive potential. Together, the experts identified and evaluated four (4) PSD postulates and 10 persuasive features cf. [11]. The postulates identified include *view* to enable people to make commitments to keep their thoughts, beliefs, values, opinions, and actions organized and consistent, *incrementality* to allows persuasion via content and tasks to be presented to users gradually, *route* (i.e., describes the methods for information via a direct route which requires conscious thought or an indirect route which relies cues for comprehension), and *unobtrusiveness* (i.e. system seamlessly integrate into users' routine without causing unnecessary disruptions). The PSD features that we identified during this process belong to three categories: *primary task, dialogue, and social support.*

Interestingly, we did not find any persuasive software features in the credibility support category in the documents analyzed. One possible reason for this absence may be the complexity involved in extracting credibility from software design documentation. We note also that the postulates were identified at a higher level of abstraction than the persuasive principles. In overall, we argue that the relevant principles should be identified and included or considered early enough rather than in hindsight to ensure a robust approach to meet user needs.

3.1 Persuasive Features in the Design Specifications

Primary Task Support. The evaluation of features identified in this category produced mixed results. However, both evaluators identified and gave similar ratings for *reduction* in the role and level of designed persuasiveness. The evaluators agreed that the role of *reduction* principle is extraordinary and requires a significant amount of effort to implement. *Reduction* is used to reduce the complex nature of the desired behavior into simple tasks to increase the probability the user will perform the desired behavior [20] and as such the role is extraordinary. For example, bits of content can be presented to users at a time. *Reduction* is used to organize the information and tasks for each goal by grouping them into sub-categories and smaller content items before presenting them to the user. This may enhance task completion rates and therefore lead toward achieving the desired behavior. See Table 1. (Tables: 3 = exemplary or extraordinary, 2 = more than ordinary, 1 = ordinary, 0 = not identified; defined for the role of the postulate and/or feature (*ROLE*) and level of designed persuasiveness (*DEPE*)).

Self-monitoring received mixed ratings from the two evaluators. While one evaluator perceived *self-monitoring* with step counters to be very persuasive, the other evaluator considered it to be ordinary. This indicates the variations in the relative importance of persuasiveness of the step counter tool itself or how it has been designed. *Self-monitoring* enables users to keep track of their performance, and this may encourage behavior modification.

Personalization gives room for individual user preferences to be catered for. Both evaluators had similar ratings for *reminders*. They considered the role and level of designed persuasiveness to be ordinary. This indicates that enabling users to customize when and how often they receive *reminders* to an extent contributes to the persuasiveness

Table 1. The persuasiveness of primary task support features

Primary task support	Description	ROLE		DEPE	
		E1	E2	E1	E2
SMO	Step counter tool for tracking steps	1	3	1	3
PER	Content presented to users is based on the preferences of users	2	0	2	0
	Application settings enable users to configure and customize the times they want to receive reminders	1	1	1	1
RED	Bulk information is organized into sub-categories and smaller content items for users	3	3	2	2
SIM	Quiz-based games for reflection	3	0	1	0

SMO: self-monitoring, PER: personalization, RED: reduction, SIM: simulation

of the app. The other instance of the implementation of *personalization* was identified by one of the evaluators. This evaluation shows that personalized content may influence the persuasiveness of the app and does not require much design effort in this application.

Also, *simulation* was identified by one evaluator, who perceived that quiz-based games are highly persuasive, even though the design effort was only ordinary. Simulation involves providing users with a system model that allows them to see how their actions relate to potential outcomes [11]. This rating could be attributed to the reflective nature of quiz-based games. The mixed results of this feature highlight the need to improve the design of this feature and increase the persuasiveness of the app.

Dialogue Support. In general, one evaluator rated features in this category higher than the other. However, both evaluators agreed on the role and level of designed persuasiveness for *reminders* for any goal. *Reminders* can persuade users to accomplish their behavioral goals and develop new habits or behaviors. Additionally, *reminders* to record step counts and review progress were identified by both evaluators but rated differently. The *reminder* to prompt users to read content was identified by only one evaluator as shown in Table 2.

Three implementations of *praise* were identified. The two evaluators identified motivation messages sent to commend users for achieving good results, but they were rated differently. This could be simply because of the individual preferences of the evaluators. While one evaluator identified and evaluated *praise* given to users for completing educational content to be persuasive, the other evaluator identified *praise* given to users for achieving high scores in reflective quizzes only as somewhat persuasive.

Two instances of *reward* were identified by both evaluators although their ratings varied. These ratings show the persuasive potential of a virtual trophy for achieving good results for step counts and a thumbs up for attaining perfect scores in the reflective exercises. *Rewards* can encourage users to engage in the desired behavior and reinforce the desired behavior. See Table 2.

Table 2. The persuasiveness of dialogue support features

Dialogue support	Description	ROLE		DEPE	
		E1	E2	E1	E2
REM	Reminders for any goal	3	3	3	3
	Reminders to read content for any goal	0	3	0	3
	Reminders to record step counts	1	3	1	3
	Reminders to review weekly/monthly step counts	1	3	1	3
PRA	Motivational messages to commend users when they achieve good results	1	3	1	3
	Congratulatory message for completing the educational content delivered	0	2	0	2
	Motivational messages users get when they get good scores in a reflective quiz	1	0	1	0
REW	Virtual trophy for users who are successful in the desired behavior	1	3	1	3
	Thumbs up (image) for users who get a perfect score on a reflective quiz	1	3	1	3
SUG	Content suggestions	1	0	1	0

REM: reminders, PRA: praise, REW: reward, SUG: suggestion

The *suggestions* feature was identified by only one evaluator, who rated the role and level of designed persuasiveness as ordinary. Hints will be displayed in the app for upcoming educational content.

Social Support. The assessment of the role and level of designed persuasiveness of *social facilitation* and *social learning* by the two evaluators shows their relative contribution to the persuasive potential of the app. *Social facilitation* had mixed ratings for both the role and the level of designed persuasiveness. Although this shows that both evaluators agree that it is present, it highlights the variations in its persuasive potential and may barely persuade users. *Social facilitation* involves providing a means for users to discern via the system that other users are performing similar behavior along with them [11] to influence their intentions and efforts. This app was leveraged to encourage users to complete educational content by enabling users to see content items that other users like.

Social learning on the other hand was identified by only one evaluator. This evaluation indicates its potential persuasiveness. This feature provides a means for users to learn from other users. This feature was planned to enable users to give recommendations, tips, and advice to other users. However, for safety reasons, this feature was only partially implemented. User-generated content will be saved to a database instead of being presented in the app for others to protect users from receiving unhealthy advice. This challenge will be explained to users to prevent any potential deception. The partial implementation of this feature may be the reason why only one evaluator identified it and its evaluation subsequently (Table 3).

Table 3. The persuasiveness of social support features

Social support	Description	ROLE		DEPE	
		E1	E2	E1	E2
SFA	Users can see other people who have completed a similar content item when they save a particular content item as a favorite	1	3	2	3
SLE	Users advise other users and learn from the advice other users give	1	0	1	0

SFA: social facilitation, SLE: social learning

3.2 Persuasion Postulates in the Design Specifications

The identification and evaluation of postulates by the two evaluators varied. From the high ratings of the *incrementality* postulate [11] by both evaluators, it was evident how educational content about the different behavioral goals is gradually presented to users. Content is presented to users in a step-by-step manner, to ensure users are not overwhelmed with too much information and activities at once. See Table 4.

Unobtrusiveness had mixed ratings. Persuasive features and content should be present at opportune moments [11]. Both evaluators found that the app's *reminders* were *unobtrusive.* Users will be able to choose the time and frequency of the notification as well as completely turn off the *reminders.* This flexibility will enable users to receive *reminders* at opportune moments and may increase their compliance with the intervention. This postulate will play an important role and was evaluated as ordinary. Also, the level of designed persuasiveness was rated as ordinary.

View and *Route* may often have subtle impact, and they were identified by only one evaluator, who evaluated them as ordinary. See Table 4. *View* was evident in the step-counting tool, in which the step counts are visualized for users to see both their progress and (in)coherence between their intention and physical activity. Step counters to track progress and encourage physical activity are a common approach to persuade users. *Route* was evident in the content and messages delivered to the users. Educational content would be provided to users via the direct *route* to appeal to their intelligence.

Table 4. The persuasiveness of postulates as evaluated by experts

Postulate	Description	ROLE		DEPE	
		E1	E2	E1	E2
View	Step counter to track their progress and stay active	0	1	0	1
Incrementality	Presenting content and activities to users gradually in a reduced manner	3	3	3	3
Route	Presenting content and messages using the direct and indirect routes	0	1	0	1
Unobtrusiveness	Providing a means for users to decide when they want to receive content and reminders	1	2	2	2

4 Discussion

Prior work on the evaluation of software specifications [10] suggests that the use of early evaluation to ensure that the intent to design a persuasive system is realized before the actual system is implemented. Validating the existence or absence of these persuasion postulates and persuasive features allows changes to be made to the design early on to increase the probability that the system will be effective.

In our study, expert reviewers critically examined the system under development for conforming with design of persuasion postulates and persuasive software features. *Self-monitoring* played a pivotal role in users' behavior change process via tracking their activities. For instance, the Patient App's step counter tool enables *self-monitoring* of steps, the meal rhythm tool tracks eating patterns, and the cigarette counter is used to track possible smoking behavior. *Self-monitoring* has been similarly employed as a central intervention component in many previous systems, too, e.g. [21, 22]. *Personalization* can increase the usefulness and adoption of an application when (1) relevant content can be presented to users, (2) users can choose the timing for content delivery, and (3) users can configure settings (e.g., reminders). *Reduction* principle is applied to lessen the effort required to do a task and increase the task completion rate. It has been used in apps, for instance, for managing chronic arthritis [23]. The role and design of persuasive features varied between settings. For example, there were different types of reminders for different purposes. Understanding the role and complexity of the design of persuasion postulates and persuasive features is critical.

In our study, we observed a relationship between certain postulates and persuasive features in the behavior change app. For instance, the *View* postulate, which emphasizes the importance of organizing information, user commitment, and consistency, was evident in the *self-monitoring* tools. Through features like the step counter, users could identify inconsistencies in their behaviors and track their progress. Another noteworthy postulate-feature relationship observed was between *Route* and *Suggestion*. The app's *Suggestion* feature primarily utilized the direct route to directly appeal to the user's intelligence. Exploring how postulates and persuasive software features work together to enhance app persuasiveness is one of the most thrilling further research topics.

In overall, this research shows that the persuasive potential of an app can be determined early from design documents. Those instances in which both evaluators identified similar features and gave high ratings emphasize their persuasive impact. Lastly, we acknowledge limitations in our work due to its subjective nature. Some features may have been missed especially due abstract nature of some persuasive features or postulates. Mixed ratings show differences in the perception of evaluators.

5 Conclusion

A well-designed persuasive system has the potential to support behavior change and improve, for instance, health outcomes. The expert review of a behavior change support system conducted here provides valuable insights into the design of persuasive systems. These kinds of early reviews may play an important role in the identification and resolution of design challenges and in enhancing the persuasiveness of the designed system. We recommend designers and researchers to adopt our approach for early assessment of the persuasive potential of their systems. This proactive approach can optimize development efforts and costs. The insights from future evaluations can complement other assessments and thus providing valuable insights to guide design decisions.

Acknowledgments. We would like to acknowledge Sami Pohjolainen and the members of the CoroPrevention project for their help in carrying out this research. This study has received funding from the European Union's Horizon 2020 research and innovation program under grant agreement No 848056. It reflects only the authors' views and the Commission is not responsible for any use that may be made of the information it contains. **Disclosure of Interests.** The authors have no competing interests to declare that are relevant to the content of this article.

References

1. Oinas-Kukkonen, H.: A foundation for the study of behavior change support systems. Pers Ubiquit. Comput. **17**, 1223–1235 (2013). https://doi.org/10.1007/s00779-012-0591-5
2. Fanning, J., Mullen, S.P., McAuley, E.: Increasing physical activity with mobile devices: a meta-analysis. J. Med. Internet Res. **14**, e161 (2012). https://doi.org/10.2196/jmir.2171
3. Ma, Y., Cheng, H.Y., Cheng, L., Sit, J.W.H.: The effectiveness of electronic health interventions on blood pressure control, self-care behavioural outcomes and psychosocial well-being in patients with hypertension: a systematic review and meta-analysis. Int. J. Nurs. Stud. **92**, 27–46 (2019). https://doi.org/10.1016/j.ijnurstu.2018.11.007
4. Stephens, J., Allen, J.: Mobile phone interventions to increase physical activity and reduce weight. J. Cardiovasc. Nurs. **28**, 320–329 (2013). https://doi.org/10.1097/JCN.0b013e318250a3e7
5. Cowie, M.R., et al.: E-Health: a position statement of the European Society of Cardiology. Eur. Heart J. **37**, 63–66 (2016). https://doi.org/10.1093/eurheartj/ehv416
6. Coorey, G.M., et al.: Implementation of a consumer-focused eHealth intervention for people with moderate-to-high cardiovascular disease risk: protocol for a mixed-methods process evaluation. BMJ Open **7**, e014353 (2017). https://doi.org/10.1136/bmjopen-2016-014353

7. Asbjørnsen, R.A., et al.: Identifying persuasive design principles and behavior change techniques supporting end user values and needs in E-health interventions for long-term weight loss maintenance: qualitative study. J. Med. Internet Res. **22**, e22598 (2020). https://doi.org/10.2196/22598
8. Matthews, J., Win, K.T., Oinas-Kukkonen, H., Freeman, M.: Persuasive technology in mobile applications promoting physical activity: a systematic review. J. Med. Syst. **40**, 1–13 (2016). https://doi.org/10.1007/s10916-015-0425-x
9. Almutari, N., Orji, R.: How effective are social influence strategies in persuasive apps for promoting physical activity? In: Adjunct Publication of the 27th Conference on User Modeling, Adaptation and Personalization, pp. 167–172. ACM, New York (2019). https://doi.org/10.1145/3314183.3323855
10. Räisänen, T., Lehto, T., Oinas-Kukkonen, H.: Practical findings from applying the PSD model for evaluating software design specifications. In: Lecture Notes in Computer Science (including subseries Lecture Notes in Artificial Intelligence and Lecture Notes in Bioinformatics), pp. 185–192 (2010). https://doi.org/10.1007/978-3-642-13226-1_19
11. Oinas-Kukkonen, H., Harjumaa, M.: Persuasive systems design: key issues, process model, and system features. Commun. Assoc. Inf. Syst. **24**, 485–500 (2009). https://doi.org/10.17705/1CAIS.02428
12. Bartlett, Y.K., Webb, T.L., Hawley, M.S.: Using persuasive technology to increase physical activity in people with chronic obstructive pulmonary disease by encouraging regular walking: a mixed-methods study exploring opinions and preferences. J. Med. Internet Res. **19**, e6616 (2017). https://doi.org/10.2196/JMIR.6616
13. Karppinen, P., et al.: Persuasive user experiences of a health behavior change support system: a 12-month study for prevention of metabolic syndrome. Int. J. Med. Inform. **96**, 51–61 (2016). https://doi.org/10.1016/j.ijmedinf.2016.02.005
14. Oyibo, K.: Investigating the key persuasive features for fitness app design and extending the persuasive system design model: a qualitative approach. Proc. Int. Symp. Human Fact. Ergon. Health Care **10**, 47–53 (2021). https://doi.org/10.1177/2327857921101022
15. Prochaska, J.O., DiClemente, C.C.: Stages and processes of self-change of smoking: toward an integrative model of change. J. Consult. Clin. Psychol. **51**, 390–395 (1983). https://doi.org/10.1037/0022-006X.51.3.390
16. Rosenzweig, E.: Usability inspection methods. In: Successful User Experience: Strategies and Roadmaps, pp. 115–130. Elsevier (2015). https://doi.org/10.1016/B978-0-12-800985-7.00006-5
17. Nielsen, J.: Finding usability problems through heuristic evaluation. In: Proceedings of the SIGCHI Conference on Human Factors in Computing Systems - CHI 1992, pp. 373–380. ACM Press, New York (1992). https://doi.org/10.1145/142750.142834
18. Chauncey, W.: Heuristic evaluation - ScienceDirect. In: User Interface Inspection Methods, pp. 1–32. Elsevier (2014). https://doi.org/10.1016/B978-0-12-410391-7.00001-4
19. Alturki, A., Gable, G., Bandara, W.: The design science research roadmap. In: Progress Evaluation. PACIS 2013 Proceedings (2013)
20. Lehto, T., Kukkonen, H.O., Pätiälä, T., Saarelma, O.: Virtual health coaching for consumers: a persuasive systems design perspective. Int. J. Netw. Virt. Organ. **13**, 24 (2013). https://doi.org/10.1504/IJNVO.2013.058440
21. Consolvo, S., et al.: Activity Sensing in the Wild: A Field Trial of UbiFit Garden (2008). https://doi.org/10.1145/1357054.1357335

22. Bickmore, T.W., Caruso, L., Clough-Gorr, K.: Acceptance and usability of a relational agent interface by urban older adults. In: CHI 2005 Extended Abstracts on Human Factors in Computing Systems, pp. 1212–1215. ACM, New York (2005). https://doi.org/10.1145/1056808.1056879
23. Geuens, J., Swinnen, T.W., Westhovens, R., de Vlam, K., Geurts, L., Vanden Abeele, V.: A review of persuasive principles in mobile apps for chronic arthritis patients: opportunities for improvement. JMIR Mhealth Uhealth **4**, e118 (2016). https://doi.org/10.2196/mhealth.6286

Exploring the Effect of Using a Single Versus Multiple Behaviour Change Strategies on Motivation to Use Gratitude App and Possible Gender Differences

Felwah Alqahtani[1,2](✉), Chinenye Ndulue[1], and Rita Orji[1]

[1] Dalhousie University, Halifax, Canada
felwah.alqahtani@dal.ca
[2] King Khalid University, Abha, Saudi Arabia

Abstract. Mental health applications (apps) have been increasingly developed to assist users to improve their mental and emotional well-being using various persuasive strategies. Although research has shown that using a single strategy in persuasive technology design can be effective, it is a common practice for designers to employ multiple strategies in their persuasive intervention design. However, the comparative effectiveness of using multiple persuasive strategies versus a single strategy in mental health apps has not been empirically investigated. To answer this question, we developed two versions of a Gratitude app to promote positive mental health and emotional well-being. The first version incorporates multiple persuasive strategies, while the second version incorporates a single strategy. We conducted a 5-week field study of 84 participants, followed by a one-on-one interview with 16 participants. The results show that overall, the Gratitude app is effective with respect to the motivational appeal toward promoting mental and emotional well-being. More importantly, employing multiple strategies in the app improves its effectiveness with respect to the motivational appeal compared to employing a single strategy. Moreover, there are gender differences in motivational appeal across the two versions of the app. Finally, interview data provided more insights, showing that participants appreciated the simplicity of the app and how the app helps them improve their mental and emotional well-being.

Keywords: Mental health · Persuasive technology · Persuasive features · Persuasive strategies · Multiple strategies · Single strategy · Health and wellness

1 Introduction

The condition of the public's mental health has recently become a major issue. One in four people may have mental health issues at some point in their lives, according to the World Health Organization (WHO) [24]. As a result, scientists and professionals are developing apps to support people dealing with a wide variety of mental health issues and to encourage positive mental health and emotional well-being in the general population. They take advantage of the widespread availability and use of technology, especially mobile and handheld devices, to create apps that provide users with constant assistance.

N. Baghaei et al. (Eds.): PERSUASIVE 2024, LNCS 14636, pp. 26–41, 2024.
https://doi.org/10.1007/978-3-031-58226-4_3

Previous research indicates that persuasive apps can be effective in helping people achieve positive lifestyle changes [17]. Games, mobile apps, website software, and desktop-based interventions have all been developed over the years with the primary goal of encouraging users to engage in health and wellness-related behaviors, such as eating healthily [28], being physically active [2], reduce alcohol consumption [14] and maintaining mental and emotional health [7]. These apps use a wide range of persuasive strategies to achieve their aims.

Although there has been a rising interest in developing persuasive mental health apps, most of the currently accessible apps use a different number of persuasive strategies, and previous research [25] has shown that using a single strategy in PTs design can be effective. Therefore, to the best of our knowledge, the comparative effectiveness of using multiple strategies versus a single strategy in persuasive mental health apps with respect to their motivational appeal to use the Gratitude app is unknown. Moreover, Previous studies show that there were gender differences regarding experiencing and expressing gratitude [8, 32]. Therefore, this study also aims to examine whether there are gender differences in motivational appeal across the two versions of the app.

To empirically answer this research question in the context of mental health and emotional well-being, we designed and implemented two versions of a Gratitude app to promote positive mental health and emotional well-being. We conducted a 5-week field randomized controlled study of 84 people and interviewed 16 of them (8 of each group). The results show that overall, the Gratitude app is effective with respect to its motivational appeal toward promoting mental and emotional well-being. Above all, employing multiple strategies in the mental health app improves its effectiveness with respect to the motivational appeal compared to employing a single strategy. Moreover, there are gender differences in motivational appeal across the two versions of the app. Finally, interview data provided more insights, showing that participants appreciated the simplicity of the app and how the app helps them improve their mental and emotional well-being.

Our research has three main contributions: First, we show a need to employ multiple strategies in mental health apps to increase their effectiveness with respect to the motivational appeal via app design, development, and empirical studies. Second, we reveal some gender differences in motivational appeal across the two versions of the Gratitude app. Third, we provide qualitative insights to explain why our app was effective. Our work is the first to empirically investigate the comparative effectiveness of implementing multiple strategies versus a single strategy in persuasive mental health apps.

2 Related Work

This section provides a brief overview of persuasive strategies in health interventions and the ARCS model of motivation.

2.1 Persuasive Strategies in Health Interventions

Persuasive technologies (PTs) are aimed at motivating or influencing people to engage in specific behaviors such as engaging in physical activity, eating healthily, and quitting smoking [12]. They are widely applied in the health and wellness domains to empower and assist users to live a healthy lifestyle. A defining characteristic of PTs is persuasion which focuses on motivating someone to change their attitude and/or behavior without force or deception [12]. These systems are made persuasive by employing persuasive strategies and behavior-change techniques. Over the years, researchers in the field of persuasive and behavior changes have focused on developing many persuasive strategies and behavior change techniques for designing effective persuasion-based technology. For instance, seven persuasive techniques were created by Fogg [12] and are known as persuasive tools. Building on Fogg's research, Harjumaa and Oinas-Kukkonen [18] proposed 28 principles of persuasive system design (PSD). Moreover, Abraham and Michie [1] developed 26 behavior change strategies, which Michie et al. [22] later expanded to include 93 strategies.

These strategies and techniques are gaining popularity in persuasive and behavior change interventions. They have been utilized in numerous apps targeting different health domains such as health and wellness [26, 29], physical activity [2, 4], alcohol and smoking reduction [21], and mental health [3, 5].

Although the previous study [27] shows that using a single strategy in persuasive app design is effective, most of the reviewed studies employed multiple strategies. This work fills that gap by examining the comparative effectiveness of using multiple strategies versus a single strategy in a persuasive mental health app.

2.2 The ARCS Model of Motivation

Motivation is an important component of health behaviour change and, consequently, an essential component of numerous motivational theories such as Self-determination theory [31], Expectancy–Value Theory [36] and Keller's ARCS model [20]. We selected ARCS for several reasons: ARCS model is a widely known and employed motivational model. It is a simple and effective macro-theory that combines a variety of theoretical bases derived from noteworthy motivational theories such as the cognitive evaluation theory, expectancy-value theory, reinforcement theory, social learning theory, and self-efficacy theory [19, 30, 35]. In addition, it highlights the essential elements of human motivation related to behaviour and behaviour change [16]. ARCS model consists of four main qualities which are build based on previous research on the psychology of human motivation:

***Attention*:** To encourage users, a system must capture and maintain their attention.
***Relevance*:** For a system to motivate users, it must represent their interests and goals. A system that is viewed as helpful and beneficial in terms of assisting users in achieving their objectives is more likely to motivate the user. For a system to be relevant, it must be goal-oriented, purpose-matching, and employ known concepts.
***Competence*:** People dislike undertaking tasks with little or no chance of accomplishment. Although success is never assured and people enjoy being challenged, a challenge that is too difficult for a user could demotivate them. Users' levels of confidence are frequently associated with their motivation and amount of effort to achieve a goal.
***Satisfaction*:** To encourage and maintain the motivation of users, they must receive some sort of satisfaction and reward for their efforts. Motivating factors include a sense of accomplishment, satisfaction, commendation, and positive reinforcement.

ARCS Model has been used to design and assess the motivational appeal of different persuasive and behaviour change interventions for various domains. For example, Stockdale et al., [33] utilized ARCS motivation model constructs to inform a persuasive breastfeeding intervention design which aims to promote the first-time mothers' confidence in their ability to breastfeed. Moreover, Dinesh et al. [23] used ARCS model to evaluate the motivational appeal of a persuasive game to promote disease awareness and prevention. In this study, we used the ARCS model to evaluate the motivational appeal of the Gratitude app and whether employing multiple strategies in the persuasive app increases the app's effectiveness towards improving mental health and emotional well-being.

2.3 Research Questions

In this paper, we explore the following research questions:

RQ1: How effective is the Gratitude app at increasing users' motivation overall?
RQ2: How effective are the individual versions of the Gratitude app with respect to their motivational appeal?
RQ3: Is there any difference in the comparative motivational appeal of the two versions (multi-strategy, single-strategy) of the Gratitude app?
RQ4: Is there a gender difference in motivational appeal across the two versions of the Gratitude app?

3 Gratitude App Design

To answer our research questions, we examined empirically whether employing multiple strategies is more effective than a single strategy on motivation to use the Gratitude app and whether there is a gender difference in motivational appeal across the two versions. Specifically, we designed and implemented a Gratitude app to encourage users to affirm and reflect on the daily good things that occur in their lives. The Gratitude app is a cross-platform app that runs on both iOS and Android mobile devices. It was created using the Flutter development framework. Flutter is an open-source, cross-platform mobile SDK that can be used to develop iOS and Android apps.

The following explains why we chose gratitude intervention as the focus of our app. First, a number of systematic reviews indicate the possible efficacy of gratitude interventions in promoting mental health and well-being [9, 11, 34]. Second, gratitude activities are easy to comprehend and perform [10] and are enjoyed by many [15]. Thirdly, gratitude activities assist individuals in recalling deeply meaningful memories, thereby improving their mental health. Fourth, focusing on the positive may also promote a positive disposition [13].

People with mental health issues tend to concentrate more on the negative. Thus, Gratitude app encourages users to express and reflect on what they are grateful for, keeping track of the positive events in their lives. The app begins with an introductory page that explains the app's primary objective, this is followed by the screen that allows users to rate their feeling before entering their gratitude for the day. Then users write what they are grateful for each day (gratitude) and can attach or capture a picture with their gratitude. The gratitude entries are displayed on the journal screen (Fig. 1.a). The app also reminds users of their previous gratitude by displaying inspirational quotes related to the previous day's gratitude. For instance, if a user was thankful for having a family the day before, the app shows a positive quote about family the following day.

Each time the user enters their gratitude, a water lily flower is added to their pond. The color of the lily flower changes depending on what the user is grateful for – the gratitude category. There are twelve primary categories of gratitude, each corresponding to a unique color of the lily flower. For instance, if a user is grateful for people, they gain a pink lily flower, and for nature, they gain a yellow lily flower. Again, each water lily flower houses/stores the corresponding gratitude for the day, and users can easily retrieve their gratitude at any time by clicking each water lily flower; gratitude appears (see Fig. 1.b).

A mood summary screen allows users to see their feeling patterns before and after expressing gratitude as faces in calendar format (Fig. 1.c). Each face houses/stores the corresponding gratitude for the day and users can easily retrieve their gratitude at any time by clicking each face in a calendar, gratitude shows up.

In the social community screen, users can read, like, comment on others' gratitude and share their gratitude with others as well if they wish to (see Fig. 1.d). Users receive random Suggestion & encouragement that motivates them to do an act of kindness. They also receive a reminder notification to enter their gratitude.

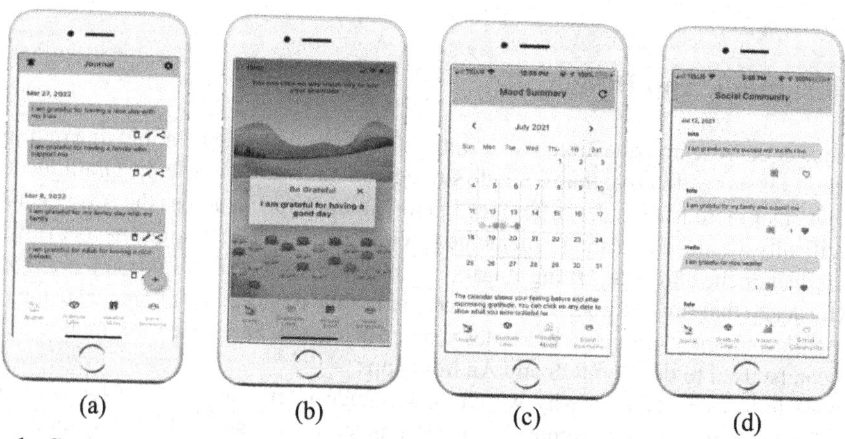

Fig. 1. Gratitude App main screens: The Journal screen (a), the Gratitude lilies screen (b), the Mood Summary screen (c), the Social Community screen (d).

3.1 Persuasive Strategies Employing in Each Version

To compare the effectiveness of multi-strategy version with the single-strategy version, we chose the common strategies implemented in mental health apps [5] and requested by users [6]: Suggestion&encouragement, Self-monitoring, Reminder, and Social support strategies are among the most frequently employed strategies by persuasive and behavior change intervention designers and they can be easily implemented in interventions.

We have combined the suggestion and encouragement strategies into a single strategy because we need to encourage people to perform the suggested acts of kindness and they often go together in most intervention designs. We then designed two versions of the Gratitude app. In one version of the intervention, we used a single strategy, Suggestion & encouragement, and in the second version, we used four strategies: Suggestion & encouragement, Self-monitoring, Reminder, and Social Support.

4 Gratitude App Evaluation

We conducted a 5-week field study to evaluate and compare the effectiveness of the two versions of the Gratitude app: the multi-strategy version and the single-strategy version. At the beginning of the study, 84 participants read and gave their consent to the study and were randomly assigned to the different app versions (42 participants used single-strategy version, 42 participants used multi-strategy version). The inclusion criteria require participants to be 18 years of age or older and to have experienced mental health issues such as stress, low mood, fear, worry, depression, anxiety, and other forms of mental health-related issues based on self-diagnosis. Before using the app, we collected participants' demographic information and assessed whether they had experienced any form of mental health issues based on self-diagnosis, including the type of mental health issues. Then participants were required to express their gratitude for at least 4 times a week over five weeks and interact with app elements. Participants received a $15.00 compensation in the form of a gift card for participating in the study, in compliance with the study's ethics approval. Table 1 shows participants' demographic information.

After the evaluation period, participants were asked to fill a post-survey to identify the participants' motivation to enhance their mental and emotional well-being. We utilized a standardized ARCS scale that included 12 items to measure ARCS constructs (attention, relevance, confidence, and satisfaction) on a 7-point Likert scale (ranging from "1 – Strongly Disagree" to "7 – Strongly Agree". Also, we randomly selected and interviewed 16 participants with the aim of eliciting more detailed feedback about the app's effectiveness in improving their mental and emotional well-being. All 16 interviews were audio recorded with participant permission.

Table 1. Demographics information

Total participants = 84	
Age	18–24 (13%), 25–34(64%), 35–44 (21%), 45–54 (2%)
Gender	Female (56%), Male (44%)
Education	High School or equivalent (6%), College diploma (4%), Bachelor's degree (50%), Master's degree (30%), PhD (10%)
Mental health issues	Stress (73%), Worry (58%), Negative feelings (45%), Negative thoughts (42%), Low moods (56%), Fear (30%) Anxiety (44%), Depression (32%)

4.1 Data Analysis

To analyze the quantitative data and answer our research questions, we employed well-known analytics techniques. We first conducted a one-sample t-test of the overall participants' responses (n = 84) as well as for individual groups (single-strategy group: n = 42, multi-strategy group: n = 42) to answer research questions RQ1 and RQ2. Then, we conducted an independent sample t-test to compare the efficacy of the two versions to answer RQ3. After that, we conducted an independent-sample t-test to investigate the gender impact in motivational appeal across the two versions of the Gratitude app which helped to answer RQ4.

To analyze the qualitative data, we transcribed the interview data. Then, we conducted a thematic analysis of the interview transcript. During the thematic analysis process, we followed steps outlined by Braun and Clarke [19]: (1) becoming familiar with the data, (2) generating initial codes, (3) searching for themes, (4) defining themes, (5) iteratively reviewing themes, and (6) writing up the results.

5 Results

In this section, we present the results of quantitative and qualitative data.

5.1 Motivational Appeal of the Gratitude App and of Individual Versions

To answer RQ1, we ran a one-sample t-test on the combined data of motivational appeal of both versions to obtain the motivational appeal of the Gratitude app. We compared the data to a neutral rating of 4 on the 7-point ARCS motivation scale. The results indicate that the Gratitude app is generally beneficial in terms of its motivating appeal. As shown in Fig. 2, the mean score of the four dimensions of the ARCS of the Gratitude app was higher than the neutral (point/mid-point) of 4.0. The p-values for the four dimensions of the ARCS were less than 0.001. Therefore, there was a significant difference between the mean obtained from the motivational appeal of the Gratitude app and the test value (neutral = 4) which answers RQ1.

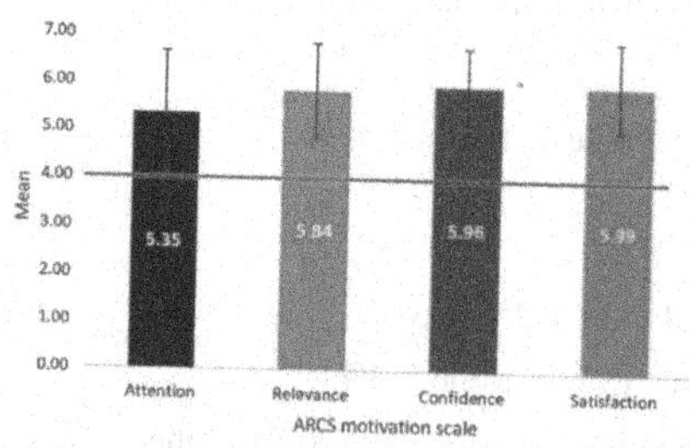

Fig. 2. A bar graph of the mean of ARCS motivation scale for the overall Gratitude app motivational appeal. Error bars represent a 95% confidence interval. The neutral rating is rep- resented by the red horizontal line

Similarly, to investigate the motivational appeal of the individual versions of the app, we performed one-sample t-tests separately on the data from using the different versions of the app. We compared this data to an optimistic-neutral rating of 4 on the 7-point ARCS motivation scale. As shown in Table 2 the ARCS scale responses were above the neutral value (4) which indicate that both versions of the Gratitude app are effective across the four ARCS motivation dimensions which answer RQ2.

Table 2. Mean (M), Standard Deviations (SD), Mean Difference (MD), t-values (t2), and significance levels on a scale from 1(low) to 7 (high) for both versions

	Single-strategy version					Multi-strategy version				
Motivation Dimensions	M	SD	MD	t2	p	M	SD	MD	t2	p
Attention	4.95	1.35	.95	4.58	<.001	5.75	1.12	1.75	10.1	<.001
Relevance	5.59	1.13	1.59	9.11	<.001	6.1	.75	2.1	18.1	<.001
Confidence	5.83	.75	1.83	15.8	<.001	6.1	.84	2.1	16.3	<.001
Satisfaction	5.78	.92	1.78	12.5	<.001	6.2	.89	2.2	16	<.001

5.2 Comparing the Motivational Appeal Between the Two Interventions (Single-Strategy Version, Multi-strategy Version) of the Gratitude App

To assess potential differences in effectiveness between the two versions (single-strategy and multi-strategy) of the Gratitude app, we conducted an independent samples t-test. This test compared the motivational appeal between the single-strategy version and the multi-strategy version.

Attention: There was a significant difference in the attention between the multi-strategy version (M = 5.75, SD = 1.12) and single-strategy version (M = 4.95, SD = 1.35); t (82) = -2.95, $p < 0.05$. The multi-strategy version captured participants' attention more than the single-strategy version.
Relevance: There was a significant difference in the relevance between the multi-strategy version (M = 6.1, SD = .75) and single-strategy version (M = 5.59, SD = 1.13); t (71.19) = -2.42, $p < 0.05$. Participants who used the multi-strategy version found the app to be more relevant to them than participants who used the single-strategy version.
Confidence: There was no significant difference in the confidence between the multi-strategy version (M = 6.1, SD = .84) and single-strategy version (M = 5.83, SD = .75); t (82) = -1.61, p = 0.11. Both versions equally increased participants' confidence in using the app to improve their mental health and emotional well-being.
Satisfaction: There was a significant difference in satisfaction between the multi-strategy version (M = 6.2, SD = .89) and single-strategy version (M = 5.75, SD = .92); t (82) = -2.13, p <. 0.05. Using the multi-strategy version increased participants' satisfaction more than using the single-strategy version.

The results indicate that the multi-strategy version is more effective than the single-strategy version for attracting and retaining participants' attention, improving the relevance of an intervention, and increasing participants' satisfaction with the intervention which answers RQ3 (see, Fig. 3).

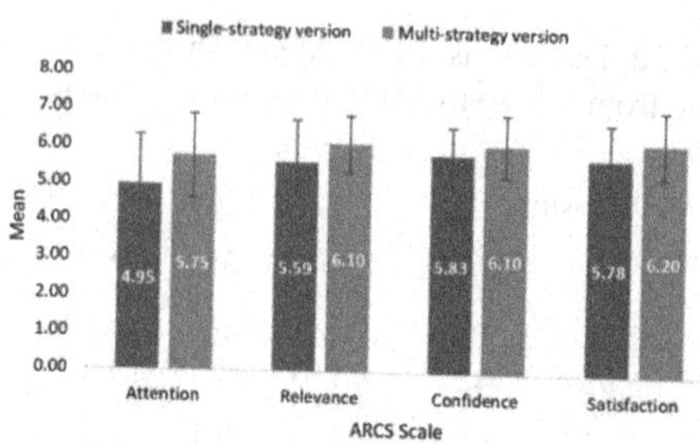

Fig. 3. Comparative motivational appeal of the two app's versions across the motivation dimensions on a scale ranging from 1 to 7

5.3 The Impact of Gender on the Two Versions (Single-Strategy Version, Multi-strategy Version) of the Gratitude App

To investigate the gender differences in motivational appeal across the two versions of the Gratitude app, we divided our participants into two groups (male and female). We compared the two versions within each group by conducting an independent-sample t-test for each group. We found that females were more satisfied with the multi-strategy version than the single-strategy version, whereas males found that the multi-strategy version held their attention and was more relevant to them than the single-strategy version (see Table 3).

Table 3. Independent-sample t-test comparing the two versions for each group (Male, Female)

Motivation Dimensions	Male	Female
Attention	$t(35) = -2.12, p < .05$	$t(45) = -1.61, p = .12$
Relevance	$t(35) = -2.12, p < .05$	$t(45) = -1.46, p = .15$
Confidence	$t(35) = -.82, p = .42$	$t(45) = -1.65, p = .15$
Satisfaction	$t(35) = -.97, p = .34$	$t(45) = -2.42, p < .05$

5.4 Thematic Analysis of the Gratitude App

We interviewed 16 participants (single-strategy group: n = 8, multi-strategy group: n = 8) who were selected randomly from people who participated in the study. We invited them for an online interview to gain more insight into their app experience. To preserve participants' privacy and anonymize the responses, I identified participants by acronym group name, and anonymized IDs (e.g., SG-P1, MG-P2, etc.) to represent participant (1) single-strategy group (SG), participant (2) multi-strategy group (MG), respectively. This section presents identified themes and sample comments from the interview.

Theme 1: Increased Awareness of Everyday Positive Aspects of Life. This theme refers to the increased capacity of the participants to notice and appreciate people and positive things in their life. The app helped participants to see life differently and refocus on the positive aspects of their lives rather than what was lacking or what went wrong, as some participants started below.

"*It made me look at the big picture as* ***I have been only focusing on what's missing rather than what I have***" [SG-P2].

"*Before using the app,* ***I used to focus on everything that bothered me, but with the app, I know I need to remind myself what I am grateful for that day which helps me to focus on good things***" [MG-P3].

Moreover, sharing gratitude in the social community and reading others increased also users' awareness of good things in their life and taught them how to be grateful for things they take for granted.

"*I also enjoyed sharing my gratitude with others in the social community and reading others' because it* ***reminded me about the thing I have, and I never thought to be grateful for***" [MG-P8].

Theme 2: Increase in Positive Emotions and the Reducing Negative Ones. This theme refers to the presence of affirmative emotions like feeling happy, calm, and optimistic and the absence of negative emotions such as stress, anger, and anxiety during using the app. Participants felt happy and optimistic while using the app because the app helped them to remember the positive moments. Moreover, thinking of the good things also helped reduce participants' anxiety, and improved their ability to cope with life as participants started below.

"*Writing what I am grateful for* ***makes me dive deeply in my mind to remember good things which make me happy and optimistic"*** [SG-P1].

"*The app helped a lot with mental health. I felt happy when it* ***reminded me what I was grateful*** *for"* [MG-P5].

"*Thinking of and counting the things I am grateful for has definitely* ***reduced my levels of anxiety and made me cope better with lif****e*" [SG-P4].

Theme 3: Positive Reframing of Situations: This theme refers to the participants' capacity to reframe their perspectives on undesirable situations and emphasize positive rationale. Participants were able to highlight the good aspects of a difficult day. Below are some of the specific responses.

"*I started to look at the good thing in my day.* ***I saw a big difference in how I think and became more positive in any situation I am in. Even if it was a busy or stressful day, that's how it affected me***. [MG-P4].

"*The app helped a lot with mental health.* ***It reminded me what I was grateful*** *for"* [MG-P5].

Theme 4: Promoted Deep Thinking in Positive Moments. This theme refers to the app's ability to prompt users to engage in in-depth reflection on their blessings. Some participants reported that the reminder notification gave them the opportunity to reflect on something for which they are grateful, even when they were feeling unhappy.

"***The reminder is good** in the sense that even **when I feel down and sees it, it makes me think deep down and find something to be grateful for***" [MG-P5].

Moreover, the previous gratitude notification also helped them to have a moment to think deeply about their previous gratitude and motivated them to be grateful.

"***I enjoyed the daily take a deep thought of gratitude** notification because **I could relate to the things I posted***" [SG-P3].

Theme 5: Suggested Act of Kindness as a Driving Force to be Kind: This theme drives from the shared feelings of the participants to have the desire and capability to be kind to others. According to participants, the encouragement quotes along with the suggested kindness activities served as motivators for participants to be kind.

"***Reading the quotes encouraged me to be kind and motivated me to improve my attitude***" [SG-P6].

"*The notification is so good and helps. **The words encourage me to be kind to others***" [MG].

However, a participant did not like the suggestion notification as they perceived it as a command.

"*I did not like the suggestion notification because **I felt it was like an order to do something,** and I did not like that*" [SG-P8].

Theme 6: Impact of Presenting Gratitude as Lily Flowers: This theme reflects participants' opinion and experiences regarding this feature. Many participants talked about how showing a lily flower for each gratitude entry attracts their attention. This feature motivated users not to miss any gratitude. Participants also reported that interacting with flowers to display the stored gratitude was enjoyable.

"*I really liked the beauty of the lily pond. The flower represents good things that happened to me **made me feel happy and encouraged me not to miss any gratitude***" [SG-P7].

"***At each time I express gratitude, one lily shows up which motivates me to do more***" [MG-P9].

"*When I clicked on any flowers, I saw something positive, which I really liked. **The ability to move from one flower to another to see my gratitude is another beautiful addition to the app***" [SG-P4].

Theme 7: Appreciation for Calendar Visualization. This theme explained why visualizing feelings leads to positive outcomes for participants in the multi-strategy group. Some participants stated that the calendar enabled them to reflect on previous days and filled them with joy for the good days they had lived. They also appreciated the visual representation of their emotions before and after expressing gratitude in a calendar format.

"*The calendar **allows me to check through my past days and know how I felt and what made me happy***" [MG-P3].

"I liked how presenting feeling before and after expressing gratitude in a calendar so I ***can see how my feeling changed over five weeks and which gratitude changed my feeling one I click on that day***" [MG-P5].

However, few participants reported that visualization was a less interesting feature.

"I do not like the visualization ***as it is irrelevant to me, and I think it is the less interesting feature***" [MG-P2].

Theme 8: Usability of the App. This theme reflects users' experiences, perceptions, and opinions of the app. Many participants appreciated the app's simplicity and ease of use, and the high-quality design of the app functions as one of its most appealing aspects. They also liked the ability to add pictures to their gratitude and how the app guided them to enter their gratitude without any effort, as shown by the sample quotes.

"I liked the simplicity of the app. ***it is not complicated. It is easy to write my gratitude***" [CS-P3].

"I liked how the ***interface was organized. It did not require any effort to be used***." [CMP8].

"I really liked the ability to ***add a picture to my gratitude. It added meaning to my gratitude***" [SG-P3].

"I enjoyed the initial of the app where it will help me on how to write what I'm grateful for instead of finding a way of putting it by myself" [TM-P7].

6 Discussion

Previous studies suggested that employing many persuasive strategies to design persuasive interventions may decrease their effectiveness [37]; while another study showed that a PT that employed a single strategy was effective. However, the comparative effectiveness of employing multiple strategies and a single strategy in PT remains an open research question. Therefore, our research investigated whether employing multiple strategies in persuasive mental health apps would be more effective than employing a single strategy concerning their motivational appeal toward promoting mental and emotional well-being using the ARCS motivational scale. To do that, we designed two different versions of a Gratitude app using different numbers of persuasive strategies. We employed the Suggestion & encouragement strategy in the single-strategy version and employed Suggestion & encouragement, Self-monitoring, Reminder, and Social Support strategies in the multi-strategy version.

Our results show that, overall, the Gratitude app was effective in terms of its motivational appeal toward enhancing mental and emotional well-being. The app encouraged users to be happy and optimistic while reducing their stress and anxiety. Additionally, it helped them to focus on the positive aspects of their lives. These findings align with the qualitative comments provided by our participants. For example, *"I* ***saw a big difference in how I think and became more positive in any situation I am in. Even if it was a busy or stressful day, that's how it affected me***". [MG-P4].

"It made me look at the big picture as I have been only focusing on what's missing rather than what I have" [CS-P2].

This supports our results that the Gratitude app was successful in motivating the participants to improve their mental and emotional well-being.

The results also showed that the two versions of the app were effective. This confirms previous research finding that a PT that employs a single strategy can be effective [25]. However, above all, the results of the comparative analysis show that a persuasive intervention designed using multiple strategies was more effective than the one designed using a single strategy in terms of motivational appeal. However, the question remains: how many strategies can be implemented in a persuasive intervention at a time to maximize effectiveness? It is essential we avoid overloading persuasive interventions with too many strategies, thereby increasing their complexity and associated cognitive load on users.

Once again, capturing participants' attention and ensuring their enjoyment while using the app increases user engagement and encourages them to spend more time within the app. The more the users use the app to express their gratitude, the more their mental health and emotional well-being improve. Therefore, ***designers of mental health apps can employ multiple strategies to increase the motivational appeal of their apps which lead to increases users' engagement***.

However, both versions increased users' confidence in using the app to improve their mental health and emotional well-being as the app is easy to understand and use and helps them to write what they are grateful for without much effort. This is particularly important, mental health apps ought to work to lower users' stress. This is evidence from participants' comment who stated that "*I liked* ***the simplicity of the app. it is not complicated.*** *It is easy to write my gratitude*" [CS-P3].

"*I liked how the* ***interface was organized. It did not require any effort to be used***." [CM-P8].

As previous studies have shown gender differences in experiencing and expressing gratitude [8, 32], our findings also indicate gender differences in motivational appeal across the two versions of the Gratitude app. Females were more satisfied with multi-strategy version as they found the app more enjoyable, felt pleasure during using the multi-strategy version and help them to express their gratitude. In contrast, males found that multi-strategy version more relevant to them and it was able to capture and retain their attention. These results show that females and males differ with their motivational appeal to the multi-strategy version.

Overall, the data analysis shows that participants found that multi-strategy of Gratitude app more effective compared to single-strategy and males perceived the motivational appeal of multi-strategy differ than female. Therefore, designers of mental health apps can employ appropriate multiple strategies to increase their app effectiveness. They also could tailor the app according to gender.

6.1 Limitation and Future Work

The first limitation of this work is that we only included participants who self-reported stress, low mood, depression, anxiety, panic attacks, and other forms of mental health-related issues. As a result, our findings may not be entirely generalizable to other patient populations. The second limitation is that most of our participants are young adults and are relatively educated; therefore, we cannot generalize the results to non-educated individuals. Our study demonstrates that employing multiple (four) strategies in mental health apps is effective. However, it is uncertain what the maximum number of strategies that can be employed in a system before reaching a point of diminishing returns. Hence, future research should investigate the breaking point (limit) to the number of strategies that can be employed in a system. Moreover, there is a need to examine how to reduce the cognitive load that may result from implementing a large number of strategies in a system to improve its effectiveness.

7 Conclusion

In recent years, there has been a rise in the development of apps aimed at boosting users' mental and emotional well-being. These apps employ various persuasive and behaviour change strategies. However, the comparative effectiveness of employing multiple strategies versus a single strategy in persuasive mental health apps is still an open research question. To answer this question, we developed two versions of a persuasive Gratitude app using a varying number of persuasive strategies in each version. We conducted a 5-week field study of 84 participants and interviewed 16 of them. The results show that overall, the Gratitude app was effective with respect to its motivational appeal. Moreover, although both versions were effective individually, the multiple strategy version emerged to be more effectiveness with respect to its motivational appeal compared to the single strategy version, Moreover, there are gender differences in motivational appeal across the two versions of the app. Furthermore, the interview data provided more insight and showed that participants appreciated the simplicity of the app and how the app improved their mental and emotional well-being.

References

1. Abraham, C., Michie, S.: A taxonomy of behavior change techniques used in interventions. Heal. Psychol. **27**(3), 379–387 (2008)
2. Aldenaini, N., Alqahtani, F., Orji, R., Srinivas, S.: Trends in persuasive technologies for physical activity and sedentary behavior: a systematic review. Front. Artif. Intell. J. Hum. Learn. Behav. Chang. **85** (2020)
3. Alhasani, M., Mulchandani, D., Oyebode, O., Orji, R.: A systematic review of persuasive strategies in stress management apps. In: CEUR Workshop Proceedings (2020)
4. Almutari, N., Orji, R.: How effective are social influence strategies in persuasive apps for promoting physical activity? A systematic review. In: ACM UMAP 2019 - Adjunct Publication of the User Modeling, Adaptation and Personalization, pp. 167–172 (2019)
5. Alqahtani, F., Al Khalifah, G., Oyebode, O., Orji, R.: Apps for mental health: an evaluation of behavior change strategies and recommendations for future development. Front. Artif. Intell. **2** (2019)
6. Alqahtani, F., Winn, A., Orji, R.: Co-designing a mobile app to improve mental health and well-being: focus group study. JMIR Form. Res. **5**(2), e18172 (2021)
7. Alslaity, A., Chan, G., Orji, R., Wilson, R.: Insights from longitudinal evaluation of moodie mental health app. In: Human Factors in Computing Systems (2022)
8. Jung Hyun Choi and Mi Yu. 2014. Correlates of gratitude disposition in middle school students: Gender differences. *Technol. Heal. Care* 22, 3 (2014), 459–466
9. Cregg, D.R., Cheavens, J.S.: Gratitude interventions: effective self-help? A meta-analysis of the impact on symptoms of depression and anxiety. J. Happiness Stud. **22**(1), 413–445 (2021)

10. Davis, D.E., et al.: Thankful for the little things: a meta-analysis of gratitude interventions. J. Couns. Psychol. **63**(1), 20–31 (2016)
11. Dickens, L.R.: Using gratitude to promote positive change: a series of meta-analyses investigating the effectiveness of gratitude interventions. Basic Appl. Soc. Psych. **39**(4), 193–208 (2017)
12. Fogg, B.J.: Persuasive Technology: Using Computers to Change What We Think and Do (2003)
13. Gaddy, M.A., Ingram, R.E.: A meta-analytic review of mood-congruent implicit memory in depressed mood. Clin. Psychol. Rev. **34**(5), 402–416 (2014)
14. Garnett, C., Crane, D., Michie, S., West, R., Brown, J.: Evaluating the effectiveness of a smartphone app to reduce excessive alcohol consumption: protocol for a factorial randomised control trial. BMC Public Health **16**(1), 536 (2016)
15. Geraghty, A.W.A., Wood, A.M., Hyland, M.E.: Attrition from self-directed interventions: investigating the relationship between psychological predictors, intervention content and dropout from a body dissatisfaction intervention. Soc. Sci. Med. **71**(1), 30–37 (2010)
16. Gopalan, V., et al.: A review of the motivation theories in learning. AIP Conf. Proc. **1891**(2017), 40002 (2017)
17. Hamari, J., Koivisto, J., Pakkanen, T.: Do persuasive technologies persuade? - A review of empirical studies. In: Lecture Notes in Computer Science (including subseries Lecture Notes in Artificial Intelligence and Lecture Notes in Bioinformatics) (2014)
18. Harjumaa, M., Oinas-Kukkonen, H.: Persuasive systems design: key issues, process model, and system features. Commun. Assoc. Inf. Syst. **24**, 1 (2009)
19. Keller, J.: Motivation in motivation in instructional design. Perform. Instr. **26**, 8 (1987)
20. Keller, J.M.: Development and use of the ARCS model of instructional design. J. Instr. Dev. **10**(3), 2–10 (1987)
21. Lehto, T., Oinas-Kukkonen, H.: Persuasive features in web-based alcohol and smoking interventions: a systematic review of the literature. J. Med. Internet Res. **13**(3), e46 (2011)
22. Michie, S., et al.: The behavior change technique taxonomy (v1) of 93 hierarchically clustered techniques: building an international consensus for the reporting of behavior change interventions. Ann. Behav. Med. **46**, 1 (2013)
23. Mulchandani, D., Alslaity, A., Orji, R.: Exploring the effectiveness of persuasive games for disease prevention and awareness and the impact of tailoring to the stages of change. Human-Computer Interact. (2022)
24. NMH Communications. World Health Organization. 2013. WHO | Mental disorders affect one in four people. WHO. https://www.who.int/whr/2001/media_centre/press_release/en/. Accessed 19 June 2020
25. Orji, R., Mandryk, R.L., Vassileva, J.: Improving the efficacy of games for change using personalization models. ACM Trans. Comput. Interact. **24**, 5 (2017)
26. Orji, R., Moffatt, K.: Persuasive technology for health and wellness: state-of-the-art and emerging trends. Health Inform. J. **24**(1), 66–91 (2018)
27. Orji, R.: Design for Behaviour Change: A Model-driven Approach for Tailoring Persuasive Technologies. Univ. Saskatchewan, Canada, pp. 1–257 (2014). https://pdfs.semanticscholar.org/40ef/72768d0858763ebf0d2ba8ccde509ac5cbd5.pdf. Accessed 6 Sept 2019
28. Orji, R., Vassileva, J., Mandryk, R.L.: LunchTime: a slow-casual game for long-term dietary behavior change. Pers. Ubiquit. Comput. **17**(6), 1211–1221 (2013)
29. Oyebode, O., Ndulue, C., Alhasani, M., Orji, R.: Persuasive mobile apps for health and wellness: a comparative systematic review. In: Gram-Hansen, S., Jonasen, T., Midden, C. (eds.) Lecture Notes in Computer Science (including subseries Lecture Notes in Artificial Intelligence and Lecture Notes in Bioinformatics), vol. 12064, pp. 163–181. Springer, Cham (2020). 10.1007/978-3-030-45712-9_13

30. Reigeluth, C.M.: Instructional-Design Theories And Models : An Overview of their Current Status Edited by J---r : SJ. (2002)
31. Ryan, R.M., Deci, E.L.: Self-determination theory: basic psychological needs in motivation, development, and wellness (2017). https://doi.org/10.1521/978.14625/28806
32. Shourie, S., Kaur, H.: Gratitude and forgiveness as correlates of well-being among adolescents. Indian J. Heal. Wellbeing **7**(8), 827–833 (2016). https://www.proquest.com/openview/326dfdd0acc17b5f55ffb491d84ca6aa/1?pq-origsite=gscholar&cbl=2032134. Accessed 30 Jan 2024
33. Sugawara, E., Nikaido, H.: Properties of AdeABC and AdeIJK efflux systems of Acinetobacter baumannii compared with those of the AcrAB-TolC system of Escherichia coli. Antimicrob. Agents Chemother. **58**(12), 7250–7257 (2014)
34. Thomas, C.: Effectiveness of gratitude intervention on selected mental health indicators : a systematic review and meta-analysis. Int. J. Allied Med. Sci. Clin. Res. **2**, 7–14 (2021). www.ijmer.in. Accessed 18 Jan 2022
35. Tsong, C.K., Samsudin, Z., Jaafar, W.A., Yahaya, W.: Designing a Motivated Tangible Multimedia System for Preschoolers Tangible Multimedia System for Preschoolers View Project. (2017). https://www.researchgate.net/publication/313903320. Accessed 17 Nov 2022
36. Wigfield, A., Eccles, J.S.: Expectancy–value theory of achievement motivation. Contemp. Educ. Psychol. **25**(1), 68–81 (2000)
37. Wildeboer, G., et al.: The relationship between persuasive technology principles, adherence and effect of web-Based interventions for mental health: a meta-analysis. Int. J. Med. Inform. **96**, 71–85 (2016)

Persuasive Design Principles for a Medication Adherence App for Chronic Arthritis Conditions

Saleh A. Altuwayrib[1,2](✉), Mark Freeman[2], Nawaf Almutairi[1,2], and Khin Than Win[2]

[1] University of Hail, Hail, Saudi Arabia
sasa948@uowmail.edu.au
[2] University of Wollongong, Wollongong, NSW, Australia

Abstract. Nonadherence to medications is a significant challenge for individuals with chronic arthritis, potentially resulting in serious health problems. Recently, the advent of mobile health apps (mHealth apps) has been promising for empowering users and facilitating health behaviour change. To motivate arthritis patients to take prescribed medications on time, the incorporation of persuasive system design (PSD) features can be beneficial. Thus, there is a need to use the PSD model in arthritis mHealth apps. This study aims to map design requirements to PSD principles to motivate arthritis patients to engage in medication management activities. Individual interviews and focus group discussions were conducted to identify design requirements from the perspectives of both arthritis patients (ATPs) and healthcare providers (HCPs). Seven distinct categories of design requirements emerged from the analysis, which includes medication management, self-monitoring, health education, motivational, integration capabilities, as well as considerations for app usability and accessibility. The significance and relevancy of these requirements in supporting adherence behaviour for Saudi arthritis patients were thoroughly discussed.

Keywords: Persuasive Design Principles · Medication Adherence · Mobile Health Applications · Chronic Arthritis Conditions

1 Introduction

Arthritis is a long-term inflammatory health condition that is characterised by joint inflammation, stiffness and swelling [1]. Medication adherence is an important behaviour that enables patients to manage the disease and prevent flare-ups and joint damage. However, nonadherence behaviour to arthritis medications remains a significant challenge for patients and healthcare systems. Nonadherence decreases the effectiveness of treatment and the individuals' quality of life. Additionally, it increases the utilisation of health services and health costs [2]. To tackle this problem, mobile health applications (mHealth apps) have emerged as promising consumer health informatics solutions that aim to support patient care and health behaviour change [3]. The design of mHealth apps plays an important role in supporting patient adherence, user engagement and health monitoring [4, 5]. Persuasive design in medication adherence apps aims to simplify medication

N. Baghaei et al. (Eds.): PERSUASIVE 2024, LNCS 14636, pp. 42–53, 2024.
https://doi.org/10.1007/978-3-031-58226-4_4

management and facilitate health behaviour change [6]. Reminders, self-monitoring and social support are examples of some persuasive features that could support medication adherence behaviour for chronic arthritis patients [7]. A previous review conducted by Geuens et al. [7] found that, on average, arthritis apps used 6 persuasive design features. Credibility was the most used category, followed by primary task support, dialogue and social support features. These features can be utilised in mHealth app design to motivate users, improve patient use of mHealth apps and adherence, and overall user satisfaction. To engage users with the use of mHealth apps, it is important to involve them in the early stages of design, understand their needs and how the app can support their health behaviour change. In this study, the user-centered design (UCD) approach was adopted to ensure that app is tailored to meet the needs and preferences of arthritis patients (ATPs) [8]. The involvement of healthcare providers (HCPs) contributes valuable information to mHealth app designers about the arthritis care aspects and assists in designing a usable app tailored to the needs of ATPs [9]. Therefore, the prototype design started with conducting a literature review and understanding the perceptions of both HCPs and ATPs to identify their requirements. This paper aims to demonstrate the incorporation of identified requirements into persuasive design features.

2 Method

This study is a part of a larger project that followed the steps of Design Science Research (DSR), which is a research methodology used to create and iteratively evaluate information systems [10]. In this paper, we present the first design cycle, progressing through the DSR steps, including problem identification, objectives of a solution, prototype design, demonstration, evaluation, and communication [11]. For the problem identification, a qualitative scoping review (SR) was conducted to identify motivational medication adherence support features, setting the groundwork for designing an app for ATPs [6]. This review informed our UCD approach, involving ten individual interviews with HCPs and two groups with 16 ATPs. The user research provided insights into medication adherence barriers, current interventions, experiences, and perceptions of using mHealth apps for arthritis and medication management. The design process commenced with developing of low-fidelity wireframes to outline the main design features, particularly navigation and the overall user flow. Figma was used to create high-fidelity mockups that visualised the design concept and allowed stakeholders to preview how the app would look and share their feedback. The Figma prototype was shared with stakeholders to gather their feedback and engage them in discussions about their preferences and expectations from the initial design iteration. Further, a third focus group discussion was conducted with 10 ATPs participated and during the session the researcher presented 21 high fidelity screen designs illustrating various aspects of the app design. Verbatim transcripts of both individual interviews and group discussions were translated from Arabic to English and subsequently coded by using NVivo 12. The analysis identified the relevant design requirements through the scoping review, individual interviews, and group discussions, and the research team mapped these requirements to the persuasive design principles.

3 Results

The results of the first design cycle identified the design requirements and initiated the design process, coupled with an evaluation of user preferences.

3.1 Stakeholder Requirements

During the user research, the necessary requirements for medication adherence apps were identified from the scoping review (SR), healthcare providers (HCPs) and arthritis patients (ATPs) perspectives (see Table 1).

Medication Management. HCPs and ATPs agreed on the importance of medication schedules, reminders, and empowering users to maintain notes associated with their medication usage. Essential features should include uploading prescriptions, tracking medication adherence, and displaying a history of previous medications. Accessing services like checking drug interactions, finding nearby pharmacies, and confirming medication availability.

Self-Monitoring. ATPs expected the app to offer diverse health trackers for systematically monitoring their condition, including symptom logging and clear visual data presentation. HCPs recommend tools for assessing disease activity, joint pain, and mood levels, along with summarizing reports. They stressed the importance of scientifically validated and recognised in the medical arthritis community.

Health Education. ATPs need detailed information about their condition, medications, and available support programs to better understand and manage their disease. HCPs emphasize providing references within health education materials for verifying information accuracy and suggest presenting content in various formats.

Motivational. ATPs consider creating an arthritis community within the app as a source of motivation for sharing experiences. Both ATPs and HCPs suggested setting medication and self-monitoring tasks as goals, with progress tracking and personalised feedback to motivate users. Features like progress bar and celebratory messages for adherence behaviour. Virtual badges for achievements and tangible rewards like discount coupons or points for unlocking features are also proposed.

Integration. The app should facilitate seamless integration with wearable devices for synchronize their health data and improve monitoring. ATPs believed that integrating the app with local health information systems to access medication related data will improve users' timely access to information.

Privacy. Provide users secure storage and management of personal health information, prioritizing patient privacy and data confidentiality. HCPs recommended that the app content be developed by non-profit organisations, adhering to ethical standards in designing health applications to ensure data confidentiality and patient privacy.

Usability. HCPs and ATPs want the app design to be appropriate to the health context with intuitive navigation, and visually appealing colours. They highlighted the importance of the app being user-friendly and easy access to main features and supportive language. The app should present educational content on arthritis using various formats, including graphics and videos and incorporate interactive elements.

Accessibility. The app should be inclusive and meet diverse users from different backgrounds, capabilities, and cultures. It should offer offline access to key features and customizable settings for calendar, language, and notifications.

Table 1. Design Requirements

	Requirements	SR	HCPs	APTs
Medication management	Provide users with the daily and weekly medication schedule	X	X	
	Allow users to track taken or missed medications and show a list of previous medications	X		X
	Provide users with reminders for medication taking	X	X	X
	Provide users with reminders for medication refill dates	X		
	Allow users to record notes related to medication use		X	X
	Provide users with ability to securely store and manage users' personal health information			X
	Allow users to access official website that enable users to check drug interactions	X		X
	Allow users to find nearby pharmacies			X
	Allow users to check the medication availability in local pharmacies			X
Self-monitoring	The app allows users to input and monitor their symptoms over time	X		X
	The app should visualize users' health measurements in a clear and comprehensible manner	X		
	Enable users to evaluate their disease activity, joint pain, and emotional well-being	X	X	

(continued)

Table 1. (*continued*)

	Requirements	SR	HCPs	APTs
	Provide reliable and relevant arthritis self-monitoring tools		X	
	The app should have various health trackers to monitor and collect comprehensive health data from users about arthritis			X
Health education	Provide detailed information about arthritis conditions, medications, and support programs	X	X	X
	Present all educational and informational content using a variety of formats to accommodate diverse user preferences		X	X
	The app should verify the credibility of educational sources and ensure they are up-to-date, and evidence based		X	X
Motivational	Allow users to connect with others in a supportive and informative environment	X		X
	Allow users to view and share arthritis-related experiences with others		X	X
	Allow users to connect with others facing similar arthritis conditions or interests	X		X
	Allow users to set, track, and achieve personalized health and treatment goals	X	X	X
	Provide users with feedback based on their interactions and achievements within the app	X	X	X
	Provide users with diverse challenges that cater to different user interests and encourage participation from a wide range of arthritis patients	X	X	
	Allow users to monitor their adherence levels and self-monitoring parameters	X	X	X
	Acknowledges and celebrates users' accomplishments and positive health behaviours	X	X	X

(*continued*)

Table 1. (*continued*)

	Requirements	SR	HCPs	APTs
	Provide users with incentives and motivate users in their adherence and treatment journey	**X**	**X**	**X**
	Celebratory messages for achievements and motivate users to continue healthy behaviours			**X**
Integration	Enable users to connect with wearable devices	**X**		**X**
	Enable users to connect with different health information systems to facilitate secure and efficient sharing of user's health-related data			**X**
Privacy	Provide users with ability to securely store and manage users' personal health information			**X**
	The app should be developed by a non-profit organisation to ensure the confidentiality of health data		**X**	
Usability	The app should be user-friendly, intuitive design and easy to navigate and interact with		**X**	**X**
	The app should be learnable and allow users to quickly understand the features		**X**	
	The app should prioritise the safety and security of user data and interactions within the app		**X**	
	Provide users with interactive elements to improve user interactions and improve engagement with the app		**X**	**X**
Accessibility	The app should be inclusive and meet diverse users from different backgrounds, capabilities, and cultures		**X**	
	The app design should be visually appealing, and colours should consider individuals with vision deficiencies			**X**
	Provide users with offline access to use essential features when the internet connection is unavailable		**X**	

(*continued*)

Table 1. (*continued*)

	Requirements	SR	HCPs	APTs
	The app should allow to adjust the text size according to user readability preferences			X
	Provide users with multiple languages to ensure inclusivity and accessibility for different arthritis patients	X	X	X

3.2 Prototype Design

After the design requirements identification, the design process commenced with creating the prototype. This step started with the ideation and visualisation of 10 app screens that were designed to satisfy user needs (see Fig. 1). These screens included: My medications, App community, Health education, Self-assessment, Calendar, Notifications, Rewards, Profile, Settings.

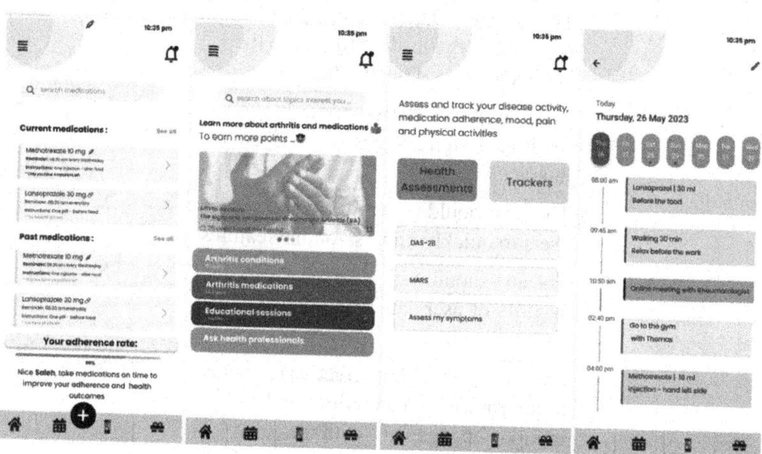

Fig. 1. Design screens

3.3 User Preferences

During the evaluation, participants expressed different opinions on prototype features, mainly focusing on medication management, self-monitoring, health education and motivational aspects. For Medication management, they advocated simplifying data entry with technologies like autocomplete, barcode, or QR code scanning, and allowing seamless management of personal health information. In self-monitoring, there was a preference for trackers to monitor joint pain, lab parameters, and mood, with reminders and informative reports generation. Health education should offer all information related to arthritis conditions and medications from reputable local and international arthritis institutions. Motivationally, participants favored having a supervised community by health professionals and volunteer users. Creating support groups tailored for specific conditions, gamified elements for earning points, level-ups with unlocking features, discount coupons for medical services, equipment, and motivational badges and messages for user engagement and positive reinforcement after taking medications or logging trackers.

3.4 Mapping Design Requirements to Persuasive Design Principles

Primary Task. ATPs would like to simplify the medication entry using QR codes and visual aids like images for easy identification. Direct users to official websites for medication management services, including drug interactions and medication availability in MOH hospitals. It is important to tailor health education to specific arthritis conditions and allow personalised medication reminders and note-taking.

Dialogue Support. Contextual reminders recommended in the app for medication adherence, linking them to daily routines like meals or prayers times. The app provides a social platform for sharing experiences and information about arthritis events and motivate users by rewarding health behaviours in medication management and self-monitoring.

Credibility Support. Both HCPs and ATPs emphasized the need for health trackers and self-assessments to be scientifically validated. They stressed the importance of sourcing information on arthritis conditions and treatments from reputable and credible arthritis organisations (see Table 2). ATPs advocated for moderated health education and community content to prevent misinformation, preferring communication with HCPs through officially regulated health institutions like MOH telehealth apps.

Social Support. Create an arthritis community for user connection and experience sharing. It can host condition-specific groups for knowledge exchange and motivation within a medically supervised environment. Provide users with anonymized medication adherence rate on each medication for benchmarking and proactively notify users about relevant arthritis events and webinars.

Table 2. Map requirements to persuasive features

	Identified requirements	PSD features
Medication management	Provide users with the daily and weekly medication schedule	Reduction (P)
	Allow users to track taken or missed medications and show a list of previous medications	Self-monitoring (P)

(continued)

Table 2. *(continued)*

	Identified requirements	PSD features
	Provide users with reminders for medication-taking	Reminders (D)
	Provide users with reminders for medication refill dates	Reminders (D)
	Allow users to record notes related to medication use	Self-monitoring (P) Personalisation (P)
	Provide users with ability to securely store and manage users' personal health information	Personalisation (P)
	Allow users to access official website that enable users to check drug interactions	Tunneling (P) Third-Party Endorsement (C)
	Allow users to find nearby pharmacies	Tunneling (P)
	Allow users to check the medication availability in local pharmacies	Tunneling (P) Third-Party Endorsement (C)
Self-monitoring	The app allows to input and monitor symptoms over time	Self-monitoring (P)
	The app should visualize users' health measurements in a clear and comprehensible manner	Self-monitoring (P)
	Enable users to evaluate their disease activity, joint pain, and emotional well-being	Self-monitoring (P) Tailoring (P) Reminders (D)
	Provide reliable and relevant arthritis self-monitoring tools	Verifiability (C)
	The app should have various health trackers to monitor and collect health data from users about arthritis	Self-monitoring (P)
Health education	Provide detailed information about arthritis conditions, medications, and support programs	Tailoring (P) Trustworthiness (C)
	Present all educational and informational content using a variety of formats to accommodate diverse user preferences	Liking (D)

(continued)

Table 2. (*continued*)

	Identified requirements	PSD features
	The app should verify the credibility of educational sources and ensure they are up-to-date, and evidence based	Verifiability (C)
Motivational	Allow users to connect with others in a supportive and informative environment	Verifiability (C) Social facilitation (S)
	Allow users to view and share arthritis-related experiences with others	Social role (D) Normative (S) Social learning (S)
	Allow users to connect with others facing similar arthritis conditions or interests	Social facilitation (S) Social learning (P)
	Allow users to set, track, and achieve personalized health and treatment goals	Personalisation (P)
	Allow users to monitor their adherence levels and self-monitoring parameters	Self-monitoring (P) Personalisation (P) Normative (S)
	Provide users with feedback based on their interactions and achievements within the app	Praise (D)
	Celebratory messages for achievements and motivate users to continue healthy behaviours	Praise (D) Recognition (S)
	Provide users with incentives and motivate users in their adherence and treatment journey	Rewards (D) Recognition (S)

P Primary; D Dialogue; C Credibility; S Social

4 Discussion

The main goal of this study was to map design requirements to PSD features that support medication adherence among ATPs. The findings revealed that primary task principles, especially personalisation with easy medication management and timely reminders are crucial. They considered a critical for chronic disease patients to prevent forgetting and optimize adherence [12]. ATPs also valued self-monitoring features to monitor disease progression, with tailored health trackers which can provide meaningful updates. Analysing user preferences helps research team in identifying what persuasive features that stakeholder find motivating and could support adherence behaviour. For ATPs, the app should focus on the social and dialogue support that makes the app engaging and enjoyable. Providing positive feedback on the user interactions within medication management, self-monitoring, and health education identified as a motivational [5]. ATPs showed a preference for rewards related to medical services and incentives linked to social participation and self-monitoring. Supervising community content and communicating with HCPs through official telehealth services. Communication channels with HCPs and self-assessment tools are generously provided at no cost by the MOH in Saudi Arabia [13]. This preference for social support features in medication management, which were less common in previous studies [14], our study revealed a preference among ATPs for such features with taking into consideration the privacy and confidentiality. Educational materials need to be visually appealing and condition-specific, and validated by local arthritis institutions for credibility [15]. However, the study's focused on Saudi Arabia limits its generalizability, and the sample size may not fully represent the broader population. Future work will refine the app's design, focusing on usability and persuasiveness, aligning with the Saudi population's preferences for health social networks [16].

5 Conclusion

The key persuasive features used were centered around primary task and dialogue support, improving the design for personalised and interactive experiences. Notably, individuals with arthritis preferred social support to learn more about their arthritis condition and seek emotional support from relevant peers. These efforts aimed to address the nonadherence behaviour caused by a lack of knowledge or motivation. Medication management features are designed to mitigate unintentional nonadherence by reminding users to take their medication, empowering them to track arthritis-related data and conveniently access information about their condition from any location.

References

1. Scott, D.L., Kingsley, G.H., Pugh, N.: Inflammatory Arthritis In Clinical Practice. Springer (2007). https://doi.org/10.1007/978-1-4471-6648-1
2. van den Bemt, B.J.F., Zwikker, H.E., van den Ende, C.H.M.: Medication adherence in patients with rheumatoid arthritis: a critical appraisal of the existing literature. Exp. Rev. Clin. Immunol. **8**(4), 337–351 (2012)
3. Marengo, M.F., Suarez-Almazor, M.E.: Improving treatment adherence in patients with rheumatoid arthritis: what are the options? Int. J. Clin. Rheumtol. **10**(5), 345–356 (2015)
4. Hamari, J., Koivisto, J., Pakkanen, T.: Do persuasive technologies persuade?-a review of empirical studies. In: Persuasive Technology: 9th International Conference, PERSUASIVE 2014. Springer (2014). https://doi.org/10.1007/978-3-319-07127-5_11
5. Almutairi, N., Vlahu-Gjorgievska, E., Win, K.T.: Persuasive features for patient engagement through mHealth applications in managing chronic conditions: a systematic literature review and meta-analysis. Inform. Health Soc. Care **48**(3), 267–291 (2023)
6. Altuwayrib, S.A., Win, K.T., Freeman, M.: Gamified medication adherence applications for chronic health conditions: scoping review. In: Persuasive Technology: 18th International Conference, PERSUASIVE 2023, Eindhoven, The Netherlands, April 19–21, 2023, Proceedings, pp. 307–321. Springer, Eindhoven (2023).https://doi.org/10.1007/978-3-031-30933-5_20

7. Geuens, J., et al.: A review of persuasive principles in mobile apps for chronic arthritis patients: opportunities for improvement. JMIR Mhealth Uhealth **4**(4), e118 (2016)
8. Göttgens, I., Oertelt-Prigione, S.: The application of human-centered design approaches in health research and innovation: a narrative review of current practices. JMIR Mhealth Uhealth **9**(12), e28102 (2021)
9. Cai, R.A., et al.: Developing and evaluating JIApp: acceptability and usability of a smartphone app system to improve self-management in young people with juvenile idiopathic arthritis. JMIR Mhealth Uhealth **5**(8), e121 (2017)
10. Hevner, A., et al.: Design science in information systems research. Manag. Inf. Syst. Q. **28**, 75 (2004)
11. Pfeffers, K., et al.: The design science research process: a model for producing and presenting information systems research. In: Proceedings of the First International Conference on Design Science Research in Information Systems and Technology (DESRIST 2006), Claremont (2006)
12. Bruera, S., et al.: PMS67 - Use of medication reminders in patients with rheumatoid arthritis. Value Health **17**(7), A384 (2014)
13. Shati, A.: Mhealth applications developed by the Ministry of Health for public users in KSA: a persuasive systems design evaluation. Health Inf. Int. J. **9**(1), 1–13 (2020)
14. Win, K.T., et al.: Persuasive systems design features in promoting medication management for consumers (2017)
15. Almutairi, N., et al.: Understanding Healthcare Providers' Value Perceptions of Content Creation and Design of a Personalized Asthma Content Creation and Design of a Personalized Asthma Management App: A Case Study in Saudi Arabia (2022)
16. El Kheir, D.Y.M., et al.: The Saudi experience of health-related social media use: a scoping review. Saudi J. Health Syst. Res. **1**(3), 81–92 (2021)

DROP DASH: A Persuasive Mobile Game to Promote Healthy Hydration Choices Using Machine Learning

Sussan Anukem(✉), Chinenye Ndulue, and Rita Orji

Dalhousie University, Halifax, NS, Canada
{sussananukem,cndulue,rita.orji}@dal.ca

Abstract. The increasing consumption of unhealthy beverages is a significant public health concern, contributing to a range of health issues. Recognized as effective tools for behavior change in various domains, persuasive games offer a promising opportunity to address these challenges. This research explores the design of "Drop Dash," a persuasive game strategically designed to encourage users to prioritize water as their primary source of hydration while discouraging the intake of unhealthy beverages through immersive gameplay focused on fostering and maintaining healthy hydration habits. Notably, the game incorporates machine learning (ML) and adopts a user-centered design approach to enhance user engagement. We developed a high-fidelity prototype of the game and evaluated it. The evaluation aimed to understand the overall usability of the game and how persuasive the strategies implemented in the game are in discouraging unhealthy hydration options and encouraging healthy hydration. The results showed that the game is highly persuasive, with the competition strategy standing out as the most effective among the eight implemented strategies. Additionally, the game received an overall usability score of 77, indicating that users generally found the game usable.

Keywords: Mobile Game · Persuasive Game · Healthy Hydration · Behavior Change · Machine Learning

1 Introduction

Over the years, our society has seen a concerning rise in the consumption of unhealthy beverages, posing a significant public health issue. The widespread availability and aggressive marketing of sugary, alcoholic, and calorie-laden drinks have led to various health problems, ranging from obesity to chronic diseases [5]. The frequent advertising and constant exposure to these types of drinks can persuade people to make unhealthy choices while omitting the healthier options.

On the other hand, the field of mobile health (mHealth) applications has witnessed substantial growth, offering numerous tools to enhance health-related habits. With over 350,000 mobile health apps available, this digital landscape has transformed how people approach dietary choices, emphasizing not only accessibility but also the persuasive

N. Baghaei et al. (Eds.): PERSUASIVE 2024, LNCS 14636, pp. 54–64, 2024.
https://doi.org/10.1007/978-3-031-58226-4_5

strategies embedded in their design [2]. These applications have become influential allies in promoting healthier lifestyles in our digital world.

Aside from mHealth applications, persuasive games have also been recognized as effective tools for promoting behavior change in various domains, including mental health [14], physical activity [1], and disease prevention [8]. They have gained popularity for their engaging nature, integrating elements of fun, excitement, and persuasive strategies to positively influence users' behavior [11].

Despite numerous initiatives attempting to address issues related to unhealthy beverage choices and poor hydration habits, changing people's behaviors, and promoting healthier choices remains a challenge.

In this paper, we introduce "Drop Dash," a persuasive game designed to leverage the potential of mobile gaming to address issues related to unhealthy beverage choices and poor hydration habits. The game emphasizes the consequences of unhealthy habits and encourages users to prioritize water as their main source of hydration. Its mechanics prompt players to gather water droplet power-ups while avoiding virtual unhealthy beverages. Machine learning is implemented to give each player a personalized daily challenge hydration target/goal recommendation. The recommendation is based on various factors, including the player's age, gender, external factors such as season and weather conditions, and their pregnancy or breastfeeding status. The personalized daily challenge serves as a strategic motivator, tailored to each player's unique circumstances and needs, thereby increasing the overall persuasiveness of the game. The game incorporates eight persuasive strategies to persuade users to make healthier choices. These include *Personalization, Reduction, Rewards, Praise, Self-Monitoring, Simulation, Suggestion, and Competition.*

To investigate the effectiveness of our design for encouraging healthy hydration habits, we developed the following three questions to guide our research:

- RQ1: What is the overall perceived persuasiveness of the Drop Dash game?
- RQ2: How usable is Drop Dash?
- RQ3: What is the perceived effectiveness of the persuasive strategies implemented in the Drop Dash game?

To answer these research questions, we created a high-fidelity prototype of the game and evaluated its perceived persuasiveness and usability, identifying potential issues before we move onto the development of the fully functional game. We conducted a study using semi-structured interviews and surveys with persuasive system design stakeholders. They evaluated the game based on the Perceived Persuasiveness Test (PPT) [15] and System Usability Scale (SUS) [3, 16].

2 Literature Review

In this section, we review existing literature on games that have been used to promote healthy behaviors in the nutrition domain. Building upon previous studies in this domain, we establish the foundation for understanding the persuasive strategies employed in these games, as identified in the reviewed literature.

Hatzigiannakoglou [6] designed a game called "Junk-Food Destroyer" targeted at adolescents with Down syndrome, aiming to encourage a balanced nutrition. The effectiveness of this tool was in the strategic implementation of rewards and feedback strategies.

Orji et al. [11] took a model-driven approach with "JunkFood Aliens," a game designed to promote healthy eating by vividly portraying the conflict between healthy and unhealthy food choices. The success of this game was attributed to the strategic implementation of persuasive strategies such as rewards, simulation, and competition.

In another study, Shiyko et al. [13] created a game called "SpaPlay" which focused on motivating women to exercise and make healthy eating choices, successfully employing strategies such as rewards and self-monitoring.

Furthermore, Orji et al. [12], designed an innovative game called "LunchTime" to educate players on how to make healthier meal choices when eating out. This game integrated elements of social learning, social influence, and goal-setting strategies.

Based on our review of existing literature, although informative, there is a lack of research on using machine learning and gameful interventions to support healthy hydration [7]. This underscores the importance of our research as a contribution to the field of Persuasive Technology and Human-Computer Interaction (HCI). By exploring the potential of gamification and machine learning in public health interventions, our work provides valuable insights into how interactive technologies can be leveraged to address nutrition related health challenges.

3 Method

In this section, we present the methodology we employed in designing our game.

3.1 Early Design Phase

To understand the problem area and the target behavior that our work should focus on, we conducted a study exploring how persuasive strategies are implemented in nutrition apps. The aim was to identify the correlation between the implementation of persuasive strategies in app design and the perceived effectiveness of these applications. We reviewed 20 nutrition apps and analyzed the persuasive strategies they implemented. We used the Persuasive Systems Design (PSD) model developed by Oinas-Kukkonen and Harjumaa [10], to identify persuasive strategies that were commonly implemented in this domain. Our findings showed that Personalization, Self-Monitoring and Suggestion were the most implemented persuasive strategies in these apps. Building on these findings, we then determined the design style and concept for the game. Opting for a minimalist design, we prioritized simplicity to ensure a clean and easily navigable interface to cater for a wider audience. Previous research suggests that persuasive games are more effective when the gaming concept is engaging, and the controls are straightforward [4]. This influenced our decision to adopt a *Linear Level Progression* and *Endless Runner* hybrid game concept in which the player character continuously moves forward through a level with a specific goal to achieve. The level ends either when the goal is achieved, or a completion criteria is not met. This design concept delivers a structured and goal-oriented gameplay experience within each level, ensuring a captivating and purpose-driven player engagement.

3.2 *Drop Dash* Overview

The game features a rich backstory, engaging gameplay, and a unique daily hydration challenge that reinforces the importance of hydration. In "*Drop Dash*," players embark on a thrilling adventure guiding Droppy, the game character, through a captivating journey to rescue HydroLand from a devastating drought. Their primary goal is to collect water droplets, needed for reviving different regions of HydroLand. Successful restoration of these regions earns players points, determining their rank on the leaderboard. Each level has a time limit and requires five health points to play. Initially, first time players are given five health points, and subsequently, they must acquire more through the daily challenge. Players must skillfully dodge unhealthy beverages to preserve health points at each level. If all five health points are depleted or the timer runs out before achieving the goal, the level terminates prematurely. The game offers an unlimited number of levels, with higher levels featuring shorter time limits and increased gameplay speed. This incremental difficulty functionality encourages players to make decisions quickly.

3.3 Machine Learning Integration

Machine learning serves as the backbone of this research, contributing significantly to user engagement. We integrated it in the game in the following ways:

1. **Logging Water Intake:** The scanning feature in "Drop Dash" is implemented to simplify the complex process of manually logging water intake for the users. To achieve this, advanced machine learning models, such as Convolutional Neural Networks (CNNs) for image classification and object detection, will be employed. These models will be seamlessly integrated into the game's scanning feature. When users scan a container, the CNNs will analyze the image, recognize the container type, estimate water levels accurately, and identify the presence of water in generic containers. This promotes accurate water intake tracking, aligning with the game's goal of encouraging healthy hydration.
2. **Personalized Daily Challenges:** One notable application of ML in "Drop Dash" is in the generation of unique daily challenge hydration targets for each player. Our game will use a combination of regression and recommendation models, such as Linear Regression and Collaborative Filtering, to tailor these challenges to each player's unique profile. We will collect and consider a range of individual factors, such as age, gender, external variables like the current season and weather conditions, and specific circumstances like pregnancy or breastfeeding status. These factors will be carefully weighed and analyzed by the ML models to provide players with daily hydration targets that are not only attainable but also align precisely with their distinct situations. This tailored approach ensures that every player receives a daily challenge that is not only achievable but also aligns with their unique circumstances, fostering a sense of personalization and motivation.

3.4 Persuasive Strategies and Their Implementations

We implemented eight Persuasive Strategies from the PSD Model [10] in the game.

1. **Suggestion:** "*This strategy recommends certain actions to users for achieving the desired goal during system use*". Players are given useful tips and recommendations on healthy hydration practices and dangers of unhealthy beverage consumption (Fig. 1a).
2. **Simulation:** "*This strategy provides the means for a user to observe the cause-and-effect linkage of their behaviour*". Players are shown a simulation of what happens when they take unhealthy beverages, (i.e., lose health points), and a simulation of the game character's health based on the player's choices during game play (Fig. 1b).
3. **Self-Monitoring:** "*This strategy allows people to track their own behaviours*". Players are shown their progress in completing the daily hydration challenge tasks at a daily, weekly, and monthly level (Fig. 1c).
4. **Reward:** "*This strategy offers virtual rewards to users for performing the target behaviour*". Players are rewarded with water droplets, health points, and badges for successfully meeting their target goal (Fig. 2a).
5. **Reduction:** "*This strategy involves simplifying complex tasks or information to facilitate user engagement*". Players are enabled to log water intake with a scanning feature instead of manual entry (Fig. 2b).
6. **Praise:** "*This strategy applauds users for performing or achieving a target action via words, images, symbols, or sounds*". Players get showered with praises for completing a task using words like 'Well-done', 'A true hero' (Fig. 2e).
7. **Personalization:** "*This strategy offers system-tailored contents and services based on the user's needs and characteristics*". Every player gets a unique daily challenge hydration target/goal recommendation based on their age, gender, external factors like the season and weather, and their pregnancy or breastfeeding status (Fig. 2c).
8. **Competition:** "*This strategy allows a player to compete against others*". Players get to compete with others globally for a rank on the leaderboard (Fig. 2d).

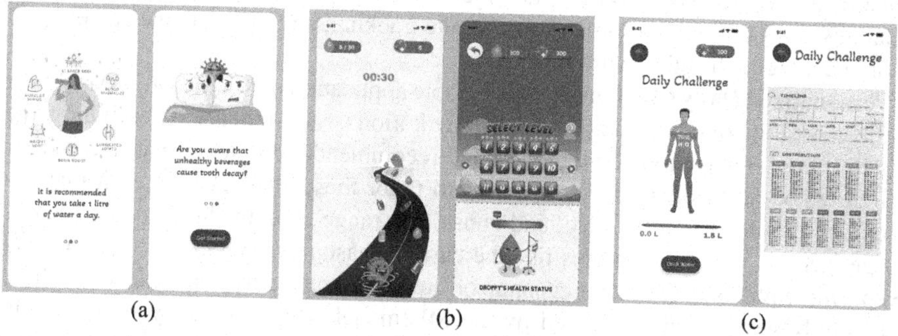

Fig. 1. Screenshots of the (a) Suggestion (b) Simulation and (c) Self-Monitoring Strategies

3.5 Study Design

To ascertain the game's persuasiveness and usability, we conducted a usability and persuasiveness evaluation we recruited five persuasive system design stakeholders, proficient in Persuasive Technology and experienced in implementing PSD model strategies

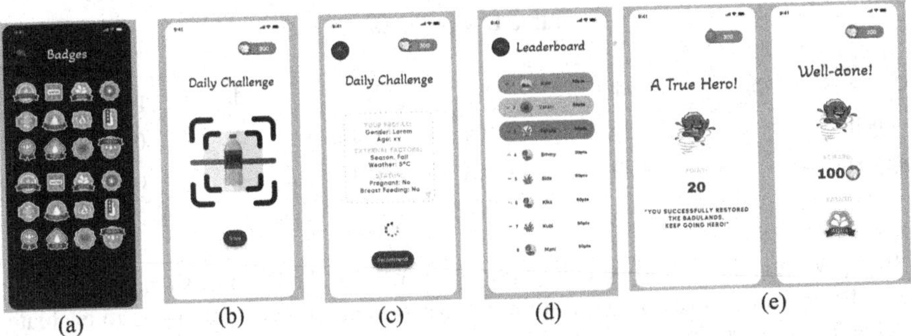

Fig. 2. Screenshots of the (a) Reward (b) Reduction (c) Personalization (d) Competition and (e) Praise Strategies

for the study. This number of participants is in line with the average number of heuristic evaluators as recommended by Jakob Nielson [9], who recommended between 3 to 5 participants since they would find about 75% of the existing usability issues. Before the study commenced, they were given an overview of the problem domain and an introduction to how the game works. The participants then played the game prototype for approximately 10 min before completing a questionnaire. The questionnaire covered a summary of each implemented persuasive strategy and presented questionnaire statements from the perceived persuasiveness scale [15] for both the overall game and each strategy, and usability using the system usability scale (SUS) [3, 17]. Participants indicated their level of agreement or disagreement with the statements on a 7-point Likert scale (ranging from 1 = strongly disagree to 7 = strongly agree). Additionally, participants were encouraged to share qualitative comments, providing valuable observations and suggestions for improvement using an open comment box.

4 Analysis and Results

In this section, we present the results from the persuasiveness and usability evaluations, and how they answer each of our research questions.

Table 1. One-sample t-test results for persuasiveness of persuasive strategies in Drop Dash

Persuasive Strategy	Mean	SD	t	df	p-value
Competition	6.00	0.559	8.000	4	0.001
Simulation	5.40	0.912	3.434	4	0.026
Personalization	5.35	1.098	2.749	4	0.051
Praise	5.25	0.848	3.297	4	0.030
Self-Monitoring	5.25	0.791	3.536	4	0.024
Rewards	5.10	0.652	3.773	4	0.020

(continued)

Table 1. *(continued)*

Persuasive Strategy	Mean	SD	t	df	p-value
Reduction	4.40	2.104	0.425	4	0.693
Suggestion	4.30	1.763	0.381	4	0.723

- RQ1: What is the overall perceived persuasiveness of the Drop Dash game?

  To answer this research question, we performed a one-sample t-test to evaluate whether our participants find the Drop Dash game significantly persuasive overall.

  The results show that Drop Dash is significantly persuasive, (t (4) = 21.915, p < .001). The mean PPT score (M = 6.05, SD = 0.209) is significantly higher than the midpoint of 4. This indicate that the game was perceived as highly persuasive.
- RQ2: How usable is Drop Dash?

  To answer this research question, we calculated the SUS score of the game based on the ratings from our evaluators. The overall System Usability Scale (SUS) score obtained was 77. According to Bangor et al. [3], the SUS score suggests that better products typically fall within the range of the high 70s to upper 80s. Therefore, a score of 77 can be interpreted as a good score, indicating that the game is above average in terms of usability. We further performed a one-sample t-test, and the results (t (4) = 4.469, p = 0.011) show that the usability score (M = 77, SD = 13.509) of Drop Dash is significantly higher than the neutral score of 50. Hence the game is very usable. Below are sample qualitative comments from evaluators that support our results:

  - "*Well designed system*" – P05; "*Nice work ...*" – P02

- RQ3: What is the perceived effectiveness of the persuasive strategies implemented in the Drop Dash game?

To answer this research question, we performed a one-sample t-test to evaluate whether there was a difference between the perceived persuasiveness of the persuasive strategies implemented in Drop Dash compared to the midpoint value of 4 (Table 1).

The results show that all the strategies are significantly persuasive except the reduction and suggestion strategies, see Table 1. For example, the mean PPT score (M = 6.0, SD = 0.559) for the competition strategy is significantly higher than the midpoint of 4 (Fig. 3), where (t (4) = 8.0, p = 0.001). This implies that this strategy was perceived as highly persuasive. On the contrary, the mean PPT score (M = 4.3, SD = 1.7625) for the suggestion strategy is not significantly higher than the midpoint of 4 where (t (4) = 0.381, p = 0.723). The result indicates that this strategy was not perceived as strongly persuasive. Sample qualitative comments from evaluators that support our result:

- "*Competition is a good strategy to employ in this app, it keeps users engaged and prolongs their use of the application.*" – P03
- "*Leaderboard would encourage me to log my daily water intake.*" – P01

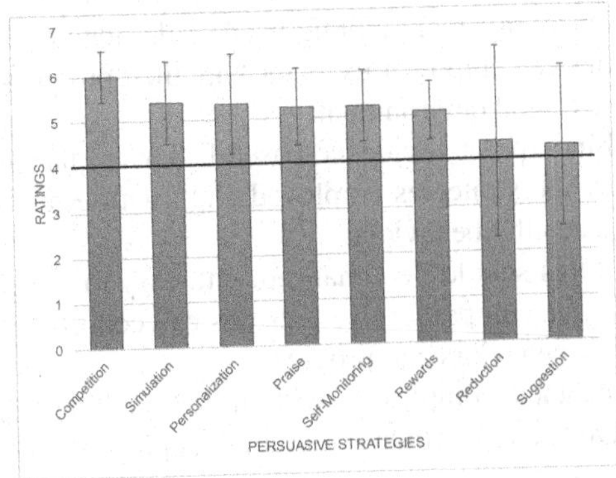

Fig. 3. Persuasiveness average rating for implemented strategies

5 Discussion

5.1 Persuasiveness of Strategies

In evaluating the persuasiveness of strategies in "Drop Dash," two strategies, Competition and Simulation, emerged as the strongest motivators and contributors to the overall effectiveness of the game as shown in Table 1. The Competition strategy, seamlessly integrated into the game dynamics, played a pivotal role in motivating players through challenges and rewards. This aligns with established research indicating that incorporating competition can motivate users to adopt a target attitude or behavior by leveraging human beings' natural drive to compete [10]. Similarly, the Simulation strategy significantly contributed to persuasiveness by providing a realistic environment reflecting the cause and effect of unhealthy choices. The interactive and realistic simulation elements effectively influenced user behavior, aligning with the game's objectives. However, the Reduction strategy exhibited lower persuasiveness as shown in Table 1, suggesting a need for enhancement. User reviews such as "*... I do not want to scan my water intake, maybe pictures of popular water bottle sizes and I preselect the image*" – P01, suggests that incorporating more interactive options and engaging elements for performing the desired behavior could elevate the strategy's effectiveness. Likewise, the Suggestion strategy demonstrated lower persuasiveness (Table 1), indicating room for improvement. Insights from existing research propose that providing meaningful content for the user could enhance the strategy [10]. Therefore, incorporating tailored recommendations based on individual user habits and progress may optimize the persuasiveness of the suggestion strategy.

5.2 Design Recommendations

Based on our findings, we offer the following design recommendations for future research.

- Features such as leaderboards, community forums, peer support networks, and collaborative challenges should be implemented more often, as these can foster a sense of community and encouragement among users. Additionally, incorporating social sharing functionalities can empower users to share their progress and achievements, creating a supportive digital environment.

- Researchers should incorporate evidence-based behavior change techniques in app design to ensure that the strategies employed align with established principles for promoting sustained healthy behaviors.
- Self-monitoring features should be enhanced with easy-to-use tools to allow users track their dietary habits comprehensively as this can contribute to a more accurate understanding of their behaviors and progress.
- Designers should balance complexity with user-friendliness in app design, by ensuring an intuitive design while integrating sophisticated behavioral change strategies.

5.3 Limitations and Future Research Directions

A notable limitation of this study is the relatively small sample size, comprised of only five participants, though it is the recommended sample size for usability evaluation. Although the gender and age group distribution offer diversity, the study's results may not be easily generalized to a larger population due to the limited sample size.

Future research should, incorporate a more substantial and diverse sample, as it could yield more robust findings. The future directions are outlined below:

- We will capitalize on the success of the Competition strategy by expanding and optimizing its impact. We will consider introducing periodic challenges or events related to the leaderboard to sustain user engagement and competitiveness.
- Since the Suggestion strategy within the Onboarding feature showed the least persuasiveness, we will analyze user feedback, and iterate on the suggestions provided during onboarding. We will ensure that suggestions are clear, relevant, and motivating to encourage users to engage with the game.
- We will address user concerns regarding the Reduction strategy by exploring other methods for logging water intake. One potential direction is to incorporate images of popular water bottle sizes, giving users the option to log water intake either by preselecting the image or by scanning.
- While enhancing the persuasive elements, we will ensure that the overall design maintains simplicity. A clean and easily navigable interface contributes to a positive user experience and facilitates usability.

5.4 Conclusion

In summary, our research addressed the pressing issue of unhealthy beverage consumption by creating "Drop Dash," a persuasive game encouraging a shift toward the healthy habit of prioritizing water for hydration. By implementing established strategies from the Persuasive System Design model and emphasizing simplicity in its design, we validated both its usability and persuasiveness. This process not only provided valuable insights but also highlighted areas for improvement. To build upon this study, future research could involve a broader and more diverse participant pool, validating and extending the current findings.

Additionally, in-depth analysis of the reasons behind the persuasiveness of certain features, and iterative user-centered design approaches, could lead to the development of more effective persuasive elements in the functional version of the game.

Furthermore, we may need to analyze specific areas where improvements can be made based on user comments and observations, then iterate on the user interface and overall usability to enhance the gaming experience. Our next step involves implementing these findings to develop the functional game platform using Unity and conducting a usability study. This iterative approach will ensure the continuous refinement of "Drop Dash" for its continual evolution.

References

1. Aldenaini, N., Alslaity, A., Sampalli, S., Orji, R.: Persuasive strategies and their implementations in mobile interventions for physical activity: a systematic review. Int. J. Hum. Comput. Interact. **39** (2023). https://doi.org/10.1080/10447318.2022.2075573
2. Alslaity, A., et al.: Mobile applications for health and wellness: a systematic review. Proc. ACM Hum. Comput. Interact. **6**, 1–29 (2022)
3. Bangor, A., Kortum, P.T., Miller, J.T.: An empirical evaluation of the system usability scale. Int. J. Hum. Comput. Interact. **24** (2008). https://doi.org/10.1080/10447310802205776
4. Briñol, P., Tormala, Z.L., Petty, R.E.: Ease and persuasion: Multiple processes, meanings, and effects. In: The Experience of Thinking: How the Fluency of Mental Processes Influences Cognition and Behavior (2013)
5. Dono, J., et al.: Intentions to reduce sugar-sweetened beverage consumption: the importance of perceived susceptibility to health risks. Publ. Health Nutr. **24** (2021). https://doi.org/10.1017/S1368980021000239
6. Hatzigiannakoglou, P.: Junk-food destroyer: helping adolescents with down syndrome to understand healthy eating through serious game. In: VS-Games 2015 - 7th International Conference on Games and Virtual Worlds for Serious Applications (2015)
7. Liska, D., Mah, E., Brisbois, T., Barrios, P.L., Baker, L.B., Spriet, L.L.: Narrative review of hydration and selected health outcomes in the general population. Nutrients **11** (2019)
8. Mulchandani, D., Alslaity, A., Orji, R.: Exploring the effectiveness of persuasive games for disease prevention and awareness and the impact of tailoring to the stages of change. Hum. Comput. Interact. **38** (2023). https://doi.org/10.1080/07370024.2022.2057858
9. Nielsen, J.: How to Conduct a Heuristic Evaluation. Useitcom (2002)
10. Oinas-Kukkonen, H., Harjumaa, M.: Persuasive systems design: key issues, process model, and system features. Commun. Assoc. Inf. Syst. **24** (2009). https://doi.org/10.17705/1cais.02428
11. Orji, R., Mandryk, R.L., Vassileva, J.: Improving the efficacy of games for change using personalization models. ACM Trans. Comput. Hum. Interact. **24** (2017). https://doi.org/10.1145/3119929
12. Orji, R., Vassileva, J., Mandryk, R.L.: LunchTime: a slow-casual game for long-term dietary behavior change. Pers. Ubiquit. Comput. **17** (2013). https://doi.org/10.1007/s00779-012-0590-6

13. Shiyko, M., Hallinan, S., Seif El-Nasr, M., Subramanian, S., Castaneda-Sceppa, C.: Effects of playing a serious computer game on body mass index and nutrition knowledge in women. JMIR Ser. Games **4** (2016). https://doi.org/10.2196/games.4977
14. Siriaraya, P., et al.: Game design in mental health care: case study–based framework for integrating game design into therapeutic content. JMIR Ser. Games **9** (2021). https://doi.org/10.2196/27953
15. Thomas, R.J., Masthoff, J., Oren, N.: Can I influence you? Development of a scale to measure perceived persuasiveness and two studies showing the use of the scale. Front. Artif. Intell. **2** (2019). https://doi.org/10.3389/frai.2019.00024
16. Will, T.: System usability scale (SUS). Iron Steel Technol. **15** (2018)

Predicting Ethical Orientation Based on Personality for Tailored Cyberethics Training

Muhammad Hassan Ali Bajwa[1(✉)], Deborah Richards[1], and Paul Formosa[2]

[1] School of Computing, Macquarie University, Sydney, NSW 2109, Australia
{hassan.bajwa,deborah.richards}@mq.edu.au

[2] School of Philosophy, Macquarie University, Sydney, NSW 2109, Australia
paul.formosa@mq.edu.au

Abstract. A lack of training in the ethical aspects of decision making among cybersecurity professionals can lead to an increased risk of cyber breaches. We have developed a serious game to provide training to increase players' awareness of five ethical principles relevant to decision making in common cybersecurity situations. By understanding what ethical principles currently drive that individual, we plan to tailor the game's scenarios and dialogues to be more persuasive in presenting alternative viewpoints in order to improve the ethical reasoning capability of players and their ability to make ethically informed cybersecurity decisions. The literature suggests that personality is a predictor of ethical behaviour. Thus, as the basis for tailoring, we seek to use personality to predict the player's priority for each of our five focus ethical principles. This paper reports our attempts to build and validate models based on data we collected from three different studies using our cyberethics game.

Keywords: Persuading ethical behavior · Personality · Tailored training · Cybersecurity · Serious game

1 Introduction

There is a significant increase in the usage of cybersecurity technologies around the world to secure cyberspaces from vulnerable attacks and threats. This gives rise to the need for skilled cybersecurity professionals and rapid decision-making, sometimes under extreme pressure [1]. Cybersecurity professionals focusing on technical or financial aspects of their decisions typically ignore the human and ethical aspects that are some of the most common causes of cyber breaches [2].

Persuading someone to take ethical considerations into account can be assisted through the use of social simulations. Serious games can provide an easily accessible and safe social simulation environment and are widely used for ethical training in different areas, such as medical ethics training [3], Ethical Disaster Management [4], and Ethical Leadership [5]. We present a serious role-playing game for training ethical decision making in cybersecurity context. The

N. Baghaei et al. (Eds.): PERSUASIVE 2024, LNCS 14636, pp. 65–74, 2024.
https://doi.org/10.1007/978-3-031-58226-4_6

aim of the game is to enable the player to identify ethical dilemmas and issues while discussing a technical cybersecurity problem. In helping players become more aware of the ethical aspects of decision-making in a technical context, the game counts as a form of persuasive technology by seeking to improve how players think and reason under pressure. We first sensitize players to five ethical principles which are relevant to cybersecurity decision-making, namely Beneficence, Non-maleficence, Justice, Autonomy, and Explicability as proposed by [6]. The players discuss two technical scenarios with intelligent virtual agents (non-player characters or NPCs). The dialogues of the agents are designed to increase the moral sensitivity of players and frame the importance and relevance of these five ethical principles. Relatedly, there is debate around the use of standardized vs tailored training [9]. However, a "one size fits all" type of training cannot be an effective approach in our case as there are many factors that impact ethical decision-making, of which personality is considered as the most influential factor [7]. Thus, we needed to identify the player's personality to tailor our training to meet their needs. Tailored training can be achieved by changing the dialogues of our agents to increase awareness about specific ethical principles which, as indicated by a player's personality, needs more focused training. To support our future goal to provide tailored training on certain ethical principles based on the player's personality, this paper seeks to answer the following research question:

RQ1: What is the relationship between personality and the five ethical principles of Beneficence, Non-maleficence, Justice, Autonomy, and Explicability?

To find this relationship, we captured the player's personality using the Five Factor Model (FFM), also known as OCEAN (Openness, Conscientiousness, Extraversion, Agreeableness, Neuroticism) [8]. We choose to model personality using FFM, as it is widely used to model the personality in agents [22,23]. Further, across three related studies, players rated how much they prioritize each of our five ethical principles. Using this data, we created models using classification algorithms. In this article we present our attempts to find this relationship in our three studies.

After reviewing background and relevant literature (Sect. 2), we present our methodology (Sect. 3), then results (Sect. 4) and discussion (Sect. 5), respectively and conclusions (Sect. 6).

2 Background and Related Literature

The research on ethical decision-making (EDM) and factors effecting EDM can be categorized into two major streams: individual and organizational factors [7,14,15]. [15] found that individual factors have the greatest influence. The individual factors impacting ethical reasoning identified by [14] include: personality, gender, education, philosophy, and nationality. Empirical research by [7] found that personality is the most important individual factor. Due to the influence of personality on an individual's ethical decision-making, it was important for us both to give our agents personalities that aligned with their ethical reasoning and explore how to provide ethical training tailored to an individual's personality.

The need for ethics training in organizations is clear [16]. Approaches to provide training vary widely and include case studies, game-based learning, role plays, lectures and more [17]. Serious roleplay game-based learning allows the player to act in a specific role (e.g., a cybersecurity specialist in our case) to explore various strategic alternatives [17]. Serious games also provide an effective experiential learning environment [18,19] and are suitable for providing training in decision-making skills at scale as the player can reason and perform action independently.

Principles are commonly adopted by professional bodies and appear in codes of ethics and professional conduct to guide its members to behave ethically. While our domain of interest is cybersecurity professionals, we aim to develop an approach that is relevant across multiple professional fields. We have drawn on the AI4People's Ethical Framework that adapts the widely accepted bioethics principles of [20] beneficence, non-maleficence, autonomy and justice, and adds the principle of explicability due to its relevance in the context of AI and other computing technologies. This framework has been previously applied to cybersecurity [6]. We therefore used these five principles and the four stages of Rest's [13] model of ethical reasoning to design our scenarios and game.

3 Methodology

The literature has identified a connection between personality and ethical behaviour, but has not yet investigated if there is a link between an individual's personality and the priority that they give to these five common ethical principles. To address this gap and answer our RQ1, we have applied machine learning to data that we have gathered over the past two years in three different ethics approved studies involving our game. All three studies collected the personality of the player and asked the player to identify the importance of the five AI4People ethical principles.

3.1 The Game and Scenarios

A serious game (V-Meet Cybersecurity) was designed to create a virtual twin of a cybersecurity organization where the player has the role of a recently hired Security Analyst. In the initial version (study 1) of the game, the player interacted with the agents as shown in Fig. 1, where the discussions between the NPCs and the player are through text-based chat. In Studies 2 and 3 we improved the design of the interaction to simulate a video meeting (V-Meet) as shown in Fig. 2. The design goal behind the change was to make it easier for the player to identify the different NPCs and their various arguments and to make the game more interactive and improve the player experience. The scenarios in Study 2 and 3 were improved to reflect the agent's personality using the dialogue cues from the literature [10]; see the examples in Table 1 and Fig. 2. Players interact with the NPCs in two different ethical scenarios based on case studies found in the literature. One scenario explored how to implement two-factor authentication

(2FA). Another scenario involved a decision of whether or not to counter-attack (AttackBack). In both situations, agents and players discuss technical as well as ethical aspects of the scenario. Agents' personas were created using all the rules defined in Fig. 3, but rules that are highlighted with solid lines were validated using data from our subsequent studies.

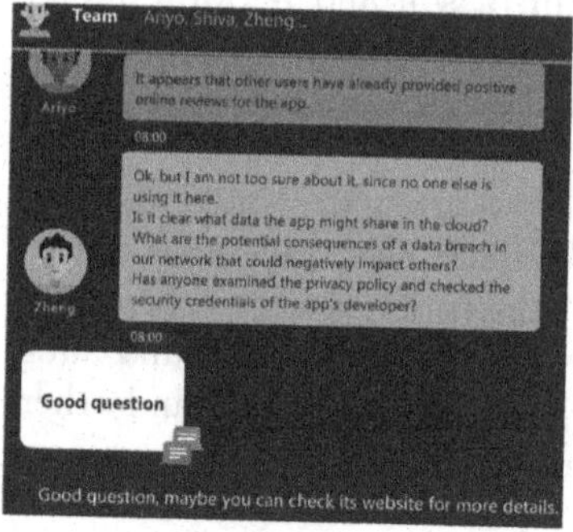

Fig. 1. Study 1 Chat Window

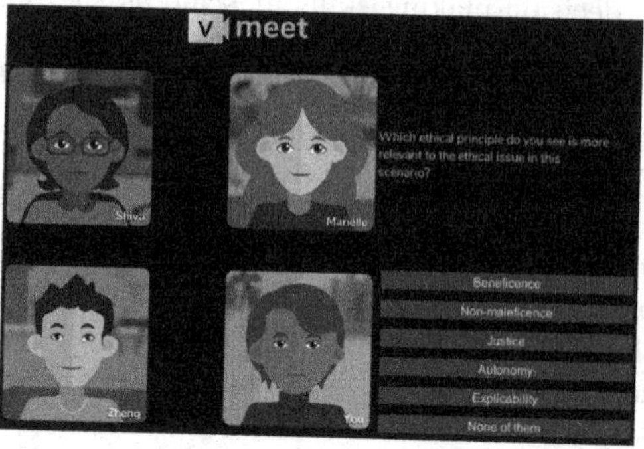

Fig. 2. V-Meet CyberSecurity (Study 2 and 3)

Table 1. Personality Cues

Personality	High	Low
Emotional stability	Don't worry, Take it easy, Calm down, I can handle	I am worried, stressed, too much for me
Conscientiousness	Be practical, Need to ensure, Elaborate, careful consideration, same page, strict policy	get it quickly, start it right away
Extraversion	I am sure, you are right, use of difficult words	This seems, I don't think, I mean, doesn't seem, I can't
Agreeableness	good initiative, I am okay with, I agree, be optimistic	bad idea/policy, not in favor, I don't agree
Openness	will try new policy, will be a good experience	don't like changes, hesitant exploring, similar to them

3.2 Recruitment

Students in all three studies participated during a workshop class in the final week of week in the unit "Introduction to Cybersecurity" and consented for their data to be used for research analysis.

3.3 Procedure and Data Collection

In Studies 1 and 2, players' demographics (gender, age, cultural background, and personality) and ethical priorities were captured using Qualtrics survey software.

To capture the FFM personality traits, we used the brief 10-item TIPI [8] on a 7-point Likert scale where 1 is rated as strongly disagree and 7 is strongly agree. Players were asked to rate each principle's importance on a scale of 1 to 5, where 5 is the most important and 1 is the least important. In Study 3, the same demographic data was captured at the beginning of the game as an onboarding survey aligned with the gameplay as the player joins the new organization and completes the initial form on their first day of joining the company.

In all studies, the players then engage with Ethbot (a virtual agent) that provides initial training to the player about the five ethical principles as part of company induction. In the first study, players engage in a chat with multiple NPCs to learn about different ethical perspectives (see Fig. 1). In Studies 2 and 3, after the EthBot training, the player attends a first video meeting in which the player and the other virtual agents discuss a technical scenario and agents provide their differing ethical perspectives on these (see Fig. 2).

Due to students' preference to play the game and reluctance to complete the Qualtrics survey (observed in Studies 1 and 2), in Study 3 all data was captured during gameplay. Players' responses in the first dialogue were designed to capture their personality and ethical priorities during the scenario. We refer to this data here as "in-game personality". To avoid order effects with repeated measures design, we counterbalanced the scenarios so that players received either the 2FA (Group A) or AttackBack (Group B) scenario first. The alternative scenario was received second.

3.4 Data Modelling

After initial preparation and cleaning of the data was done using MS Excel, SPSS modeler V18.0 was used to run the classification algorithm to find the relationships between traits and principles. To find which ethical principle is the best predictor for which personality trait, we applied the C5.0 classification algorithm after each target output (principle) using five inputs (personality traits). We used C5.0 as it is a widely used and high-performance classification algorithm that can produce highly understandable models. Three equal-sized bins were created based on the dataset for High, Medium, and Low values. C5 also provides us with a decision tree which helps us to extract the rules as shown in Fig. 3. Five models were then created for each principle (target) to provide us with the best predictor from five personality traits (input) as shown in Fig. 3.

The approach used in Study 1 was also followed in Study 2. The results of Studies 1 and 2 were validated in Study 3. However, in the third study, we captured the player's personality and ethical priorities in two different ways: explicitly (as in the first two studies) and implicitly (in-game). This means, along with capturing the players' personality and ethical priorities in the same way as in study 1 and 2, in study 3 we also asked players to respond to a set of questions during the dialogue to capture personality and ethical prioritization implicitly. We adopted this approach to see if there were any differences in either type of response. The results of this evaluation have been presented in another article [26]. Another difference between the three studies is that in evaluating the results in Study 2, instead of only using the C5.0 classification algorithm, we applied the auto-classifier option in SPSS Modeller to evaluate the results with different algorithms. The classifiers that were applied by SPSS included C&R Tree1, Logistic Regression, C5.1, Bayesian Network and Neural Net 1. Accuracy rates of around 68% were achieved with these algorithms that provide more accurate results. The best predictors based on these algorithms that provide more accurate results (Neural Nets for in-game responses and C5.0 for all others) are presented in Table 2.

4 Results

4.1 Demographics

The total number of participants (N) in the first, second and third study were 444, 219 and 304, respectively, after removing participants who did not give consent for their data to be used. Demographics distribution in all studies can be found in [24–26].

4.2 Validation of Personality-Principle Relationship

Figure 3 shows the relationship between each personality trait and ethical principle that was found in Study 1. As explained in Sect. 3.1, this relationship was used to create the agent's personas (personality-principle combinations) that were implemented in Studies 2 and 3.

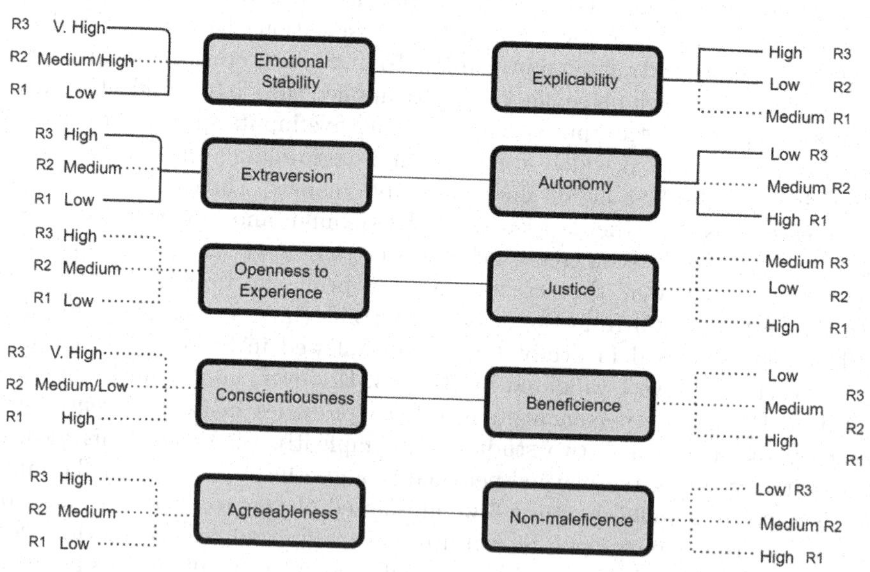

Fig. 3. Study 1 Personality-Principle Relationships (solid line=confirmed in Study 3)

Following the same approach used in Study 1, we generated rules from the data collected in Study 3 to clarify the relationship between principles and personality traits. The results from Study 3, which confirm the Study 1 rules, are shown in Fig. 3 as solid lines. The dotted lines are the rules found in Study 1 but which were unconfirmed in the subsequent studies. Figure 2 shows that we were only able to confirm the rules for Autonomy and Explicability. We extracted the following rules from the decision trees produced by SPSS Modeller.

1. If Emotional Stability is **High** then Explicability is **High**
2. If Emotional Stability is **Low** then Explicability is **Low**
3. If Extraversion is **Low** then Autonomy is **High**
4. If Extraversion is **High** then Autonomy is **Low**

A comparison of the relationships found between the first, second and third studies is provided in Table 2. Table 2 also compares the in-game player personality responses captured during V-Meet discussion, as explained in Sect. 3.1. It can be seen from Table 2 that emotional stability is the only consistent best predictor in all the studies, including the in-game responses for Explicability. Extroversion was found to be consistent in the first and third studies, and was found to be the second best predictor in Study 2 with a minor (0.1) difference on a scale of (0=Worst, 1=Best) with the first best predictor. Openness was consistent between Studies 1 and 2. Conscientiousness was consistent between Studies 1 and in-game responses in Study 3. We were not able to find any consistent personality trait for the Non-maleficence ethical principle.

Table 2. Personality-Principle Relationship Validation (*2nd by .1)

Trait/Study	Study 1	Study 2	Study 3 - TIPI	Study 3- Ingame
Beneficence	Conscientiousness	Extraversion	Emotions stable	Conscientiousness
Non-Malef	Agreeableness	Not Found	Extraversion	Conscientiousness
Justice	Openness	Openness	Extraversion	Conscientiousness
Autonomy	Extraversion	Extraversion*	Extraversion	Conscientiousness
Explicability	Emotions stable	Emotions stable	Emotions stable	Emotions stable

5 Discussion

A persuasive gamified approach to training in ethical decision-making aims to help players to consider the relevant ethical issues and consequences of their decisions. This entails evaluating the potential positive or negative impacts of decisions on both the decision-maker and others. There are many factors that affect an individual's ethical decision-making, of which personality is the most influential factor according to the literature. We presented our attempts to find the relationship between player personality and ethical principles during three studies conducted over the last two years with cybersecurity students.

In our initial study with 444 participants [24], we were able to associate each personality trait with each principle based on the C5 classification algorithm. The rules were formed from the decision tree. Figure 3 shows all the rules found in Study 1. We sought to verify the association between each principle and personality (RQ1) using unseen cases based on new datasets of subsequent studies conducted with different cohorts. We also sought to validate that the rules created in our initial studies, which were used to define the relationship between personality and principle, were consistent and reliable.

In answering RQ1, it can be seen from Table 2 that emotional stability is the most consistent predictor for the explicability principle. The rules between the emotional stability and explicability relationship were also verified, and this tells us that an emotionally stable person tends to prioritize being transparent and open in their decision making. This is relevant to the cybersecurity context, as an emotionally stable person can handle stress [21] from stakeholders and can be more transparent in explaining a cyber incident such as a cyber-attack. Extraversion, Openness and Conscientiousness were verified an equal number of times in our later studies. Extraversion can be considered the second-best predictor in Study 2 with a minor difference of 0.1 with the best predictor on a scale of 0 to 1, where 0 is considered as the worst and 1 is considered as the best predictor for the principle. The difference can be largely ignored because we were able to validate the relationship rules between extraversion and autonomy. A different study [11] found a positive correlation between extraversion and autonomy at work, but we have found a negative correlation between these two factors. This is explained by the other study [11] understanding autonomy in terms of the individual's own autonomy, whereas in our study it is largely about considering the autonomy of others. This is further supported with the finding of another study [12], where individuals high on the extroversion scale tended to be contradictory, thus lowering other's autonomy. Further, individuals lower on the extroversion scale were more likely to be collaborative in developing a creative solution, thus raising the autonomy of others.

6 Conclusion and Future Work

Due to the rise in cybersecurity breaches caused by ignoring the human, rather than the technical, aspects of cybersecurity, it is essential to provide training to cybersecurity professionals to help them aware of the ethical ramifications of their decisions. Ethical decision making is most significantly impacted by an individual's personality. Thus, tailored ethical training via serious games needs to take players' personalities into account. For that reason, in this article we present our attempts to predict the prioritization of ethical principles of players based on their personality to tailor our cyberethics training. In our three studies, we were able to find only one consistent relationship between emotional stability and explicability. This relationship will be used in future versions of our game.

For the other principles training will be tailored on run-time user responses according to their ethical orientation and not according to their personality.

References

1. Singh, T., Johnston, A.C., D'Arcy, J., Harms, P.D.: Stress in the cybersecurity profession: a systematic review of related literature and opportunities for future research. Organ. Cybersecur. J. Pract. Process People (2023)
2. Datto. Datto's Global State of the Channel Ransomware Report (2020). https://www.datto.com/resource-downloads/Datto-State-of-the-Channel-Ransomware-Report-v2-1.pdf
3. Lorenzini, C., Faita, C., Barsotti, M., Carrozzino, M., Tecchia, F., Bergamasco, M.: ADITHO – a serious game for training and evaluating medical ethics skills. In: Chorianopoulos, K., Divitini, M., Hauge, J.B., Jaccheri, L., Malaka, R. (eds.) ICEC 2015. LNCS, vol. 9353, pp. 59–71. Springer, Cham (2015). https://doi.org/10.1007/978-3-319-24589-8_5
4. Wahyudin, D., Hasegawa, S.: Mobile serious game design for training ethical decision making skills of inexperienced disaster volunteers. J. Inf. Syst. Educ. **14**(1), 28–41 (2015)
5. Certuche, U.B., Lopez, M.D.R., Vasquez, L.M.L.: Design of a serious game to teach organizational ethical leadership. In Developments in Business Simulation and Experiential Learning: Proceedings of the Annual ABSEL Conference, vol. 46 (2019)
6. Formosa, P., Wilson, M., Richards, D.: A principlist framework for cybersecurity ethics. Comput. Secur. **109**, 102382 (2021)
7. Craft, J.L.: A review of the empirical ethical decision-making literature: 2004–2011. J. Bus. Ethics **117**(2013), 221–259 (2013)
8. Costa, P.T., McCrae, R.R.: The revised neo personality inventory (neo-pi-r). SAGE Handb. Pers. Theory Assess. **2**(2), 179–198 (2008)
9. Kassab, H., Scott, K., Boyd, M.R., Puspitasari, A., Endicott, D., Lewis, C.C.: Tailored isn't always better: impact of standardized versus tailored training on intention to use measurement-based care. Implement. Res. Pract. **3**, 26334895221087476 (2022)
10. John, O.P., Srivastava, S., et al.: The Big-Five trait taxonomy: history, measurement, and theoretical perspectives (1999)
11. Farfán, J., Peña, M., Fernández-Salinero, S., Topa, G.: The moderating role of extroversion and neuroticism in the relationship between autonomy at work, burnout, and job satisfaction. Int. J. Environ. Res. Public Health **17**(21), 8166 (2020)
12. Nussbaum, E.M.: How introverts versus extroverts approach small-group argumentative discussions. Elem. Sch. J. **102**(3), 183–197 (2002)
13. Rest, J.R.: Moral development: advances in research and theory (1986)
14. Casali, G.L., Perano, M.: Forty years of research on factors influencing ethical decision making: Establishing a future research agenda. J. Bus. Res. **132**, 614–630 (2021)
15. Ford, R.C., Richardson, W.D.: Ethical decision making: a review of the empirical literature. J. Bus. Ethics **13**, 205–221 (1994)
16. Perri, D.F., Callanan, G.A., Rotenberry, P.F., Oehlers, P.F.: Education and training in ethical decision making: comparing context and orientation. Educ.+ Train. **51**(1), 70–83 (2009)

17. Martin, B.O., Kolomitro, K., Lam, T.C.: Training methods: a review and analysis. Hum. Resour. Dev. Rev. **13**(1), 11–35 (2014)
18. Gentry, J.W.: What is experiential learning. Guide Bus. Gaming Experient. Learn. **9**, 20 (1990)
19. Oblinger, D.: The next generation of educational engagement. J. Interact. Media Educ. **2004**(1) (2004)
20. Floridi, L., et al.: AI4People-an ethical framework for a good AI society: opportunities, risks, principles, and recommendations. Minds Mach. **28**(4), 689–707 (2018)
21. Ramesar, S., Koortzen, P., Oosthuizen, R.M.: The relationship between emotional intelligence and stress management. SA J. Ind. Psychol. **35**(1), 39–48 (2009)
22. Ahrndt, S., Aria, A., Fähndrich, J., Albayrak, S.: Ants in the OCEAN: modulating agents with personality for planning with humans. In: Bulling, N. (ed.) EUMAS 2014. LNCS (LNAI), vol. 8953, pp. 3–18. Springer, Cham (2015). https://doi.org/10.1007/978-3-319-17130-2_1
23. Mairesse, F., Walker, M.A.: Can Conversational Agents Express Big Five Personality Traits Through Language?: Evaluating a Psychologically-Informed Language Generator. Cambridge University Engineering, Cambridge & Sheffield (2009)
24. Sadeghi, B., et al.: Modelling the ethical priorities influencing decision-making in cybersecurity contexts. Organ. Cybersecur. J. Pract. Process People (2023)
25. Bajwa, M.H.A., Richards, D., Formosa, P.: Providing alternative ethical perspectives through intelligent agents in a serious game for cybersecurity ethical training. Games Change Asia-Pac. J. **2**, 149–178 (2023)
26. Ali Bajwa, M. H., Richards, D., Formosa, P.: Evaluation of embodied conversational agents designed with ethical principles and personality for cybersecurity ethics training. In: Proceedings of the 23rd ACM International Conference on Intelligent Virtual Agents, p. 1–8 (2023)

Design and Development of mHealth App: Eye Donor Aust

Waraporn Chumkasian[1,3](✉), Khin Than Win[1], Elena Vlahu-Gjorgievska[1], Mark Freeman[1], Ritin Fernandez[2], Heidi Green[1], and Con Petsoglou[3]

[1] University of Wollongong, Wollongong, Australia
wc817@uowmail.edu.au, win@uow.edu.au
[2] University of New Castle, Gosford, Australia
[3] Sydney Eye Hospital, Sydney, NSW, Australia

Abstract. The aim of this study is to increase users' eye donation knowledge and awareness through the design and development of the Eye Donor Aust app. Its development is based on the Design Science Research methodology adopting Persuasive Systems Design. Three cycles of iterative design and development are applied to develop an artefact Eye Donor Aust app. The app content is created based on mapping the meta-requirements into design requirements and design and development. The requirements are identified from the literature, consumer surveys and stakeholder consultations. The app is available from the Apple App Store and Google Play Store. This study is useful as guidance in designing and developing an educational app for other organ donation apps and similar.

Keywords: Mobile App · mobile health · Eye Donation · Persuasive Systems Design · Design Science Research

1 Introduction

Corneal scarcity is a global issue caused by system impediments, including opt-in consent systems and limited services [1]. Significant barriers to cornea donation have been identified in multiple studies, such as inadequate knowledge about the donation and transplantation process, including false religious beliefs and lack of cornea donation awareness [2, 3]. As the opt-in system is used for eye donation in Australia, consent for eye donation from prospective donors remains vital. Providing appropriate eye donation education can overcome cornea donation barriers and improve willingness to consent to donate.

Studies indicated that promoting health education through online and mobile applications has improved awareness of relevant health conditions and provided positive outcomes [4–6]. A strategy in some countries to increase public health awareness, including organ donation, is through smartphone applications (apps) [7, 8]. Apps are widely used in healthcare to inform the public on a range of health topics, including physical activity [6], medication management [9], diabetes [10], asthma [5, 11], and breastfeeding [4].

N. Baghaei et al. (Eds.): PERSUASIVE 2024, LNCS 14636, pp. 75–88, 2024.
https://doi.org/10.1007/978-3-031-58226-4_7

Such apps are also used in the organ donation fields to educate patients about kidney [12], blood [13], and organ [7] donation. Similarly, several apps have been developed for eye donation; however, these apps provide eye donation information that is specific to the country in which the app was created, including being in their native language [14]. In Australia, the Australian Organ and Tissue Registry website and the DonateLife website and app provide general information about organ donation but not specifically about eye donation. Thus, there is a need for a specific eye donation educational app with essential eye donation information and features supporting potential donors donating.

Applying the Persuasive Systems Design model (PSD) [15], Persuasion could be provided to the consumers through digital health technology through the Primary task support category, such as tailoring and communication to users through Dialogue support, such as suggestions and features from each category of the Persuasive Systems Design [16]. While Persuasive Systems Design has been applied in blood donation [17] and organ donation [18] apps, there is no study that adopted PSD for eye donation education application. These studies emphasized social persuasion [18], motivating people to adopt the targeted behaviour and cultural tailored PSD [17].

Studies indicated providing knowledge, skills and confidence through mobile applications could enhance consumers engagement and motivation towards targeted behaviour [19, 20] and PSD has been adopted in breastfeeding education [21] and asthma education to consumers [5]. Thus, this study aimed to design and develop an educational eye donation app called "Eye Donor Aust" to increase users' eye donation knowledge and improve donation awareness among Australians.

2 Methodology

The eye donation app's design and development process was guided by a Design Science Research (DSR) methodology [22], which comprises six design process steps: Problem definition, Objective of the solution, Design and development, Demonstration, Evaluation, and Communication. Three phases of DSR processes were involved in the design and development of this application. The first phase involved identifying the meta-requirements for the application; the second phase involved the design and development of the prototype, and the third phase involved the final application development (Fig. 1). The study was approved by the relevant Health and Medical Research Ethics Committee.

2.1 The First Phase

A systematic literature review was conducted in search of eye donation barriers and solutions [2]. It was performed using the following search terms: "smartphone application, organ donation, mobile, apps, handheld device, app, eye donation". Articles published in English between 2004 and 2022 included scholarly papers on quantitative randomised controlled trials and primary research. The quality appraisal of the included studies was conducted.

To understand stakeholder requirements and values for the eye donation app design and development, a survey of users and consultations with the stakeholders were conducted.

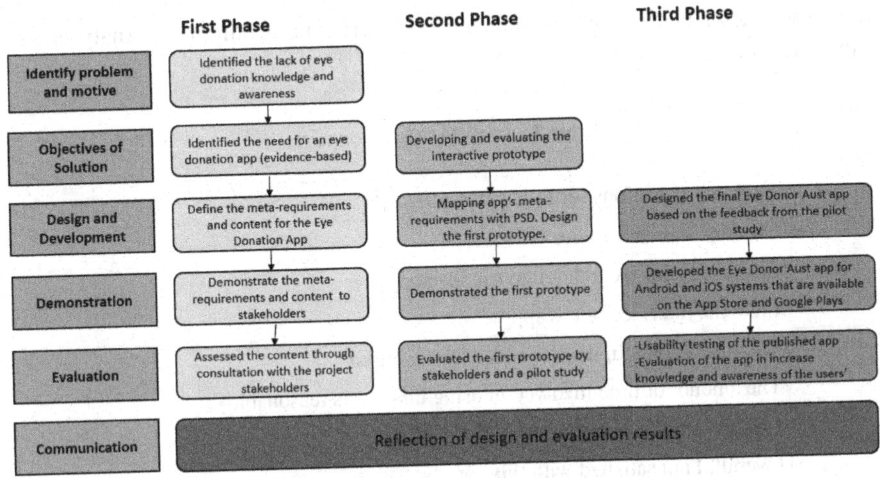

Fig. 1. Design Science Research Process

Identifying the eye donation knowledge was conducted by surveying a convenient sampling of 166 patients and carers at the Eye Clinics in the tertiary Hospital in Sydney. The valid questionnaire was adapted to evaluate the eye donation knowledge [23]. The data were analysed using SPSS V24.

Relevant stakeholders were identified to obtain the study requirements. The stakeholders involved a manager and staff from the NSW Eye and Tissue Bank, an educator from Australian Organ and Tissue Donation Services (DonateLife), a cornea transplant surgeon, a medical officer, a clinical nurse specialist, a Human-centered IT specialist, and an app developer were consulted. Content creation and analysis were conducted. Further, stakeholders evaluated the app's content related to meta-requirements and whether the content and design were appropriate for the users.

2.2 The Second Phase

The meta-requirements identified from the literature review and the survey were translated into the design requirements and app features (Table 2). The wireframes were developed to ensure the prototype represented the necessary content. Those were presented to the seven stakeholders. After that, the app was further developed on the iOS platform. A pilot study was conducted to assess the prototype published in Testflight. The study was conducted with 20 participants who downloaded and installed the prototype.

2.3 The Third Phase

The final app was developed for both the iOS and the Android platforms. App usability evaluation was conducted with patients at the eye clinic in Sydney. Each participant was provided with an iPad with the EyeDonor Aust app installed. A valid tool for the app's usability testing was created from a previously validated study of the mHealth App Usability Questionnaire (MAUQ) [24]. The survey questions are presented in Table 1.

Exploratory factor analysis was conducted using Principal Component Analysis with Varimax Rotation.

Table 1. Usability Questionnaire

item	Usability Questions for EyeDonor Aust App
1	The app was easy to use
2	It was easy for me to learn to use the app
3	I like the interface of the app
4	The information in the app was well organised
5	The amount of time involved in using this app is reasonable
6	I would use this app again
7	Overall, I am satisfied with this app
8	Whenever I made a mistake using the app, I could recover easily and quickly
9	This app provided an acceptable way to receive eye donation information
10	The navigation was consistent when moving between screens
11	The app moves easily to different screens
12	This app has all the functions and capabilities I expect it to have
13	The app would be useful to increase my eye donation knowledge
14	The app helped me to understand the process of eye donation
15	The app made it convenient for me to register as an eye donor

3 Results

A user-friendly and visually appealing eye donation app called "Eye Donor Aust" was developed and is available on the Apple App Store and Google Play Store.

3.1 Design Cycle First Phase

The content design was conducted in the first cycle. The systematic literature review identifies eye donation knowledge and lack of awareness [2]. Inadequate eye donation knowledge, such as religious beliefs regarding eye donation [25], criteria for eye donation [26, 27], lack of eye donation awareness [3], and poor attitudes towards donation [28] contribute to low donation rates and have led to reducing eye donation consent. The app evaluation also highlighted the need for more high-quality eye donation apps. Additionally, the survey results from the consumers' eye donation knowledge indicated the need for relevant eye donation knowledge for consumers.

Adopting the Persuasive Systems Design model, the intent and context analysis identified the relevant stakeholders, such as the persuader (a manager and staff from the NSW Eye and Tissue Bank, an educator from Australian Organ and Tissue Donation Services (DonateLife), a cornea transplant surgeon, a medical officer, a clinical nurse specialist, a Human-centered IT specialist, and an app developer), and the persuader or app users (consumers). Secondly, the event context analysis identified the purpose of the app (use context) and the users' needs, such as motivation and user interests. Additionally, the strategy context analysis helped to (1) design content that convinces users to change their attitudes and behaviour (message) and (2) choose the way to convey the message (route).

Stakeholder consultations were conducted to develop appropriate content and identify the meta-requirements. The Meta-requirements identified are presented in Fig. 2, which include 1) promoting eye donation education, 2) motivating potential donors to provide consent, 3) enabling them to register for eye donation, and 4) ensuring ethical perspectives.

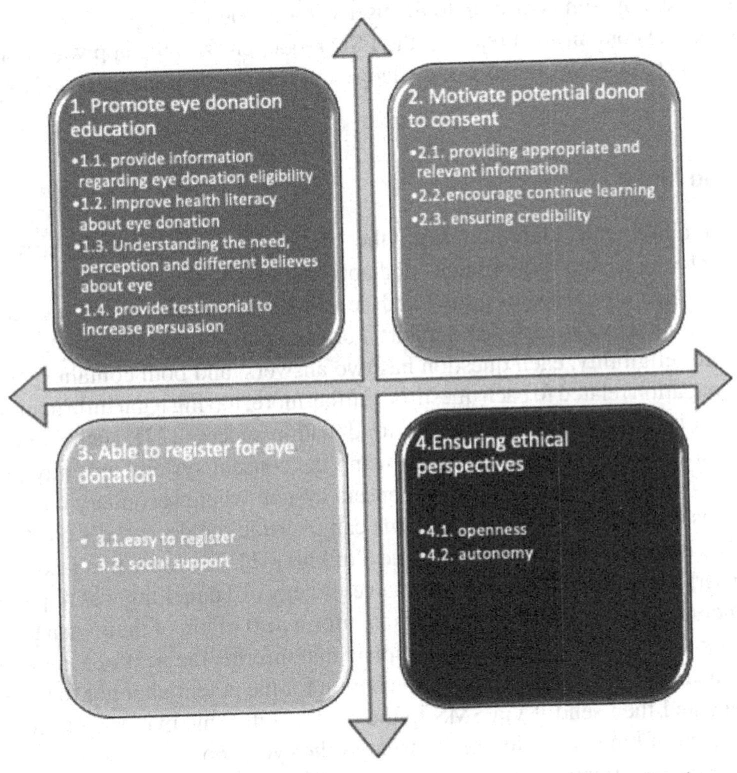

Fig. 2. Meta-requirements for the eye donation information application

This Eye Donor Aust app was developed to provide information and overcome misconceptions regarding eye donation, thus changing the user's attitude towards eye donation.

The content was tested for readability using the Flesch-Kincaid Reading Ease/Flesch-Kincaid Grade Level [29]. These tests have been widely used to assess how easily the reader understands the reading content. The content of this app has a Flesch-Kincaid Grade Level of 5.2.

As identified by the [3], belief, knowledge and misconceptions related to eye donation need to be addressed. Thus, the application presented content related to eye donation, cornea transplant-related information, eye donation-related information based on different religions, and testimonials from the transplant recipients. Moreover, the information related to whether the person would be eligible to donate or not also is included. Users can go directly to the Donate Life page through the app when they decide to donate. Thus, user can provide their consent easily.

The ethical value perspectives were considered. The app content should benefit users and not discriminate against specific ethnic groups or be unbiased. The app must maintain fidelity by ensuring confidentiality, being upfront with users, and indicating what information should be collected. Moreover, the users' autonomy should be respected, and the users should be able to decide to accept or refuse to use the app. The decision to register for eye donation is also up to the user without coercion.

Mapping the content features with the PSD model ensures the app was designed to influence users to increase donation knowledge and voluntarily improve users' awareness [30].

3.2 Second Phase

The meta-requirements identified from the literature review and the survey were translated into the design requirements and app features (Table 2).

The app's features were designed and developed to enhance users' eye donation knowledge, guided by primary task support. For example, in the seven questions assessing eye donor eligibility, each question has two answers, and both contain specific eye donation education related to each question. Furthermore, having legal information about eye donation is essential for users to ensure donation success [27], such as the age of a person that can consent to donation, knowing the consent system currently practised in the user's country (such as the opt-in consent system where secondary consent from next of kin is required for donation and this can override the deceased's consent if the deceased's wishes were unknown to their next of kin) [31]. To ensure that next of kin are aware of users' donation wishes, the persuasive strategy of Tunnelling was implemented. The app includes a texting feature for users to inform next of kin of their wish to become an eye donor in two simple steps. The template that informs the next of kin of the wish to become an eye donor is created, with the option for the potential donor to personalise the message and then send it via SMS to the next of kin. This may help to reduce the number of next of kin to override the consent of the eye donor.

The persuasive strategies of 'System credibility', 'Verifiability', and 'Third party endorsement' were embedded in the app's features by disclosing the list of trusted stakeholders and including their organisational logos on the app's terms and conditions screen. Studies highlight that to motivate potential donors to donate their eyes, an app developed by trusted sources gains more credibility and persuades users to use it [32]. To increase the app's credibility, the persuasive strategies of 'Trustworthiness' and 'Expertise' were implemented to motivate potential donors to donate eyes. The app informs users of the scientific and academic reliability of the content in multiple places on the app's screens, with further reading and references provided to support the content [32].

A persuasive strategy was implemented to influence users to register for eye donation by providing links to the National Organ and Tissue Donation website in multiple places throughout the app as a reminder to the user.

This stage aimed to demonstrate and present the wireframes to the expert stakeholders, such as the corneal surgeon, NSW Tissue Bank educator, IT specialist, DonateLife educator and app developer. Throughout the meetings, input from stakeholders was used to identify content appropriateness and whether the design was suitable for the users. The expert review identified further improvements, including rewording two sub-screen titles to be more engaging and precise and ensuring all the reference links are working and the video clips that could only be watched vertically as they did not rotate with the phone.

In addition, a pilot study was conducted to evaluate the app prototype (published in Testflight). 20 participants from the Sydney Eye Hospital, which consists of healthcare providers and patients, were recruited as a convenience sample. Positive feedback from the pilot study was that the app was easy to use, and the content was well-organised using colour coding.

Table 2. The table demonstrates the app's meta requirements based on the Persuasive System Design (PSD) model.

Meta-requirements	Design Requirements	Features	Principles
1.1. Donation eligibility	The seven eligibility questions for becoming an eye donor	Reduction	T
1.2 Health literacy	Guiding users to access different information sections based on their navigation	Tunnelling	T
	Providing additional information content and presents them in a different format	Tailoring	T
	Reading text feature to assist the user with visual impairment	Tailoring	T
1.3 Understanding needs	Provide essential information commonly asked by potential eye donors	Tailoring	T
1.4 Testimonials	App allows users to continue exploring or to register to be an eye donor	Suggestion	D

(continued)

Table 2. (*continued*)

Meta-requirements	Design Requirements	Features	Principles
	Recipients and family testimonies, as well as the religious statements presented	Similarity	D
	A colour-coded app content flow is being used	Liking	D
2.1. Relevant information	Providing information related to eye donation only and content that suits with the user's age ranges	Tailoring	T
	The eligibility questions leading towards registration	Tunnelling	T
2.2. Encourage continue learning	Providing videos using simple language and plays by people of different ages and genders	Similarity	D
	Presents meaningful images related to the eye donation	Liking	D
2.3. Credibility	The app shows the trusted source of stakeholders who are involved in app development	Expertise	C
	The app displays reliable sources of information	Trustworthiness	C
	The app exhibits list of the experts within organisations	Authority	C
	Includes reliable stakeholder logo and list of respective third-party information in part of terms and conditions	3rd party endorsed	C
	Link to national organ donation registry for donation	verifiability	C
3.1. Easy to register	The app guides the user to register at DonateLife after the eye donation eligibility questions	Tunnelling	T
3.2. Social support	Sending SMS to their family and starting eye donation conversation with their family	Cooperation	S
4.1. Openness	Provide comprehensive information and related cornea issues	Tailoring	T
4.2. Autonomy	Ability to decide or refuse to accept the term of use, freely navigate within the app and decide to register without coercion	Reduction	T

T: Primary Task Support, D: Dialogue Support, C: Credibility Support, S: Social Support

3.3 Phase Three

The final eye donation app was developed based on input and feedback from relevant stakeholders and the outcomes of the pilot study. The two sub screen titles were more precise: '*Common myths for eye donation*' was changed to '*Eye disease and eye donation*', and '*Common family concerns*' was changed to '*Religious and personal statement about eye and organ donation*'. Broken links to references were fixed, and the technical issue that prevented video clips from being played horizontally following phone rotation was addressed. Following these changes, the Eye Donor Aust app (Fig. 3) was developed and published on iOS and Android platforms, making the app available for users to download free of charge.

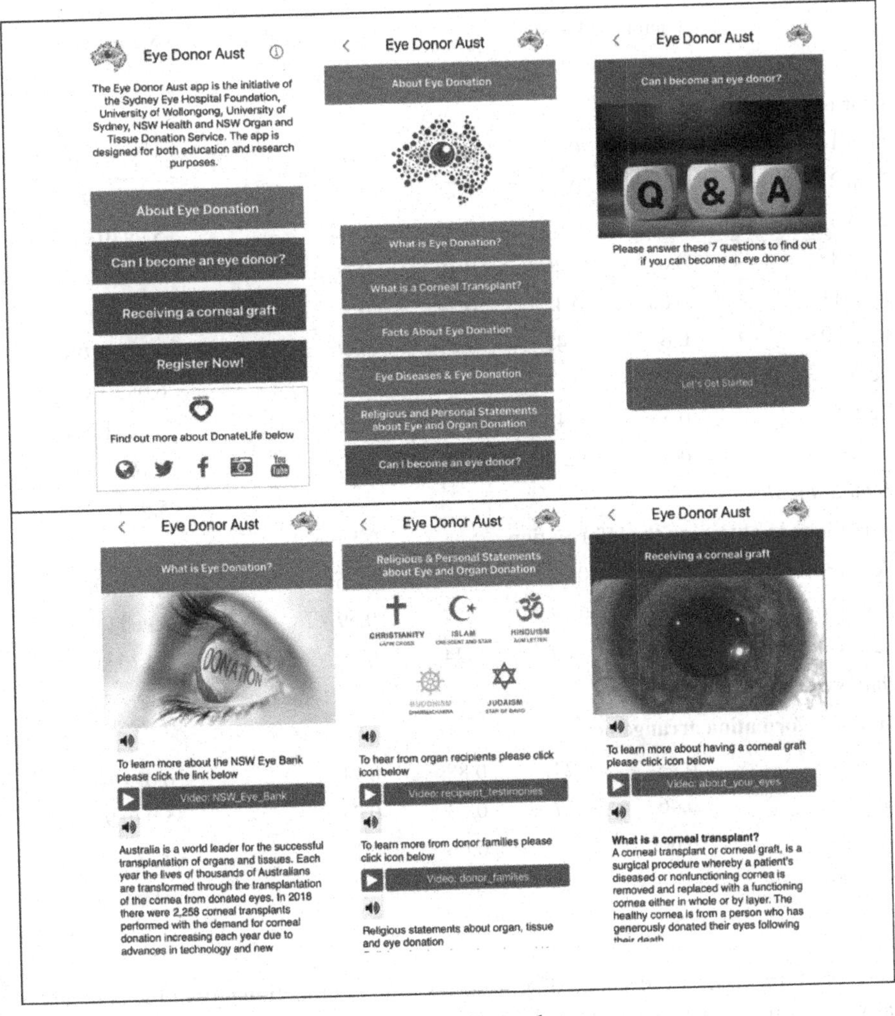

Fig. 3. App Screenshots

The app's usability test was conducted using a validated questionnaire adapted from a previous study of the mHealth App Usability Questionnaire (MAUQ) [24].

The results of exploratory factor analysis were presented in Table 3. Three subscales with 68.4% of total variance were obtained from the analysis, which were identified as 'Ease of use and satisfaction' (9 items, Cronbach alpha 0.9), 'Usefulness in obtaining information' (3 items, Cronbach alpha 0.82), and 'System information arrangement' (3 items, Cronbach alpha 0.85). The internal consistency for the full MAUQ was high (*a* = 0.93). The internal consistency evaluation, Cronbach alpha was satisfactory for all, as the values are between 0.7 and 0.9 [33].

Table 3. Exploratory Factor Analysis

	Factor loadings			Communalities	Mean (SD)
	1	2	3		
Ease of use and satisfaction					
Item 1	0.78	0.25	0.19	0.72	6.23 (0.90)
Item 2	0.76	0.20	0.25	0.69	6.24 (0.98)
Item 5	0.74	0.03	0.38	0.69	5.99 (0.97)
Item 8	0.69	0.26	0.10	0.56	5.66 (1.29)
Item 11	0.68	0.42	0.24	0.7	6.11 (0.85)
Item 10	0.66	0.42	0.21	0.66	6.17 (0.78)
Item 7	0.57	0.17	0.52	0.62	6.05 (0.83)
Item 12	0.55	0.42	0.27	0.56	5.82 (1.04)
Item 6	0.52	0.36	0.25	0.47	5.16 (1.67)
Total Subscale					5.96 (.79)
Usefulness in obtaining the information					
Item 13	0.35	0.77	0.19	0.76	6.1 (0.98)
Item 15	0.19	0.72	0.17	0.59	5.96 (1.04)
Item 9	0.59	0.62	0.24	0.79	6.1 (0.89)
Total subscale					6.06 (.82)
System information arrangement					
Item 4	0.28	0.24	0.88	0.91	6.09 (0.89)
Item 3	0.46	0.17	0.73	0.78	5.9 (0.99)
Item 14	0.06	0.57	0.66	0.78	6.12 (0.99)
Total Subscale					6.06 (.84)

Overall, the users were satisfied with the content and functionality of the app, and it was well-designed and easy to use. The content was well presented and reliable as it was evidenced-based, and input was received from the experts in eye donation and support from trusty organisations such as NSW Eye and Tissue Bank and the Australian Organ and Tissue Donation Authority.

4 Discussion

One of the advantages of using the app to increase donations is that it is an online technology that easily navigates users to register as eye donors [7]. This study demonstrated the design and development of an evidence-based eye donation app. Four main features of the app assist users to overcome eye donation barriers in this study, which proved by previous studies that are essential for good quality eye donation apps such as providing eye donation education using multiple media and having easy access to register to Australian Organ and Tissue Donation Service. Persuasion context analysis helped shape and create the app's content [15].

To the best of our knowledge, this is the only eye donation application developed for Australian use. In this study, eye donation knowledge content is included in the app in multiple forms such as text, image, graphics, and animation to suit the needs of a wide range of user age groups. Design perspectives were carefully considered to encourage users to provide consent to donate. Relevant features related to primary task support, dialogue support, credibility support and social support categories were presented. Primary task support principles such as reduction and tailoring have been applied mostly in this app, providing self-assessment eligibility for eye donation and providing tailored information containing corneal transplant surgery. This information assists users with decision-making to register for eye donation.

Due to its educative approach, it is envisioned that users of the Eye Donor Aust app will likely consent to eye donation. The app presents credible information following national guidelines, research literature and expert advice. The great advantage of this app is that it is endorsed and supported by trusted experts in eye donation, such as the NSW Eye and Tissue Donation Service and the Australian Organ and Tissue Donation Service. This improves the app's credibility immensely.

Additionally, the strength of the Eye Donor Aust app drew on scientific, reliable and professional sources. It provides accurate depictions and explanations of the anatomy and physiology of the eye, and the National Organ and Tissue Donation Guidelines were used to ensure the accuracy of its content for Australian users. Outstanding features of the app includes the easy shareability of the app; use of videos and imagery; flexible font size for the visually impaired; eligibility self-assessment; easy access to register to DonateLife registration; and the next of kin SMS notification by users who wish to become an eye donor. Further strengths included testing, ethical considerations and specialist input. The app's usability testing was conducted using valid instruments [34] and satisfactory results were received. Also, users can explore the app without using mobile data. The content and functions were developed with ethical considerations that supported the autonomy, privacy, trust.

Future work will be the study on persuasiveness of the application and understand how PSD features utilized in the application could provide eye donation knowledge and motivation towards consent to donate.

5 Conclusion

Using an app to provide eye donation education and to improve attitudes towards eye donation in the community could help to close the gap between the demand for and supply of donated corneas, ultimately increasing the independence and quality of life of Australians needing cornea transplantation. This study presented the design and development of the first specific eye donation app for the Australian population, the Eye Donor Aust app, which aims to promote eye donation information that would assist users in overcoming some known barriers to donation, such as lack of donation knowledge and poor attitudes toward donation.

The knowledge gained from using PSD and DSR to design and develop the app can potentially be applied to guide the development of other organ donation apps and websites, as well as other health apps, including for users from diverse backgrounds, specific cultural groups or with particular religious beliefs.

The findings of our usability testing strongly suggest that the methodology used has resulted in an app that is user-friendly, visually appealing, and appropriate for users across a wide age range. The tool used in this study to create and assess our eye donation app ensured that the app's meta requirements were supported and that the app's design and functions were ethically developed. This tool can be utilised to create and assess similar apps. Further evaluation of the app's impact in increasing eye donation rates is required.

References

1. Ezaz, G., Lai, M.: How the "Opt-in" option optimizes organ donation rates. Dig. Dis. Sci. **64**, 1067–1069 (2019)
2. Chumkasian, W., et al.: Prevalence and predictors of knowledge and attitudes toward eye donation among the general population: a systematic review. Cornea **10**, 1097 (2022)
3. Wong, K., Kam, K., Chen, L., Young, A.: Corneal blindness and current major treatment concern graft scarcity. Int. J. Ophthalmol. **10**, 1154–1162 (2017)
4. Almohanna, A., Win, K., Meedya, S., Vlahu-Gjorgievska, E.: Design and content validation of an instrument measuring user perception of the persuasive design principles in a breastfeeding mHealth app: a modified Delphi study. Int. J. Med. Informatics **164**, 104789 (2022)
5. Almutairi, N., Win, K.T., Vlahu-Gjorgievska, E., Alangari, A.A.: Understanding healthcare providers' value perceptions of content creation and design of a personalized asthma management app: a case study in Saudi Arabia (2022)
6. Win, K.T., Roberts, M.R.H., Oinas-Kukkonen, H.: Persuasive system features in computer-mediated lifestyle modification interventions for physical activity. Inform. Health Soc. Care **44**, 376–404 (2019)
7. Kumar, K., et al.: A smartphone app for increasing live organ donation. Am. J. Transplant. **16**, 3548–3553 (2016)
8. Bramstedt, K.A., Cameron, A.: Beyond the billboard: the Facebook-based application, donor, and its guided approach to facilitating living organ donation. Am. J. Transplant. **17**, 336–340 (2017)
9. Win, K.T., Mulan, J., Howard, S., Oinass-Kukkonen, H.: Persuasive systems design features in promoting medication management for consumers. In: Proceeding of the 50th Hawaii International Conference on System Science HICSS, pp. 3326–3335, Hawaii (2017)

10. Modave, F., et al.: DiaFit: the development of a smart app for patient with Type 2 diabetes and obesity. JMIR Diabetes **1**, e5 (2016)
11. Davis, S.R., Peters, D., Calvo, R.A., Sawyer, S.M., Foster, S.M., Smith, L.: "Kiss myAsthma": using a participatory design approach to develop a self-management app with young people with asthma. J. Asthma **55**, 1018–1027 (2017)
12. Gordon, E.J., et al.: Effect of a mobile web app on kidney transplant candidates' knowledge about increased risk donor kidneys: a randomized controlled trial. Transplantation **101**, 1167 (2017)
13. Ouhbi, S., Fernández-Alemán, J.L., Toval, A., Idri, A., Pozo, J.R.: Free blood donation mobile applications. J. Med. Syst. **39**, 1–20 (2015)
14. Chumkasian, W., Fernandez, R., Petsoglou, C., Win, K.: Smartphone technology to promote eye donation: the evidence clinical and experimental ophthalmology, vol. 44, p. 113. Wiley-Blackwell 111 RIVER ST, HOBOKEN 07030-5774, NJ, USA (2016)
15. Oinass-Kukkonen, H., Harjumaa, M.: Persuasive system design: key issues, process model, and system features. Commun. Assoc. Inf. Syst. **24**, 485–500 (2009)
16. Win, K.T., Ramaprasad, A., Syn, T.: Ontological review of Persuasion Support Systems (PSS) for health behavior change through physical activity. J. Med. Syst. **43**, 1–12 (2019)
17. Müller, H.M., Reuter-Oppermann, M.: Persuasive blood donation app design for individualist and collectivist cultures. In: Gerber, A., Baskerville, R. (eds.) Design Science Research for a New Society: Society 5.0, pp. 157–172. Springer, Cham (2023). https://doi.org/10.1007/978-3-031-32808-4_10
18. Barbier, M., Moták, L., De Gasquet, C., Girandola, F., Bonnardel, N., Lo Monaco, G.: Social representations and interface layout: a new way of enhancing persuasive technology applied to organ donation. PLoS ONE **15**, e0244538 (2020)
19. Almutairi, N., Vlahu-Gjorgievska, E., Win, K.T.: Persuasive features for patient engagement through mHealth applications in managing chronic conditions: a systematic literature review and meta-analysis. Inform. Health Soc. Care **48**, 267–291 (2023)
20. Alhubayshi, A., Almutairi, N., Win, K.T.: Patient engagement through mobile health interventions of diabetes: a systematic literature review. In: ACIS 2022 (2022)
21. Almohanna, A.A.S., Meedya, S., Vlahu-Gjorgievska, E., Win, K.T.: A study of women's perceptions and opinions of a persuasive breastfeeding mHealth app. In: Meschtscherjakov, A., Midden, C., Ham, J. (eds.) International Conference on Persuasive Technology, pp. 142–157. Springer, Cham (2023). https://doi.org/10.1007/978-3-031-30933-5_10
22. Peffers, K., Tuunanen, T., Rothenberger, M.A., Chatterjee, S.: A design science research methodology for information systems research. J. Manag. Inf. Syst. **24**, 45–77 (2007)
23. Hyde, M.: Determining the psychosocial predictors of living, living-related, and posthumous organ donation, vol. Doctor of Philosophy, p. 523. Queensland University of Technology, Brisbane, Australia (2009)
24. Zhou, L., Bao, J., Setiawan, I.M.A., Saptono, A., Parmanto, B.: The mHealth app usability questionnaire (MAUQ): development and validation study. JMIR Mhealth Uhealth **7**, e11500 (2019)
25. Singh, A., Gupta, N., Ganger, A., Vashist, P., Tandon, R.: Awareness regarding eye donation in an urban slum population: a community-based survey. Exp. Clin. Transplant. **6**, 730–735 (2017)
26. Paraz, C.M.A., Truong, H.T.T., Sai, D.K., Cajucom-Uy, H.Y., Chan, C.L.L., Kassim, S.M.: Knowledge and attitudes toward corneal donation among Singaporean youth: a cross sectional study. Eye Vision **3**, 1–10 (2016)
27. Bugis, A., et al.: Knowledge and attitudes regarding eye donation and corneal transplants in Saudi Arabia: a cross-sectional study. Int. J. Med. Res. Professionals **4**, 271–275 (2018)
28. Williams, A.M., Muir, K.W.: Awareness and attitudes toward corneal donation: challenges and opportunities. Clin. Ophthalmol. **12**, 1049–1059 (2018)

29. Walsh, T., Volsko, T.: Readability assessment of internet-based consumer health information. Respir. Care **53**, 1310–1315 (2008)
30. Oinas-Kukkonen, H., Harjumaa, M.: A systematic framework for designing and evaluating persuasive systems. In: Oinas-Kukkonen, H., Hasle, P., Harjumaa, M., Segerstahl, K., Ohrstrom, P. (eds.) Persuasive 2008. LNCS, vol. 5033, pp. 164–176. Springer, Heidelberg (2008). https://doi.org/10.1007/978-3-540-68504-3_15
31. Delgado, J., Molina-Pérez, A., Shaw, D., Rodríguez-Arias, D.: The role of the family in deceased organ procurement: a guide for clinicians and policymakers. Transplantation **103**, e112–e118 (2019)
32. BinDhim, N.F., Hawkey, A., Trevena, L.: A systematic review of quality assessment methods for smartphone health apps. Telemed. e-Health **21**, 97–104 (2015)
33. Tabachnick, B.G., Fidell, L.S., Ullman, J.B.: Using Multivariate Statistics. Pearson, Boston (2013)
34. Chumkasian, W., Fernandez, R., Win, K.T., Petsoglou, C., Lord, H.: Adaptation of the MAUQ and usability evaluation of a mobile phone–based system to promote eye donation. Int. J. Med. Inform. **151**, 104462 (2021)

Persuasive Systems Features in Digital Health Interventions for Diabetes Management: A Scoping Review

Renata Savian Colvero de Oliveira(✉) and Harri Oinas-Kukkonen

Oulu Advanced Research on Service and Information Systems, University of Oulu, Oulu, Finland

{renata.deoliveira,harri.oinas-kukkonen}@oulu.fi

Abstract. Type 2 diabetes mellitus (T2DM) is a global health problem. Studies have shown that using mobile applications can help reduce the burden of this disease and contribute to its self-management. However, there is no full agreement on which persuasive features are most effective or have the greatest impact in promoting behavior change among these patients. Based on the Persuasive Systems Design (PSD), this study aimed to conduct a scoping review to investigate and identify essential PSD features in the context of T2DM. Excluding the duplicates, of the 638 records, 24 were selected and included. During our analysis, primary task support features self-monitoring (n = 22) and personalization (n = 11), computer-human dialog support feature known as reminders (n = 13), and credibility support expertise (n = 10) were found to be the most utilized in the studied applications. Other notable occurrences comprised credibility support feature authority (n = 7) and dialog support feature praise (n = 6). Eleven other less commonly utilized features were found.

Keywords: Type 2 Diabetes Mellitus · mobile applications · Persuasive Systems Design · PSD · persuasive features

1 Introduction

While computers lack intentions, genuine persuasion necessitates intentional influence, prompting creators of such technology to have the deliberate intention to influence others [1]. This deliberate design is observable in persuasive technology, which includes computers, websites, smartphones, apps, tablets, wearables, and computer games that are purposefully designed to induce changes in attitudes or behaviors. Still, effective behavior change requires converging motivation, ability, and triggers [2]. Oinas-Kukkonen and Harjumaa [3] proposed essential steps in developing persuasive systems for behavioral change: analyzing persuasion context, selecting persuasive design principles, defining software requirements, and finally implementing the software.

Four main categories are included in the PSD framework. Primary Task Support is the first category, focusing on design principles that directly help the user fulfill one's original reason for starting to use the app. The second category, Dialogue Support,

N. Baghaei et al. (Eds.): PERSUASIVE 2024, LNCS 14636, pp. 89–99, 2024.
https://doi.org/10.1007/978-3-031-58226-4_8

focuses on principles related to human-computer dialogue implementation in a way that facilitates users in achieving their objectives or exhibiting target behavior. The third category, Credibility Support, focuses on design principles that help create dependable systems with a higher chance of persuading users. The fourth category, Social Support, covers principles for designing a system that uses social influence to motivate users [3].

T2DM is a chronic disease that requires diverse approaches. From this perspective, in addition to diabetes education and the support of a multidisciplinary team [4], establishing behavioral goals is also a vital technique to encourage self-management behaviors [5]. Some strategies available to help patients are digital health interventions, which can, for example, increase patients' physical activity level [6]. Still, mobile, and web-based interventions can show positive changes in some eating behaviors and health outcomes in patients with this comorbidity [7].

This study aims to investigate and identify essential PSD features in the context of T2DM, proposing key elements for implementing digital health interventions. By exploring the spectrum of PSD features in this context, we hope to provide meaningful insights into the ongoing efforts to leverage technology for effective behavior change and diabetes management.

2 Research Method

This is a scoping review study developed following the methodology of the Joanna Briggs Institute [8], which establishes five steps: 1) Identification of the research question; 2) Identification of relevant studies; 3) Selection of studies; 4) Data analysis; and 5) Grouping, synthesis, and presentation of data.

Search Strategy. Bibliographic research was conducted on the sixth of October 2023, consulting the databases PubMed®, Scopus®, Web of Science®, and Science Direct® (Elsevier®). In these databases, descriptors and their synonyms obtained in the Medical Subject Headings (MESH), ("Mobile Applications") OR ("Electronic Application") AND ("Diabetes Mellitus, Type 2") AND ("Persuasion") OR ("Behavior Change"), in English were used. Depending on the database consulted truncation symbols were used to search for words with the same root, increasing the chances of rescuing more articles. All localized studies were imported and organized in the Rayyan® selection platform [9] to organize the articles' reading and selection.

Inclusion and Exclusion Criteria. Articles available in full and addressing our research question "What are the most prevalent persuasive features in mobile and web applications designed for the self-management of Type 2 Diabetes Mellitus based on the Persuasive System Design?", were considered eligible. Those who did not answer the research question, patients in risk or high risk to develop T2DM, prevention of T2DM, gestational diabetes mellitus, editorials, notes/letters to the editor, opinion articles, study protocols, book chapters, guidelines, review articles, qualitative studies, usability studies, self-categorized mixed method studies, studies with other interventions (SMS messages, phone calls, phone counseling or email), and no results were excluded. Studies without full text available (conference abstracts or posters) were also excluded.

Final Selection. One researcher used the inclusion and exclusion criteria for the articles rescued from the databases, starting the selection by reading the titles and abstracts and, finally, the full texts.

Data Extraction. From the selected studies, the following information was extracted and organized in tables: author, year of publication, the identification and interpretation of the four PSD features: Primary task support (PRIM), Computer-human dialogue support (DIAL), Credibility Support (CRED) and Social Support (SOCI). Interpretations concerning the PSD features were initially proposed by the first author, but then all authors discussed these and any uncertainties together until a consensus was reached. Notably, only the features clearly described in the studies could be included, and no inferences or assumptions were made. The articles were also categorized with an ID number regarding the oldest to newest and the alphabetic order.

3 Results

After the searches, the files were organized in the Rayyan® [9] selection platform, where 219 duplicates were excluded, leaving 638 articles to be investigated by title and abstract. After this first stage, 32 articles were selected for full reading. Eight records were excluded by the following reasons: did not answer the research question (n = 1), mixed methods study (n = 1), included coaching telephone calls (n = 1), involved two different diseases (n = 1), involved pre T2DM (n = 1), was not related to persuasion (n = 2) and was a conference abstract after all (n = 1). As a result, 24 studies remained.

Of the 28 features, which comprise the 4 main areas (PRIM, DIAL, CRED, SOCI), 17 were identified among the studies: self-monitoring (SMO), personalization (PER), tailoring (TAI), reduction (RED), tunneling (TUN), reminders (REM), praise (PRA), rewards (REW), liking (LIK), social role (SRO), suggestions (SUG), expertise (EXP), authority (AUT), trustworthiness (TRU), real-world feel (RWF), verifiability (VER) and social learning (SLE) (Table 1). Eleven features (Simulation, Rehearsal, Similarity, Surface Credibility, Third Party-Endorsements, Normative Influence, Cooperation, Competition, Social Recognition, Social Comparison and Social Facilitation) were not identified in the included studies.

The most frequently reported feature was SMO. Only studies 23 [32] and 17 [26] did not include it in its application. Instead, study 23 emphasized how users could track daily steps, sedentary minutes, active minutes, calories burned, and resting heart rate using a watch sensor. However, whether this information was also visible to users on the application screen or if they only consulted it on their watch remained unclear. Therefore, respecting the research method, in this study we did not interpret that the application would have utilized SMO. This should have been explicitly stated in the text.

Still considering the PRIM category, a widely used feature was PER. Sometimes papers describe that an application "tailors" on an individual level based on the user's progress, as observed in study 5 [14]. However, this was considered here as PER rather than TAI. Also, in study 9 [18], differentiating between TUN and RED was found difficult as both seek to reduce cognitive load [3].

REM, a DIAL feature, was the second most used. The most frequently used types were reminders to take medication [14, 17, 26, 30]; reminders to engage in physical

Table 1. PSD Features in Type 2 Diabetes Mellitus digital health interventions.

ID	PRIM	DIAL	CRED	SOCI
1 [10]	SMO, RED, PER	REM	AUT	
2 [11]	SMO	PRA		
3 [12]	SMO, PER		TRU, EXP, RWF	
4 [13]	SMO, PER	REM, SUG		
5 [14]	SMO, PER	REW, REM, PRA, LIK	AUT	
6 [15]	SMO	REM	TRU, EXP, VER	
7 [16]	SMO, TAI, PER, RED	REW, REM		SLE
8 [17]	SMO, PER	REM		
9 [18]	SMO, TUN, RED, TAI	SUG	AUT, VER	SLE
10 [19]	SMO			
11 [20]	SMO	REW, REM, PRA,SRO	EXP, AUT, RWF	
12 [21]	SMO	SRO		
13 [22]	SMO		RWF, EXP	
14 [23]	SMO			
15 [24]	SMO	PRA, SUG	EXP	
16 [25]	SMO, PER	REM	AUT	
17 [26]		REM, PRA, REW		
18 [27]	SMO		EXP	
19 [28]	SMO, PER	REM	EXP	
20 [29]	SMO, PER	REM	AUT	
21 [30]	SMO	REM	EXP	
22 [31]	SMO		RWF, AUT, EXP	
23 [32]	PER	REM	EXP	
24 [33]	SMO, PER	PRA		

activity, such as workouts or a reduction in sitting [14, 16, 19, 30]; and reminders to complete or fill in their primary task-related goals [20, 25, 29, 30]. This demonstrates that reminders are a crucial role in reinforcing communication between the user and the system. In study 12, the application composed of two subsystems, out of which the one called mySugr utilized SRO but the other called Glucose Buddy didn't.

Regarding CRED, it is not surprising that EXP was a widely utilized feature given the applications under study—which are health aids for individuals with T2DM—as applications in this domain need to exhibit knowledge, experience, and competence to convince users of their potential. Exploring AUT, a common aspect found between the applications is the description that health professionals participated in developing them (study 9, 16) [18, 25], in addition to using other reliable sources, such as official guidelines (study 1, 5, 11, 20, 22) [10, 14, 20, 29, 31].

Furthermore, the software may be reported to be secure and guarantee privacy. However, the articles did not always state whether this information was visible and available to users, as it was in study 3 [12]. Brief but clear statements of how the features were used and represented in the systems would be essential for better interpreting the studies. A similar situation could be identified in study 15 [24], where the term "messages of support" is briefly mentioned but was not included as a premium feature of the system. We therefore interpreted that PRA was available to both patients with and without access to what they called as forecasts.

Study 7 [16] mentioned that application users were offered optional information about how they can obtain support from their partner, friends, family, or colleagues, exploring social support. However, since this information was not directly related to peers or other users, it could not be interpreted as SOCI. Nevertheless, they included a few stories about what people in similar circumstances believe, so we could identify this as a case of SLE. The lack of specific details makes it challenging to accurately identify the SOCI, because for it to exist within a system, it must leverage the influence of peers or other users, such as comparing results and thus improving outcomes [3].

There was one notable similarity between studies 16 [25] and 20 [29], which both used data from "The Livongo for Diabetes" program, a digitally remote chronic condition management initiative that uses mobile technology to provide participants with information and resources to help them manage their diabetes on their own. However, they had different study types, samples, and objectives. Also, the same PSD features were described, however some of them were not illustrated in the same way. SMO and REM were described as the same. Regarding AUT, study 16 [25] did not mention the Association of Diabetes Care and Education Specialists and American Diabetes Association as study 20 [29] did, but they mentioned access to certified diabetes care and education specialists. PER had the same description, citing the delivery of personalized insights related to glycemic management, but only study 20 [29] added that the members could set their own step goals.

Finally, the small distinctions in the descriptions of PSD features between studies 16 [25] and 20 [29] highlight the significance of focusing careful attention to details when examining and describing the functionalities of applications for chronic condition management. To promote a thorough understanding and prevent any misunderstandings, this observation necessitates the careful and transparent definition and illustration of particular features. It can also imply that the application analyzed most likely did not contain any persuasive elements other than those that were methodically found. This finding strengthens the validity of the findings of our investigation by emphasizing the consistency and stability in identifying and analyzing PSD features within the specified research framework.

Three distinct sets of features emerged based on the frequency of the utilization during our analysis (Table 2). The statement of three sets arose due to the clear observation of differentiation, highlighting notable variability in the prevalence of these features across the examined interventions. With significant occurrences (n = 22, n = 13, n = 11 and n = 10), the first set of features composing of SMO, REM, PER and EXP respectively stands out as the most often utilized features throughout the chosen apps. This suggests that these features are being adopted quite consistently within the problem domain at hand. The second set also showed important frequencies, AUT (n = 7) and PRA (n = 6). Lastly, the third set comprised REW (n = 4), RWF (n = 4), SUG (n = 3), RED (n = 3), TRU (n = 2), VER (n = 2), SRO (n = 2), TAI (n = 2), SLE (n = 2), LIK (n = 1) and TUN (n = 1).

Table 2. Summary of the number of the PSD features recognized.

PRIM		DIAL		CRED		SOCI	
SMO	22	REM	13	EXP	10	SLE	2
PER	11	PRA	6	AUT	7		
RED	3	REW	4	RWF	4		
TAI	2	SUG	3	TRU	2		
TUN	1	SRO	2	VER	2		
		LIK	1				

4 Discussion

This study identified the most prevalent PSD features in T2DM mobile and web applications and emphasized the rational use of each asset in a PSD. Among the three distinct sets of features recognized, the first set comprised SMO, REM, PER and EXP were the most used features, followed by AUT and PRA. Not surprisingly, the most frequently reported feature was SMO, which had already been established as one of the most used in previous publications [34–36].

While there is no agreement on the most effective PSD features, examining similar digital health interventions with comparable goals would provide valuable insights for this. A previous study that applied to four different more general health domains—diet, emotional and mental health, physical activity and fitness, and health assessment and healthcare—provides insight into relevant treatments that could also be implemented for T2DM patients. Their findings, derived from an assessment of 80 mobile health apps, revealed that PER was the most frequently employed persuasive feature (n = 77), followed by surface credibility (n = 69), TRU (n = 66), and SMO (n = 64) [37]. These results show PRIM as one of the most important categories, composed of PER and SMO, which is consistent with our current research. The role of TRU and surface credibility may grow when going from diabetes management to other health subdomains. It also highlights the need for patients to verify the accuracy of the information presented in the application and understand who is responsible for their creation, as CRED also stood out. This may be related to the fact that health-related applications require greater care and attention to detail because the content can seriously affect people's lives and may even cause harm if it is not well-planned or supported by serious evidence.

Prior research additionally examined risk factors closely associated with T2DM, including obesity [38] and metabolic syndrome [39]. These studies also employed PSD analyses and reported findings similar to the present study. According to Sittig et al. [38], PRIM was the most often used category in research on obesity interventions; DIAL, CRED, and then SOCI followed it. In line with our findings, the most applied principle was SMO. In the meantime, SMO and REM are among the features that users believe to be particularly helpful and persuasive, according to a qualitative study that describes how users perceive the features implemented in an application for metabolic syndrome [39]. A comparative analysis between these studies holds the potential to establish a hierarchy of recommended features for developing effective digital health interventions, contributing to the ongoing discourse on optimizing persuasive features for health-related mobile and web applications.

Unfortunately, one of the challenges faced is the lack of use of SOCI features in health applications, even though their potential benefits have already been demonstrated. In a meta-analysis of 13 RCTs (n = 2712) whose objective was to summarize the existing evidence on the impact of peer coach-led T2DM self-management interventions showed that HbA1c significantly reduced in the intervention group (standard mean difference – 0,14% 95%CI −0,25, −0,03) [40]. Positive results were also found regarding quality of life, self-efficacy, and diabetes distress. Similar to our study, Geirhos et al. [41] also discovered that the least used PSD feature category was SOCI. There could be several reasons for this, such as implementation challenges, ethical and privacy dilemmas with data sharing, or issues with a potentially incorrect tip or peer suggestion that could be interpreted as valid. Consequently, financing a mediator to supervise the messages' content and ensure ethical issues would be required.

Considering each target population has unique characteristics and outcomes may differ, this article does not offer a full agreement on the best PSD features for all diseases and circumstances. As an example of this, according to a study aiming to examine persuasive system features in web-based interventions for substance abuse, RED was the most frequently mentioned PRIM feature. SMO and simulation, which are also PRIM features, were next in importance [35]. However, given the physiological aspects of chronic non-communicable diseases, this research can guide the development of new digital health interventions targeted at T2DM, obesity, and metabolic syndrome—closely related subjects, offering assistance across different fields.

It is also noteworthy that not all studies found significant results in their primary outcome (studies 2, 3, 4, 6 and 19) [11–13, 15, 28]. However, studies 2 [11], 3 [12] and 6 [15] achieved only their secondary objectives. Study 2 showed significant positive changes in self-management reflected by the skill and technique acquisition scale in a specific mobile app with a health counseling group. Study 3 achieved a significant between-group difference in HbA1c at the 3-month time point (0.52%, p = 0.03), significant decreases in weight (p = 0.006) and waist circumference (p = 0.01). Notably, results considered positive by clinicians should not only aim to reduce exam parameters since treating diabetes mellitus is holistic [42, 43]. Finally, study 6 dropout analyses comparing study completers with dropouts revealed that 6-month use was associated with being younger, lower self-efficacy concerns, lower internal locus of control concerns, and lower adherence behaviors. However, it is important to note that the authors of these papers used 0.1 for the significance level for Mann-Whitney U tests. One possible reason for failing to achieve the primary objective could be the small sample size from a single clinic, as well as the self-reported levels of adherence.

Study 4 [13] failed to achieve the primary and secondary outcomes. A possible explanation is the low participation in the trial (9.9%–17.0%). The authors highlighted the application as not personalized enough since participants only chose the frequency of the messages and the topics of the intervention (dietary habits, physical activity, prevention of hypoglycemia, and glucose control), with the topic of hypo-glycemia being a mandatory topic. Limited results were also observed in Study 19 [28], as there was no significant difference in HbA1c between the supervised and technology groups combined, nor between the mobile app and smartwatch groups. Between the supervised and technology groups, similar percentages of participants achieved a clinically meaningful difference (46% vs. 43%), and the associated Odds ratio was 0.87 with a wide confidence interval (95%CI 0.34–2.28), providing an uncertainty associated with the presented estimate. Regarding secondary and explanatory outcomes, the groups were identical.

This work has some limitations, as we might not have reported all the applications' features because each characteristic decision may be subjective. Nevertheless, we respected the method of only reporting what was explicitly stated in the paper, and to prevent misunderstandings the final interpretation was reached together by both reviewers/authors with careful attention being paid to all anomalies found. Additionally, not all studies produced the anticipated results; however, this could be due to the ineffectiveness of the features or to some biases, including sample size and study design.

It should also be noted that analyzing PSD features based on literature is quite difficult a task, as features are not always clearly reported. There is still prevalent misunderstanding regarding PER and TAI. While they seem to be quite similar, there is a difference between them. PER addresses the individual user level, while TAI is about the user group profile, which requires recognizing profiles for different user groups [3]. These circumstances ought to motivate authors to enhance their explanations and carefully consider the feature descriptions. This would facilitate the PSD analysis and, consequently, better recommendations, and the development of protocols that application developers can apply.

5 Conclusion

This scoping review highlights the evolving landscape of digital interventions in managing Type 2 diabetes mellitus (T2DM). By focusing on usage patterns, particularly the prevalence of Persuasive Systems Design (PSD) features such as *self-monitoring, reminders, personalization and expertise*, this study identifies key areas where digital applications can actively facilitate behavior change among diabetes patients. These findings lay the groundwork for further investigation into the effectiveness of these features, which is crucial for advancing our understanding of their utilization and impact on diabetes management.

Understanding what makes an effective intervention requires first identifying the most used features, as was the focus of this research. Our results serve as the foundation for researching and developing new digital health interventions while expanding our understanding of persuasion strategies and technological advancements in persuasive systems design.

Acknowledgments. This study has received funding from the Research Council of Finland under decision 351670 with theme "Persuasive digital health interventions: Software features as key predictors for successful prevention and treatment of overweight, obesity, metabolic syndrome and cardiovascular diseases".

Disclosure of Interests. The authors have no competing interests to declare that are relevant to the content of this article.

References

1. Fogg, B.J.: Persuasive Computers: Perspectives and Research Directions (1998)
2. Fogg, B.J.: A behavior model for persuasive design. In: Persuasive 2009: Proceedings of the 4th International Conference on Persuasive Technology, vol. 40, pp. 1–7 (2009)
3. Oinas-Kukkonen, H., Harjumaa, M.: Persuasive systems design: key issues, process model, and system features. Commun. Assoc. Inf. Syst. **24**(1), 28 (2009)
4. Funnell, M.M., et al.: National standards for diabetes self-management education. Diab. Care **33**(1), S89–S96 (2010)
5. Bodenheimer, T., MacGregor, K., Sharifi, C.: Helping Patients Manage Their Chronic Conditions. California Healthcare Foundation, Oakland (2005)
6. Mönninghoff, A., et al.: Long-term effectiveness of mHealth physical activity interventions: systematic review and meta-analysis of randomized controlled trials. J. Med. Internet Res. **23**(4), e26699 (2021)
7. Karimi, N., Opie, R.S., Crawford, D., O'Connell, S., Ball, K.: Digitally-delivered interventions to improve nutrition behaviours among people from ethnic minority and socioeconomically disadvantaged groups with type 2 diabetes: systematic review. J. Med. Internet Res. **26**, e42595 (2022)
8. Peters, M.D.J., Godfrey, C., McInerney, P., Munn, Z., Tricco, A.C., Khalil, H.: Scoping reviews. In: Aromataris, E., Lockwood, C., Porritt, K., Pilla, B., Jordan, Z. (eds.) JBI Manual for Evidence Synthesis. JBI 2024 (2020). https://doi.org/10.46658/JBIMES-24-09. https://synthesismanual.jbi.global
9. Ouzzani, M., Hammady, H., Fedorowicz, Z., Elmagarmid, A.: Rayyan-a web and mobile app for systematic reviews. Syst. Rev. **5**(1), 210 (2016)
10. Orsama, A.L., et al.: Active assistance technology reduces glycosylated hemoglobin and weight in individuals with type 2 diabetes: results of a theory-based randomized trial. Diabetes Technol. Ther. **15**(8), 662–669 (2013)
11. Holmen, H., et al.: A mobile health intervention for self-management and lifestyle change for persons with type 2 diabetes, Part 2: one-year results from the Norwegian randomized controlled trial renewing health. JMIR Mhealth Uhealth **2**(4), e57 (2014)
12. Wayne, N., Perez, D.F., Kaplan, D.M., Ritvo, P.: Health coaching reduces HbA1c in type 2 diabetic patients from a lower-socioeconomic status community: a randomized controlled trial. J. Med. Internet Res. **17**(10), e224 (2015)
13. Boels, A.M., Rutten, G., Zuithoff, N., de Wit, A., Vos, R.: Effectiveness of diabetes self-management education via a smartphone application in insulin treated type 2 diabetes patients - design of a randomised controlled trial ('TRIGGER study'). BMC Endocr. Disord. **18**(1), 74 (2018)

14. Höchsmann, C., Infanger, D., Klenk, C., Königstein, K., Walz, S.P., Schmidt-Trucksäss, A.: Effectiveness of a behavior change technique-based smartphone game to improve intrinsic motivation and physical activity adherence in patients with type 2 diabetes: randomized controlled trial. JMIR Serious Games **7**(1), e11444 (2019)
15. Kjos, A.L., Vaughan, A.G., Bhargava, A.: Impact of a mobile app on medication adherence and adherence-related beliefs in patients with type 2 diabetes. J. Am. Pharm. Assoc. **59**(2), 44–51 (2019)
16. Poppe, L., et al.: Efficacy of a self-regulation-based electronic and mobile health intervention targeting an active lifestyle in adults having type 2 diabetes and in adults aged 50 years or older: two randomized controlled trials. J. Med. Internet Res. **21**(8), e13363 (2019)
17. Bailey, D.P., Mugridge, L.H., Dong, F., Zhang, X., Chater, A.M.: Randomised controlled feasibility study of the MyHealthAvatar-diabetes smartphone app for reducing prolonged sitting time in type 2 diabetes mellitus. Int. J. Environ. Res. Public Health **17**(12), 4414 (2020)
18. Sittig, S., Wang, J., Iyengar, S., Myneni, S., Franklin, A.: Incorporating behavioral trigger messages into a mobile health app for chronic disease management: randomized clinical feasibility trial in diabetes. JMIR Mhealth Uhealth **8**(3), e15927 (2020)
19. Zheng, Y., et al.: Actual use of multiple health monitors among older adults with diabetes: pilot study. JMIR Aging **3**(1), e15995 (2020)
20. Krishnakumar, A., et al.: Evaluating glycemic control in patients of South Asian origin with type 2 diabetes using a digital therapeutic platform: analysis of real-world data. J. Med. Internet Res. **23**(3), e17908 (2021)
21. Maharaj, A., Lim, D., Murphy, R., Serlachius, A.: Comparing two commercially available diabetes apps to explore challenges in user engagement: randomized controlled feasibility study. JMIR Form Res. **5**(6), e25151 (2021)
22. Zaharia, O.P., Kupriyanova, Y., Karusheva, Y., Markgraf, D.F., Kantartzis, K., Birkenfeld, A.L., et al.: Improving insulin sensitivity, liver steatosis and fibrosis in type 2 diabetes by a food-based digital education-assisted lifestyle intervention program: a feasibility study. Eur. J. Nutr. **60**(7), 3811–3818 (2021)
23. Coombes, J.S., et al.: Personal activity intelligence e-Health program in people with type 2 diabetes: a pilot randomized controlled trial. Med. Sci. Sports Exerc. **54**(1), 18–27 (2022)
24. Imrisek, S.D., et al.: Effects of a novel blood glucose forecasting feature on glycemic management and logging in adults with type 2 diabetes using one drop: retrospective cohort study. JMIR Diab. **7**(2), e34624 (2022)
25. Kamath, S., Kappaganthu, K., Painter, S., Madan, A.: Improving outcomes through personalized recommendations in a remote diabetes monitoring program: observational study. JMIR Form Res. **6**(3), e33329 (2022)
26. Nadadur, S.: Medication adherence app for food pantry clients with diabetes: a feasibility study. J. Nurse Pract. **18**(8), 897–903 (2022)
27. Raghavan, A., et al.: Improvement in glycaemic control in patients with type 2 diabetes with treatment using an interactive mobile application - a pilot study from India. Prim. Care Diab. **16**(6), 844–848 (2022)
28. Timurtas, E., Inceer, M., Mayo, N., Karabacak, N., Sertbas, Y., Polat, M.G.: Technology-based and supervised exercise interventions for individuals with type 2 diabetes: randomized controlled trial. Prim. Care Diab. **16**(1), 49–56 (2022)
29. Wang, Y., et al.: Association of physical activity on blood glucose in individuals with type 2 diabetes. Transl. Behav. Med. **12**(3), 448–453 (2022)
30. Jafar, N., Huriyati, E., Haryani, Setyawati, A.: Enhancing knowledge of Diabetes self-management and quality of life in people with Diabetes Mellitus by using Guru Diabetes Apps-based health coaching. J. Public Health Res. **12**(3), 22799036231186338 (2023)

31. Joshi, S., et al.: Fitterfly diabetes CGM digital therapeutics program for glycemic control and weight management in people with type 2 diabetes mellitus: real-world effectiveness evaluation. JMIR Diab. **8**, e43292 (2023)
32. Joshi, S., et al.: Digital twin-enabled personalized nutrition improves metabolic dysfunction-associated fatty liver disease in type 2 diabetes: results of a 1-year randomized controlled study. Endocr. Pract. **29**, 960–970 (2023). 1530-891x, https://doi.org/10.1016/j.eprac.2023.08.016. Accessed 17 Nov 2023
33. Sjöblom, L., Bonn, S.E., Alexandrou, C., Dahlgren, A., Eke, H., Trolle, L.Y.: Dietary habits after a physical activity mHealth intervention: a randomized controlled trial. BMC Nutr. **9**(1), 23 (2023)
34. Agyei, E., Miettunen, J., Oinas-Kukkonen, H.: Effective interventions and features for coronary heart disease: a meta-analysis, Behav. Inf. Technol. (2023)
35. Lehto, T., Oinas-Kukkonen, H.: Persuasive features in web-based alcohol and smoking interventions: a systematic review of the literature. J. Med. Internet Res. **13**(3), e46 (2011)
36. Win, K.T., Roberts, M.R.H., Oinas-Kukkonen, H.: Persuasive system features in computer-mediated lifestyle modification interventions for physical activity. Inform. Health Soc. Care **44**(4), 376–404 (2019)
37. Oyebode, O., Ndulue, C., Alhasani, M., Orji, R.: Persuasive mobile apps for health and wellness: a comparative systematic review. In: Gram-Hansen, S.B., Jonasen, T.S., Midden, C. (eds.) PERSUASIVE 2020. LNCS, vol. 12064, pp. 163–181. Springer, Cham (2020). https://doi.org/10.1007/978-3-030-45712-9_13
38. Sittig, S., McGowan, A., Iyengar, S.: Extensive review of persuasive system design categories and principles: behavioral obesity interventions. J. Med. Syst. **44**(7), 128 (2020)
39. Karppinen, P., et al.: Persuasive user experiences of a health Behavior Change Support System: a 12-month study for prevention of metabolic syndrome. Int. J. Med. Inform. **96**, 51–61 (2016)
40. Verma, I., et al.: The impact of peer coach-led type 2 diabetes mellitus interventions on glycaemic control and self-management outcomes: a systematic review and meta-analysis. Prim. Care Diab. **16**(6), 719–735 (2022)
41. Geirhos, A., et al.: Standardized evaluation of the quality and persuasiveness of mobile health applications for diabetes management. Sci. Rep. **12**(1), 3639 (2022)
42. Juanamasta, I.G., Aungsuroch, Y., Gunawan, J., Suniyadewi, N.W., Nopita Wati, N.M.: Holistic care management of diabetes mellitus: an integrative review. Int. J. Prev. Med. **12**, 69 (2021)
43. Hashim, M.J.: The art of diabetes care: guidelines for a holistic approach to human and social factors. J. Yeungnam Med. Sci. **40**(2), 218–222 (2023)

Collaboratively Setting Daily Step Goals with a Virtual Coach: Using Reinforcement Learning to Personalize Initial Proposals

Martin Dierikx[1], Nele Albers[1](✉), Bouke L. Scheltinga[2], and Willem-Paul Brinkman[1]

[1] Intelligent Systems, Delft University of Technology, Delft, Netherlands
{n.albers,w.p.brinkman}@tudelft.nl

[2] Biomedical Signals and Systems, University of Twente, Enschede, Netherlands

Abstract. Goal-setting is commonly used in behavior change applications for physical activity. However, for goals to be effective, they need to be tailored to a user's situation (e.g., motivation, progress). One way to obtain such goals is a collaborative process in which a healthcare professional and client set a goal together, thus making use of the professional's expertise and the client's knowledge about their own situation. As healthcare professionals are not always available, we created a dialog with the virtual coach Steph to collaboratively set daily step goals. Since judgments in human decision-making processes are adjusted based on the starting point or anchor, the first step goal proposal Steph makes is likely to influence the user's final goal and self-efficacy. Situational factors impacting physical activity (e.g., motivation, self-efficacy, available time) or how users process information (e.g., mood) may determine which initial proposals are most effective in getting users to reach their underlying previous activity-based recommended step goals. Using data from 117 people interacting with Steph for up to five days, we designed a reinforcement learning algorithm that considers users' current and future situations when choosing an initial step goal proposal. Our simulations show that initial step goal proposals matter: choosing optimal ones based on this algorithm could make it more likely that people move to a situation with high motivation, high self-efficacy, and a favorable daily context. Then, they are more likely to achieve, but also to overachieve, their underlying recommended step goals. Our dataset is publicly available.

Keywords: Physical activity · Behavior change · Reinforcement learning · Conversational agent · Goal-setting

1 Introduction

Goal-setting is commonly used in behavior change applications for physical activity (e.g., [3,6,39,44,50]). It helps to stay focused on a desired outcome, spend effort toward that outcome, and find effective strategies [37]. However, for goals

N. Baghaei et al. (Eds.): PERSUASIVE 2024, LNCS 14636, pp. 100–115, 2024.
https://doi.org/10.1007/978-3-031-58226-4_9

to be effective, it is recommended that they satisfy criteria such as being specific, measurable, achievable, relevant, and time-bound (SMART) [21] as well as being (re-)evaluated [5,37]. Current physical activity applications commonly do not satisfy these criteria, especially when it comes to tailoring the goal difficulty to a user's ability and re-evaluating goals based on the user's progress [5].

In a traditional offline setting, one way to set goals satisfying these criteria is for a client and healthcare professional to agree on a goal in a collaborative process [10]. Involving clients in the goal-setting process can not only increase their self-efficacy [37], but it also offers the opportunity to combine the expertise of the healthcare professional and the client's knowledge about their own situation. Such collaborative goal-setting has, for example, been recommended for people with diabetes [14] and been applied in the context of asthma management [47]. Since virtual coaches can take the role of such a healthcare professional in eHealth applications for behavior change, we thus wanted to design a collaborative goal-setting dialog with a virtual coach. Besides providing guidance where traditionally healthcare professionals would have, virtual coaches also have the potential to combat the low adherence common to eHealth applications for behavior change [7,26] by fostering engagement, discussing relevant and timely information, showing understanding, and connecting with people [2,27,38].

When designing such a collaborative goal-setting dialog, attention needs to be paid to the starting point. This is because, in a human decision-making process, judgments are commonly made based on the starting point of the process (i.e., an anchor) [52]. All subsequent judgments are then made by adjusting away from that anchor. For example, the first offer in a negotiation has been shown to be a strong predictor of the settling price for purchasing a pharmaceutical plant or the assigning bonus for a new employee [25]. And anchoring values have also been shown to affect self-efficacy in a problem-solving task [12]. This means that the first goal option that is discussed in the goal-setting dialog is likely to influence both the final goal the virtual coach and the user set and the user's self-efficacy regarding achieving that goal.

Since a suitable physical activity goal for the user depends on their current situation (e.g., previous physical activity, depressive symptoms, self-efficacy [42]), the starting point of the goal-setting process should hence also be adapted to a user's current situation. Previous work has, for example, adapted physical activity goals based on a user's routine [11], previous performance [33], or location, step count variation, number of app screens yesterday, and past push notifications [36]. Moreover, since we want to adapt initial goal proposals rather than fixed goals, factors that influence how people process information can also play a role. For instance, a user's mood may influence the degree of message elaboration [8]. When setting multiple short-term (e.g., daily) goals over an extended period of time, however, it is not only the *current* situation of the user that matters but also the *future* one. For example, while setting higher physical activity goals may result in higher physical activity levels, it may also lead to lower goal achievement [13] and thus potentially lower engagement in the future [49]. Setting initially lower goals, on the other hand, may allow people to make small wins and thus increase their motivation [4].

One framework that allows us to consider both current and future user situations (i.e., states) is Reinforcement Learning (RL) [48]. RL, with a consideration of current and future states, has previously been applied to adapt weekly step goals to people's previous activity and self-efficacy [59] or determine when to send physical activity notifications [53]. Here, we investigate whether RL is also useful when choosing initial goal proposals in a collaborative dialog for physical activity. To this end, we conducted a study in which 117 people interacted with the text-based virtual coach Steph for up to five days. Each day, participants and Steph collaboratively set a daily goal for walking, which is easily accessible to most people [34], has documented health benefits [34], and is one of the easiest and most acceptable forms of physical activity since it can be integrated into everyday life [15]. In this collaboration, Steph first determined people's current situation with regard to mood, sleep quality, available time, motivation, and self-efficacy before giving a step goal proposal that could be iteratively refined afterward. The proposal could thereby take five different forms, each based on adjusting an underlying previous activity-based recommended goal in a different way (i.e., ± 0, 200, or 400 steps). On the next day, Steph asked the user about the number of steps they took the previous day before initiating the setting of a new goal. Based on this study's data, this paper's contribution is threefold. First, we provide insights into the effects of initial goal proposals in a collaborative goal-setting dialog. Second, we contribute an RL model that optimizes the choice of initial proposals based on people's current and future states. And third, we publish our dataset to aid future work on adaptive collaborative goal-setting.

2 Materials and Methods

2.1 Virtual Coach

We developed the text-based virtual coach Steph [18] in Rasa [9]. Steph introduced itself as helping people set daily step goals toward the ultimate goal of taking 10,000 steps every day [55]. In each session, Steph asked about people's current state based on their mood, sleep quality, available time, motivation, and self-efficacy. Afterward, Steph computed a recommended daily step goal based on the user's previous walking behavior using the percentile algorithm by Adams et al. [1][1]. Based on this recommended step goal, Steph gave the user three goal options, each 100 steps apart, as well as the possibility to indicate that they wanted a different goal. This way, users were given a say in determining their goal and nudged toward picking one of the three options. If users indicated wanting a higher goal, Steph congratulated them for wanting to challenge themselves but also warned them that taking too many steps might lead to injuries; if users

[1] We rounded the resulting number to the nearest 100 since people tend to need more time to process non-rounded numbers [31] and to put extra effort into completing a rounded goal if they are close to it [43].

indicated wanting a lower goal, Steph expressed understanding but said that taking at least some steps is good for them. Users could indicate wanting a lower or higher goal up to five times with a minimum goal of 2,000 and a maximum goal of 10,000 steps[2]. Once the user had decided on a goal, Steph congratulated them on their choice, gave a few examples of how to easily take steps during the day, and sent a reminder message with the goal on Prolific. The next session started by asking users about the number of steps they took on the previous day. In its dialog style, Steph followed principles from motivational interviewing such as expressing empathy and acknowledging answers [51]. As part of a social communication style, Steph further used informal language (e.g., "Aww, that's annoying") and emojis, made use of positively valenced words (e.g. "great", "cool"), and reacted enthusiastically to users' inputs. Such a social communication style has, for example, been shown to increase customer satisfaction with chatbots [58]. A demo video of the dialog can be found online [16].

2.2 Personalizing Initial Step Goal Options

We can define our approach as a Markov Decision Process (MDP) $\langle S, A, R, T, \gamma \rangle$. The action space A consisted of five ways of personalizing the step goal proposals, the reward function $R : S \times A \rightarrow \mathbb{R}$ was determined by the difference between the recommended step goal and the number of steps a person took, $T : S \times A \times S \rightarrow [0, 1]$ was the transition function, and the discount factor γ was set to 0.85 to favor rewards obtained earlier over rewards obtained later. The finite state space S described the state a user was in and was captured by their mood, sleep quality, available time, motivation, and self-efficacy. The goal of an agent in an MDP is to learn an optimal policy $\pi^* : S \rightarrow \Pi(A)$ that maximizes the expected cumulative discounted reward $\mathbb{E}\left[\sum_t^\infty \gamma^t r_t\right]$ for acting in the environment. The optimal Q-value function $Q^* : S \times A \rightarrow \mathbb{R}$ describes the expected cumulative discounted reward for executing a in state s and π^* in all subsequent states. Figure 1 shows how our RL approach is embedded in the goal-setting dialog.

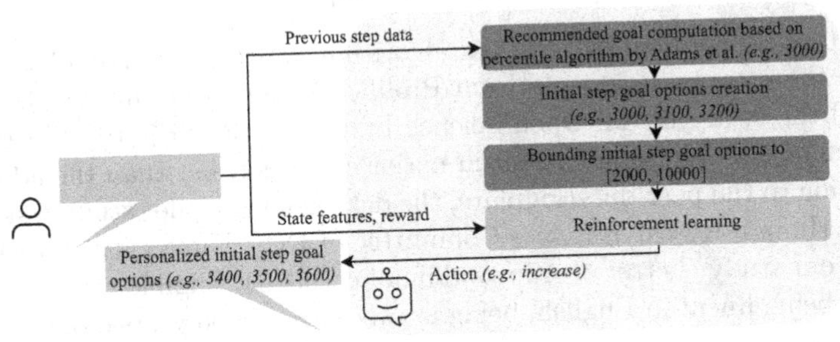

Fig. 1. Pipeline for arriving at personalized initial step goal options.

[2] Few people take less than 2,000 daily steps [22,28,56], and taking more than 10,000 steps does not offer much further benefit while making injuries more likely [35,41].

State Space. In each session, users provided answers to questions about their mood valence based on the adjectives by Russell [46] mapped to a valence score using the emotion wheel by Kollias et al. [32], sleep quality from the previous night based on Dzierzewski et al. [23], available time and motivation based on the physical activity barrier descriptions by Robbins et al. [45], and self-efficacy based on the definition by Park and Kim [42]. The latter four variables were all measured on 11-point scales from 0 to 10. Mood valence, sleep quality, and available time were subsequently added to create a "daily context"-state that described factors that could influence the effectiveness of the actions but were unlikely to also be affected by the actions. This "daily context"-state could take values between 0 and 30. The intuition is that the higher the value, the more favorable is the daily context for physical activity.

Actions. Our action space consisted of five ways of personalizing the initial step goal options: *decrease*, *slightly decrease*, *do not change*, *slightly increase*, and *increase*. *Slightly decrease* and *slightly increase* decreased or increased the three initial goal options by 200 steps, *decrease* and *increase* changed the initial options by 400 steps, and *do not change* kept the original options.

Reward. The reward r was based on the absolute difference Δ between the recommended goal G and the actual number of steps a user took ($Steps$). Taking more steps than recommended is penalized half as much as taking fewer steps:

$$r = \begin{cases} 1 - \frac{\Delta}{G} & if\ Steps \leq G \\ 1 - \frac{\Delta}{2G} & if\ Steps > G. \end{cases}$$

The intuition behind this reward signal is that we primarily want users to reach the recommended number of steps, but also penalize taking too many steps to some degree since this can lead to injuries.

2.3 Data Collection and Model Training

Study. To collect training data for our algorithm, we conducted an observational study on the crowdsourcing platform Prolific in June and July 2023. We pre-registered the study in the Open Science Framework (OSF) [19]. Since a pilot study with 34 people did not result in major changes other than the addition of one question to the post-questionnaire, the data from the pilot study was used as well. The Human Research Ethics Committee of Delft University of Technology approved our study (Letter of Approval number: 3016). Eligible were people who indicated being fluent in English, being between 18 and 65 years old, engaging in physical exercise for at most 150 min per week, having taken no more than 9,000 steps on average per day in the last week, not participating in a physical activity program, having a low risk of getting injured because of walking according to the Physical Activity Readiness Questionnaire 2023 [54], being contemplating or preparing to become more physically active, and having a way to track their steps. Moreover, we used the quality measures on Prolific to choose people who had completed at least one previous study and had an approval rate of at least 90%. Participants further had to live in one of five time zones (GMT, GMT+1, GMT+2, GMT+3, or GMT+4) to ensure that the daily step goals were set in the morning. The way the step goal options were personalized was chosen randomly in all five sessions. 235 people were invited to the first session and 77 people successfully completed all five sessions. Of the 117 participants with at least one transition sample, 60 (51%) were female, 55 (47%) were male, and 2 (2%) indicated another gender. The age ranged from 18 to 56 (M = 28, SD = 8) years. Participants most commonly reported using an iPhone health app (32%), the Samsung Health app (31%), or a smartwatch (24%) to track their steps. The average number of steps per day before the study ranged from 30 to 9,000 (M = 4,402, SD = 2,383). Participants who successfully completed a study part were paid based on the minimum payment rules on Prolific (i.e., six GBP per hour). Participants were informed that their payment was independent of their achieving their step goals.

Collected Data. We collected 381 $\langle s, a, r, s' \rangle$-samples from 117 people, where s is the state, a the action, r the reward, and s' the next state. Across all 381 samples, the initially proposed step goals were rejected a total of 100 times (M = 0.26, SD = 0.67). People reached their goals 66% of the time and found their goals relatively easy to reach. Specifically, the mean goal difficulty rating provided after the five sessions was 2.04 (SD = 2.06), rated on a scale from −5 ("It was very difficult to reach the daily goals") to 5 ("It was very easy to reach the daily goals"). The average number of steps taken per day before the study was 4,549 (SD = 4,350) for the 75 people who completed the post-questionnaire. On the fifth and final day of the study, these people took an average of 5,367 steps (SD = 3,353). Based on a paired Bayesian t-test, this corresponds to a mean increase of 1,087 steps (SD = 1,298, 95%-HDI = [710, 1,478]). Furthermore, we collected data on people's experiences of their interaction with Steph after the five sessions using the short form of the Artificial Social Agent (ASA) Questionnaire [24]. We obtained a mean score of 19.32, which is higher than the scores of 9 of the 14 agents tested by Fitrianie et al. [24].

State Space Reduction. To reduce the size of the state space and thus the amount of required data, we transformed the three state features (motivation, self-efficacy, and the "daily context"-state) into binary features based on whether a value was greater than or equal to the median (1) or less than the median (0). The final state space thus had size $|S| = 2^3 = 8$. We refer to states with binary strings such as 001 (here motivation and self-efficacy are 0 and the "daily context"-state is 1).

Model Training. Using the reward and transition functions estimated from the data, we computed Q^* using value iteration. Since some states were much more common than others, we had fewer than ten samples for some state-action combinations. To reduce overfitting, we added samples with the overall mean reward for the reward prediction for those state-action combinations with few samples. Similarly, we balanced with an equal probability of all next states when estimating the transition function. Overall, we imputed 125 samples.

3 Results

We now investigate each of our analysis questions. For each of them, we first describe our setup, followed by our findings and the resulting answer to the question. Our data and analysis code are available online [20].

AQ1: How well do states predict behavior after proposing personalized step goals?

Setup. Knowing the state a user is in may help to predict their behavior after using different ways of personalizing their initial step goals (i.e., actions). The behavior in our case is how close people get to their underlying recommended step goal, which is captured by the reward function. We compared two approaches for predicting the reward: 1) the mean reward per action, and 2) the mean reward per action and state. We used leave-one-out cross-validation for the 117 participants with at least one transition sample to compare the two approaches based on the mean L_1-error and its Bayesian 95% credible interval (CI) [40] per state. In contrast to the often used frequentist confidence intervals, Bayesian CIs provide information on the most likely values (i.e., a likely range) [29]. If the mean of one of the approaches is outside of the credible interval of the other approach, we regard this as a credible indication that values are different.

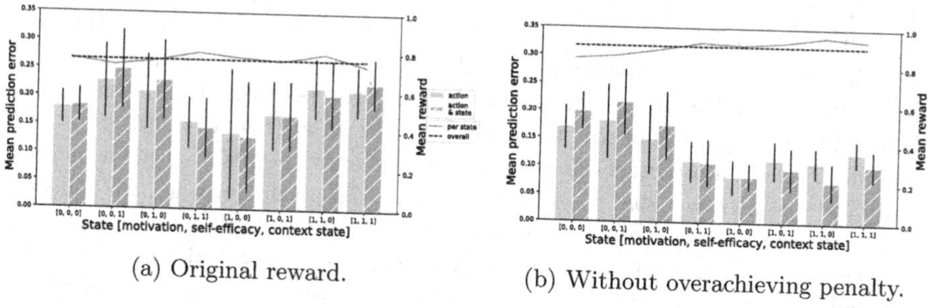

(a) Original reward.

(b) Without overachieving penalty.

Fig. 2. Left axis: Mean L_1-error with 95%-CIs for predicting rewards based on 1) the mean reward per action and 2) the mean reward per action and state. Right axis: Mean reward overall and per state.

Results. Figure 2a shows that none of the two approaches for predicting the reward clearly performs better for any of the eight states. The mean rewards per state also are very similar, ranging from 0.73 for state 001 to 0.80 for state 011. However, if, for exploratory purposes, we modify the original reward by removing the penalty for overachieving (i.e., taking more steps than the recommended goal), considering the state a user is in does improve the reward prediction in some states (Fig. 2b). The mean modified reward also differs more clearly between states, with the mean modified reward being generally higher when more state features are high. This can be explained by the observation that even though the mean rewards are similar in the eight states (Fig. 2a), the underlying behaviors differ. Specifically, many people *under*achieve their recommended goals in states with low state features, whereas many people *over*achieve their goals in states with high state features (Fig. 3). Thus, more people reach their recommended goals in states with high state features.

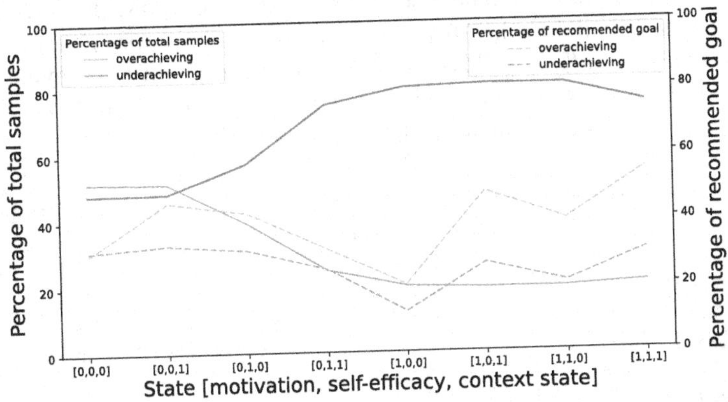

Fig. 3. Left axis (*continuous lines*): percentage of samples where more or fewer steps were taken than the recommended goal per state. Right axis (*dashed lines*): percentage of the recommended goal that was over- or underachieved.

Answer to AQ1. Knowing a user's state does not provide a clear benefit for predicting their behavior after proposing personalized step goals. If, however, we remove the penalty for taking more steps than one's recommended goal, knowing a user's state does offer a benefit for some states. So states do matter when it comes to predicting whether people reach their recommended goal.

AQ2: How well do states predict next states after proposing personalized step goals?

Setup. By making a personalized initial proposal, we would ideally want people to move to a next state in which they are very likely to reach their recommended step goal and thus make more progress toward the long-term goal of 10,000 steps per day. Thus, we need to be able to predict the state after proposing personalized step goals. We again used leave-one-out cross-validation to compare three ways of predicting the next states for the samples from the left-out person: 1) assigning an equal probability to all states, 2) predicting that people stay in their current state, and 3) using the transition function estimated from the training data. We compared the three approaches based on the mean likelihood of the next state and its 95%-CI per state. A higher likelihood suggests that next states can be predicted better. Again, if the mean of one of the approaches lies outside of the credible interval of another approach, we regard this as a credible indication that values are different.

Results. Figure 4 shows that considering the current state, either by predicting that people stay in their current state or by using the estimated transition function to predict next states, generally helps to predict the next state. This suggests that state transitions do not occur uniformly at random. In two states, namely, 000 and 111, predicting that people stay in their current state leads to the highest mean likelihood of next states. In both these states, the corresponding means are clearly outside the 95%-CIs of the other two approaches, suggesting that the values are different. This shows the high probability of staying in these two states, which are states in which people either commonly underachieve their recommended goals or overachieve them by a lot (Fig. 3).

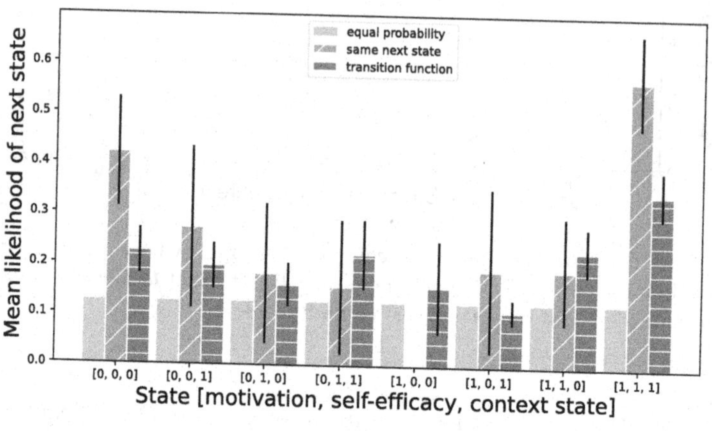

Fig. 4. Comparison of three approaches to predicting next states with regard to the mean likelihood of next states with 95%-CIs for each state.

Answer to AQ2. Our results show that considering the current state a user is in helps to predict their next state after proposing personalized step goals. Furthermore, once people are in states with low or high values for all three state features, they tend to stay there. This suggests that it is difficult to move people out of the state where more than half of them do not reach their recommended goal (i.e., state 000). However, once people are in a state where almost 80% reach or overachieve their goal (i.e., state 111), they tend to stay there.

AQ3: What is the effect of (multiple) optimal step goal proposals on users' states?

Setup. We would like users to ultimately move to states in which they are most likely to reach their recommended goals. Starting from an equal distribution of 8,000 simulated people across the states, we calculated the percentage of people in each state after following the optimal policy π^* for a certain number of time steps.

Results. Figure 5a shows that after 20 time steps, the largest percentage of people (36.5%) is in state 111, which is a state in which most people reach or overachieve their goal. However, the number of people in state 000, which is the state where most people do not reach their goal, also slightly increases to 15.7%.

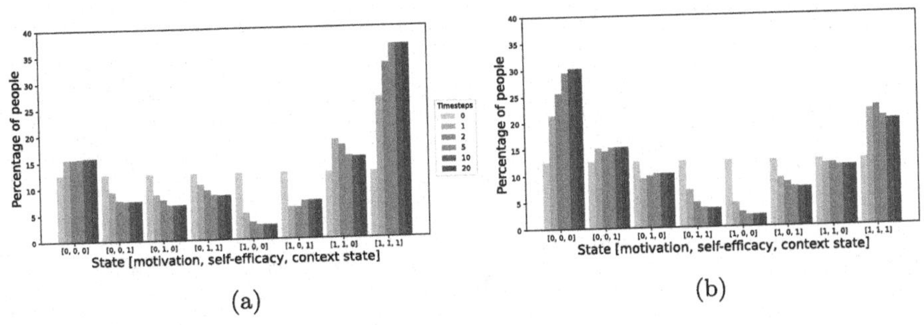

Fig. 5. Percentage of people in each state after following (a) the optimal policy π^* and (b) the worst policy π^- for varying numbers of time steps.

Answer to AQ3. While choosing the optimal way of personalizing step goals multiple times allows most people to move to and stay in states where they are most likely to reach or overachieve their recommended goal, a considerable number of people also remain in the state in which they are least likely to reach their recommended goal.

AQ4: How do optimal and sub-optimal step goal proposals compare in their effects on behavior?

Setup. So far, we are, to some degree, able to predict next states and choose sequences of personalized step goal proposals that move people to better states. However, how much does the choice of step goal proposal personalization matter? To examine this, we calculated the mean reward per transition over time when following 1) the optimal policy π^*, 2) the worst policy π^-, and 3) the average policy $\pi^\sim$. $\pi^\sim$ is a theoretical policy for comparison purposes in which each action is taken $\frac{1}{|A|}$ times for each person at each time step, where $|A|$ is the number of actions. We simulated 117 people, initially distributed across the states as in the first session of our study.

Results. The mean reward per transition for π^* is 0.11 (15.8%) higher than for π^- and 0.06 (8.0%) higher than for $\pi^\sim$ after 100 time steps (Fig. 6). This suggests that when it comes to obtaining a higher reward, the choice of goal proposal personalization is not so important. If, however, we again remove the penalty for overachieving (i.e., only consider whether people reach their recommended goal), the choice of goal proposal personalization does matter. This can be seen by comparing Fig. 5b to Fig. 5a. Specifically, following the worst policy leads to more people in state 000 and fewer people in state 111 after 20 simulated time steps, which means that fewer people reach their recommended goals.

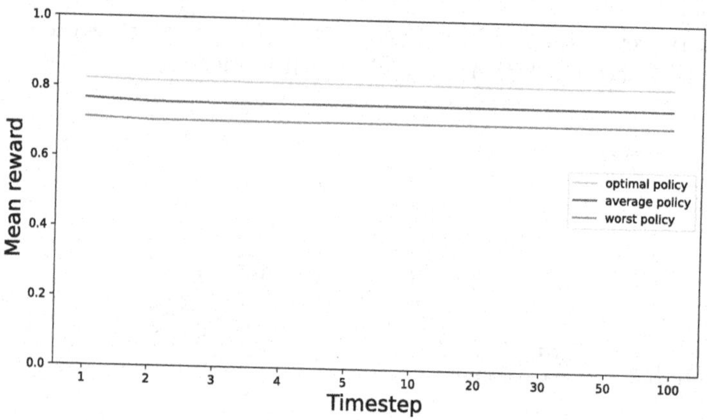

Fig. 6. Mean reward per transition over time for three policies.

Answer to AQ4. If we want people to achieve their goal and penalize both under- and overachieving, personalizing step goal proposals optimally poses an advantage of between 8.0% and 15.8% compared to doing so in an average or the worst possible way. Following the worst policy does, however, cause people to more frequently move to states in which they are more likely to underachieve. Thus, if we do not mind people overachieving their goals and just want people to reach their goals, optimally personalizing step goal proposals does matter.

4 Discussion and Conclusion

This work presented a dialog to collaboratively set daily step goals with a virtual coach and specifically examined the effect of initial step goal proposals that are created by adjusting an underlying previous activity-based recommended goal in one of five possible ways (i.e., ± 0, 200, or 400). We find that user states based on their mood, sleep quality, available time, motivation, and self-efficacy help to predict whether people reach their recommended goal after these proposals are made (*AQ1*). Moreover, these current user states are also predictive of the user states on the next day and thus of whether people reach their recommended goals in the future (*AQ2*). Regarding long-term effects, our simulations show that choosing optimal step goal proposals based on an RL algorithm that considers people's current and future states allows most people to move to and stay in states where they are very likely to reach their recommended goal (*AQ3*). However, some people always remain in the state in which they are least likely to reach their recommended goal. Our simulations further show that it matters which initial step goal proposal the virtual coach makes (*AQ4*). Specifically, more people move to good states (i.e., states where more people reach their recommended goal) if an initial proposal that is optimal based on the RL algorithm is made than in the case of a sub-optimal proposal.

While the likelihood of users reaching their recommended goal differs between user states, this is not the case for our originally devised reward signal that also penalizes taking more steps than one's recommended goal. This is because people in good states often not only reach their recommended goal but substantially exceed it, which also means that our RL algorithm over time tends to move people to states where they overachieve the number of steps they are recommended to take. We had originally decided to penalize overachieving because of the risk of injuries that exists especially for physically inactive people like our participants due to low strength and cardiovascular fitness levels [30]. However, it is not yet sufficiently clear at which point the injury risk outweighs the benefits of more physical activity, particularly because this also depends on the walking speed [30]. Instead of penalizing overachieving in the reward signal, it may be better to more thoroughly educate users on the potential risks of exceeding recommended step goals (e.g., by reminding overachieving users of injury risks and how they can become more physically active in a healthy way).

Besides the handling of overachieving recommended goals, our study has several further limitations. First, due to the high cost of collecting human data like ours, we obtained a relatively limited dataset of 381 samples. We thus turned our state features into binary features, but we still had relatively few samples for some states. It would be interesting to repeat our analysis with more data. To facilitate this, we have made our dataset publicly available [20]. In addition, while we did gather data from human subjects, we did not study the actual long-term effects of making optimal initial step goal proposals based on our RL algorithm. Moreover, even though our participants were informed that their payment for completing the daily goal-setting dialogs was independent of their achieving their step goals, they might have felt at least some obligation to take daily steps. Future work should compare the long-term effects of different ways of choosing initial step goal proposals in the wild. Lastly, there might be other factors that influence the effectiveness of different initial step goal proposals, such as people's social environment [42] and their traits (e.g., personality [57]).

In summary, we have created a virtual coach to collaboratively set daily step goals with users and an RL algorithm that adapts initial step goal proposals based on current and future user states. Simulations show that initial proposals matter: using RL to optimize initial step goal proposals could make it more likely that people move to a state with high motivation, high self-efficacy, and a favorable daily context. In such a state, people are more likely to reach, but also to exceed, their recommended number of steps. Designers of collaborative goal-setting dialogs should thus choose the first proposal carefully and based on users' situations while accounting for the possibility that users exceed their physical activity recommendations.

Acknowledgments. This work is based on the publicly available Master's thesis by Dierikx [17]. The Master's thesis was written as part of the multidisciplinary research project Perfect Fit, which is supported by several funders organized by the Netherlands Organization for Scientific Research (NWO), program Commit2Data - Big Data & Health (project number 628.011.211). Besides NWO, the funders include the Netherlands Organisation for Health Research and Development (ZonMw), Hartstichting, the Ministry of Health, Welfare and Sport (VWS), Health Holland, and the Netherlands eScience Center. The authors acknowledge the help they received from Kristell Penfornis and Anke Versluis in designing the goal-setting dialog.

References

1. Adams, M.A., Sallis, J.F., Norman, G.J., Hovell, M.F., Hekler, E.B., Perata, E.: An adaptive physical activity intervention for overweight adults: a randomized controlled trial. PLoS ONE **8**(12), e82901 (2013). https://doi.org/10.1371/journal.pone.0082901
2. Aggarwal, A., Tam, C.C., Wu, D., Li, X., Qiao, S.: Artificial intelligence-based chatbots for promoting health behavioral changes: systematic review. J. Med. Internet Res. **25**, e40789 (2023). https://doi.org/10.2196/40789
3. Albers, N., Hizli, B., Scheltinga, B.L., Meijer, E., Brinkman, W.P.: Setting physical activity goals with a virtual coach: vicarious experiences, personalization and acceptance. J. Med. Syst. **47**(1), 15 (2023). https://doi.org/10.1007/s10916-022-01899-9
4. Amabile, T., Kramer, S.: The Progress Principle: Using Small Wins to Ignite Joy, Engagement, and Creativity at Work. Harvard Business Press, Brighton (2011)
5. Baretta, D., Bondaronek, P., Direito, A., Steca, P.: Implementation of the goal-setting components in popular physical activity apps: review and content analysis. Digit. Health **5**, 2055207619862706 (2019). https://doi.org/10.1177/2055207619862706
6. Beinema, T., op den Akker, H., van Velsen, L., Hermens, H.: Tailoring coaching strategies to users' motivation in a multi-agent health coaching application. Comput. Hum. Behav. **121**, 106787 (2021). https://doi.org/10.1016/j.chb.2021.106787
7. Beun, R., et al.: Improving adherence in automated e-coaching - a case from insomnia therapy. In: Meschtscherjakov, A., de Ruyter, B.E.R., Fuchsberger, V., Murer, M., Tscheligi, M. (eds.) PERSUASIVE 2016. LNCS, vol. 9638, pp. 276–287. Springer, Heidelberg (2016). https://doi.org/10.1007/978-3-319-31510-2_24
8. Bless, H., Bohner, G., Schwarz, N., Strack, F.: Mood and persuasion: a cognitive response analysis. Pers. Soc. Psychol. Bull. **16**(2), 331–345 (1990). https://doi.org/10.1177/0146167290162013
9. Bocklisch, T., Faulkner, J., Pawlowski, N., Nichol, A.: Rasa: open source language understanding and dialogue management. arXiv preprint arXiv:1712.05181 (2017)
10. Bodenheimer, T., Handley, M.A.: Goal-setting for behavior change in primary care: an exploration and status report. Patient Educ. Couns. **76**(2), 174–180 (2009). https://doi.org/10.1016/j.pec.2009.06.001
11. Cabrita, M., op den Akker, H., Achterkamp, R., Hermens, H.J., Vollenbroek-Hutten, M.M.R.: Automated personalized goal-setting in an activity coaching application. In: Postolache, O., van Sinderen, M., Ali, F.H., Benavente-Peces, C. (eds.) SENSORNETS 2014 - Proceedings of the 3rd International Conference on Sensor Networks, Lisbon, Portugal, 7–9 January 2014, pp. 389–396 (2014)
12. Cervone, D., Peake, P.K.: Anchoring, efficacy, and action: the influence of judgmental heuristics on self-efficacy judgments and behavior. J. Pers. Soc. Psychol. **50**(3), 492–501 (1986)
13. Chevance, G., et al.: Goal setting and achievement for walking: a series of n-of-1 digital interventions. Health Psychol. **40**(1), 30–39 (2021)

14. Davis, J., et al.: 2022 national standards for diabetes self-management education and support. Sci. Diab. Self-Manag. Care **48**(1), 44–59 (2022). https://doi.org/10.1177/26350106211072203
15. Department of Health and Social Care: UK chief medical officers' physical activity guidelines (2019). https://assets.publishing.service.gov.uk/media/5d839543ed915d52428dc134/uk-chief-medical-officers-physical-activity-guidelines.pdf. Accessed 13 Nov 2023
16. Dierikx, M.: Example dialog with the virtual coach steph for setting daily step goals (2023). https://youtu.be/FSpG-G0zc-o
17. Dierikx, M.: Using reinforcement learning to personalize daily step goals for a collaborative dialogue with a virtual coach. Master's thesis (2023). http://resolver.tudelft.nl/uuid:4f2c12de-9b9f-4e3f-ad3a-902947d693bb
18. Dierikx, M.: Using Reinforcement Learning to Personalize Daily Step Goals for a Collaborative Dialogue with a Virtual Coach: code for the virtual coach (2023). https://doi.org/10.5281/zenodo.8382413
19. Dierikx, M., Albers, N., Brinkman, W.P.: Daily collaborative personalized step goal-setting with a virtual coach (2023). https://doi.org/10.17605/OSF.IO/6JQPK
20. Dierikx, M., Albers, N., Scheltinga, B.L., Brinkman, W.P.: Collaboratively setting daily step goals with a virtual coach: using reinforcement learning to personalize initial proposals - data and analysis code (2023). https://doi.org/10.4121/53f2d238-77fc-4045-89a9-fb7fa2871f1d
21. Doran, G.T.: There's a smart way to write management's goals and objectives. Manage. Rev. **70**(11), 35–36 (1981)
22. Dwyer, T., et al.: The inverse relationship between number of steps per day and obesity in a population-based sample-the ausdiab study. Int. J. Obes. **31**(5), 797–804 (2007)
23. Dzierzewski, J.M., et al.: Exercise and sleep in community-dwelling older adults: evidence for a reciprocal relationship. J. Sleep Res. **23**(1), 61–68 (2014). https://doi.org/10.1111/jsr.12078
24. Fitrianie, S., Bruijnes, M., Li, F., Abdulrahman, A., Brinkman, W.P.: The artificial-social-agent questionnaire: establishing the long and short questionnaire versions. In: Martinho, C., Dias, J., Campos, J., Heylen, D. (eds.) Proceedings of the 22nd ACM International Conference on Intelligent Virtual Agents, IVA 2022. Association for Computing Machinery, New York (2022)
25. Galinsky, A.D., Mussweiler, T.: First offers as anchors: the role of perspective-taking and negotiator focus. J. Pers. Soc. Psychol. **81**(4), 657–669 (2001). https://doi.org/10.1037/0022-3514.81.4.657
26. Greenhalgh, T., et al.: Beyond adoption: a new framework for theorizing and evaluating nonadoption, abandonment, and challenges to the scale-up, spread, and sustainability of health and care technologies. J. Med. Internet Res. **19**(11) (2017). https://doi.org/10.2196/jmir.8775
27. He, L., Balaji, D., Wiers, R.W., Antheunis, M.L., Krahmer, E.: Effectiveness and acceptability of conversational agents for smoking cessation: a systematic review and meta-analysis. Nicotine Tobacco Res. **25**(7), 1241–1250 (2022)
28. Hirvensalo, M., et al.: Daily steps among finnish adults: variation by age, sex, and socioeconomic position. Scand. J. Public Health **39**(7), 669–677 (2011). https://doi.org/10.1177/1403494811420324
29. Hoekstra, R., Morey, R.D., Rouder, J.N., Wagenmakers, E.J.: Robust misinterpretation of confidence intervals. Psychon. Bull. Rev. **21**, 1157–1164 (2014). https://doi.org/10.3758/s13423-013-0572-3

30. Hootman, J.M., Macera, C.A., Ainsworth, B.E., Addy, C.L., Martin, M., Blair, S.N.: Epidemiology of musculoskeletal injuries among sedentary and physically active adults. Med. Sci. Sports Exerc. **34**(5), 838–844 (2002)
31. Jain, G., Gaeth, G.J., Nayakankuppam, D., Levin, I.P.: Revisiting attribute framing: the impact of number roundedness on framing. Organ. Behav. Hum. Decis. Process. **161**, 109–119 (2020)
32. Kollias, D., et al.: Deep affect prediction in-the-wild: aff-wild database and challenge, deep architectures, and beyond. Int. J. Comput. Vision **127**(6), 907–929 (2019). https://doi.org/10.1007/S11263-019-01158-4
33. Konrad, A., et al.: Finding the adaptive sweet spot: balancing compliance and achievement in automated stress reduction. In: Proceedings of the 33rd Annual ACM Conference on Human Factors in Computing Systems, CHI 2015, pp. 3829–3838. Association for Computing Machinery, New York (2015)
34. Lee, I.M., Buchner, D.M.: The importance of walking to public health. Med. Sci. Sports Exerc. **40**(7), S512–S518 (2008)
35. Lee, I.M., Shiroma, E.J., Kamada, M., Bassett, D.R., Matthews, C.E., Buring, J.E.: Association of step volume and intensity with all-cause mortality in older women. JAMA Intern. Med. **179**(8), 1105–1112 (2019)
36. Liao, P., Greenewald, K.H., Klasnja, P.V., Murphy, S.A.: Personalized heartsteps: a reinforcement learning algorithm for optimizing physical activity. Proc. ACM Interact. Mob. Wearable Ubiquitous Technol. **4**(1), 18:1–18:22 (2020)
37. Locke, E.A., Latham, G.P.: Building a practically useful theory of goal setting and task motivation: a 35-year odyssey. Am. Psychol. **57**(9), 705–717 (2002)
38. Montenegro, J.L.Z., da Costa, C.A., da Rosa Righi, R.: Survey of conversational agents in health. Expert Syst. Appl. **129**, 56–67 (2019)
39. Muellmann, S., Forberger, S., Möllers, T., Bröring, E., Zeeb, H., Pischke, C.R.: Effectiveness of ehealth interventions for the promotion of physical activity in older adults: a systematic review. Prev. Med. **108**, 93–110 (2018)
40. Oliphant, T.E.: A bayesian perspective on estimating mean, variance, and standard-deviation from data (2006)
41. Paluch, A.E., et al.: Daily steps and all-cause mortality: a meta-analysis of 15 international cohorts. Lancet Public Health **7**(3), e219–e228 (2022). https://doi.org/10.1016/S2468-2667(21)00302-9
42. Park, H., Kim, N.: Predicting factors of physical activity in adolescents: a systematic review. Asian Nurs. Res. **2**(2), 113–128 (2008)
43. Pope, D., Simonsohn, U.: Round numbers as goals: evidence from baseball, sat takers, and the lab. Psychol. Sci. **22**(1), 71–79 (2011)
44. Rhodes, A., Smith, A.D., Chadwick, P., Croker, H., Llewellyn, C.H., et al.: Exclusively digital health interventions targeting diet, physical activity, and weight gain in pregnant women: systematic review and meta-analysis. JMIR Mhealth Uhealth **8**(7), e18255 (2020). https://doi.org/10.2196/18255
45. Robbins, L.B., Pender, N.J., Kazanis, A.S.: Barriers to physical activity perceived by adolescent girls. J. Midwifery Women's Health **48**(3), 206–212 (2003)
46. Russell, J.A.: A circumplex model of affect. J. Pers. Soc. Psychol. **39**(6), 1161–1178 (1980)
47. Smith, L., et al.: The contribution of goal specificity to goal achievement in collaborative goal setting for the management of asthma. Res. Social Adm. Pharm. **9**(6), 918–929 (2013). https://doi.org/10.1016/j.sapharm.2013.02.002
48. Sutton, R.S., Barto, A.G.: Reinforcement learning: An introduction. Bradford Books (2018)

49. Swann, C., Rosenbaum, S., Lawrence, A., Vella, S.A., McEwan, D., Ekkekakis, P.: Updating goal-setting theory in physical activity promotion: a critical conceptual review. Health Psychol. Rev. **15**(1), 34–50 (2021)
50. Tong, H.L., et al.: A personalized mobile app for physical activity: an experimental mixed-methods study. Digital Health **8**, 20552076221115016 (2022)
51. Treasure, J.: Motivational interviewing. Adv. Psychiatr. Treat. **10**(5), 331–337 (2004)
52. Tversky, A., Kahneman, D.: Judgment under uncertainty: heuristics and biases. Science **185**(4157), 1124–1131 (1974)
53. Wang, S., Zhang, C., Kröse, B., van Hoof, H.: Optimizing adaptive notifications in mobile health interventions systems: reinforcement learning from a data-driven behavioral simulator. J. Med. Syst. **45**(12) (2021)
54. Warburton, D.E., Jamnik, V.K., Bredin, S.S., Gledhill, N.: The physical activity readiness questionnaire for everyone (par-q+) and electronic physical activity readiness medical examination (eparmed-x+). Health Fitness J. Canada **4**(2), 3–17 (2011). https://doi.org/10.14288/hfjc.v4i2.103
55. Wattanapisit, A., Thanamee, S.: Evidence behind 10,000 steps walking. J. Health Res. **31**(3), 241–248 (2017)
56. White, D.K., et al.: The association of obesity with walking independent of knee pain: the multicenter osteoarthritis study. J. Obes. **2012** (2012). https://doi.org/10.1155/2012/261974
57. Wilson, K.E., Dishman, R.K.: Personality and physical activity: a systematic review and meta-analysis. Personality Individ. Differ. **72**, 230–242 (2015)
58. Xu, Y., Zhang, J., Chi, R., Deng, G.: Enhancing customer satisfaction with chatbots: the influence of anthropomorphic communication styles and anthropomorphised roles. Nankai Bus. Rev. Int. **14**(2), 249–271 (2023)
59. Zhou, M., et al.: Personalizing mobile fitness apps using reinforcement learning. In: CEUR Workshop Proceedings, vol. 2068. NIH Public Access (2018)

Persuasive System Design Features for Mobile Mental Health Applications

Yonas Deressa Guracho[1,2](✉), Susan J. Thomas[1], Nawaf Almutairi[1,3], and Khin Than Win[1]

[1] University of Wollongong, Northfields Avenue, Wollongong, NSW 2522, Australia
yonasderessa19@gmail.com
[2] College of Medicine and Health Sciences, Bahir Dar University, Bahir Dar, Ethiopia
[3] Faculty of Public Health and Health Informatics, University of Hail, Hail, Saudi Arabia

Abstract. Mobile mental health applications show promise and may be suitable for low-resource contexts, however, they remain underutilized. Designing and developing mental health applications that consider users' preferences and experts' recommendations and integrate with persuasive design principles may increase uptake. However, research in the field is scarce in low-income contexts including Ethiopia.

Our research involved five main steps. First, we performed a literature review to identify existing evidence and recommendations. We adapted 15 app features from the existing literature. Second, we conducted two rounds of a modified Delphi study with 21 experts in the first and 16 in the second rounds to reach a consensus on the 15 adapted key app features. Third, we surveyed 419 individuals in Ethiopia with mental disorders to understand their needs and preferences for the adapted app features. Fourth, we integrated persuasive system design principles into the adapted app features. Fifth, we collaborated with experts to code the application content and finalize the prototype. The next step will be the development of the app in the Ethiopian official language, and usability testing of the application.

Keywords: Mental Health · Mental Health Application · Persuasive Technology · Mobile Health

1 Introduction

1.1 Background

According to the Global Burden of Disease study, approximately 15% of years of life lost are attributed to mental disorders, solidifying their position as one of the primary causes of disability on a global scale [1, 2]. By the year 2030, mental disorders are expected to be the emerging predominant global cause of mortality and morbidity [3, 4]. Individuals with mental illness and their families often face stigma, discrimination, and human rights abuses. These challenges can make it difficult for them to access the support and care they need. Furthermore, the limited availability of mental health services and support systems is also challenging [5–7]. To decrease this gap, new technology like self-directed mental health app interventions offers opportunities to supplement face-to-face mental health intervention [8].

N. Baghaei et al. (Eds.): PERSUASIVE 2024, LNCS 14636, pp. 116–132, 2024.
https://doi.org/10.1007/978-3-031-58226-4_10

A recent systematic review and meta-analysis suggest that smartphone app-assisted intervention can effectively treat symptoms of mental disorders. Roth et al. [9] confirmed that providing psychoeducational information via technology-based mental health care improved clients' attitudes toward technology-based care. Other research findings have confirmed that people who use mobile apps for mental health are more aware of their psychological state and are less likely to suffer from depression [10], and anxiety [11]. For instance, simple mindfulness practices significantly improved their quality of life. Despite the proven benefits, the usage of mental health apps remains relatively low. Only about one in four smartphone users currently utilize these apps for their mental health conditions. This limited usage could be attributed to various factors such as doubts about benefits, negative attitudes towards mental health apps, app feature preference, lack of knowledge about apps, app complexity, and potential language barriers [12, 13].

1.2 Literature Review

Users most often choose mental health apps for their features. This determines their preference to use them. The most preferred features of mental health apps include symptom-tracking, psychoeducational components [14], self-assessment [15], stress management techniques, profiling, meditation [16], daily mood tracker [34], appointments tracker, and progress tracker [17]. However, most mobile applications used for mental health disorders fail to meet users' requirements and needs [17, 18]. For instance, Nelson Shen et al. [19] found that among apps developed for depression, only one-third adhere to depression-related content. Also, most of the apps do not disclose the organizational affiliation behind them and the source of the content, which makes establishing their credibility and reliability more challenging [19].

A systematic review of mobile app features and content quality conducted by Nicholas and colleagues found that only 31% of apps cite their sources, and only 40% of apps employ validated screening tools. Furthermore, the majority of apps fail to track crucial data, such as medication use and adherence [20].

Another systematic review and content analysis study conducted by Shen and colleagues found that only 32.1% of depression apps address psychoeducation [19]. Although the content of many mental health apps is important, they often fail to address the issues that users care about most like trustworthiness [21].

Users also claim many barriers to using mobile mental health apps. For instance, individual experience, privacy, confidentiality, awareness, knowledge, connectivity, lack of guidance, tailored feedback, and information on how to access the app are some of the barriers to using the app [10, 22]. Therefore, integrating persuasive system principles into mental health applications by addressing key stakeholders' preferences plays a paramount role in the sustainability and credibility of the mHealth apps utilizations. In addition, users' attitudes have significantly impacted technology utilization [23]. Some theories also support this concept. For example, according to self-determination theory [24], the theory of planned behavior [25], and the Fogg behavior model [26], individual abilities, autonomy, motivation, interest, and positive attitude play key roles in mHealth application utilization.

A survey conducted by Alqahtani et al. [27] found that self-monitoring, personalization, and reminders are the most common persuasive principles used in mental health apps. However, general information about diseases, instructions about behavior, tailoring, establishing surface credibility, giving feedback, and goal setting are rarely used [27].

Mental health apps may be particularly useful in low-resource contexts where needs are high and access to mental health services is particularly limited. For example, several studies have provided evidence indicating that mHealth interventions in Ethiopia have a positive impact on maternal services, and newborn care [28, 29]. However, there is a lack of research in Ethiopia that integrates mental health descriptions with persuasive system principles. To the authors' knowledge, no mental health app has been designed or developed in an Ethiopian context by engaging experts, users, and persuasive system design principles. Therefore, this paper is aimed at integrating persuasive principles into mobile mental health applications to design an app prototype. The prototype will serve as a baseline for app developers, mental health policymakers, and researchers in low-income countries like Ethiopia.

2 Methods

To address the research questions, we performed five steps (see Fig. 1):

Step 1: To identify the use patterns, interests, and perceived usefulness of mental health apps by patients, we conducted a systematic literature review and meta-analysis [30]. We also reviewed the literature on mHealth app features for mental health conditions and the availability of such apps in the Ethiopian context. We used the following keywords to search the existing app stores: "depression," "anxiety," "psychological distress," "stress," "mood disorder," "bipolar disorder," "manic-depressive," "sleep disorder," "PTSD," "cognitive disorder," "somatic disorder," "psychosis," and "schizophrenia." Through the literature review, we identified 15 app features.

Step 2: Using 15 mental health app features derived from the findings in the literature review of step one, we conducted two rounds of Modified Delphi studies to gain expert evaluation of the proposed mental health app features between July 15, 2023, and August 12, 2023. Experts included mental health professionals, health informatics experts, researchers in persuasive technology and specialists from the Ethiopian Psychiatrist Association, Mental Health Association, Medical Association, and Health Informatics Association.

For analyzing, Content Validity Ratio (CVR) was applied. $CVR = (Ne - N/2)/(N/2)$, where Ne is the number of experts who responded on the items "important or very important" and N is the total number of experts. CVR value greater than 0.5 was considered as acceptable [31].

Step 3: A cross-sectional survey on 419 Ethiopian patients with mental disorders was conducted at the outpatient department of an Ethiopian mental health hospital. Systematic sampling methods were employed to select study participants. All individuals older than 18 years were included.

Step 4: The persuasive system design was applied for the app design and development. The proposed app features incorporated persuasive system principles that aimed to support the primary task (such as reduction, tunnelling, tailoring, personalization, self-monitoring, simulation/demonstration, and goal setting), enhance the system credibility (through trustworthiness, expertise, authority, and third-party endorsement), provide dialogue support (with praise, reminders, and suggestions/recommendations), and foster social support (by enabling social facilitation and cooperation).

Step 5: Prototyping and iterations of the prototype app were conducted. Software engineers, academics, and mental health experts were involved in the iteration process. Furthermore, throughout the design and development process, we considered human values in relation to Ethiopia's cultural, social, and economic contexts.

To uphold the app's trustworthiness, privacy, autonomy, continuity, humaneness, and usability, we based our design on the insights of local experts, healthcare professionals involved in patient care, and guidelines from the Ethiopian Ministry of Health's mental health gap manual. This approach ensured that our app would not only be functional but also respectful of the local context and values. Also, the app has been designed in the Ethiopian official and national language – Amharic. Furthermore, the therapeutic features used in the application had to take the Ethiopian cultural situation into account.

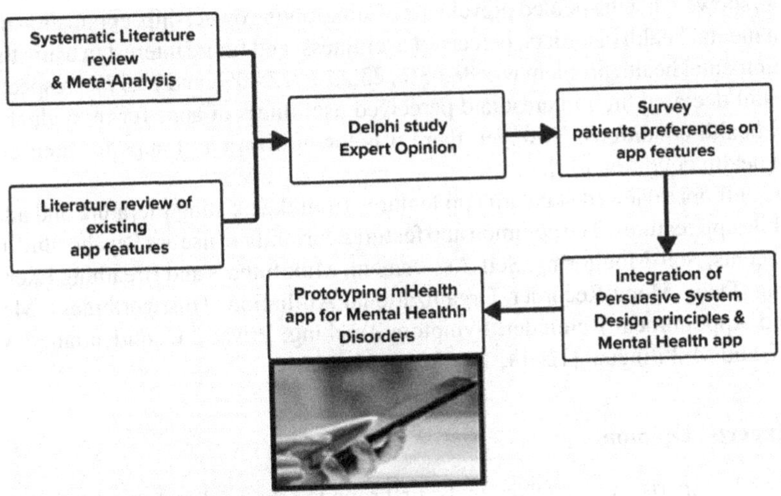

Fig. 1. A schematic illustration of the process involved in designing a mental health app

2.1 Data Analysis

We used Stata (meta-analysis) to analyze the pooled prevalence for Step One; an Excel spreadsheet was used to analyze experts' opinions. Survey data was analyzed using SPSS version 25. NVivo-12 is also applied. Descriptive statistical analysis was used. Finally, data were presented in text, tables, and figures.

2.2 Ethical Considerations

Ethical approval was obtained from the University of Wollongong, Health, and Medical Human Research Ethics Committee (2023/122), and Bahir Dar University School of Medicine and Health Sciences Institutional Review Board (797/2023). St. Amanuel Mental Specialized Hospital Review Board also consented, with reference number AM/146/416. All necessary ethical considerations were adhered to, such as ensuring voluntary participation and informed consent, maintaining privacy and confidentiality, and upholding the right to withdraw or refuse to participate.

3 Results

3.1 Systematic Literature Review and Literature Review of Existing App Features

Ten articles were eligible for the systematic literature review and meta-analysis. The findings showed that the pooled prevalence of smartphone ownership, application use for current mental health disorders, perceived usefulness, and future interest in using the app for their mental health problem was 88.63%, 23.29%, 72.80%, and 78.97%, respectively. The result declared high interest and perceived usefulness of apps for individuals with mental health conditions. However, there was low utilization of apps for their current mental health condition [30].

The authors reviewed standard app features from the existing literature and adapted 15 mobile app features. The common app features currently in use are Psychoeducational Components, Self-Monitoring, Self-Assessment, Mindfulness and Breathing Exercises, Profiling, Daily Mood Recorder, Organizational Affiliation, Trustworthiness, Medication and Appointment Reminder, Symptom Tracking, Privacy, Confidentiality, Visual Appeal, and Multilingual [12, 14, 15, 17, 22, 32, 33].

3.2 Experts' Opinion

A total of 21 experts were involved in the first round of the modified Delphi study, while 16 experts were involved in the second round. Among the 16 experts involved in both rounds one and two, ten were from Ethiopia, four from Australia, one from Canada, and one from the United States. In these Delphi studies, 15 app features were presented to experts to evaluate the relevance of the app feature. The CVR for all 15 items was found to be 0.88 or higher. Therefore, all 15 app features are relevant for mental health app design and development. Our result is also supported by other studies [34–38]. (See Table 1).

Table 1. Experts' opinion and patients' preferences of mental health app features

Mental Health App Features Adapted to Ethiopian Context	Expert opinion: CVR (n = 15)	Patient's App Features Preferences (n = 419)	
		Somewhat relevant	Quite/Highly relevant
1. Information on depression, anxiety, psychological distress	0.88	193 (46.1%)	226 (53.9%)
2. Information on management of depression, anxiety, psychological distress	1	193 (46.1%)	226 (53.9%)
3. Test for depression, anxiety, psychological distress	1	186 (44.4%)	233 (55.6%)
4. Based on the level of severity of depression, anxiety, and psychological distress, the app suggests treatment options	1	186 (44.4%)	233 (55.6%)
5. Monitor symptoms and provide feedback	1	130 (31%)	289 (69%)
6. Progressive muscle relaxation techniques and or breathing exercise techniques for self-management	1	123 (29.4%)	296 (70.6%)
7. Reminder for medication and upcoming appointments	1	121 (28.9%)	298 (71.1%)
8. Cognitive behavioural therapy, meditation, and mindfulness techniques as supportive therapy	1	122 (29.1%)	297 (70.9%)
9. Interactive and engaging (multiple languages, text, audio)	1	131 (31.3%)	288 (68.7%)
10. Emergency contact number	1	131 (31.3%)	288 (68.7%)
11. Private (protected by security or password)	1	140 (33.4%)	279 (66.6%)
12. Confidential (not shared to the third party without the consent of the user)	1	142 (33.9%)	277 (66.1)

(*continued*)

Table 1. (*continued*)

Mental Health App Features Adapted to Ethiopian Context	Expert opinion: CVR (n = 15)	Patient's App Features Preferences (n = 419)	
		Somewhat relevant	Quite/Highly relevant
13. Safe to use or free of harm. There is no potential risk in using the app	1	139 (33.2%)	280 (66.8%)
14. Connecting with doctors	1	141 (33.7%)	278 (66.3%)
15. Trusted source of information	1	137 (32.7%)	282 (67.3%)

Note: CVR = Content validity ratio. The content validity ratio and universal agreement among experts on the app features were evaluated [31]. The preference scale had the following options: 1 = not relevant, 2 = somewhat relevant, 3 = quite relevant, and 4 = highly relevant [39]

3.3 Patients' App Features Preferences

A cross-sectional study was carried out from September 25, 2023 to November 5, 2023, involving a sample of 419 patients with mental disorders in Ethiopia. The survey was conducted in the outpatient department at St. Amanuel Mental Specialized Hospital. The study participants' ages ranged from 18 to 63, with a mean age of 34.69 and a standard deviation of +22.19. About 59% (248 participants) were male, and 41% (171 participants) were female. In the study, 24.8% (104 participants) had major depressive disorder, 21.5% (90 participants) had an anxiety and related disorder, 15% (63 participants) trauma and trauma related disorders, 22.9% (96 participants) had bipolar disorder, and 15.8% (66 participants) had been diagnosed with schizophrenia or other forms of psychosis. The participants' level of preference ranged from somewhat relevant to highly relevant on the 15 recommended app features for mental disorders. The responses of all study participants ranged from somewhat relevant to highly relevant. This means that proposed app features are suitable to be incorporated when designing a prototype of the app (see Table 1).

3.4 Mental Health Apps Based on Persuasive Systems Design Principles

The authors integrated descriptions of mental health app features with persuasive system design principles. Among 28 persuasive design features only 17 were considered in this study. Among the suggested principles for persuasive systems, six were related to primary task support (including reduction, tunnelling, tailoring, self-monitoring, simulation, and rehearsal), five were associated with system credibility support (such as trustworthiness, expertise, real-world feel, third-party endorsement, and verifiability), five pertained to dialogue support (covering praise, reminders, suggestions, liking, and social role), and one was linked to social support (cooperation). The details of the integration are shown in Table 2.

Table 2. Integrating persuasive system strategies with mental health app descriptions in the context of Ethiopia.

Requirements	Mental Health App Description	Persuasive System Principles
1. General information on depression, anxiety, psychological distress	Providing effortless access to information, enabling users to evaluate and manage their behavior independently without intermediaries Supporting awareness of depression, anxiety, and psychological disorders Providing information on how patients lead healthy lives by combating depression, anxiety, and psychological disorders	Reduction Suggestion
2. Information on management	Providing information on treatments and their benefits	Reduction
3. Test for depression, anxiety, psychological distress	Allowing patients to assess/evaluate their current mental health status using a validated self-reported questionnaire called DASS-21 (depression, anxiety, psychological distress, and stress level using 21 Likert items)	Tunnelling
4. Based on the level of severity of depression, anxiety, and psychological distress, the app suggests treatment options	Self-assessment results give users suggestions of which self-management technique will work best for them based on their self-assessment score	Suggestion Tailoring
5. Monitor symptoms and provide feedback	This feature is a portfolio. This folder records consecutive assessment results and every treatment taken or missed Presenting the result in text, table, or line graph	Self-monitoring

(continued)

Table 2. (*continued*)

Requirements	Mental Health App Description	Persuasive System Principles
6. Progressive muscle relaxation techniques and or breathing exercise techniques for self-management	Providing self-management techniques with easy instructions on how the patient does progressive muscle relaxation techniques and breathing exercises Guiding the user step-by-step on how s/he practices self-help Acknowledging the users by text/voice for using it	Tailoring Suggestion Praise
7. Reminder for medication and upcoming appointment	Helping users remember medication timings and doctor appointments and encouraging regular self-care. Implementing as an alert or pop-up box and sounds	Reminders
8. Cognitive behavioral therapy, meditation, and mindfulness techniques as supportive therapy	The app guides the user on how to practice cognitive behavioral, mindfulness, and meditation techniques Apps consistently offer the same or similar self-care strategies for managing specific symptoms. Patients will do meditation, mindfulness, or breathing exercises as part of self-management Doing this lets the patient see the difference between before and after meditation, mindfulness, or breathing exercises	Tunnelling Rehearsal Simulation

(*continued*)

Table 2. (*continued*)

Requirements	Mental Health App Description	Persuasive System Principles
9. Interactive and engaging (multiple languages, text, audio)	The app lets users switch between Amharic and English, convert text to voice, change the screen's background, or adjust font size Offering audio recordings of texts in multiple languages significantly reduces the effort required for reading	Liking
10. Emergency contact number	Help the user easily access emergency contact and call without typing the numbers	Social role
11. Private (protected by security or password)	Only the user can access his/her assessment results, medications, and portfolio Personal files and treatment are protected by security/password	Trustworthiness
12. Confidential (the portfolio is not shared with a third party without the users' consent)	The app portfolio is not shared with a second or third party without the user's consent or willingness. Therefore, the user is the only one who can share his/her status if willing to share	Trustworthiness
13. Safe to use or free of harm. There is no potential risk for using the app	There are no risks associated with using the app. It can be downloaded and used for free. Furthermore, it is designed to assist patients, prevent complications, reduce stigma, and promote mental health and well-being. If users have any queries, they can contact the authors through email	Verifiability

(*continued*)

Table 2. *(continued)*

Requirements	Mental Health App Description	Persuasive System Principles
14. Connecting with doctors	The app enhances communication between patients and doctors. By maintaining monthly records of treatment adherence or self-assessments, patients can engage in more meaningful discussions with their doctors, paving the way for a quicker recovery from their illnesses	Cooperation
15. Trusted source of information	The text uploaded into the app has been sourced from the *Ethiopian Mental Health Gap Manual* and the 11th Edition of the *Diagnostic and Statistical Manual of Mental Disorders* (DSM-5). Experts thoroughly evaluated this content before it was incorporated into the app The app may use logos from respected institutions such as Bahir Dar University and the University of Wollongong. Users can explore further information by following the provided links	Third-party trustworthiness, real-world feel
	Individuals with expertise in various fields, including psychiatrists, mental health nursing professionals, personnel from mental health associations, clinical psychologists, health informatics specialists, software engineers, and researchers were involved in the process	Expertise

3.5 Information Architecture

The information architecture shows the diagrammatic flow of the proposed information. The app's home screen displays six main themes. The first four – mental health concepts, depression, anxiety, and psychological distress – are aimed at raising mental health awareness. Every user can access these themes without creating an account or logging in. The purpose is to create mental health awareness for anyone who intends to use the app, whether they have a mental health disorder or not.

The second part – the profiling and self-test (DASS-21) [40] – is password protected, and the user is invited to create an account. In this section, the patient adds his/her identity, medication type, dose, and frequency and sets reminders for his/her medication and upcoming appointments. The other section is the patient portfolio. This section saves assessment results and medication adherence (see Fig. 2).

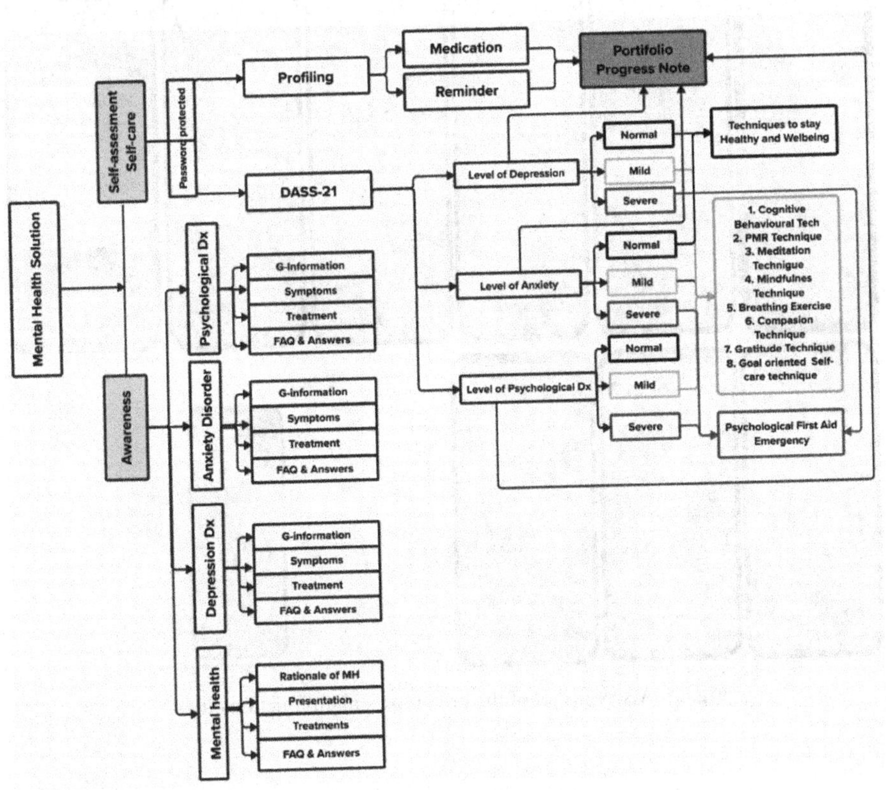

Fig. 2. Information architecture of the app

3.6 App Prototype

This app prototype is designed for depression, anxiety, and psychological disorders. Software engineers, professors and academic researchers with relevant expertise, and mental health experts were involved in the design process. We held a series of eight Zoom meetings over ten weeks to design the prototype. The features included basic concepts, misconceptions, causes, symptoms, treatments, and commonly asked questions with answers. The app incorporates an assessment of current symptoms through the DASS-21 tool, which measures the level of depression, anxiety, and psychological stress. Based on the assessment results, the app suggests self-management strategies. For example, if the user has a normal score level, the app offers tips for wellbeing. If the user has a mild to moderate score, the app recommends mindfulness and meditation techniques, compassion, gratitude, breathing exercises, and progressive muscle relaxation techniques. In addition, if the score shows severe symptoms, psychological first aid, self-care and contacting emergency phone calls will be suggested. (See Fig. 3).

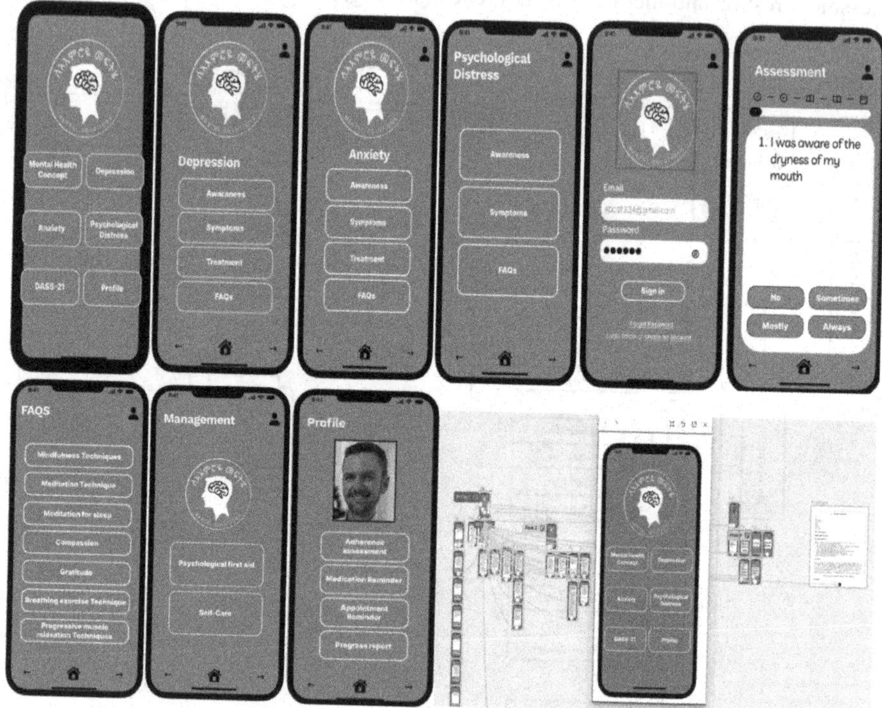

Fig. 3. A screenshot of the prototype's main functionalities

4 Discussions

To the best of our knowledge, the app is the first of its kind to be developed for a low-income country like Ethiopia. The finding showed a high interest in mental health app use but low mental health app utilization. Experts in the field and health professionals suggested 15 app features that are best suited for low-income countries. Furthermore, the authors also found the importance of incorporating persuasive system design principles with mental health app descriptions. A unique feature of this app prototype is that it involved multiple key stakeholders in the design process. This has the potential to improve the quality of mental health apps. Our rigorous approach is consistent with recommendations in the literature. For example, Marcu et al. [41], and Fleming et al. [42] reported that the involvement of stakeholders such as users, experts, and professionals is a crucial part of the design process.

Our designed app provides multiple features. Our finding is in line with a study conducted by Alqahtani and Orji [43]. The author found that users tend to choose mental health apps with a wide range of features as the main choice [43]. For instance, Fleming et al. [42] reported in their findings that app features with visual appeal, mindfulness, and meditation features have extremely high uptake and priority for the users. Additionally, mental health apps with multiple features like screening or self-testing, providing educational information and follow-up, and apps with behavioral support are commonly considered beneficial for users [44]. Therefore, findings suggest that the app is promising and may be interest for policymakers, researchers, and evidence-based practice in low-income countries like Ethiopia.

Even though participatory design improves mental health app utilization [45], in many cases, mental health app designs do not meet patients' needs and requirements, resulting in the apps having low trustworthiness [17, 18]. Therefore, our app prototype presents comprehensive features to meet multiple needs such as mental health awareness, treatment information, symptom tracking, meditation, breathing exercises, cognitive behavioral therapy, treatment adherence, self-care strategies, profiling, and mental health first aid.

Persuasive features are applicable and effective in mobile health applications [46, 47]. Therefore, incorporating mental health descriptions with persuasive design principles is crucial to the design process. A systematic review of recent articles found that the most common persuasive design principles for mental health conditions are tailoring, self-monitoring, personalization, reminders, and social roles [48]. Our resultant prototype also integrated those two main pillars to make the prototype more reliable. As a result of this paper, recommendations are made for improving mental health app design and development by incorporating mental health descriptions with persuasive design principles.

5 Strengths and Limitations

This paper used a five-step process to design the app prototype, which consisted of 1) a systematic literature review and meta-analysis, 2) a modified Delphi study, 3) surveying, 4) integrating persuasive design principles into mental health app descriptions, and 5) iterative prototyping. The heterogeneity of experts and the large sample size used in Delphi and the survey are the paper's strengths, while the study's cross-sectional nature is a potential limitation.

6 Conclusion

This prototype has been designed, using rigorous methods, for countries like Ethiopia, where fewer than 10% of individuals with mental disorders get mental healthcare due to resource shortages. Therefore, this prototype has been designed to develop a quality mHealth application that helps individuals with mental disorders. Our future work involves app development, usability testing, and evaluating its effectiveness with patients who have common mental disorders. In addition, the authors suggest that future researchers should consider usability tests and adapt the prototype to another area of mental disorders.

Disclosure of Interests. The authors have no competing interest in the submitted paper. We, all the authors, fully agree to submit to the 19th International Conference on Persuasive Technology 2024 and Publication.

References

1. Arias, D., Saxena, S., Verguet, S.: Quantifying the global burden of mental disorders and their economic value. EClinicalMedicine **54**, 101675 (2022)
2. Vigo, D., Thornicroft, G., Atun, R.: Estimating the true global burden of mental illness. Lancet Psychiatry **3**(2), 171–178 (2016)
3. Walker, E.R., McGee, R.E., Druss, B.G.: Mortality in mental disorders and global disease burden implications: a systematic review and meta-analysis. JAMA Psychiat. **72**(4), 334–341 (2015)
4. Funk, M.: Global burden of mental disorders and the need for a comprehensive, coordinated response from health and social sectors at the country level, Retrieved 30 2016
5. Fekadu, A., et al.: Excess mortality in severe mental illness: 10-year population-based cohort study in rural Ethiopia. Br. J. Psychiatry **206**(4), 289–296 (2015)
6. Kassa, G.M., Abajobir, A.A.: Prevalence of common mental illnesses in Ethiopia: a systematic review and meta-analysis. Neurol. Psychiatry Brain Res. **30**, 74–85 (2018)
7. Giorgis, K.S.T.W.: National Mental Health Strategy 2020–2025: Ministry of Health, Ethiopia (2020)
8. Ben-Zeev, D.: Technology in mental health: creating new knowledge and inventing the future of services. Psychiatr. Serv. **68**(2), 107–108 (2017)
9. Roth, C.B., et al.: Psychiatry in the digital age: a blessing or a curse? Int. J. Environ. Res. Public Health **18**(16), 8302 (2021)
10. Serrano-Ripoll, M.J., et al.: Impact of smartphone app-based psychological interventions for reducing depressive symptoms in people with depression: systematic literature review and meta-analysis of randomized controlled trials. JMIR Mhealth Uhealth **10**(1), e29621 (2022)
11. Levin, M.E., et al.: Evaluating an adjunctive mobile app to enhance psychological flexibility in acceptance and commitment therapy. Behav. Modif. **41**(6), 846–867 (2017)
12. Lipschitz, J., et al.: Adoption of mobile apps for depression and anxiety: cross-sectional survey study on patient interest and barriers to engagement. JMIR Ment Health **6**(1), e11334 (2019)
13. Hsu, M., et al.: Smartphone ownership, smartphone utilization, and interest in using mental health apps to address substance use disorders: literature review and cross-sectional survey study across two sites. JMIR Form Res **6**(7), e38684 (2022)
14. Magee, J.C., et al.: Mobile app tools for identifying and managing mental health disorders in primary care. Curr. Treat. Options Psych. **5**(3), 345–362 (2018)

15. Larsen, M.E., et al.: Using science to sell apps: evaluation of mental health app store quality claims. NPJ Digit. Med. **2**(1), 1–6 (2019)
16. Islam, M.A., Choudhury, N.: Mobile apps for mental health: a content analysis. Indian J. Mental Health **7**(3), 222–229 (2020)
17. de Almeida, R.S., et al.: Patients' perspectives about the design of a mobile application for psychotic disorders = Perspetivas dos pacientes sobre o design de uma aplicação móvel para perturbações psicóticas (2018)
18. Goodwin, J., et al.: Development of a mental health smartphone app: perspectives of mental health service users. J. Ment. Health **25**(5), 434–440 (2016)
19. Shen, N., et al.: Finding a depression app: a review and content analysis of the depression app marketplace. JMIR mHealth uHealth **3**(1), e16 (2015)
20. Nicholas, J., et al.: Mobile apps for bipolar disorder: a systematic review of features and content quality. J. Med. Internet Res. **17**(8), e198 (2015)
21. Torous, J., et al.: Clinical review of user engagement with mental health smartphone apps: evidence, theory and improvements. BMJ Ment. Health **21**(3), 116–119 (2018)
22. Pywell, J., et al.: Barriers to older adults' uptake of mobile-based mental health interventions. Digit. Health **6**, 2055207620905422 (2020)
23. Oinas-Kukkonen, H.: Behavior change support systems: a research model and agenda. In: Ploug, T., Hasle, P., Oinas-Kukkonen, H. (eds.) PERSUASIVE 2010. LNCS, vol. 6137, pp. 4–14. Springer, Heidelberg (2010). https://doi.org/10.1007/978-3-642-13226-1_3
24. Ajzen, I.: Understanding Attitudes and Predicting Social Behavior. Englewood Cliffs, Prentice-Hall (1980)
25. Ajzen, I.: The theory of planned behavior. Organ. Behav. Hum. Decis. Process. **50**(2), 179–211 (1991)
26. Fogg, B.J.: A behavior model for persuasive design. In: Proceedings of the 4th International Conference on Persuasive Technology (2009)
27. Alqahtani, F., et al.: Apps for mental health: an evaluation of behavior change strategies and recommendations for future development. Front. Artif. Intell. **2**, 30 (2019)
28. Shiferaw, S., et al.: Designing mHealth for maternity services in primary health facilities in a low-income setting - lessons from a partially successful implementation. BMC Med. Inform. Decis. Mak. **18**(1), 96 (2018)
29. Nigussie, Z.Y., et al.: Using mHealth to improve timeliness and quality of maternal and newborn health in the primary health care system in Ethiopia. Glob. Health Sci. Pract. **9**(3), 668–681 (2021)
30. Guracho, Y.D., Thomas, S.J., Win, K.T.: Smartphone application use patterns for mental health disorders: a systematic literature review and meta-analysis. Int. J. Med. Inform. **179**, 105217 (2023)
31. Zamanzadeh, V., et al.: Design and implementation content validity study: development of an instrument for measuring patient-centered communication. J. Caring Sci. **4**(2), 165–178 (2015)
32. Pung, A., Fletcher, S.L., Gunn, J.M.: Mobile app use by primary care patients to manage their depressive symptoms: qualitative study. J. Med. Internet Res. **20**(9), e10035 (2018)
33. Schueller, S.M., et al.: Discovery of and interest in health apps among those with mental health needs: survey and focus group study. J. Med. Internet Res. **20**(6), e10141 (2018)
34. Squires, A.: A valid step in the process: a commentary on Beckstead (2009). Int. J. Nurs. Stud. **46**(9), 1284 (2009)
35. Scrivin, R., et al.: Development and validation of a questionnaire investigating endurance athletes practices to manage gastrointestinal symptoms around exercise. Nutr. Diet. **78**(3), 286–295 (2021)
36. Lynn, M.R.: Determination and quantification of content validity. Nurs. Res. **35**(6), 382–386 (1986)

37. Almathami, H.K.Y., Win, K.T., Vlahu-Gjorgievska, E.: Development and validation of a new tool to identify factors that influence users' motivation toward the use of teleconsultation systems: a modified Delphi study. Int. J. Med. Inform. **157**, 104618 (2022)
38. Almohanna, A.A.S., et al.: Design and content validation of an instrument measuring user perception of the persuasive design principles in a breastfeeding mHealth app: a modified Delphi study. Int. J. Med. Inform. **164**, 104789 (2022)
39. Davis, L.L.: Instrument review: getting the most from a panel of experts. Appl. Nurs. Res. **5**(4), 194–197 (1992)
40. Tsegaye, B.S., Asemu, M.M., Hailu, H.B.: Construct validity and Reliability of Amharic version of DASS-21 scale among Ethiopian Defense University College of Health Science Students (2023)
41. Marcu, G., Bardram, J.E., Gabrielli, S.: A framework for overcoming challenges in designing persuasive monitoring and feedback systems for mental illness. In: 2011 5th International Conference on Pervasive Computing Technologies for Healthcare (PervasiveHealth) and Workshops. IEEE (2011)
42. Fleming, T., et al.: Digital Tools for Mental Health and Wellbeing: Opportunities & Impact. Findings from the literature and community research (2022). https://www.hpa.org.nz/news/digital-tools-for-mental-health-and-wellbeing
43. Alqahtani, F., Orji, R.: Insights from user reviews to improve mental health apps. Health Informatics J. **26**(3), 2042–2066 (2020)
44. Howard, A., et al.: Adult experts' perceptions of telemental health for youth: a Delphi study. JAMIA Open **1**(1), 67–74 (2018)
45. Aryana, B., Brewster, L.: Design for mobile mental health: exploring the informed participation approach. Health Informatics J. **26**(2), 1208–1224 (2019)
46. Matthews, J., et al.: Persuasive technology in mobile applications promoting physical activity: a systematic review. J. Med. Syst. **40**, 1–13 (2016)
47. Win, K.T., et al.: Persuasive systems design features in promoting medication management for consumers (2017)
48. Portz, J.D., et al.: Persuasive features in health information technology interventions for older adults with chronic diseases: a systematic review. Heal. Technol. **6**, 89–99 (2016)

How Would I Be Perceived If I Challenge Individuals Sharing Misinformation? Exploring Misperceptions in the UK and Arab Samples and the Potential for the Social Norms Approach

Selin Gurgun[1(✉)], Muaadh Noman[2], Emily Arden-Close[1], Keith Phalp[1], and Raian Ali[2]

[1] Faculty of Science and Technology, Bournemouth University, Poole, UK
{sgurgun,eardenclose,kphalp}@bournemouth.ac.uk
[2] College of Science and Engineering, Hamad Bin Khalifa University, Doha, Qatar
{muno32967,raali2}@hbku.edu.qa

Abstract. Research conducted in the UK explored the presence of misperceptions, revealing that people anticipated more negative consequences for challenging misinformation on social media. These misperceptions include the anticipation of harming relationships, causing embarrassment and offense to others, the belief that challenging may not yield success and the perception that such behaviour is unacceptable. As the UK culture is characterised as individualistic, we replicated this investigation in a collectivistic culture-Arab societies. Our aim is to explore the differences and similarities of these misperceptions across cultures and to examine whether applying the social norms approach can be a solution to address the inaction towards challenging misinformation. Comparing the UK (N = 250) and Arabs (N = 212), we showed that, in both cultures there are misperceptions towards challenging misinformation. While misperceptions regarding concerning relationship costs and futility remain consistent across cultures the concerns about causing harm to others and the acceptability of the behaviour differ. Participants in the UK show a higher concern about offense or embarrassment, in contrast, participants in Arab countries exhibit higher misperceptions about injunctive norms, perceiving challenging misinformation as less socially acceptable than it actually is. This study also shows that participants' likelihood to challenge misinformation is influenced by their misperceptions about potential harm to others and perceived injunctive norms. These findings present an opportunity to apply the social norms approach to behaviour change by addressing these misperceptions. Messages emphasising social acceptability of correcting misinformation and highlighting that people appreciate being corrected could serve as powerful tools to encourage users to challenge misinformation.

Keywords: Misinformation · Challenging Misinformation · Social Norms · User Corrections · Behaviour Change

N. Baghaei et al. (Eds.): PERSUASIVE 2024, LNCS 14636, pp. 133–150, 2024.
https://doi.org/10.1007/978-3-031-58226-4_11

1 Introduction

As misinformation spreads faster than genuine news [1] the need to combat misinformation has become an important topic. Various solutions have been proposed to combat the spread of misinformation. While most solutions focus on technologies such as automated detection and correction [2–4], blockchain technologies [5] and natural language processing [6, 7], these solutions often view users as passive recipients rather than active participants [8]. However, users' detection and correction can also be an effective way to combat misinformation [9, 10] and can be as effective as algorithmic corrections [11]. Despite this, people generally do not challenge misinformation they encounter on social media [12–17].

User behaviour on social media is complex and can be influenced by numerous factors with regard to challenging misinformation, such as diversity in individuals' cognitive processes [18] and users' concerns regarding their image on social media or their relationship with others [19].

Social norms, often described as informal rules and standards guiding social behaviours [20], are linked to perceived social pressures that can encourage or discourage specific behaviour [21]. These norms are typically categorised into two dimensions: a) what is common (descriptive norms) and b) what is approved or disapproved (injunctive norms) [22]. In both cases norms inform people's anticipations of others' behaviours and promote conformity. Through the lens of these established norms, people perceive and judge the actions and attitudes of others [23]. Understanding the user perceptions on challenging behaviour on social media and addressing potential misperceptions allows for correcting them which is an important step to ensure that the decisions related to challenging misinformation are based on reality, rather than misperceptions.

In prior research, scholars have explored the presence of misperceptions towards challenging misinformation on social media [24]. Their findings indicated that people on social media overestimate the negative reactions they would face when challenging others, a perception that does not align with the actual reactions. However, it is important to note that this sample chosen was drawn from the UK, characterised by a high level of individualism [25] which may potentially diminish the adherence to social norms [26, 27] and therefore influence the decision to challenge. Consequently, these results may or may not be applicable in other cultural contexts, such as Arab culture, characterised by high collectivism where high level of empathy and the concerns about preservation of relationships [25, 28] may also pose challenges to correcting misinformation. A prevalent critique asserts that psychological studies often rely on WEIRD samples predominantly sourced from Western, Educated, Industrialized, Rich, and Democratic backgrounds [29]. To overcome this critique, we collected data from Arabs.

This study is a replication of the prior research that investigates the misperceptions in the UK to Arab participants to explore the differences and similarities of these misperceptions across cultures. The motivation of this work is to pave the way for effective strategies, such as the social norms approach, to mitigate the dissemination of misinformation across diverse cultural contexts.

In the U.K. one of the main reasons preventing people from challenging misinformation is adherence to the norm of conflict avoidance [30]. Research suggests that Western cultures, characterised by high individualism [28] value open discussion and direct confrontation, whereas collectivistic cultures like Arab culture use avoidance as a conflict management strategy [31, 32]. Therefore, a comparative analysis of these cultures can provide valuable insights into variations in misperceptions between the two cultures and their potential impact on people's likelihood to challenge misinformation.

Drawing from the prior research we used three potential misperceptions that were identified before. The first is "relationship consequences", where users hold negative assumptions about how challenging others might affect their interpersonal relationships. This is based on the idea that confrontation might lead to tension or conflict, potentially negatively impacting relationships [33, 34]. Another aspect involves assumptions users hold regarding the potential harm people experience when they are challenged. This includes the risk of people feeling offended or embarrassed when their ideas are contradicted [14, 35], which we categorised as "negative impact". In addition, users' beliefs regarding the effectiveness of challenging misinformation represent another misperception, which we named "futility". This conveys a sense of hopelessness or ineffectiveness people may experience with regard to challenging misinformation [36, 37]. Lastly, we investigate the acceptability of challenging behaviour referred to as "injunctive norms" [23, 38, 39]. We aim to gain insights into whether users' perceptions of challenging misinformation differ across various cultures.

Identifying perceived norms and discrepancies between perceived and actual norms are the first steps in utilising social norms approach [40]. Social norms approach is based on the idea of correcting these misperceptions to alleviate the social pressure associated with conforming incorrectly perceived as the norm. Consequently, in this study we also examine whether applying the social norms approach can serve as a solution to address the inaction towards challenging misinformation.

Our contribution lies in replicating and extending prior research conducted in the UK, characterised by individualism, to Arab societies characterised by collectivism. By comparing both cultures, we aim to explore whether the observed misperceptions in the UK are a culturally specific phenomenon or if they occur similarly in a more collectivistic culture. This provides insights into the interaction between cultural norms and individuals' likelihood to challenge misinformation on social media. Furthermore, this research investigates the potential of the social norms approach as a cross-cultural solution to address inaction towards challenging misinformation. Ultimately, our work aims to foster an environment conducive to making more informed decisions when encountering misinformation.

2 Theoretical Underpinnings

2.1 Social Norms Approach

Social norms theory refers to situations where people hold incorrect perception of the attitudes and behaviours of others. This theory has been applied in health related areas [22] particularly to peer substance use [40–42] where the majority tends to overestimate the frequency and amount of substance use and its acceptability among their peers, leading to an increase in their own consumption. This misperception is identified by comparing their own behaviour and their perception of the norm held by the majority of their peers [41]. Such perceptions act like social influences on people, increasing their consumption to conform the estimated norm [43]. In short, individuals behaviour is significantly shaped by their assumption of what is considered "normal" [44].

In terms of prevention and intervention of substance use, social norms approach involves challenging students' misperceptions about peer substance use and attitudes [40, 41]. The foundation of these interventions is to highlight the actual norm, which is often healthier and safer than the perceived norm. As an example, if students think that their peers typically consume six alcoholic drinks at parties, when in reality, they only have three, a social norms campaign might give the message that the majority of students typically have no more than three alcoholic drinks when they party. The idea is that correcting these misperceptions reduces the social pressure to follow what is incorrectly perceived as the norm, leading to reduced e.g., alcohol use and more negative attitudes toward it [40] (See Fig. 1).

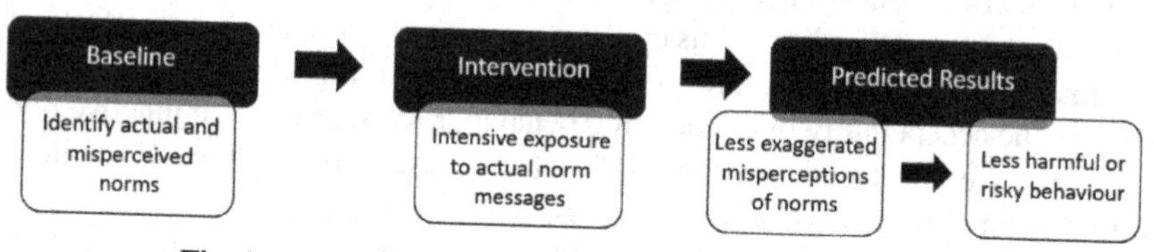

Fig. 1. Model of Social Norms Approach to Prevention [40]

Social norms theory can also be applied to different situations where individuals avoid confronting others' problem behaviour due to their misperceived belief that such behaviour is socially acceptable within their peer group [45]. In other words, people who underestimate how much their peers are uncomfortable with problematic behaviour might choose not to express their discomfort regarding that behaviour. However, if people were made aware of the actual level discomfort their peers feel about that behaviour, they might become more willing to voice their concerns. For instance, research in the U.S. indicates that most college students tend to underestimate how accepting and supportive their peers are of gay, lesbian and bisexual students. They believe their peers are less tolerant and supportive than they actually are [46]. Another study in the U.S. found that, college students tend to misperceive the risky sexual behaviour norms of their peers, believing that their peers engage in riskier sexual behaviour than they actually do. These misperceptions have been positively associated with students' sexual behaviour [47]. Social norms theory has also been applied in the context of distracted driving behaviour. Adolescents tend to perceive that their parents and peers engage in distracted driving more frequently than they do and this misperception can lead them to underestimate the risks associated with distracted driving, leading to their engagement in such behaviour [48].

Considering the influence of misperceptions on shaping behaviour, exploring their impact on challenging misinformation can provide valuable insights. It stands to reason that people may be hesitant to challenge misinformation when they encounter it. Expanding upon prior research, this study aims to provide insights into informed interventions and strategies that transcend specific cultural contexts. Since the social norms approach has effectively influenced a wide range of behaviors, this research expanded its application to investigate how users perceive the act of challenging misinformation with a particular emphasis on the examination of cultural differences.

3 Method

3.1 Participants

A total of 462 participants (age range 18–77 years, 176 female, 283 male and 3 non-binary, 250 from the U.K. and 212 from Arab countries (Egypt 22.2%, Saudi Arabia 12.3%, Iraq 10.8%, Jordan 9.9%, Syria 9%, Bahrain 9%, Lebanon 7.5%, Oman 6.6%, Palestine 4.2%, Kuwait 3.3%, Algeria 1.4%, Morocco 1.4%, Tunisia 0.9%, Sudan 0.5%, Yemen 0.5%, and the United Arab Emirates 0.5%) were recruited through Prolific™ (www.prolific.co) and Cint (www.cint.com), well-established online recruitment platforms for research studies. Inclusion criteria were being 18 years or older, fluency in the English or Arabic language, using Facebook with their identity, prior exposure to misinformation on Facebook, and being based in the UK or an Arabic country-based.

3.2 Data Collection

The survey was conducted online using Qualtrics, an online survey design platform. Participants were informed about the study objectives and asked for their consent before proceeding. They were given information regarding data confidentiality, their freedom to participate and the right to withdraw from the study and their access to the study findings. The ethics approval was obtained by Bournemouth University and Hamad Bin Khalifa University. The questionnaire included three attention checks, and participants who failed at least two of them were excluded from the analysis. In recognition of their participation, eligible participants were compensated for their participation.

3.3 Questionnaire Design

The questionnaire for this study was created using Qualtrics™ (https://www.qualtrics.com), an online survey platform. To ensure participants had a clear and common understanding, we included the key concepts' definitions such as "misinformation", "challenging" and "acquaintance". The questions asking challenging acquaintances was intentional as we tried to maintain a neutral stance between total strangers and loved ones in social relationships, since people's behaviour can vary when interacting with strangers and loved ones [14]. Facebook was chosen due to its global base with approximately 2.91 billion monthly active users [49] and being the most frequent mentioned (67%) to be a platform where users encountered fake news [50]. It is also an appropriate platform for investigating social norms as it is a semi-public space where comments and likes can be seen by others apart from friends. Facebook also consists of both strong ties (e.g., family) and weak ties (e.g., acquaintances like neighbours) [51]. Therefore, it is a convenient platform to investigate the attitudes towards acquaintances. Weak ties are significant as people are more likely to encounter different opinions through such connections [52] people they find it more difficult to confront them than to confront those with whom they have strong ties [53].

The survey evaluated Arab and UK participants' attitudes and their perceptions of others regarding challenging misinformation on social media. Participants were first asked about their attitudes towards challenging misinformation which we term "self-term" in this paper and after they were asked about their opinions about others which we term "perceived". The questionnaire along with the data can be found in OSF (https://osf.io/p2yav/).

3.4 Measures

Demographic Characteristics.
Participants answered questions about their age, gender and educational level.

Relationship Consequences. We utilised the items from a novel scale of Perceived Relationship Costs [54, 55]. Example of self-reported items included are "*It would offend me*" and "*I would think that they are aggressive*". Internal reliability was high for both UK ($\alpha = 0.92$) and Arabs ($\alpha = 0.91$). For the perceived items, we changed the items as "It would offend them" and "They would think that I am aggressive". Internal reliability was also high for both UK ($\alpha = 0.92$) and Arabs ($\alpha = 0.93$).

Negative Impact on the Person Being Challenged. Self-reported negative impact and perceived negative impact were assessed with two items on a 7-point Likert scale from Strongly Disagree to Strongly Agree. The items are for self-report "*I would feel embarrassed*" and "*I would feel that they will be viewed as untrustworthy by other social contacts*". The items for perceived are "*They would feel embarrassed*" and "*They would feel that I will be viewed as untrustworthy by other social contacts*". The items were derived from previous research [14, 56, 57]. Given the acknowledged limitations associated with using Cronbach's alpha for two-item scales, we did not include it in our results [58].

Futility of the Act of Challenging. Actual futility and perceived futility were assessed with two items on a 7-point Likert scale from Strongly Disagree to Strongly Agree adapted from Milliken et al.'s [56] study on employee silence. Self-reported items include "*challenging would change my mind that the information I shared is true*" and for perceived "*challenging would change their mind that the information they shared is true*".

Injunctive Norms. Participants were asked to respond to the self-report item, "*how do you find challenging others on Facebook when they share misinformation?*" and the perceived item "*how would a typical person from your Facebook network find challenging others when they share misinformation?*". The responses were recorded on a 7-point scale from (1) very unacceptable to (7) very acceptable.

3.5 Data Analysis

Data were analysed using SPSS version 28. Descriptive statistics were used to report demographic information and the range, mean, and standard deviation for the misperception variable in both Arab and UK populations. As both Arab and UK data was not normally distributed, non-parametric tests were used. A Mann-Whitney U test was run to determine if there were differences in misperception scores between the UK and Arab countries. Misperception score was calculated for each participant by subtracting the self-report mean from the perception of the participants (them score). A result of a positive misperception score was interpreted as an overestimation (further details on the method can be found in [59–61]. Ordinal logistic regression was used to assess the impact of the misperceptions on the likelihood to challenge.

4 Results

4.1 Participant Demographics

In total, 585 participants (324 from the Arab region, 261 from the UK) completed the online survey. Of those who completed, 462 participants (212 Arab, 250 UK) provided valid answers, passed three attention checks, and not being considered speeders or duplicates. Demographic characteristics of the participants, including age, gender, and educational background, are presented in Table 1.

Table 1. Participants demographics

		Arab (N = 212)		UK (N = 250)	
		Count	%	Count	%
Gender	Male	140	66.0	104	41.6
	Female	72	34.0	143	57.2
	Non-binary	0	0	3	1.2
Age	18–24	31	14.6	44	17.6
	25–34	113	53.3	94	37.6
	35–44	50	23.6	67	26.8
	Over 45	18	8.5	45	18.0
Education	Primary	14	6.6	36	14.4
	Further	29	13.7	57	26.8
	Higher	169	79.7	157	62.8

4.2 Misperceptions of Relationship Costs, Negative Impact on Others, Futility, and Injunctive Norms

A paired-samples t-test was used to examine the discrepancy between participants' actual attitudes and their perceptions of others' attitudes towards being challenged when posting misinformation. The significant difference between their self-report and perceived responses indicates that there is a misperception.

During data screening, only four outliers were identified for the UK and one outlier was identified for the Arabs each falling more than 1.5 box-lengths from the edge of the box in a box plot. However, their values did not classify as extreme, so they were kept in analyses. For both data assumption of normality was not violated, as assessed by a normal Q-Q plot for all the analysis. Inspection of their values did not reveal them to be extreme and they were kept in the analysis. The assumption of normality was not violated, as assessed by a normal Q-Q plot for all the analysis.

Table 2 shows the statistically significant differences in Arab participants for all six perceived relationship cost items ($p < .01$). This is in line with the UK findings [24]. Arab participants reported greater anticipation of other's negative reactions regarding their relationships compared to their actual reactions when being challenged. The mean of self-report for the relationship costs was 3.09 (SD = 1.57) and for perceived relationship costs, it is 3.70 (SD = 1.53) with a significant t-value of −6.11 ($p < .001$). This suggests that Arab participants perceive challenging others as more detrimental to their relationships compared to how they would react if they were challenged.

In terms of the items relating to negative impact on others, the misperceptions for the negative impact was not statistically significant for either cultural group.

For the items around futility of challenging misinformation, the analysis involved reverse-coding positively framed items. For Arab participants, the results indicated a significant difference for all the items ($p < .001$) in the Arab sample whereas in the UK only one item "It would make me (them) delete the post" was significant (p < .01). The mean of self-report for futility was 2.59 (SD = 1.43) and for perception of others it was 3.12 (SD = 1.22), with a significant t-value of −4.65 (p < .001). This suggests that Arab participants think that their effort will be futile as others are unlikely to change their mind and delete their post; however they themselves are more inclined to change their mind and delete their post.

Similar to the UK results, among Arab participants there was a significant difference between participants' self-reported answers and their perception of others answers regarding the acceptability of challenging misinformation (p < .001). The mean of self-report for injunctive norms was 4.79 (SD = 1.80) compared to 4.4 (SD = 1.55) for perception of others, with a significant t-value of 2.71 (p < .01). This indicates that, participants perceive that others consider it less acceptable to challenge misinformation than they find it to be.

A Mann-Whitney U test was run to determine any differences in degree of misperception between UK and Arab countries. In line with prior research on misperceptions [60–62], we computed misperception scores as the perceived ("them" score) minus average self-reported scores (average of all "me" scores). Misperception scores for UK participants ranged from −3.95 to 3.69 and for Arab participants ranged from −3.74 to 4. Distributions of the scores for UK and Arab countries were similar, as assessed by visual inspection. There was no statistically significantly difference between Arabs (median 0.59) and UK (median 0.97) regarding the misperception of relationship costs score, U = 23874, z = −1.84, p = 0.07. Similarly, there was no statistically significant difference between Arabs (0.41) and UK (0.54) regarding the misperception of futility, U = 25244, z = −0.88, p = 0.38. For the misperception of negative impact on others, median was statistically significantly higher in the U.K (0.08) than in Arab countries (−0.42), U = 22185, z = −3.04, p = 0.002. The results indicates that, participants in Arab countries tend to underestimate the negative impact on others when challenged, perceiving that they themselves will experience more negative harm than their perception of others. In contrast, in the UK, participants are in an overestimation, thinking that others will experience more negative harm from them than they actually do. However, it

Table 2. Mean and SD values of self-reported and perceived items across UK and Arab samples

	Self-Report		Perceptions		t-value	
	Arab (N = 212)	U.K (N = 250)	Arab (N = 212)	U.K (N = 250)	Arab (N = 212)	U.K (N = 250)
Relationship Consequences	M (SD)	M (SD)	M (SD)	M (SD)		
It would offend me (them)	3.51 (1.96)	3.78 (1.83)	4.04 (1.79)	4.72 (1.46)	-3.75***	-7.98***
I (They) would think that they are (I am) aggressive	2.87 (1.72)	3.64 (1.71)	3.76 (1.83)	4.36 (1.57)	-6.63***	-7.08***
I (They) would think that they are (I am) unfriendly	3.07 (1.83)	3.66 (1.7)	3.76 (1.88)	4.48 (1.52)	-5.13***	-7.55***
I (They) would think that they are (I am) not empathetic	3.04 (1.87)	3.44 (1.67)	3.7 (1.87)	4.3 (1.47)	-4.97***	-8.2***
The relationship between us will deteriorate	2.74 (1.84)	3.58 (1.77)	3.25 (1.73)	4.26 (1.55)	-4.17***	-7.02***
We will interact less frequently afterwards	3.3 (1.9)	4.11 (1.79)	3.68 (1.76)	4.52 (1.52)	-3.12**	-3.96***
Average perceived relationship costs	3.09 (1.57)	3.71 (1.49)	3.7 (1.53)	4.43 (1.29)	-6.11***	-8.94***
Negative impact on the person being challenged						
I (They) would feel embarrassed or upset	4.19 (2.02)	4.86 (1.58)	4.44 (1.69)	4.79 (1.63)	-2.04*	-0.69
I (They) would feel that I will be viewed as untrustworthy by other social contacts	3.9 (2.01)	4.62 (1.65)	4.02 (1.73)	4.4 (1.44)	-0.97	2.28*
Average perceived negative items	4.04 (1.87)	4.74 (1.48)	4.23 (1.5)	4.6 (1.27)	-1.77	-1.65

(continued)

Table 2. (*continued*)

	Self-Report		Perceptions		t-value	
	Arab (N = 212)	U.K (N = 250)	Arab (N = 212)	U.K (N = 250)	Arab (N = 212)	U.K (N = 250)
Futility						
It would change my (their) mind (R)	2.67 (1.72)	3.6 (1.47)	3.2 (1.48)	3.88 (1.36)	-3.79***	-1.94
It would make me (them) delete the post (R)	2.52 (1.67)	3.31 (1.74)	3.04 (1.44)	4.01 (1.45)	-3.86***	-4.24**
Average perceived futility items	2.59 (1.43)	3.46 (1.40)	3.12 (1.22)	3.95 (1.21)	-4.65***	-3.57**
Injunctive Norms						
How do you (would a typical person) find challenging others on Facebook when they share misinformation?	4.74 (1.8)	4.95 (1.42)	4.4 (1.55)	4.29 (1.34)	2.71**	6.83***

* p < 0.05, ** p < 0.01, *** p < 0.001

is also worth noting that the effect size was 0.14 which is a small effect based on Cohen's classification [63]. For the injunctive norms, median was statistically significantly lower in the UK (−0.95) than in Arab countries (−0.74), $U = 33136$, $z = 4.67$, $p < 0.001$. This indicates that, in the Arab countries there is a greater misperception that challenging others is unacceptable compared to the UK. The effect size was 0.22 which is small to medium effect size category (Table 3).

Table 3. Comparisons of misperception results by the Mann-Whitney U test

Variables	Median	Median	U	z	p
Misperception relationship costs	0.97	0.59	23874	−1.84	0.07
Misperception futility	0.54	0.41	25244	−0.88	0.38
Misperception negative impact on others	0.08	−0.42	22185	−3.04	0.002
Misperception injunctive norms	−0.95	−0.74	33136	4.67	<0.001

4.3 The Affect of Misperception on the Likelihood to Challenge

For the purposes of this study, prior to the regression analysis, we treated misperception data as overestimation as on average, participants are more likely to overestimate the negative reactions from other when they challenge. To operationalise the data, we categorised the misperception scores. A positive misperception score (i.e., actual attitude of participants < perceived attitude of others) indicated a tendency to overestimate others' negative attitude in terms of challenging misinformation. We classified the negative misperception score (i.e., actual attitude of participants > perceived attitude of others) and zero score (i.e., actual attitude of participants = perceived attitude of others) as having no overestimation. This approach allowed for grouping of participants based on whether they overestimated.

A cumulative odds ordinal logistic regression with proportional odds was run to determine the extent to which overestimation of others' negative reactions impacts likelihood to challenge across the two cultures, controlling for age and gender (See Table 4).

Table 4. Ordinal logistic regression results for predicting the likelihood to challenge with predictors including age, gender, overestimating the three negative consequences and injunctive norms

Predictors	UK			Arab Countries		
	B	SE	Odds Ratio	B	SE	Odds Ratio
Age	0.034	0.01	1.034*	0.011	0.015	1.011
Gender (Female)	−0.38	0.231	0.684	−0.287	0.261	0.75
Overestimating Relationship Consequences	−0.063	0.285	0.939	−0.451	0.288	0.637
Overestimating Futility	0.166	0.241	1.181	0.107	0.268	1.113
Overestimating Negative Impact (offending others)	−0.536	0.259	0.585*	−0.198	0.285	0.82
Overestimating Injunctive Norms (acceptability)	0.458	0.233	1.581*	0.582	0.255	1.790*

* $p < 0.05$, ** $p < 0.01$, *** $p < 0.001$

For the Arab countries, the assumption of proportional odds was met, as assessed by a full likelihood ratio test comparing the fit of the proportional odds model to a model with varying location parameters, $\chi 2(210) = 232.484$, $p = .137$. However, for the U.K, this assumption was not met, $\chi 2(255) = 676.862$, $p < .001$. Therefore, an examination of the assumption of proportional odds was undertaken by running separate binomial logistic regressions on cumulative dichotomous dependent variables. This examination showed that for most of the variables the assumption of proportional odds appears tenable. The deviance goodness-of-fit test indicated that for both cultures, the model was a good fit to the observed data, for the UK $\chi^2(1203) = 736.312$, $p = 1$ and Arab countries. $\chi^2(1050) = 661.438$, $p = 1$. For both cultures, the final model statistically significantly predicted the dependent variable over and above the intercept-only model, UK $\chi^2(51) = 99.733$, p $< .001$ and for Arabs $\chi^2(42) = 61.494$, p = .026. Regarding the independent variables, for the UK age, overestimating negative impact and overestimating injunctive norms significantly predicted likelihood to challenge (odds ratio of 1.034 (95% CI, 1.013 to 1.056) $p < .01$, odds ratio of 0.585 (95% CI, 0.352 to 0.971), $p < .05$ and odds ratio of 1.581 (95% CI, 1.001 to 2.498), $p = .05$ respectively). For the Arab countries, only overestimating injunctive norms significantly predicted likelihood to challenge (odds ratio of 1.790 (95% CI, 1.085 to 2.951) $p < .05$).

5 Discussion

Our findings highlight the presence of misperceptions in both cultural contexts, highlighting the potential for Social Norms Approach to address and correct these misperceptions. Prior research showed the existence of misperceptions across these variables in the UK [24]. The new results from Arab participants are aligned with those from the UK, indicating the existence of these misperceptions. In both cultures, participants believed that, through challenging misinformation, their relationship with others will be harmed and people will be offended or embarrassed. They also perceive that challenging misinformation is not socially acceptable. Our study showed that these perceptions do not align with reality. Based on the difference between their self-report and perceptions, we can conclude that, in both cultures, participants overestimate the potential harm of challenging misinformation to their relationships, the negative impact on others and the lack of potential success while underestimating the acceptability of this behaviour. Recognising these misperceptions is important as it allows for their correction, in turn leading to an environment where people are more motivated to engage in correcting misinformation. This provides an opportunity for the social norms approach, which aims to correct misperceptions of norms and promote more positive behaviours. The social norms approach predicts that interventions to correct misperceptions by revealing the actual, beneficial norm will have a positive impact on individuals, leading to a decrease in problem behaviours [23, 40]. Therefore, by addressing misperceptions and promoting accurate norms, the social norms approach can be an effective strategy for behaviour change in both individualistic and collectivist cultures.

The analysis of differences in misperception scores between the UK and Arab cultures revealed that participants from both cultures have the tendency to overestimate or underestimate the negative consequences and social norms associated with challenging misinformation.

While some misperceptions did not differ across cultures, such as misperception of relationship costs and futility; negative impact on others and injunctive norms were significantly different across both cultures. Cultural values and tendencies of the participants towards confrontation and conflict would provide further context to understand these similarities and differences.

The concern regarding causing harm to others, including offense or embarrassment when challenging is higher in the UK. This might be due to differences in communication styles. According to Hofstede's dimensions [25], the UK has been defined as an individualistic culture which places a high value on open communication and direct confrontation which may manifest in a more assertive approach to challenging misinformation [31, 64]. This approach, however, in contrast with the politeness norm in the UK which is characterised by values like respect, respecting privacy, keeping distance and being reserved [65]. This communication style is often perceived as avoidance-based and hearer oriented [66] which promote indirectness and subtlety in communication. While individuals in the UK may prioritise open communication, they may also be mindful of social norms and have concerns more about others when they challenge and aim to avoid causing embarrassment or offense when correcting.

Participants in Arab countries displayed higher misperceptions about injunctive norms, indicating they believe that challenging misinformation is less socially acceptable than it actually is. In collectivistic cultures such as Arab culture, there is a greater emphasis on maintaining social harmony and indirect communication [31, 55, 67]. One key feature that defines the people in collectivist cultures is their strong emphasis on relationships [55]. Challenging misinformation therefore can be perceived less acceptable due to the cultural norm of preserving the existing interpersonal relationships. Another aspect to consider might be the role of power distance which refers to the extent to which less powerful members of society accept and expect that power is distributed unequally [28]. In hierarchical societies with high power distance such as many Arab countries, challenging misinformation can be perceived as less acceptable, especially if misinformation is propagated by authority figures or those perceived to hold higher status, due to respect for hierarchical structures.

Our results demonstrate that certain misperceptions have an impact on likelihood of challenging misinformation, in line with previous research highlighting the significant impact of misperceptions on behaviour and individuals' decision to engage in specific behaviour [68].

In the UK participants who overestimated the negative impact on others of challenging misinformation were less inclined to challenge misinformation. The concern for the potential harm on others significantly influenced their decision to challenge. Additionally, in both cultural contexts, perceived injunctive norms, the acceptability of the behaviour, play an important role in likelihood of challenging misinformation. When people perceive challenging others is socially acceptable, they are more inclined to challenge misinformation.

These findings pave the way for tailoring interventions and strategies to address these misperceptions. In addition to its success in various domains such as health related behaviour [22, 69], substance use [40, 41] and smartphone use [68], the social norms approach can be applied to different situations where individuals refrain from a behaviour due to their misperceived belief that such behaviour is not socially acceptable within their peer group [45]. In our study, although many participants reported that they find challenging misinformation is socially acceptable, they believe that others do not consider it socially acceptable. However, research revealed that people are reluctant to share misinformation due to fear of potential damage to their reputation that they are only willing to do so in exchange for a monetary incentive [57]. In this case, this contradiction suggests, people might value being challenged as it can help protect their own reputation as opposed to participants' perception.

When implementing the social norms approach, messages that convey the idea that challenging misinformation is socially acceptable and that people appreciate being corrected, hold the premise to motivate people to challenge misinformation more confidently. Through this approach, an environment where challenging misinformation is not seen as personal and recognised as common can be cultivated. This can help alleviate misperceptions such as fear of causing offense or the belief that it is socially unacceptable.

5.1 Threats to Validity

There are potential threats to validity that could impact the quality and generalisability of our findings. First, when asking people about their behaviour, one must consider the Hawthorne effect [70] which refers to the situations where individuals change their behaviour when they are aware of being observed. The discrepancies could also be due to self-enhancement biases such as illusory superiority where people tend to overstate their positive characteristics and underestimate their negative characteristics compared to the average other or most others [71, 72]. Self-reports of experience might be subject to recall error [73] or social desirability bias [74]. To address these, future work should consider an experimental study or observational research to gain a better understanding of participants' behaviour. We selected specific cultures such as the UK and Arab countries as representations of individualistic and collectivistic cultures. The results might not be generalisable to other cultures with similar or different characteristics. To address this limitation, future work should consider comparative studies involving a broader range of cultures.

6 Conclusion and Future Work

Our study reveals misperceptions about challenging misinformation in both UK and Arab cultural contexts. Despite cultural differences, participants in both settings tend to overestimate harm to relationships and underestimate the social acceptability and effectiveness of challenging misinformation. The difference between self-reported and actual norms is crucial for motivating challenging behaviour. The social norms approach emerges as a promising strategy to address these misperceptions, correcting norms and promoting positive behaviours. Although the differences in misperception scores between the UK and Arab cultures highlight cultural nuance, interventions based on the social norms approach, revealing the healthy norm, can positively impact individuals in both cultures, fostering a reduction in problem behaviours. Our findings have broader implications extending the application of the social norms approach to online interactions where interventions should emphasise the social acceptability of the behaviour. Additional to self-reports, future work could consider observational data to increase the validity of the findings. Moreover, this study's findings can be applied to understand whether the misperceptions identified are common across various cultures beyond the UK and Arab context. Additionally, future studies might explore the implementation of the social norms approach in the design of social media platforms to assess its potential positive impact on the frequency of challenging misinformation in online sphere.

Acknowledgments. This publication was supported by NPRP 14 Cluster grant # NPRP 14C-0916–210015 from the Qatar National Research Fund (a member of Qatar Foundation). The findings herein reflect the work and are solely the responsibility of the authors.

References

1. Vosoughi, S., Roy, D., Aral, S.: The spread of true and false news online. Science **359**(6380), 1146–1151 (2018)
2. Garrett, R.K., Weeks, B.E.: The promise and peril of real-time corrections to political misperceptions. In: Proceedings of the 2013 Conference on Computer Supported Cooperative Work (2013)
3. Tanaka, Y., Sakamoto, Y., Matsuka, T.: Toward a social-technological system that inactivates false rumors through the critical thinking of crowds, pp. 649–658. IEEE (2013)
4. Guo, Z., Schlichtkrull, M., Vlachos, A.: A survey on automated fact-checking. Trans. Assoc. Comput. Linguist. **10**, 178–206 (2022)
5. Paul, S., et al.: Fake news detection in social media using blockchain. In: 2019 7th International Conference on Smart Computing & Communications (ICSCC). IEEE (2019)
6. Nakov, P., et al.: Overview of the CLEF–2021 CheckThat! lab on detecting check-worthy claims, previously fact-checked claims, and fake news. In: Candan, K.S., et al. (eds.) CLEF 2021. LNCS, vol. 12880, pp. 264–291. Springer, Cham (2021). https://doi.org/10.1007/978-3-030-85251-1_19
7. de Oliveira, N.R., et al.: Identifying fake news on social networks based on natural language processing: trends and challenges. Information **12**(1), 38 (2021)
8. Fernandez, M., Alani, H.: Online misinformation: challenges and future directions. In: Companion Proceedings of the The Web Conference (2018)
9. Vraga, E.K., Bode, L.: Using expert sources to correct health misinformation in social media. Sci. Commun. **39**(5), 621–645 (2017)
10. Walter, N., Murphy, S.T.: How to unring the bell: a meta-analytic approach to correction of misinformation. Commun. Monogr. **85**(3), 423–441 (2018)
11. Bode, L., Vraga, E.K.: See something, say something: correction of global health misinformation on social media. Health Commun. **33**, 1131 (2018)
12. Tully, M., Bode, L., Vraga, E.K.: Mobilizing users: does exposure to misinformation and its correction affect users' responses to a health misinformation post? Soc. Media + Soc. **6**, 205630512097837 (2020)
13. Chadwick, A., Vaccari, C.: News sharing on UK social media: misinformation, disinformation, and correction. In: 2019: Loughborough: Online Civic Culture Centre, Loughborough University (2019)
14. Tandoc, E.C., Lim, D., Ling, R.: Diffusion of disinformation: how social media users respond to fake news and why. Journalism **21**(3), 381–398 (2020)
15. Vicol, D.O.: Who is most likely to believe and to share misinformation? Full Fact. (2020)
16. Bode, L., Vraga, E.K.: Correction experiences on social media during COVID-19. Soc. Media + Soc. **7**, 205630512110088 (2021)
17. Bode, L., Vraga, E.K.: Value for correction: documenting perceptions about peer correction of misinformation on social media in the context of COVID-19. J. Quant. Description Digit. Media **1** (2021)
18. Swire, B., Ecker, U.: ELEVEN misinformation and its correction: cognitive mechanisms and recommendations for mass communication. In: Misinformation and Mass Audiences, pp. 195–211. University of Texas Press (2018)

19. Gurgun, S., et al.: Why do we not stand up to misinformation? Factors influencing the likelihood of challenging misinformation on social media and the role of demographics, in factors influencing the likelihood of challenging misinformation on social media and the role of demographics. Technol. Soc. **76**, 102444 (2023)
20. Cialdini, R.B., Trost, M.R.: Social influence: social norms, conformity and compliance. In: Gilbert, D.T., Fiske, S.T., Lindzey, G. (eds.) The Handbook of Social Psychology, 4th edn., vol. 1–2, pp. 151–192. McGraw-Hill, New York, NY (1998)
21. Ajzen, I.: The theory of planned behavior. Organ. Behav. Hum. Decis. Process. **50**(2), 179–211 (1991)
22. Dempsey, R.C., McAlaney, J., Bewick, B.M.: A critical appraisal of the social norms approach as an interventional strategy for health-related behavior and attitude change. Front. Psychol. **9**, 2180 (2018)
23. Berkowitz, A.D.: The social norms approach: theory, research, and annotated bibliography. Citeseer (2004)
24. Gurgun, S., et al.: Challenging Misinformation on Social Media: Users' Perceptions and Misperceptions and Their Impact on the Likelihood to Challenge. Available at SSRN 4600006 (2023)
25. Hofstede, G.: Country Comparison Tool (2023). https://www.hofstede-insights.com/country-comparison-tool. Cited 2023
26. Heinrichs, N., et al.: Cultural differences in perceived social norms and social anxiety. Behav. Res. Ther. **44**(8), 1187–1197 (2006)
27. Schreier, S.S., et al.: Social anxiety and social norms in individualistic and collectivistic countries. Depress. Anxiety **27**(12), 1128–1134 (2010)
28. Hofstede, G.: Culture's Consequences: International Differences in Work-Related Values, vol. 5. Sage (1984)
29. Henrich, J., Heine, S.J., Norenzayan, A.: The weirdest people in the world? Behav. Brain Sci. **33**(2–3), 61–83 (2010)
30. Chadwick, A., Vaccari, C., Hall, N.-A.: Covid vaccines and online personal messaging: the challenge of challenging everyday misinformation. Loughborough University (2022)
31. Tjosvold, D., Sun, H.F.: Understanding conflict avoidance: relationship, motivations, actions, and consequences. Int. J. Confl. Manage. **13**, 142–164 (2002)
32. Adair, W.L., Okumura, T., Brett, J.M.: Negotiation behavior when cultures collide: the United States and Japan. J. Appl. Psychol. **86**(3), 371 (2001)
33. Mutz, D.C.: The consequences of cross-cutting networks for political participation. Am. J. Polit. Sci. **46**, 838–855 (2002)
34. Sleeper, M., et al.: The post that wasn't: exploring self-censorship on Facebook (2013)
35. Steen-Johnsen, K., Enjolras, B.: The fear of offending: social norms and freedom of expression. Society **53**(4), 352–362 (2016). https://doi.org/10.1007/s12115-016-0044-2
36. Van Houtte, M., Stevens, P.A.J.: Sense of futility: the missing link between track position and self-reported school misconduct. Youth Soc. **40**(2), 245–264 (2008)
37. Brookover, W.B., et al.: Elementary school social climate and school achievement. Am. Educ. Res. J. **15**(2), 301–318 (1978)
38. Lapinski, M.K., Rimal, R.N.: An explication of social norms. Commun. Theory **15**(2), 127–147 (2005)
39. Rimal, R.N., Real, K.: Understanding the influence of perceived norms on behaviors. Commun. Theory **13**(2), 184–203 (2003)
40. Perkins, H.W.: The emergence and evolution of the social norms approach to substance abuse prevention. In: The Social Norms Approach to Preventing School and College Age Substance Abuse: A Handbook for Educators, Counselors, and Clinicians, pp. 3–17 (2003)

41. McAlaney, J., et al.: Personal and perceived peer use of and attitudes toward alcohol among university and college students in seven EU countries: project SNIPE. J. Stud. Alcohol Drugs **76**(3), 430–438 (2015)
42. McAlaney, J., McMahon, J.: Normative beliefs, misperceptions, and heavy episodic drinking in a British student sample. J. Stud. Alcohol Drugs **68**(3), 385–392 (2007)
43. Borsari, B., Carey, K.B.: Descriptive and injunctive norms in college drinking: a meta-analytic integration. J. Stud. Alcohol **64**(3), 331–341 (2003)
44. Bandura, A.: Social Foundations of Thought and Action, pp. 23–28, Englewood Cliffs (1986)
45. Berkowitz, A.D.: Applications of social norms theory to other health and social justice issues. In: Perkins, H.W. (ed.) The Social Norms Approach to Preventing School and College Age Substance Abuse: A Handbook for Educators, Counselors, and Clinicians, pp. 259–279. Jossey-Bass/Wiley, Hoboken, NJ (2003)
46. Bowen, A.M., Bourgeois, M.J.: Attitudes toward lesbian, gay, and bisexual college students: the contribution of pluralistic ignorance, dynamic social impact, and contact theories. J. Am. Coll. Health **50**(2), 91–96 (2001)
47. Lewis, M.A., et al.: Gender-specific normative misperceptions of risky sexual behavior and alcohol-related risky sexual behavior. Sex Roles **57**(1–2), 81–90 (2007)
48. Carter, P.M., et al.: Social norms and risk perception: predictors of distracted driving behavior among novice adolescent drivers. J. Adolesc. Health. **54**(5), S32–S41 (2014)
49. Statista, Q.: Number of monthly active Facebook users worldwide as of 4th quarter 2015 (2016)
50. Centre for International Governance, I. and Ipsos, CIGI-Ipsos Global Survey on Internet Security and Trust (2019)
51. Ellison, N.B., Boyd, D.: Sociality Through Social Network Sites. The Oxford Handbook of Internet Studies, pp. 151–172 (2013)
52. Kim, Y.: The contribution of social network sites to exposure to political difference: the relationships among SNSs, online political messaging, and exposure to cross-cutting perspectives. Comput. Hum. Behav. **27**(2), 971–977 (2011)
53. Valenzuela, S., Kim, Y., Gil de Zúñiga, H.: Social networks that matter: exploring the role of political discussion for online political participation. Int. J. Public Opinion Res. **24**(2), 163–184 (2012)
54. Zhang, Z.-X., Wei, X.: Superficial harmony and conflict avoidance resulting from negative anticipation in the workplace. Manag. Organ. Rev. **13**(4), 795–820 (2017)
55. Zhang, Z.-X., Zhang, Y., Wang, M.: Harmony, illusory relationship costs, and conflict resolution in Chinese contexts. In: Leung, A.K.Y., Chiu, C.-Y., Hong, Y.-Y. (eds.) Cultural Processes: A Social Psychological Perspective, pp. 188–209. Cambridge University Press, New York, NY (2011)
56. Milliken, F.J., Morrison, E.W., Hewlin, P.F.: An exploratory study of employee silence: issues that employees don't communicate upward and why. J. Manage. Stud. **40**(6), 1453–1476 (2003)
57. Altay, S., Hacquin, A.-S., Mercier, H.: Why do so few people share fake news? It hurts their reputation. New Media Soc. **24**, 1461444820969893 (2022)
58. Hulin, C., Cudeck, R.: Cronbach's alpha on two-item scales. J. Consum. Psychol. **10**(1/2), 55 (2001)
59. Sandstrom, M., Makover, H., Bartini, M.: Social context of bullying: do misperceptions of group norms influence children's responses to witnessed episodes? Soc. Influ. **8**(2–3), 196–215 (2013)
60. Perkins, J.M., Perkins, H.W., Craig, D.W.: Peer weight norm misperception as a risk factor for being over and underweight among UK secondary school students. Eur. J. Clin. Nutr. **64**(9), 965–971 (2010)

61. Kenney, S.R., LaBrie, J.W., Lac, A.: Injunctive peer misperceptions and the mediation of self-approval on risk for driving after drinking among college students. J. Health Commun. **18**(4), 459–477 (2013)
62. Duong, H.T., Parker, L.: Going with the flow: young motorcyclists' misperceived norms and motorcycle speeding behaviour. J. Soc. Mark. **8**(3), 314–332 (2018)
63. Cohen, J.: Statistical Power Analysis for the Behavioral Sciences. Academic Press, New York (2013)
64. Morris, M.W., et al.: Conflict management style: accounting for cross-national differences. J. Int. Bus. Stud. **29**(4), 729–747 (1998)
65. Kamehkhosh, N., Larina, T.V.: Cultural values and politeness strategies in British and Persian family discourse. In: Proceedings of INTCESS, p. 7 (2020)
66. Larina, T.: Directness, imposition and politeness in English and Russian. Cambridge ESOL Res. Notes **33**, 33–38 (2008)
67. Triandis, H.C.: Culture and social behavior (1994)
68. McAlaney, J., et al.: Perceptions and misperceptions of smartphone use: applying the social norms approach. Information **11**(11), 513 (2020)
69. Reid, A.E., Aiken, L.S.: Correcting injunctive norm misperceptions motivates behavior change: a randomized controlled sun protection intervention. Health Psychol. **32**(5), 551 (2013)
70. Wickström, G., Bendix, T.: The "Hawthorne effect"—what did the original Hawthorne studies actually show? Scand. J. Work Environ. Health **26**, 363–367 (2000)
71. Hoorens, V.: Self-enhancement and superiority biases in social comparison. Eur. Rev. Soc. Psychol. **4**(1), 113–139 (1993)
72. Brown, J.D.: Evaluations of self and others: self-enhancement biases in social judgments. Soc. Cogn. **4**(4), 353–376 (1986)
73. Sudman, S., Bradburn, N.M., Schwarz, N.: Thinking About Answers: The Application of Cognitive Processes to Survey Methodology. Jossey-Bass, San Francisco (1996)
74. Grimm, P.: Social Desirability Bias. Wiley International Encyclopedia of Marketing. Wiley, New York (2010)

Persuasive Technology Through Behavior and Emotion with Pet-Type Artifacts

Rio Harada(✉) and Kaoru Sumi

Graduate School of Systems Information Science, Future University Hakodate, Hakodate, Japan
g2123049@fun.ac.jp, kaoru.sumi@acm.org

Abstract. This study examined the behaviors and emotional expressions that artifacts such as four-legged pets use to persuade people. On the basis of a preliminary study, we created six types of emotional expressions (joy, sadness, confusion, anger, surprise, and neutral) by combining each part of a dog's face and tail, voice, and speed of movement. We also selected several behaviors and created 12 types of animations combining the behaviors and emotional expressions. We conducted experiments using actual trash and trash cans in a mixed reality space in which participants were asked to wear Hololens2. The results showed that emotional expressions such as "sadness" and "confusion" were effective when the pet-like artifact was utilized to encourage participants to throw away the trash, while expressions that gave the impression of "joy" or "anger" were not effective. In addition, there was little difference in ratings based on whether the combination of actions was longer or shorter.

Keywords: Persuasive Technology · persuasion · behavior changes · pet-type artifact · emotion · behavior · movement

1 Introduction

Persuasive Technology [1] deals with research on human persuasion by computers, and in this study, we utilize it to examine how a four-legged artifact can persuade humans. Although there have been studies on humanoid artifacts such as character agents and robots that persuade humans, there have been relatively fewer works using four-legged artifacts. A variety of animal-inspired robots have been developed in recent years, including so-called pet robots, entertainment pets, and robotic pets, such as AIBO [2] NeCoRo [3], MiRo [4], Paro [5, 6], PaPeRo [7], LOVOT [8] and NICOBO[1]. This current research landscape indicates that there are many pet-like robots being developed and that there are various user needs, such as wanting to be able to accept robots without resistance and wanting to enjoy and be healed by them.

Research has been conducted on robot therapy [9] using such robots. Several studies on human interaction with a dog-shaped robot have also been conducted, comparing animal-assisted therapy with robot-assisted therapy. Animal-assisted therapy is an

[1] https://www.engadget.com/panasonic-companion-robot-nicobo-164059256.html.

N. Baghaei et al. (Eds.): PERSUASIVE 2024, LNCS 14636, pp. 151–160, 2024.
https://doi.org/10.1007/978-3-031-58226-4_12

alternative or complementary type of therapy that involves the use of animals in treatment [10, 11]. Studies have been conducted to determine the effects of supplementing animal-assisted therapy animals with robots. A comparison of animal-assisted therapy and robot-assisted therapy with children and adults as subjects showed that the robot has a limited ability to engage in temporally structured behavioral interactions with humans. Similar studies have experimented with the importance of framing the robot as a puppy as a way to improve interaction. However, robot-assisted therapy is promising because "the robotic pet hygienic standard is higher than that of live animals [12]".

In commercial entertainment robots, the ability to communicate naturally with humans has been emphasized. However, not much research has been conducted on pets persuading humans or encouraging behavioral change, other than as communication partners. On the other hand, actual dogs can appeal to their owners to bring them food when they are hungry or can encourage their owners to take them for a walk when they need to be exercised. This is the limitation of current pet robots, and we believe that overcoming this limitation may be the key to unlocking greater intimacy and trust between robots and humans. Therefore, this study investigates the possibility of four-legged canine artifacts persuading humans by means of emotional and behavioral expressions.

One study [13] that investigated the effects of specific emotions in negotiation confirmed that emotional expressions can have a significant influence on negotiation outcomes. Another study on the effects of "anger" and "joy" in negotiation [14] showed that angry facial expressions encouraged the other party to make more concessions compared to joyful expressions. An experiment [15] was conducted in which a character agent interacted with a subject using words and facial expressions in a situation where the subject was in a particular emotional state and then attempted to persuade the subject to do work. The results suggested that subjects were more likely to be persuaded if the character agent made a good impression on them during the emotional interaction. Other research has been conducted on humanoid virtual agents persuading people. Although various studies have utilized facial expressions [16], gestures [17], and facial expressions and gestures in combination [18, 19, 20], relatively fewer studies have utilized four-legged artifacts.

One study using a weak robot [21] examined the use of emotions designed to make others want to help the robot when it used feeble expressions. In that study, a trashcan-type robot encouraged the user, a child, to throw away the trash by performing feeble actions such as picking at the trash or staring at it, since the robot does not have a trash collection function. The results showed that "moving" and "going to the location of the trash can" were the factors that prompted the desired behavior, and that the child predicted the intention from the shape and movement of the robot. It is important to examine the effects of persuasion through the emotional expression and behavior of pet robots using such methods, just as people sometimes make puppy dog eyes when they ask for something. There are many interesting studies in this vein regarding canine behavior. Dogs can successfully communicate their intentions to their owners by means of nonverbal communication techniques such as vocalizations, touch, and body and head movements [22,23, 24, 25]. In a study on auditory robots [26], a companion robot was developed utilizing behaviors based on canine communication. In that study, participants were asked to open and close a microwave oven door to get the robot to pay attention to them, move toward the target, and alternate between looking at the user and the target. The results of these experiments showed that head movement and gaze direction are important in communicating the robot's intentions when using visual communication signals. The results also suggested that a combination of the dog's behavior and emotional expressions could be helpful in persuading the user more effectively.

Table 1. Sadness (E2).

Emotion	Sad(E2)
Neck	Tilt down
Head	Tilt down
Ears	Tilt outward at an angle
Tail	Tilt down
Voice	Pronounce "whine" in a high-pitched voice.
Movement speed	Move slowly

Table 2. Anger (E3).

Emotion	Anger (E3)
Neck	Tilt down
Head	Tilt up
Ears	Tilt backward and outward
Tail	Tilt up
Voice	Pronounce "woof " in a low voice
Movement speed	Move slightly and slowly

Table 3. Joy (E4).

Emotion	Joy (E4)
Neck	Tilt slightly down
Head	Tilt up
Ears	Tilt backward and outward
Tail	Swing left and right loudly and quickly
Voice	Pronounce " ruff " in a high voice
Movement speed	Move quickly

Table 4. Surprise (E5).

Emotion	Surprised (E5)
Neck	Tilt slightly up
Head	Tilt frontward
Ears	Tilt inward diagonally
Tail	Tilt up
Voice	Pronounce " bow " in a high voice
Movement speed	Move at normal speed

In the current study, we propose a method to evoke the behavior of a dog-shaped artifact to ask humans to throw away trash through its movements and emotional expressions. We created an animated artifact that is capable of rich motion and emotional expression, displayed it in a real space utilizing mixed reality technology, and examined what kind of behavior the dog-shaped artifact could persuade people to take.

Table 5. Confusion (E6).

Emotion	Confused (E6)
Neck	Tilt slightly down
Head	Tilt slightly down
Ears	Tilt outward at an angle
Tail	Tilt down
Voice	Pronounce " Kuhn" in a high-pitched voice.
Movement speed	Move quickly

2 Methods of Persuasion via Movement and Emotional Expression

Our ultimate goal is to achieve persuasion through the actions of artifacts such as robots, but due to the current limitations of robot actions, we decided to use mixed reality technology, which displays animations of dogs in a real space. This section describes how we prepared the emotional actions of the four-legged artifact.

2.1 Emotional Expressions of Dog Model

We created an animation of a dog utilizing combinations of neck, head, ear, and tail movements, vocalizations, and movement speed. With these combinations, six types of emotional expressions were created: a neutral expression (E1), sadness (E2), anger (E3), joy (E4), surprise (E5), and confusion (E6), as summarized in Tables 1, 2, 3, 4 and 5. These emotional expressions were chosen on the basis of prior research [22] detailing emotional expressions and actual dog movements. The emotional expressions in these dog animations were evaluated as relevant by most of the subjects in a preliminary experiment.

2.2 Creation of Animations

Using a prior study on a hearing robot [26] as a guide, we created animations with both many and few combinations of actions. For example, the first animation pattern, denoted as M1, was a combination of a small number of movements in the following order: squeal at the subject; walk away from the subject and toward the trash while sometimes turning toward the subject; walk back and forth between the trash and the trash can; and squeal at the subject in front of the trash. The second pattern, M2, combined more movements than M1, in the following order: look alternately at the trash, the trash can, and the subject in front of the trash; squeal at the subject in front of the trash; walk back and forth between the trash and the trash can; and squeal at the subject in front of the trash.

By comparing these two movement patterns, we investigated how the number of squeals and the number of combinations of squeals affected the impression conveyed and the persuasion of people. In addition, by combining the two movement patterns (M1 (few) and M2 (many)) and the six emotional expressions (neutral, joy, sadness, confusion, anger, and surprise), we created 12 different animations denoted from A1 (few/ neutral) to A12 (many/ confusion).

2.3 MR-Based Experimental Applications

We utilized HoloLens2, a Mixed Reality (MR) technology, to reproduce a pet-like artifact in the real world. Specifically, we prepared trash and trash cans in real space and displayed a dog artifact in virtual space, thereby allowing the user to see a combination of real and virtual spaces.

To facilitate the experiment using Hololens2, we developed an app for playing back animations. A hand menu was implemented as a user interface to play, change, and stop the animation. This menu was displayed when a camera recognized the user's palm. The menu could be scrolled by moving the hand with the palm facing outward, and it could be closed by moving the palm slowly away from the camera.

3 Experiment

We recruited ten university students majoring in computer science aged 20–23 for this experiment. In the real space in the experiment there is a trash and a bin, and in the virtual space an animation of a dog is shown, allowing the user to see both. Audio can be heard through Hololens2.

First, the participants were asked to sit on a chair and wear the HoloLens2. We explained how to open and close the menu, and how to operate the buttons. After explaining the experimental flow, we instructed participants to respond to a questionnaire when "Go Next" was displayed. Specifically, each participant was asked to press the play button to start the animation, and after the animation ended, they answered the questionnaire and pressed "Go Next" to move on to the next animation. Participants were asked to watch the animations and respond to the questionnaire from A1 (few/ neutral) to A12 (many/confusion). Few and many indicate the length of the animation, while neutral and confusion indicate the emotional expression. To evaluate the method of evoking behavior, the 12 specific animation combinations were as follows: A1 (few/ neutral, i.e., M1/E1), A2 (few/sadness, M1/E2), A3 (few/anger, M1/E3), A4 (few/joy, M1/E4), A5 (few/surprise, M1/E5), A6 (few/confusion, M1/E6), A7 (many/ neutral, M2/E1), A8 (many/sadness, M2/E2), A9 (many/anger, M2/E3), A10 (many/joy, M2/E4), A11 (many/surprise, M2/E5), and A12 (many/confusion, M2/E6).

The questionnaire items are as follows; *Q1: Did the dog seem sad?, Q2: Did the dog seem happy?, Q3: Did the dog seem angry?, Q4: Did the dog seem surprised?, Q5: Did the dog seem expectant?, Q6: Did the dog seem impatient?, Q7: Did the dog seem troubled?, Q8: Did you understand what the dog was trying to tell you?, Q9: Did you feel like throwing out the trash?, Q10: Did the dog's behavior make you want to throw out the trash? If the answer is "yes", please explain why., Q11: Please describe your impression of the dog's movements, your thoughts, and any other impressions you have.*

For Q1–Q7, we used a 5-point semantic differential (SD) method to ask the participants what impression they got from the dog. For Q8–Q9, we used a 5-point SD method to ask the participants whether they understood the dog's intention to ask them to throw away the trash and whether they wanted to throw away the trash. Lastly, Q10 asked the participant's reason for the answer to Q9, and Q11 asked about overall impressions.

4 Result

The results for Q1–Q9 were scored from 1 (“not applicable”) to 5 (“applicable”) and then tabulated. An alternative hypothesis that the median was greater than 3 was formulated for questions on which at least 50% of the respondents responded with 4 or higher; in such cases, a one-sample test was conducted using Wilcoxon’s signed-rank test. Questions for which all respondents answered “yes” were not tested. For A1 (few/ neutral) and A7 (many/ neutral), more than 50% of the respondents gave 4 or higher on Q5, and there was no significant difference in the scores for Q5 ($df = 9$, $p > .05$). For A2 (few/ sadness) and A8 (many/sadness), more than 50% of respondents gave 4 or higher on Q1 and Q7, and there was a significant difference in the scores for both Q1 and Q7 ($df = 9$, $p < .05$). Next, for A3 (few/ anger) and A9 (many/anger), more than 50% of respondents gave 4 or higher on Q3, and there was a significant difference in the scores for Q3 ($df = 9$, $p < .05$). For A4 (few/ joy) and A10 (many/joy), more than 50% of respondents gave 4 or higher on Q2 and Q5, and there was a significant difference between the scores for both Q2 and Q5 ($df = 9$, $p < .05$). For A5 (few/ surprise) and A11 (many/surprise), more than 50% of respondents gave 4 or higher on Q3, and there was no significant difference in the scores for Q3 ($df = 9$, $p > .05$). Finally, for A6(few/ confusion) and A12 (many/confusion), more than 50% of respondents gave 4 or higher on Q1 and Q7, and there was a significant difference in the scores for both Q1 and Q7 ($df = 9$, $p < .05$). This result indicates that A12 (many/confusion) gave the impression that the dog was “sad” or “troubled”.

In the free responses for A2, A6, A8, and A12, many participants reported that they thought the dog looked sad from the sound of its cry and its ears and tail. As for A3 and A9, many respondents reported that the dog looked angry from its. Lastly, in the free responses for A4 and A10, many respondents commented on the dog’s tail-wagging behavior.

For Q8, the percentage of respondents who gave a score of 4 or higher under all conditions was more than 50%. Significant differences were found for all conditions except A3 (few/anger), A4 (few/joy), A5 (few/surprise), and A10 (many/joy) ($df = 9$, $p < .05$). These results indicate that the dog communicated its intention to have the trash thrown away under all conditions except A3, A4, A5, and A10. We also compared the differences in behavior patterns M1 (few) and M2 (many) for each of emotions E1 through E6 using Wilcoxon’s signed-rank test and found there were no significant differences for any of the combinations ($df = 9$, $p > .05$).

Next, for Q9, the percentage of respondents who gave 4 or higher under all conditions was more than 50%. Significant differences were found for A1 (few/ neutral), A2 (few/sadness), A8 (many/sadness), A11 (many/surprise), and A12 (many/confusion) ($df = 9$, $p < .05$). A6 (few/confusion) was not tested because all the respondents answered “yes” on this question. The results thus demonstrate that animations A1, A2, A6, A8, A11, and A12 increased the participants’ desire to throw the trash away. For Q9, we again compared the differences in behavior patterns M1 and M2 for E1 through E6 using Wilcoxon’s signed-rank test and found significant differences for combinations A4 (few/joy) and A10 (many/joy) ($df = 9$, $p > .05$). We also found that the scores were higher for A10 than for A4. No significant differences were found for any of the other combinations ($df = 9$, $p > .05$).

As for the free responses, we analyzed the reasons for giving a score of 4 or 5 on Q9 in the cases of A1 (few/ neutral), A2 (few/sadness), A6 (few/sadness), A8 (many/sadness), A11 (many/surprise), and A12 (many/confusion), for which significant differences were found. For A1 and A11, the reasons were that the dog seemed concerned about the trash because of its back-and-forth movement between the trash and the trash can and because of its gaze. On the other hand, for A3 (few/anger), A4 (few/joy), A5 (few/surprise), A7 (many/ neutral), A9 (many/angry), and A10 (many/joy), no significant differences were found. In these cases, the reasons for giving a score of 1 to 3 on Q9 were not significantly different between A3 and A9. For A4 and A10, the reasons were that the dog looked like it wanted to be played with and did not look like it wanted the participant to throw away the garbage. Lastly, for A7, the reason was that the dog's behavior did not look like a request to throw away the trash.

5 Discussion

The emotional expressions of E2 (sadness, for A2 and A8) and E6 (puzzlement, for A6 and A12) gave the impression that the dog was "sad" and "troubled", respectively. In the free responses for these cases, many respondents indicated that the dog looked sad from the sound of its cry and from its ears and tail, and there was not much difference between the E2 (sadness) and E6 (puzzlement). Hence, we conclude that the degree of head tilt and the speed of head movement had little influence on the participants' impressions. In addition, some respondents indicated that the dog looked weak, suggesting that the emotional expression of E3 (anger) indeed gave the impression that the dog "looked angry". Many respondents also stated that they were afraid of the dog, suggesting that the sound of its squeal had a significant influence on their impression of the dog being "angry". In the free responses for A4 (few/joy) and A10 (many/joy), there were many comments about the tail wagging, suggesting that it had a large influence on the impression of the dog seeming "pleased" and "expectant". In addition, many respondents said that the tail wagging was cute.

The only combinations for which the results differed depending on the difference in movement patterns were A1 (few/ neutral) and A7 (many/ neutral). One reason for the differing results was that the animations were presented in a fixed order. In addition, A5 (few/surprise) and A11 (many/surprise) did not give the impression that the dog was in fact "surprised". In this study, we attempted to express the dog's emotions by means of six combinations of neck, head, ear, and tail movements, vocalizations, and movement speed, but to express surprise, it would be necessary to add movements such as a "quick retreat" and "tilting the ears inward in the middle of a movement", as well as changes in the ears and tail during movement.

The experimental results showed that the evaluation of intentionality transfer differed depending on the emotional expression. In the free responses for A4 (few/joy) and A10 (many/joy), for which no significant differences were found, many respondents said that the dog looked like it wanted to be played with. This suggests that the emotional expression of E4 (joy), which gave the impression that the dog "seemed to be pleased", is not appropriate in a situation where the intention is to ask the user to throw away trash, as it conveys a false intention. In addition, there was no significant difference between

M1 (few) and M2 (many) in any of the combinations. The differences between A3 (few/anger) and A9 (many/anger), and between A4 (few/joy) and A11 (many/surprise), were presumably due to the small sample size.

As for persuasion, the experimental results showed that A1 (few/ neutral), A2 (few/sadness), A6 (few/confusion), A8 (many/sadness), A11 (many/surprise), and A12 (many/confusion) increased the participants' motivation to throw away the trash. This was because the dog seemed concerned about the trash on account of its movements (such as gazing back and forth between the trash and the trashcan) for A1 and A11. As for A2, A6, A8, and A12, the reasons were that the dog seemed to be in trouble and that the dog looked sad. This suggests that the emotional expressions of E2 (sadness) and E6 (puzzlement) may have given impressions of "sadness" and "troubled" for the dog, which increased the participants' motivation to throw away the trash. Therefore, animations A2, A6, A8, and A12, which gave the impressions of "sad" and "troubled", can be considered suitable as persuasion techniques to elicit help from the user and to encourage action, as in the case of a weak robot [21].

On the other hand, A3 (few/anger), A4 (few/joy), A5 (few/surprise), A7 (many/ neutral), A9 (many/anger), and A10 (many/joy) were found to be less effective in motivating the user to throw away the trash. Regarding the reason, the free responses for A3 and A9 indicated that the participants did not want to approach an angry animal, thus suggesting that the emotional expression of E3 (anger) made the dog seem more ferocious. Therefore, we conclude that this emotional expression enhances the impressions of "fear" and "not wanting to approach" for those who have a fear or dislike of dogs, making it more difficult to motivate them to throw away the trash. On the other hand, if the intention was not to get people to throw away trash but rather to keep away from the animal or to warn that the animal was dangerous, a higher persuasive effect would be expected. This suggests that the emotional expression of E4 (joy) may have conveyed the wrong intention that the dog wanted to play. Alternatively, if the intention was not to throw away trash but to play along, the correct intention would be conveyed, and a higher persuasive effect could thus be expected. As for A5 (few/surprise) and A7 (many/ neutral), the results presumably stemmed from the fact that the dog did not seem to want or expect the garbage to be thrown away. This suggests that conveying the correct intention through behavior is important in persuasion using pet-like robots.

Finally, regarding the comparison between M1 (few) and M2 (many), the scores for A10 (many/joy) were higher than those for A4 (few/joy). However, there were no significant differences among the other combinations, which may have been due to the high evaluation of persuasion from the beginning. That is, the low scores for A4 may have led to the high scores for A10. It is therefore conceivable that a combination of actions may increase the evaluation of persuasion for other emotional expressions, as well.

6 Conclusion

This study investigated the behaviors and emotional expressions of a four-legged pet-like artifact to persuade people. Since currently available pet-like robots do not allow for rich expressions, participants were asked to wear Hololens2 and were tested using actual trash and trash cans in a mixed reality space. The experimental results showed that emotional expressions such as "sadness" and "confusion" were effective when participants were prompted to throw away the trash using artificial objects such as pets. On the other hand, emotional expressions such as "joy" and "anger" were not effective. In addition, there was little difference in ratings based on whether the combination of actions was long or short.

References

1. Fogg, B.J.: Persuasive Technology: Using Computers to Change What We Thinly and Do. Morgan Kaufmann (2002). https://doi.org/10.1145/764008.763957
2. Fujita, M.: AIBO: Towards the era of digital creatures. In: Hollerbach, J.M., Koditschek, D.E. (eds.) Robotics Research. Springer, London (2000). https://doi.org/10.1007/978-1-4471-0765-1_38
3. Tamura, T., et al.: Is an entertainment robot useful in the care of elderlypeople with severe dementia? J. Gerontology Ser. Biol. Sci. Med. Sci. **59**(1), M83–M85 (2004)
4. Collins, E.C., Prescott, T.J., Mitchinson, B.: Saying it with light: a pilot study of affective communication using the MIRO robot. In: Wilson, S.P., Verschure, P.F.M.J. (ed.) Biomimetic and Biohybrid Systems: 4th International Conference, Living Machines 2015, pp. 243–255. Springer International Publishing, Cham (2015). https://doi.org/10.1007/978-3-319-22979-9_25
5. Inoue, K., Wada, K., Shibata, T.: Exploring the applicability of the robotic seal PARO to support caring for older persons with dementia within the home context. Palliat Care Soc Pract. **14**(15), 26323524211030284 (2021). https://doi.org/10.1177/26323524211030285, PMID:34350398;PMCID:PMC8287345
6. Rashid, N.L.A., Leow, Y., Klainin-Yobas, P., Itoh, S., Wu, V.X.: The effectiveness of a therapeutic robot, 'Paro', on behavioural and psychological symptoms, medication use, total sleep time and sociability in older adults with dementia: a systematic review and meta-analysis. Int. J. Nurs. Stud.Nurs. Stud. **145**, 104530 (2023). https://doi.org/10.1016/j.ijnurstu.2023.104530. (2023 19 May), PMID: 37348392
7. Fujita, Y.: Development of prototype personal robot "PaPeRo." NEC Res. Developm. **43**, 41–44 (2002)
8. Tan, C.K.K., Lou, V.W.Q., Cheng, C.Y.M., He, P.C., Mor, Y.Y.: Technology acceptance of a social robot (lovot) among single older adults in hong kong and singapore: protocol for a multimethod study. JMIR Res, Protoc. **17**(12), e48618 (2023). https://doi.org/10.2196/48618, PMID:37590084;PMCID:PMC10472167
9. Stiehl, W.D., Lieberman, J., Breazeal, C., Basel, L., Lalla, L., Wolf, M.: De-sign of a therapeutic robotic companion for relational, affective touch. In: IEEE International Workshop on Robot and Human Interactive Communication, ROMAN 2005, pp. 408–415. IEEE (2005)
10. Kruger, K.A., Serpell, J.A.: 3 - Animal-assisted interventions in mental health: definitions and theoretical foundations. In: Fine, A.H (ed.) Handbook on Animal-Assisted Therapy, 3rd edn., pp. 33–48. Academic Press (2010). https://doi.org/10.1016/B978-0-12-381453-1.10003-0, ISBN 9780123814531,
11. Fine, A.H.: Handbook on animal-assisted therapy. Theoretical foundations and guidelines for practice. Elsevier, Amsterdam (2010)
12. Kerepesi, A., Kubinyi, E., Jonsson, G.K., Magnusson, M.S., Miklósi, A.: Behavioural comparison of human-animal (dog) and human-robot (AIBO) interactions. Behav. Processes. **73**(1), 92–99 (2006). https://doi.org/10.1016/j.beproc.2006.04.001. (6 Apr 2006), PMID: 16678360

13. Morris, M.W., Kelner, D.: How emotions work: An analysis of the social functions of emotional expression in negotiations. Res. Organiz. Behav. **22**, 1–50 (2000). https://doi.org/10.1016/S0191-3085(00)22002-9
14. Sinaceur, M., Tiedens, L.Z.: . Get mad and get more than even: When and why anger expression is effective in negotiations. J. Experim. Soc. Psychol. **42**(3), 314–322 (2006). https://doi.org/10.1016/j.jesp.2005.05.002
15. Sumi, K., Nagata, M.: Evaluating a Virtual agent as persuasive technology. In: Csapó, J., Magyar, A. (eds.) Psychology of Persuasion. Nova Science Publishers (2010)
16. Poggi, I., Niewiadomski, R., Pelachaud, C.: Facial deception in humans and ECAs. In: Wachsmuth, I., Knoblich, G. (ed.) Modeling Communication with Robots and Virtual Humans, pp. 198–221. Springer, Heidelberg (2008). https://doi.org/10.1007/978-3-540-79037-2_11
17. Poggi, I., Pelachaud, C.: Persuasion and the expressivity of gestures in humans and machines. In: Wachsmuth, I., Lenzen, M., Knoblich, G. (eds.) Embodied Communication in Humans and Machines. Oxford Academic, Oxford (2008) (22 Mar. 2012), https://doi.org/10.1093/acprof:oso/9780199231751.003.0017, (Accessed 17 June 2023)
18. Pelachaud, C.: Modelling multimodal expression of emotion in a virtual agent. Philos. Trans. R. Soc. Lond. B Biol. Sci. **364**(1535), 3539–3548 (2009). https://doi.org/10.1098/rstb.2009.0186, PMID:19884148;PMCID:PMC2781894
19. Martin, J., Niewiadomski, R., Devillers, L., Buisine, S., Pelachaud, C.: Multimodal complex emotions: gesture expressivity and blended facial expressions. Int. J. Humanoid Robotics **3**, 269–291 (2006)
20. Pelachaud, C.: Studies on gesture expressivity for a virtual agent. Speech Commun. **51**(7) 2009, 630–639. https://doi.org/10.1016/j.specom.2008.04.009, ISSN 0167–6393
21. Yamaji, Y., Miyake, T., Yoshiike, Y., De Silva, P.R.S., Okada, M.: STB: child-dependent sociable trash box. Int. J. Soc. Robot. **3**(4), 359–370 (2011). https://doi.org/10.1007/s12369-011-0114-y
22. Emert, P.B.: Hearing-ear Dogs. Crestwood House Publishing, NY (1985)
23. Lakatos, G., Gácsi, M., Topál, J., Miklósi, A.: Comprehension and utilisation of pointing gestures and gazing in dog-human communication in relatively complex situations. Anim. Cogn. **15**(2), 201–213 (2012). https://doi.org/10.1007/s10071-011-0446-x
24. Miklósi, A., Polgárdi, R., Topál, J., Csányi, V.: 2002 Intentional behaviour in dog-human communication: an experimental analysis of"showing" behaviour in the dog. Anim. Cogn. **3**, 159–166 (2000). https://doi.org/10.1007/s100710000072
25. Mowry, R.L., Carnahan, S., Watson, D.: A National Study on the Training, Selection and Placement of Hearing Dogs. Little Rock, AR. University of Arkansas Rehabilitation Research and Training Center for Persons Who are Hard of Hearing (1994)
26. Koay, K.L., et al.: Hey! there is someone at your door. a hearing robot using visual communication signals of hearing dogs to communicate intent. In: Proceedings of the 2013 IEEE Symposium on Artificial Life, pp. 90–97 (2013). https://doi.org/10.1109/ALIFE.2013.6602436

An Embodied Conversational Agent to Support Wellbeing After Injury: Insights from a Stakeholder Inclusive Design Approach

Katherine Hopman[1](✉), Deborah Richards[1], and Melissa N. Norberg[2]

[1] School of Computing, Macquarie University, 4 Research Park Drive, Sydney, NSW 2109, Australia

katherine.hopman@hdr.mq.edu.au, deborah.richards@mq.edu.au

[2] Centre for Emotional Health, Australian Hearing Hub, Level 1, Macquarie University, 16 University Avenue, Sydney, NSW 2109, Australia

melissa.norberg@mq.edu.au

Abstract. Embodied conversational agents (ECAs) are increasingly being included in digital health and wellbeing programs. Whilst initial evaluations of ECAs in this field have been promising, there has been a lack of detail as to how stakeholders and end users have been included in the design process. Stakeholder inclusion has been acknowledged as essential to ensure that ECAs meet expectations, maximize engagement and facilitate behavior change. This study describes an iterative coproduction process used to develop an emotion regulation intervention conversational agent (ERICA) to support people following injury. The coproduction process followed an accelerated creation approach with 13 qualitative interviews being conducted with people who had a lived experience of recovering from injury/adversity. Interviews were completed with the goal to understand barriers and facilitators to engagement, user experience and to identify opportunities for program improvement. Four broad themes emerged from the data: visual look, voice, content and experience. A key finding from this study was a high level of stakeholder apprehension of generative AI and the need for ECA designers to make explicit the specific technology and functions being used within programs. Findings highlight the value of timely stakeholder inclusion in digital intervention design, particularly when knowledge and expectations of generative technology is rapidly changing.

Keywords: Embodied Conversational Agents · Stakeholder Inclusive Design

1 Introduction

Despite many people making a good recovery after injury, a small but significant group experience long-term psychological distress and disability [1, 2]. Studies examining health outcomes following traumatic injury, indicate that somewhere between 20–60% of injured people experience poor psychological outcomes [2, 3] with the vast majority never seeking psychological treatment [2]. This has led to authors suggesting a need to prioritise the development of early, psychological interventions for this cohort [4].

N. Baghaei et al. (Eds.): PERSUASIVE 2024, LNCS 14636, pp. 161–175, 2024.
https://doi.org/10.1007/978-3-031-58226-4_13

Access and motivation to engage with mental health services and treatment are however well-recognised issues in many countries [5]. Digital technology has been widely promoted as offering potential opportunity to tackle these issues with its particular advantages addressing both structural (location and availability of services) and attitudinal (perceived stigma in accessing psychological services) barriers [6, 7]. Consequently, there has been a significant increase in the development of digital enabled interventions in the mental health and wellbeing domain.

In particular, there has been a growing interest in the design and evaluation of digitally enabled interventions that promote adaptive emotion regulation [8]. Whilst the preliminary evidence for the efficacy of these interventions is promising, they do not appear to be immune to the challenges of engagement and adherence faced by many digital mental health programs [9]. This is a significant issue that needs to be resolved if such programs are to facilitate positive behaviour change.

A possible solution to these challenges is embodied conversational agents (ECAs). ECAs are software-based dialogue systems with a visual representation or embodiment. They are designed to simulate conversational-like behavior with a human to provide support with particular tasks [10] and have been deployed successfully in a wide variety of health and health coaching domains [11]. As support for ECAs has grown, so too has the knowledge that there are still significant gaps in our understanding as to key design features [11] and how these contribute to user experience, engagement [10] and behavior change [12]. In addition, many chatbots and ECAs are discontinued due to their inability to meet user expectations [12]. Thus, there is a need for dedicated research examining the user experience and users' perception of quality of conversational agents [10] as well as a greater adoption of coproduction methods to facilitate end user collaboration in ECA design [13].

In response to the above, the research team has developed an ECA to deliver an emotion regulation intervention following injury via the Emotion Regulation Intervention Conversational Agent (ERICA). Development of the ERICA program followed an accelerated creation approach similar to that proposed by Mohr and colleagues [14], whereby an interdisciplinary team, including stakeholders responsible for implementing the program, developed an initial prototype based on literature review, expert knowledge and system/service knowledge. A detailed description of the initial ERICA prototype is provided elsewhere [15]. This study describes the second cycle of creation within the accelerated creation approach which encompassed iterative testing with people who had a lived experience of injury recovery.

2 Background and Related Work

Research demonstrates that humans have strong social reactions to ECAs [12] and are willing to disclose more to ECAs [16], regardless of their health literacy levels [17]. Further, ECAs can establish a therapeutic alliance with users [18], which is a robust mechanism of change in psychotherapy interventions [19]. Noting these key attributes there has been a steady growth of ECA studies in healthcare [12]. A systematic review conducted in 2018, identified 33 studies using ECAs across areas including, but not limited to, physical activity, mental health, substance use and nutrition [11]. With the first study deploying an ECA to promote emotion regulation being described in 2018 [20].

Emotion regulation has been identified as playing a critical role in health and illness [21] and is believed to be a central mechanism underpinning a person's ability to adapt to challenging life events [22]. A recent literature review and meta-analysis [23] assessed 48 health and wellbeing apps and noted six specifically targeted emotion regulation. On average, these six apps were moderately better at improving emotion regulation than control conditions ($g = 0.49$, 95%CI 0.23–0.74) suggesting digital technologies may offer an effective approach to promote emotion regulation and ultimately reduce psychological distress in vulnerable populations [24].

Despite growing evidence for the clinical efficacy of ECAs in the health and well-being domains, end users have generally had limited to no involvement in the design of their delivery (such as modality, visual appearance, format, frequency, etc.) or content [25]. Recent analysis of ECA use has identified that many are discontinued due to their inability to meet user expectations and to develop positive ongoing user experiences [12], potentially due to using a top-down approach, involving experts specifying interventions and having limited end user input in the design process [14]. Although in its infancy, current evidence suggests collaboration with service users may predict subsequent engagement with digital interventions [13].

Codesign with end users is recognised as invaluable for optimising products and services [26]. Codesign within the rapidly changing digital health space however can be challenging. Challenges include balancing the time and resources to locate and develop collaborative relationships with end users with the need to develop products efficiently. An approach that addresses this issue is the Accelerated Creation to Sustainment (ACTS) Model [14]. This model recognises that success in creating an effective, implementable, and sustainable technology enabled health services or intervention must take place in the settings where they are expected to be deployed. The model begins with stakeholder collaboration to design a minimally viable product and then moves into a comprehensive trial and evaluation phase which allows for continuous improvement.

In this paper we describe the create phase of a codesign approach to develop an intervention to empower people to self-manage emotional distress following injury. Through in-depth qualitative interviews we aimed to explore end user's experiences of engaging with a conversational agent and their perception of key design features.

Research Question: What design factors affect engagement with the ERICA program amongst people who have the lived experience of recovering from injury or an adverse event?

3 Methods

3.1 Study Design

A qualitative design, using semi-structured interviews following use of ERICA, was used to gain a deeper understanding of the target users' experience of engaging with ERICA and to collect recommendations for program enhancement. Aligning with the ACTS model, an iterative methodology was used to allow for suggested design changes to be added to the program for further testing within the study timeframe. This allowed for continuous improvement and evaluation [14]. The 30-min study was approved by Macquarie University Human Research Ethics Committee (Reference Number: 520231195346852). The study did not evaluate usability of the program as this had previously been established [15].

3.2 Recruitment and Procedure

Study participants were recruited from a community of insurance customers who had expressed an interest in testing of products and services. Members of the community were eligible to participate if they had finalised a personal injury or significant home claim within the last 5 years.

Following consent, study participants were randomly assigned to interact with ERICA via one of three different emotion regulation skill conversations. All interviews were conducted from April 2023 to July 2023 on Zoom by Author1, an occupational therapist with over 20 years' experience. The questions asked during the interview are presented with the results. Participants received a $50 gift card following participation.

3.3 Materials

The ERICA prototype was developed through an interdisciplinary collaboration of stakeholders including experts in computer science, clinical psychology and the insurance industry. A summary of key program features is provided below. See [15] to find out more about the initial design of our agent characteristics, user interaction and agent dialogue with an overview of the three dialogues and example dialogue. Sample dialogue of ERICA after our updates can be found at https://web.science.mq.edu.au/~richards/ERICAdemo.

Visual Design

Guided by evidence that a female physician resulted in users being quicker to talk and to converse with more emotional statements [27], the virtual agent ERICA is a female character created in Adobe Fuse and implemented in the Unity 3D Game Engine. Nonverbal behaviours are limited to blinking, smiling and minor head movement using the online service mixamo.com and utilises the SALSA lip-synching plugin using an ECA dialogue generator developed by our lab. An Action Interpreter and Dialogue Generator process dialogue files. An iterative process between the primary researchers, was used to develop a backdrop representing an informal healthcare consulting environment.

Communication Methods

ERICA interacts with participants using both voice (text to speech) and text on screen. The agent does not use natural language processing or generative AI and participants interact with ERICA via a decision tree system of constrained pre-set options. This simple design approach was selected for two key reasons. Firstly, the research team's goal was to develop a "minimally viable product" to allow for rapid deployment to trial stage [14]. Secondly the highly regulated nature of the insurance industry necessitated an approach that ensured end users (claimants) did not receive incorrect or invalid ECA responses that could arise from natural language processing errors [28].

Dialogue Content

ERICA's dialogues were constructed with a specific focus of providing psychoeducation to a population at risk of developing mental health symptoms, but not currently experiencing a disorder. The interactive dialogues were scripted with a focus on increasing a person's understanding of the negative health impacts that can arise from experiencing strong and enduring negative emotions. They also aimed to facilitate users to self-reflect on the way they currently manage emotions with a goal of increasing participants' self-awareness of mood states.

Three separate dialogues were designed to promote three adaptive cognitive emotion regulation strategies; Positive refocusing, Reappraisal and Putting it into Perspective. Each dialogue focussed on promoting self-management and self-efficacy by providing users with knowledge, and practice examples to build confidence in their ability to implement the three adaptive strategies.

3.4 Data Analysis

All interviews were digitally recorded and transcribed verbatim by the first author. A conventional content analysis approach, similar to that described by [29] was adopted. Conventional content analysis involves a systematic process of coding and identifying themes or patterns. In this approach researchers avoid using preconceived categories and instead allow categories to flow from the data. This has also been described as inductive category development [30].

Thematic analysis of the data was conducted independently by Author1 and Author2. Data was read word for word to derive codes and a process of constant comparison was used to generate and refine categories and sub categories. Cohen's Kappa for inter-rater reliability was conducted after all transcripts had been independently coded. The codes that did not coincide at follow-up were discussed and reorganized until consensus was reached on all themes.

4 Results

4.1 Sample/Study Participants

Thirteen participants were interviewed in this study. 54% of the sample was male and participants were recruited from every state in Australia except Tasmania and the Northern Territory. 9 of the participants had personal injury claims and 4 had significant home claims. Just over half the sample were aged 50 years or older with ages ranging from the category of 20–29 through to 70 +.

4.2 Quantitative Ratings

Table 1 shows results for the Session Rating Scale [31]. The scale rates the four components of therapeutic alliance on a sliding scale from 0 through to 10. Figure 1 provides participants ratings of ERICA's function and design goals using a five-point Likert scale from Strongly Disagree through to Strongly Agree.

Table 1. Session Rating Scale (sliding scale 0–10)

Subscale	9–10	5–8	0–5
Relationship- I did not / did feel heard, understood or respected	3	7	3*
Goals – We did/did not work on or talk about what I wanted work on or talk about	4	6	3
Approach – The therapist's approach was/ was not a good fit for me	4	6	3
Overall- There was something was missing /session was right for me	2	6	4

* The same three people scored ERICA between 0–5 for all subscales

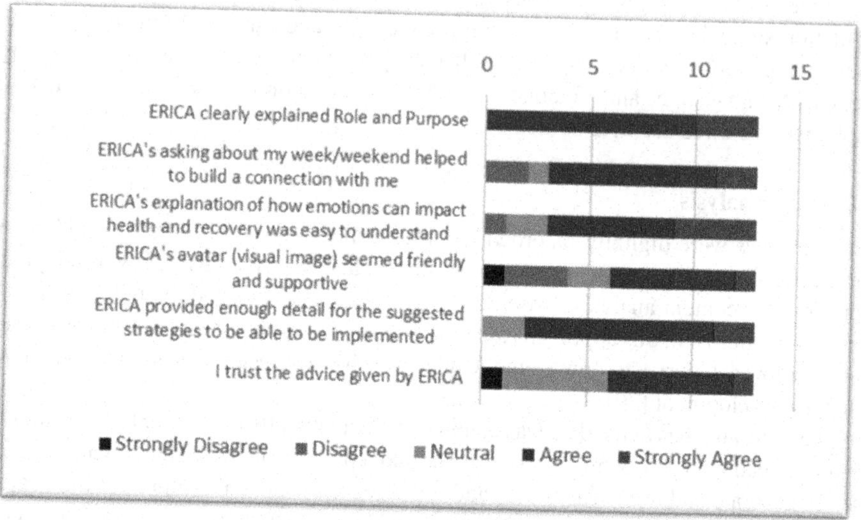

Fig. 1. ERICA component ratings

4.3 Qualitative Themes and Subthemes

Themes that emerged from the qualitative data were grouped into four domains: Visual design, Voice, Content and Experience. Tables 2, 3 and 4 present the sub themes within each domain for subthemes with frequency 2 or above with an illustrative quote. In each table, subthemes are grouped according to whether they resulted in a negative, positive or neutral effect on participant engagement. Cohen's kappa for each theme were 95.6%, 100%, 87.2% and 93.2% respectively, indicating a high inter-rater reliability.

Visual Design

18 of the 29 coded interview excerpts relating to visual design were negative with just under 50% of the study participants reporting that they disliked ERICA's animation and lip synchronization and 3/13 found the avatar too robotic. Two participants discussed the background (setting), with one indicating that they liked the setting and one indicating that the setting was a "bit bland". One person identified that they felt the Helpline resources should be more visible.

Table 2. Theme: Visual Design

Sub Theme	Freq	Verbatim
Disliked Animation	6	I am not sure if you can improve on the facial features or the animation to make it more realistic. I would just glance at her moving her eyes and lips and head and that movement seemed disjointed
Too Robotic	3	Need to feel like I am speaking and interacting more with a human, still felt like a robot. I think there's more need to make her look facially more real
Poor Lip Synching	6	Her mouth moved funny though so I couldn't stop staring at her funny face. It was like watching those movies when the mouth comes out different to the words
Liked avatar	4	ERICA seemed nice
Preference for a female avatar	5	I think having the feminine touch is important, you can actually open up easier if you are speaking to a female
Option to choose avatar gender	2	I think letting people choose gender of the avatar

Voice

Three participants identified that they found that ERICA's voice was a barrier to engagement with the program. All three felt that the voice was too robotic:

"More human voice and modulation, you know I actually found myself tuning out. In the last couple of screens, I actually put my volume off, and we just moved to next page. I would read it again. The voice just got to me".

One also identified that the speaking pace was too slow:

"Found I was reading the text rather than listening to ERICA's voice, thereby having to wait for ages for each page to move to the next one".

Content

Just over half of the participants (7/13) identified that they found the ERICA program helpful and/or useful and 4/13 participants reported the content being interesting. In contrast 3/13 expressed apprehension of the program content and 6/13 were apprehensive of interacting with AI. There was an even split with regards to whether participants perceived that there was enough "small talk" to build a connection. One comment expressed the need for a greater focus on the user's current state, with other single comments including, "oversimplified", "recovery can be a lifelong process" and a "need for screening".

Table 3. Theme content

Sub Theme	Freq	Verbatim
Negative	21	
Apprehension of AI	6	It wouldn't entice me personally because I am like anti AI. I think it's gone too far
Apprehension of content	3	If I knew it was programmed by a trusted organisation or a trusted entity that is qualified to provide assistance, in these sorts of spaces, then you have more trust as a result
Need for script refinement	4	there are points where it's kind of a little bit judgy/ you really want to be doing is empowering people and sometimes she presents it as 'Well now you know what thought challenging is your all good"
Not tailored	2	How does she tailor it to me and my situation? I like the interaction but I want it tailored to my specific thing. One size isn't going to fit everybody
More small talk	2	If you want to improve on the small talk it would make it a bit more realistic and a bit more engaging
Responses inadequate	2	There were times when none of the responses suited me/ There were times that she asked a question, and I input an answer and then that answer wasn't used in the next question
More content	2	So instead of just doing CBT… I'd encourage you to look at cognitive processing therapy and trauma based therapies, so that the thought challenging tool isn't the only tool your giving people
Positive	24	
Useful/ Helpful	7	I think it was helpful, I've been on workers comp since the end of last year
Interesting	4	It was interesting to hear what she had to say
Good amount of small talk	3	Question about you week or weekend was a good icebreaker and well balanced
Good flow	2	I mean they, the answers that were given are pretty good because the way it's been structured it flows, there is definitely continuity there
Liked examples	2	That's good that she walks through an example with you. I like the fact that she would go through the strategies with you and talk through, that's' very good instead of just here it is

(*continued*)

Table 3. (*continued*)

Sub Theme	Freq	Verbatim
Relatable	2	You can identify with it/ It connected with the way of thinking, so you may have felt something and reading that you thought Oh Yes you know that makes sense
Trust Content	2	Surprisingly, yes, I trust the advice given by ERICA/I thought she was very trustworthy
Appropriate responses	2	When I answered the questions, I felt that I was understood, she captured everything correctly with the drop down boxes

Experience
21 of the 32 coded interview excerpts in the domain of experience were positive (Table 4 first 6 rows, bottom 4 row are negative) with the most frequent themes being that the ERICA program was accessible, engaging and innovative. Participants who commented on whether they felt supported by the program were evenly split with 2 feeling the program did feel supportive while 2 did not feel the program was supportive. 3 people expressed that they would prefer to interact with a human and 2 people expressed feeling some apprehension about the potential for their health information to be disclosed to an insurer. Two comments called the experience weird or sterile.

4.4 Suggested Program Enhancements

A range of suggestions were made by participants to enhance the ERICA program. Those that were feasible to be implemented quickly were actioned halfway through testing. Seven participants tested the following program changes (See Fig. 2):

- Adding a Help and Resources button on the screen which linked to information regarding Helplines (contact numbers and availability).
- Addition of a Menu on screen which enables navigation and return to conversations and topics. As each topic was completed the Menu was ticked.
- Addition of a pop up "tool tip" which alerts users to click on text boxes to move ahead (if waiting for ERICA to finish speaking).

Additional suggestions that require further consideration/resources or were unable to be added within the study timeframe are listed below:

- Addition of video content and/or peer interaction
- Provision of a downloadable summary of discussed cognitive strategies
- Conversion of the web-based program into an app
- Use of a video of real person rather than the digital avatar image
- Provide the option for a user to tailor the gender of the avatar
- Inclusion of additional activities to promote positive mental health e.g. discussing the importance of physical exercise
- Greater emphasis that a clinical psychologist helped to design the program

Table 4. Theme experience

Theme	Freq	Verbatim
Enjoyable	5	I was pleasantly surprised by the time I got to the end of it
Innovative	4	New and fresh I think. I've never come across a sort of bot experience like that before
Accessible	6	Yeah, its spontaneous, as in you could have it whenever you want. Otherwise you'd have to make an appointment and I mean a month from now
Good way to Learn	2	I still felt like it was a good way to learn, like it's taking the information and its turning it into like a sort of conversation and I think that's really helpful
Self help	2	Some people don't know that they need help, this is more of a self-help journey
Supported	2	It's nice to know that someone cares a little bit. Send it out reasonably soon after an incident so that you can feel cared for
Not Supported	2	Supportive, I don't think it was. It still felt like I was talking to a robot. I don't know how to get around that supporting factor
Prefer to talk to a human	3	I prefer to have a social interaction, face to face/You can't replace a human being
Not enough interaction	2	I must admit I lost interest after about 5 min, there was no interaction…you weren't asking questions back
Health data privacy	2	There is always that concern about how does disclosure of health-related things to an insurer impact upon your claim

4.5 Program Deployment

ERICA has been designed with three different dialogues. During the interview, participants were asked to suggest their preferred method for completion. The majority identified that they felt it would be too much to complete all three at once. A range of different deployment methods were suggested with five participants indicating preference for a staggered approach, where a link to a new dialogue was sent out over a specified timeframe. Suggested timeframes ranged from twice a week to once a week to once a fortnight with one participant suggesting that it would be good to be able to nominate which date you would like to receive the next dialogue. Three participants identified a preference to have all the dialogues available at program commencement and to receive reminders within a few days to complete outstanding dialogues.

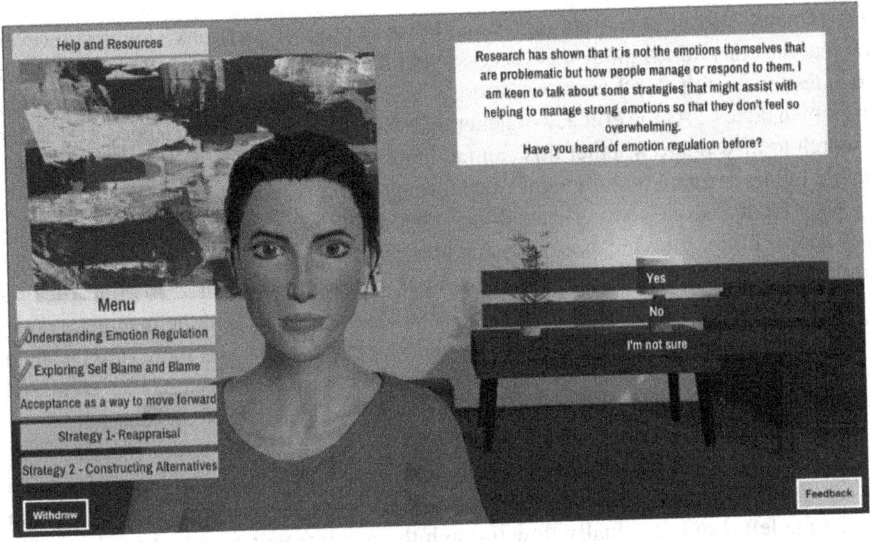

Fig. 2. ERICA prototype enhancements

5 Discussion

This study documents the iterative trial phase of an ECA delivered emotion regulation intervention. Qualitative interviews were completed with 13 people with a lived experience of recovering from an injury/adversity and identified four key themes impacting the user's perception of and engagement with the ECA. Firstly, results relating to visual design indicated that many participants perceived the simple animation and limited lip synchronization as a significant barrier to engagement. Two participants indicated that they expected better graphics and one questioned whether a static image might provide a better experience. The ability to create precise lip synchronization in agent design has been recognized as challenging [32] and our findings indicate further work is needed to understand optimal configuration for engagement. The research group has recently commenced a study comparing behavioural outcomes for a static (i.e. no lip synching) versus animated ECA delivering psychoeducation.

In contrast to visual design, data collected on the psychoeducational content was evenly balanced, with just over half the study participants identifying that they found the program content useful or helpful. Interestingly, 6/13 participants expressed apprehension of engaging with AI. Although no generative AI or NLP was included in the ERICA prototype, participants expressed a general mistrust of AI being used to generate responses, with one participant also expressing concern about whether the program was collecting their biometric data. Mistrust and misunderstanding of AI in healthcare is an issue increasingly being discussed and highlights the need for designers to provide visibility and transparency of AI functions within programs [33].

Participants also identified opportunities to refine the program content, with one person suggesting specific phrases requiring re-scripting to reduce the perception of the agent being "judgy" and another highlighting terminology that was not user friendly e.g. "catastrophizing". The constrained user input, was identified by some as a barrier to engagement with one person stating "I couldn't ask the agent questions". Others however felt that the constrained input was successful with one person stating "When I answered the questions, I felt that I was understood, she captured everything correctly with the dropdown boxes". As the efficacy of generative AI grows, there will be a need for further research to investigate whether this can facilitate greater engagement in a safe way and enable ECA's to adapt to individual users during an interaction [12].

User feedback in the experience domain had the most positive comments including easy accessibility, enjoyment, novelty and innovative approach. One person specifically acknowledged they enjoyed the conversational approach to learning. In contrast, two participants were concerned about the potential sharing of data with an insurance company. Data transparency in technology is an evolving concept and increasingly being acknowledged by technology users. Our findings confirm that users expect clear and upfront acknowledgement of how their data is being collected, used and shared.

Use of the ACTS model enabled testing of some suggested program changes in an efficient way. For example, we were able to assess the impact of the addition of a menu function with one participant reporting "I remember I watched my progress on the menu bar on the left. I didn't actually flow through the menu from top to bottom. I actually ended up, I think I skipped one or two sections… but I'm glad that I never got to miss it, because I then went back". Adopting such an approach enables quality assurance during the design phase with a goal of creating more effective resources [26].

Lastly, results from the Session Rating Scale indicate people with a lived experience of recovery had similar levels of satisfaction with the ERICA program to those involved in preliminary prototype/piloting of program (see [15]). In this study just over 30% rated the program approach as 9 or 10 out of 10 while just over 27% in the pilot study scored ERICA in the same range. This is interesting as both cohorts had a significantly different median ages with the pilot being 21.7 years and this study having an average age over 50. It is also noted that both studies had participants who expressed a strong level of discomfort engaging with an ECA and preference for human interaction. This aligns with results from previous work [7] which indicated that a virtual agent might not be a suitable addition for everybody.

5.1 Limitations

This study used an ACTS approach for codesign of the ERICA intervention. Whilst this approach has advantages related to time efficiency, it does not include engagement with end users at design inception. Many authors suggest that this is an essential component of codesign and critical to ensuring user engagement in the real world [13, 33]. Comprehensive codesign approaches are however resource intensive and may be more achievable in health service design, where more resourcing and longer timeframes can be planned and budgeted. Also, it is difficult for users to envisage and provide feedback on technology without any prototype to refer to.

6 Conclusion and Future Work

Inclusion of end users in the design of ERICA has enabled development of deeper understating of design factors that impact users' perceptions of ECAs. Currently there appears to be a high level of apprehension and misunderstanding about AI which is acting as a barrier to ECA engagement. In addition, users have high expectations for the fidelity of ECA animation and lip synchronization. It will be important to monitor and address this in technology enabled services and interventions going forward. We are currently further reviewing the outstanding recommendations and the results from an additional study conducted to evaluate user engagement and satisfaction with two different versions of ERICA, with and without lip syncing.

Acknowledgments. Thanks to Meredith Porte for technical assistance and to all participants involved in the study.

Funding. This project is supported by Digital Health CRC Limited ("DHCRC"). DHCRC is funded under the Australian Commonwealth's Cooperative Research Centres (CRC) Program.

References

1. Collie, A., Simpson, P.M., Cameron, P.A., et al.: Patterns and predictors of return to work after major trauma: a prospective, population-based registry study. Annals Surgery **269**(5), 972–978 (2019)
2. Kenardy, J., Edmed, S.L., Shourie, S., et al.: Changing patterns in the prevalence of post-traumatic stress disorder, major depressive episode and generalized anxiety disorder over 24 months following a road traffic crash: results from the UQ SuPPORT study. J. Affect. Disord. **236**, 172–179 (2018)
3. Bryant, R.A., O'Donnell, M.L., Creamer, M., et al.: The psychiatric sequelae of traumatic injury. Am. J. Psychiatry **167**(3), 312–320 (2010)
4. Pozzato, I., Craig, A., Gopinath, B., et al.: Outcomes after traffic injury: mental health comorbidity and relationship with pain interference. BMC Psychiatry **20**(1), 189 (2020)
5. Rathnayaka, P., N. Mills, D. Burnett, et al.: A mental health chatbot with cognitive skills for personalised behavioural activation and remote health monitoring. Sensors (Basel) **22**(10) (2022)
6. Daley, K., Hungerbuehler, I., Cavanagh, K., et al.: Preliminary evaluation of the engagement and effectiveness of a mental health chatbot. Front Digit Health **2**, 576361 (2020)
7. Tielman, M.L., Neerincx, M.A., van Meggelen, M., et al.: How should a virtual agent present psychoeducation? influence of verbal and textual presentation on adherence. Technol. Health Care **25**, 1081–1096 (2017)
8. Slovak, P., Antle, A., Theofanopoulou, N., et al.: Designing for emotion regulation interventions: an agenda for HCI theory and research. ACM Trans. Comput.-Hum. Interact. **30**(1), Article 13 (2023)
9. Linardon, J., Cuijpers, P., Carlbring, P., et al.: The efficacy of app-supported smartphone interventions for mental health problems: a meta-analysis of randomized controlled trials. World Psychiatry **18**(3), 325–336 (2019)
10. Motger, Q., Franch, X., Marco, J.: Software-based dialogue systems: survey, taxonomy, and challenges. ACM Comput. Surv. **55**(5), Article 91 (2022)

11. ter Stal, S., Kramer, L.L., Tabak, M., et al.: Design Features of embodied conversational agents in ehealth: a literature review. Int. J. of Hum-Comp. Studies **138**, 102409 (2020)
12. Diederich, S., Brendel, A.B., Morana, S., et al.: On the design of and interaction with conversational agents: an organizing and assessing review of human-computer interaction research. J. Assoc. Info. Syst. **23**(1), 96–138 (2022)
13. Berry, N., Machin, M., Ainsworth, J., et al.: Developing a theory-informed smartphone app for early psychosis: learning points from a multidisciplinary collaboration. Front. Psych. **11**, 602861 (2020)
14. Mohr, D.C., Lyon, A.R., Lattie, E.G., et al.: Accelerating Digital mental health research from early design and creation to successful implementation and sustainment. JMIR **19**(5), e153 (2017)
15. Hopman, K., Richards, D., Norberg, M.M.: A Digital coach to promote emotion regulation skills. Multimodal Technologies and Interaction **7**(6), 57 (2023)
16. Lucas, G.M., Gratch, J., King, A., et al.: It's only a computer: virtual humans increase willingness to disclose. Comput. Hum. Behav. **37**, 94–100 (2014)
17. Bickmore, T.W., Pfeifer, L.M., Byron, D., et al.: Usability of conversational agents by patients with inadequate health literacy: evidence from two clinical trials. J. Health Commun. **15**(Suppl. 2), 197–210 (2010)
18. Bickmore, T., Gruber, A., Picard, R.: Establishing the computer-patient working alliance in automated health behavior change interventions. Pt. Educ Couns **59**(1), 21–30 (2005)
19. Flückiger, C., Del Re, A.C., Wampold, B.E., et al.: The alliance in adult psychotherapy: a meta-analytic synthesis. Psychotherapy (Chic.) **55**(4), 316–340 (2018)
20. Suganuma, S., Sakamoto, D., Shimoyama, H.: An embodied conversational agent for unguided internet-based cognitive behavior therapy in preventative mental health: feasibility and acceptability pilot trial. JMIR Ment Health **5**(3), e10454 (2018)
21. Gross, J.J.: The extended process model of emotion regulation: elaborations, applications, and future directions. Psychol. Inq. **26**(1), 130–137 (2015)
22. Kobylińska, D., Kusev, P.: Flexible emotion regulation: how situational demands and individual differences influence the effectiveness of regulatory strategies. Front. Psychol. **10**(72) (2019)
23. Eisenstadt, M., Liverpool, S., Infanti, E., et al.: Mobile apps that promote emotion regulation, positive mental health, and well-being in the general population: systematic review and meta-analysis. JMIR Ment Health **8**(11), e31170 (2021)
24. Hasking, P., Chen, N.T.M., Chiu, V., et al.: Managing emotion: Open label trial and waitlist controlled trial of an emotion regulation program for university students. J. Am. College Health, 1–11 (2023)
25. Kramer, L.L., Ter Stal, S., Mulder, B.C., et al.: Developing embodied conversational agents for coaching people in a healthy lifestyle: scoping review. J. Med. Internet Res. **22**(2), e14058 (2020)
26. Fylan, B., Tomlinson, J., Raynor, D.K., et al.: Using experience-based co-design with patients, carers and healthcare professionals to develop theory-based interventions for safer medicines use. Res. Social Adm. Pharm. **17**(12), 2127–2135 (2021)
27. Schmid Mast, M., Hall, J.A., Roter, D.L.: Disentangling physician sex and physician communication style: their effects on patient satisfaction in a virtual medical visit. Patient Educ. Counseling **68**(1), 16–22 (2007)
28. Bickmore, T.W., Ólafsson, S., O'Leary, T.K.: Mitigating patient and consumer safety risks when using conversational assistants for medical information: exploratory mixed methods experiment. J. Med. Internet Res. **23**(11), e30704 (2021)
29. Hsieh, H.F., Shannon, S.E.: Three approaches to qualitative content analysis. Qual. Health Res. **15**(9), 1277–1288 (2005)

30. Mayring, P.: Qualitative Content Analysis. Forum Qualitative Sozialforschung/Forum: Qualitative Soc. Res. **1**(2) (2000)
31. Duncan, B.L., Miller, S.D., Sparks, J.A., et al.: The session rating scale: preliminary psychometric properties of a "working" alliance measure. J. Breif Ther. **3**(1), 3–12 (2003)
32. Kolivand, H., Ali, I.R., Sulong, G.: Realistic lip synching for virtual character using common viseme set. Comput. Inform. Sci. (8) (2015)
33. Lupetti, M.L., Hagens, E., Maden, W.V.D., et al.: Trustworthy Embodied Conversational Agents for Healthcare: A Design Exploration of Embodied Conversational Agents for the periconception period at Erasmus MC. In: Proceedings of CUT 2023, Article 25. ACM Eindhoven, NL (2023)

Exploring Self-competition as a Viable Motivation to Promote Physical Activity

Henna Hyypiö, Sarthak Giri(✉), and Harri Oinas-Kukkonen

Oulu Advanced Research on Service and Information Systems, University of Oulu, 90570 Oulu, Finland
{sarthak.giri,harri.oinas-kukkonen}@oulu.fi

Abstract. Persuasive systems design encompasses a wide range of concepts that may help users be motivated to achieve the targeted goal or behavior change. This study evaluates contemporary applications that seek to promote physical activity and finds that, although there are different implementations of competition-related features, they are not designed for individuals motivated by self-competition, a type of competition that allows individuals to compete against themselves to beat their own personal best performance. Furthermore, it explores how the psychological construct of competitive orientation can be used as a basis for personalizing persuasive systems. The paper then conceptualizes the design features of a system that addresses and caters to the self-competitive orientation of a user.

Keywords: Persuasive Systems Design · Behavior Change Support Systems · Competition Strategy · Self-Competition · Competitive Orientation · Personalization

1 Introduction

Lack of physical activity (PA) is one of the leading risk factors for mortality and is connected with poorer quality of life [25] World Health Organization (WHO) reports that more than a quarter of the world's adult population is insufficiently active [30]. This increase in sedentary lifestyle [30], is related to various health problems such as cardiovascular diseases and type-2 diabetes [25, 30] and the costs associated to the treatments of such diseases fall largely on society. It is estimated that the direct costs caused by inactivity constitute about 1,5–3,8% of all direct healthcare costs in developed countries [12]. The increasing sedentary behavior and lack of physical activity are battled against with various health interventions. Such interventions, including face-to-face contact with doctors or other professionals, are expensive and not available to everyone.

Thus, the development of mobile applications for physical activity (hereafter referred to as applications or apps) and the increasing global smartphone use promise to address these problems by offering cost-effective solutions with a wider reach [16]. However, data suggests that there are still a lot of shortcomings in the applications, which negatively impacts their use and effectiveness. For example, intervention studies have reported only small to moderate increase in physical activity measured in number of minutes

N. Baghaei et al. (Eds.): PERSUASIVE 2024, LNCS 14636, pp. 176–189, 2024.
https://doi.org/10.1007/978-3-031-58226-4_14

per day with the use of wearables and mobile applications [6, 24]. Moreover, many papers have reported that application use tends to decrease over time [2, 10, 13]. In order to resolve these issues of engagement and effectiveness, studies have suggested personalizing the intervention content to match individual characteristics [23, 26, 29]. Furthermore, approaching different personality types based on Myers-Brigg Type Indicator (MBTI) with different persuasive features was also found to help with receptiveness of the application [21].

Persuasive strategies, techniques, and principles aimed at changing or shaping attitudes and behaviors without coercion or deception, can also help address the problem of engagement and effectiveness with these applications [17]. Competition is one such persuasive strategy. In previous literature, the persuasive strategy of competition has been reported controversially as both motivating and demotivating for users [20, 21]. For instance, a study by Fukuoka et al. [4] stated that competition was reported among one of the four most motivating system features by the study participants [4]. On the contrary, most of the study participants in the D'Addario study [1] expressed avoidance to competition features. These studies made it clear that more insight was needed to understand individual characteristics in order for them to function as the basis for personalizing persuasive strategies [3]. Orji et al. [20] tried to address the issue in a study that confirmed that competition strategy in mobile applications does not motivate all users equally; however, the study was unable to take into account the multidimensional characteristics of humans in relation to competition [20]. Individual competitiveness is not binary: having a desire to compete or a lack thereof [22], but instead, is multidimensional and more complex.

Given that there is a dearth of studies exploring personalizing persuasive strategy of competition to different individuals, this paper seeks to fill this gap by unearthing the following question: what are mobile applications promoting PA currently doing to personalize the persuasive strategy of competition, and how can these strategies be improved? In order to explore this question, we use empirical analysis to analyze the competition strategy of mobile apps through the Persuasive System Design (PSD) and use conceptual analysis to identify and address gaps in the design of these apps. Theories and frameworks such as Behavior change support system, PSD and competition research are used for conceptual analysis.

2 Background

2.1 Competition Research

Competitive orientation refers to a person's thoughts, emotions and behaviors in competitive situations. Competitive orientation is known to have significant effects on achievement motivation and performance in achievement situations. Individuals are different in terms of their competitive orientation, which can have an impact on a variety of practical settings, including education, health, organizations, and sport [22].

In this paper, we look at different competitive orientations outlined by Orosz et al. [20]: hypercompetitive orientation, self-developmental competitive orientation, anxiety-driven competition avoidance and lack of interest toward competition. Hypercompetitive orientation is strongly result-oriented and hypercompetitive individuals desire and prefer to work hard. The focus is on winning over others even in ways where the end does not justify the means. Anxiety-driven competition avoidance orientation is associated with general anxiety related to the process of competition. Anxiety-driven individuals tend to avoid competition, while they fear failure. Self-developmental competitive orientation is focused on the self and the ability improvement. The focus is on personal growth and mastery of the task. Lack of interest in competition orientation is related to the disinterest towards competition. Finally, individuals with a lack of interest towards competition are less concerned with others' expectations in competitive situations. In other words, they do not care about winning or losing. These orientations, which can coexist within an individual, can not only influence their behaviour but can also change over one's lifetime. Studying and applying insights from an individual's competitive orientation in different contexts like education, health, and sports and across different stages of their life can be very useful for application designers. Table 1 presents examples for different competitive orientations in the context of playing tennis.

Table 1. Comparing competitive orientations via examples of playing tennis

Competitive orientation	Examples
Hypercompetitive orientation	In a game of tennis, Person A is not just content with winning, but aims to dominate each game even by bending the rules or engaging in unsportsmanlike conduct
Self-developmental competitive orientation	Person A's main goal is to improve their skills, like serving and backhand, regardless of whether they win or lose against others in tennis
Anxiety-driven competition avoidance orientation	Person A practices tennis but avoids playing with peers due to anxiety over losing against them
Lack of interest in competition orientation	When playing tennis with friends, Person A is indifferent to the competitive elements of the game, participating more for the social interaction and exercise

2.2 Behavior Change Support Systems (BCSSs) and Persuasive Systems Design (PSD) Model

Behavior change support system is defined as "a socio-technical information system with psychological and behavioral outcomes designed to form, alter or reinforce attitudes, behaviors or an act of complying without using coercion or deception" [18]. A BCSS can be evaluated and designed using the persuasive systems design (PSD) model proposed by Oinas-Kukkonen and Harjumaa [17].

The PSD model discusses the process of evaluating and designing persuasive systems through three steps. This model comprises three critical steps: understanding the core principles or postulates of persuasive technology, analyzing the persuasion context (intent of the system, the persuasion event and the persuasion strategy), and selecting the most suitable persuasive content and functionality from an array of 28 options across four categories: primary task, dialogue support, system credibility, and social support. Many mobile applications already include PSD features like self-monitoring (primary task) and social comparison (social support), but there is no consensus on which features contribute most significantly to their effectiveness [14, 15]. Experts, however, agree that personalization, whereby the applications are designed to align with user characteristics, goals and desires, can substantially enhance their persuasive power, effectiveness, and user engagement [1, 26].

In general, language personalization and tailoring are used interchangeably but within the discussion of persuasive systems, it is important to differentiate between tailoring and personalization. As defined by Oinas-Kukkonen et al. [19], tailoring is a weaker level of personalization. Personalization, on the other hand, involves offering genuinely individualized content or services, deeply integrated with the PSD model's user context [19]. This form of personalization requires a thorough understanding of the individual user, including aspects such as lifestyle, life circumstances, and personality traits. Table 2 explains the distinction with examples. Currently most systems use tailoring (low-level personalization) where all users receive the same set of features although the content of these features is personalized [19]. The challenge lies in elevating this approach by extending high-level personalization to the software features themselves, based on individual user characteristics. Appealing to the competitiveness of a user is one way to achieve high level personalization in software features.

Table 2. Personalization strategies according to the depth and level of personalization [19]

		Depth	
		Low	High
Level	**Feature**	Low-level personalization, i.e. tailoring of features. Different user segments might have different sets of features employed in their applications	High-level personalization of features. Depending on their personal characteristics, different users might have different sets of features employed in their applications
	Contents	Low-level personalization, i.e. tailoring of the contents of the feature. All users have the same set of features, but the contents of the features might vary with different user groups	Strong personalization of the contents of the feature. All users have the same set of features, but the contents of the features might vary according to the personal characteristics of the user

Three PSD features, social comparison, rewards and praise can be analyzed to understand how they facilitate personalization such that it appeals to the competitiveness of a user. Social comparison offers the user an opportunity to view and compare results with other users but does not involve winning or losing [17]. This feature can be implemented, for example, by providing a leaderboard to show users where they rank relative to other users. Although the feature doesn't reward the user directly for outperforming others, it does stimulate competition. Reward is a feature that enhances system persuasiveness by providing users virtual rewards for performing a target behavior. While earning rewards by definition doesn't have to involve competition, since it can be awarded for merely completing a task, it is often implemented to induce competition. For example, only the winner gets awarded points, badges or trophies or at least gets more of it than others. Praise is defined as words, images, symbols or sounds that are provided to the user to give them feedback based on their behavior. Similar to reward, praise feature can be implemented independently of, or, in conjunction with competition.

3 Study Setting

3.1 Conceptual Analysis

The purpose of conceptual analysis is to create new connections between existing theories, link research across disciplines and provide the scope of thinking [7]. To create new knowledge, conceptual analysis involves assimilation and combination of evidence from previous research [8]. There are two alternative starting points for a conceptual study: start from a phenomenon that can be observed but is not adequately explained by existing literature, or start from a theory, argue its uncompletedness, and introduce other theories to fill in the gaps [9].

In this study, the starting point for the research is the observed phenomenon that the competition strategy in persuasive systems is perceived differently by different users; some users find it motivating while others find the feature right down off-putting. While the phenomenon has been observed in numerous studies, there is no adequate explanation for it [1, 4, 11, 20, 21]. In order to conceptualize an explanation, different theories were considered. To clarify the roles of these different theories, a distinction between domain theories and method theories was made. Domain theories are theories that provide the "data" analogous to data in empirical research. Domain theory refers to a set of knowledge on a substantive topic area in a field or domain. Method theories, in turn, are used for studying the domain theory phenomenon. i.e., the role of method theories is to provide some new insight into the domain theory. Method theories can offer explanations to concepts and relationships in the domain theory. In this paper, by examining domain theories such as PSD and method theories such as competitive orientation construct, we gained nuanced insights into the varying responses to competition strategies. This comprehensive analysis allowed us to identify distinct competitive orientations, propose personalized strategies based on these orientations, and develop a framework for tailoring competition features to individual user needs.

3.2 Empirical Analysis

The empirical phase involved a systematic examination of mobile applications designed to promote physical activity. The selection of the applications was limited to the Google Play Store since the researcher only had access to an Android device to test the applications. Applications promoting physical activity were searched in the Google Play Store by using keywords such as activity, exercise, fitness, and steps. Potential applications for review were also identified by searching on the internet. Sites that have reviewed and rated activity applications were utilized in the initial screening. Since higher ratings and a larger number of downloads add credibility to applications, those that had an above 4 rating and number of downloads exceeding 10 million were selected as candidates for review. To enhance the accessibility of the application, only those that had English as one of the working languages within the app were chosen. Also, the research was limited to apps that were free to use so only those that had a free trial period were considered. Furthermore, only applications intended for adults were looked at. Once these criteria were met, the application was downloaded and checked for further criteria such as being able to use without any further equipment such as a heart rate sensor or a sports watch. Finally, only applications making use of the competition feature were selected for review. This sampling method combines elements of convenience sampling (relying on readily available applications from the Google Play Store and internet searches) and purposeful sampling (applying specific criteria such as number of downloads and star ratings). Figure 1 depicts the screening process.

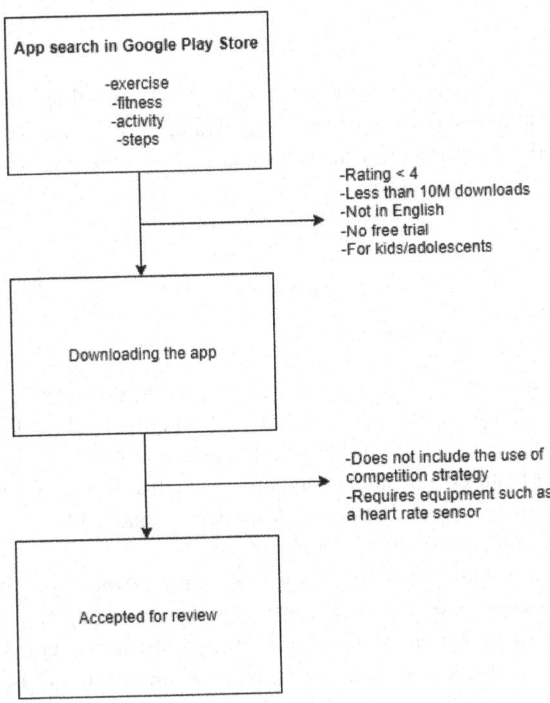

Fig. 1. Methodology of the screening process

After the screening process, as shown in Table 3, four applications: Samsung Health, Strava, Fitbit, and Relive were selected. These four applications were downloaded by the researcher and another user. To ensure that rigorous data about the functionalities of the applications was obtained, at least one walking activity was recorded by the users with each application. In addition, to test the competition feature of the application, besides the researcher, another user was always asked to participate in the competition. Comparing and analysing the use and interaction with the application among the two users also gave information about the possible personalization of the applications. In addition to downloading and exploring the applications themselves, the application web pages were searched for relevant information regarding competition and self-competition features and personalization of the application and its features. The applications were used from 3–12 weeks depending on the application.

Table 3. Reviewed applications

App name	No. of downloads	Rating	Date of data extraction
Samsung Health	1B+	4.0	24.11.2022
Fitbit	50M+	4.0	24.11.2022
Strava	50M+	4.4	2.12.2022
Relive	10M+	4.6	8.12.2022

We employed the Persuasive Systems Design (PSD) model as our analytical lens, focusing on the implementation of competition strategies within these apps. The analysis also identified self-competition features and assessed the level of personalization implemented.

4 Results

4.1 Competition Features Analysis

Our analysis primarily focused on the competition features of these applications, noting significant similarities in their design and functionality. Each application included a "Challenges" section, which allowed users to engage in customizable competitions. These competitions featured adjustable components, such as participant numbers, objectives (e.g., steps or distance), and duration. Moreover, users had the flexibility to invite friends or open the competition to all app users.

Strava, Samsung Health, and Relive also hosted their own competitions, engaging users in global challenges with extensive participation. For example, Samsung Health's Global Challenges invited users worldwide to a monthly step count contest, offering digital badges as incentives. Strava Challenges, in some instances, provided physical prizes for winners.

A common element across all applications was the inclusion of leaderboards, which displayed users' rankings and scores adjacent to the other competitors. These leaderboards typically featured participants' names and profile pictures, along with their rankings and current scores. Figure 2 depicts three varied leaderboard implementations.

Regarding rewards, all applications incorporated virtual prizes, such as trophies or badges, to recognize competition winners. The nature of these rewards varied across

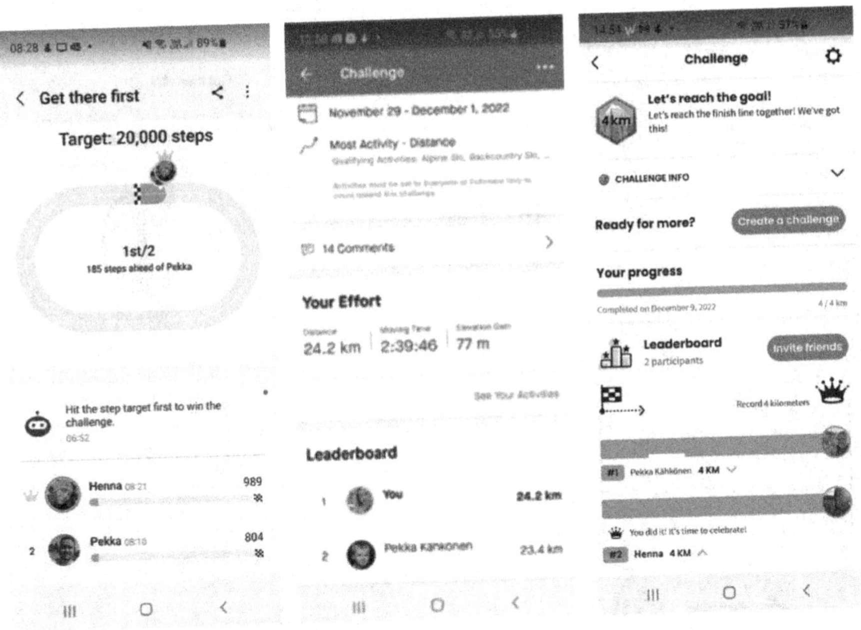

Fig. 2. Leaderboards in Samsung Health (left), Strava (middle) and Relive (right).

applications, with some rewarding all participants who achieved a predetermined goal, while others reserved rewards for top performers only. Figure 3 presents three different applications with their rewards.

Through the above analysis, we were able to identify gaps in competition strategy, and level of personalization which we then continued to explore with conceptual analysis to come up with possible solution and implementation within mobile applications.

4.2 Competitive Orientation and Self-competition Strategy

Our study explored the implementation of competition strategies within these applications and found that it did not cater to people who had self-developmental competitive orientations. Individuals with this competitive orientation are concerned about self-improvement, not about how their potential rivals are doing. A strategy that improves perceived persuasiveness amongst these people would be what we call self-competition strategy. Self-competition is defined as a type of competition that allows the individual to compete against himself to beat his own personal best performance.

We found that while direct features for self-competition were not prominently integrated, elements supporting this concept were present. For example, Fitbit allowed users to create solo competitions aimed at achieving personal bests, although it didn't explicitly track or display personal records within the competition framework. Samsung Health provided a clear display of personal best results but did not integrate features explicitly encouraging users to surpass these records. Relive, on the other hand, prompted users upon achieving personal records like the longest or furthest activity, which aligns with the idea of self-competition but lacks direct encouragement for pursuing such goals.

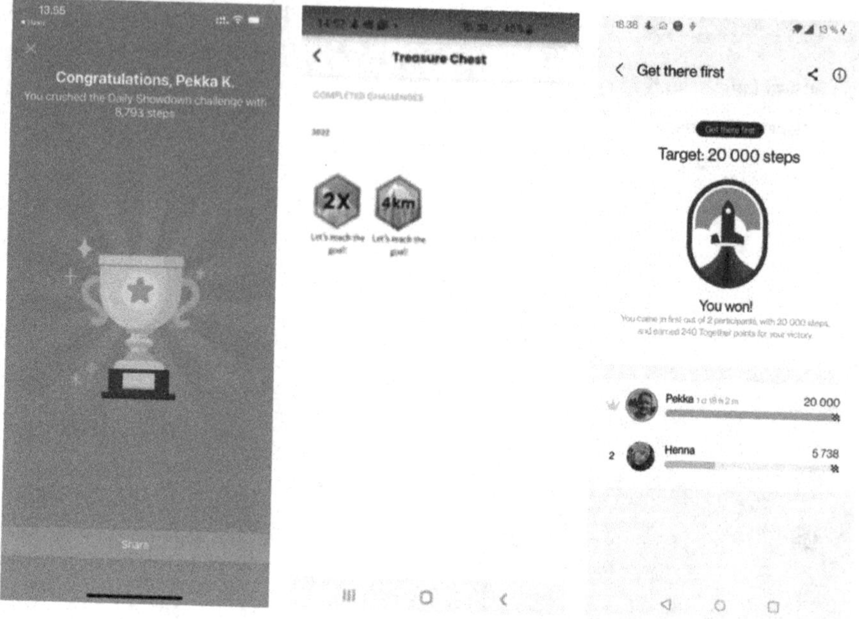

Fig. 3. Virtual competition rewards in Fitbit (left), Relive (middle) and Samsung Health (right)

By coalescing the domain theories and method theories identified in this paper, we came up with at least one self-competition strategy to improve on each of these applications' failure to cater to people with self-developmental competitive orientation. Fitbit could address its limitation by adding a longitudinal self-monitoring feature where the person can go back in history and compare the current statistics to last week, last month or even last year's statistics. This would enable the user to track his own progress and set goals to surpass his/her last personal records or beat his/her improvement deltas. Samsung Health could implement the PSD feature of praise for beating one's own personal records, not just beating other competitors' records. This could be valuable in encouraging users to stay on their self-development journey and improve every day. Relive could implement giving rewards to make people with self-development-oriented also feel a sense of accomplishment.

4.3 Personalization Analysis

Personalization is suggested by previous literature to have an impact on persuasive strategy preference, intervention engagement and effectiveness [1, 23, 26–29]. Thus, to maximize the persuasive power of the competition strategy, and that way to increase the system effectiveness, the competition strategy should be personalized.

Our review found that none of the applications employed feature-level personalization where the set of features offered to users are personalized to match a certain user group (low-level personalization or tailoring) or the individual characteristics of the particular user (high-level personalization). It also didn't have content personalization strategies (low-level or high-level). Despite collecting basic user information like name, age, gender, and interests, this data was not used to tailor the competition feature's content to individual users. It only allowed customization in the sense that users could modify certain aspects of the competition, such as participant numbers and competition objectives, but this did not extend to personalization based on user characteristics or preferences.

The empirical findings of this study indicate that the reviewed applications do not have any means to find out the competitive orientation of the user. To overcome this, sensors or direct questionnaires can be designed to uncover facts about the user that can be used for personalization. When using the strategy of asking information directly from the users, competitive orientation could be defined by asking the user a set of questions relating to competitiveness, and users' behavioral and emotional reactions to winning and losing. If the user confirms to have self-development competitive orientation, then self-competition features should be introduced with the possibility to measure and view data relating to one's performance record.

Table 4 shows the personalization at a high-level and low-level with the competition strategy encompassing the self-competition strategy at both the feature and the content.

Table 4. Personalization strategies encompassing self-competition

		Depth	
		Low-level	High-level
Level	**Feature**	Competition feature is only employed in the applications of those user groups which are determined to benefit from the feature. E.g., the feature is only employed for Canadians since they are a nation characterized with a high level of individualism and competitiveness [5]	Competition feature is only employed in the applications of those users who are recognized as being hypercompetitive since hypercompetitive individuals are motivated by competition Users recognized as having a self-developmental competitive orientation receive a feature that uses a self-competition strategy
	Contents	All users have the competition feature, but the contents of the feature is tailored based on user demographics, such as age, gender and level of activity. E.g., the user is competing only against those rivals whose physical fitness is similar to that of the user	Detailed information about the user is used to personalize the competition feature's contents to match the user's specific needs to gain optimal motivational effect. The competition components, e.g. type of competition, rivals and competition reward should be personalized to achieve optimal motivational effect

5 Discussion

This study explores how competition strategies in mobile apps promoting physical activity are implemented and personalized, and their support for individual competitive orientations. Our empirical investigation of four popular applications revealed that their competition features shared many similarities, such as the inclusion of leaderboards, message boards, and virtual rewards. Custom competitions were a common feature, with some apps also hosting provider-initiated challenges, showcasing minor variations like physical rewards and pre-set competition goals.

A significant finding was the lack of personalization in these competition strategies. The absence of personalized features in the reviewed apps aligns with the complexities of implementing high-level personalization, such as the need for machine learning techniques or detailed user questionnaires. This challenge is compounded by the evolving nature of users' goals and preferences, and the observation from prior research that individuals' competitiveness can change over time.

Our analysis also highlighted that the competition features in these apps did not cater to the varied competitive orientations of users. Specifically, none of the applications employed a self-competition strategy, which could be particularly motivating for users with a self-developmental competitive orientation. This oversight suggests a missed opportunity to leverage the motivational potential of addressing different competitive orientations. While the apps offered customization options, they fell short of providing true personalization at both feature and content levels.

From the conceptual standpoint, it becomes clear that users' competitive orientation is crucial in determining the effectiveness of competition strategies. Ideally, apps should tailor their competition features to align with users' competitive orientations. For instance, hyper-competitive individuals might benefit from more intense competitive features, whereas users with a self-developmental orientation might find more value in self-competition strategies.

5.1 Implications for Research and Practice

The study suggests that the Persuasive Systems Design (PSD) model could be expanded to include self-competition features, catering to users with different competitive orientations. Understanding that competitive orientation influences the effectiveness of competition strategies implies that these strategies can be more personalized at both the feature and content levels.

For system designers, this underscores the importance of personalizing competition features. Recognizing the diverse competitive orientations can lead to the development of more engaging and effective applications. Offering users the choice of their preferred mode of competition, whether it's against others, against themselves, or opting out of competition altogether, could increase user satisfaction and app effectiveness. Additionally, aspects like competition type, goals, and participant composition should be tailored to individual user preferences.

End-users stand to gain from these insights as well. By choosing applications that align with their competitive orientation, users can more effectively engage in behavior change initiatives. For example, individuals who identify with a self-developmental competitive orientation might seek out apps with self-competition features.

6 Conclusion

This study contributes to a deeper understanding of competition strategies in health and fitness apps, highlighting the need for more personalized approaches. We've identified a gap in how these strategies are currently implemented, particularly in catering to diverse competitive orientations. Despite the limitations of our approach, including a small sample size, a focus limited to the physical activity domain and use of only free versions of applications, our findings offer valuable insights for future app development.

Disclosure of Interests. Authors have no competing interests.

References

1. D'Addario, M., Baretta, D., Zanatta, F., Greco, A., Steca, P.: Engagement features in physical activity smartphone apps: focus group study with sedentary people. JMIR mHealth uHealth **8**(11) (2020). https://doi.org/10.2196/20460
2. Direito, A., et al.: Tailored daily activity: an adaptive physical activity smartphone intervention. Telemed. e-Health **26**(4), 426–437 (2020). https://doi.org/10.1089/tmj.2019.0034
3. Enwald, H.: Combining personalization, tailoring, persuasive design and gamification – where do we stand? In: 8th International Workshop on Behavior Change Support Systems, BCSS 2020: Behavior Change Support Systems. (CEUR workshop proceedings), vol. 2662. CEUR-WS.org (2020). http://ceur-ws.org/Vol-2662/BCSS2020_short3.pdf
4. Fukuoka, Y., Kamitani, E., Bonnet, K., Lindgren, T.: Real-time social support through a mobile virtual community to improve healthy behavior in overweight and sedentary adults: a focus group analysis. J. Med. Internet Res. **13**(3) (2011). https://doi.org/10.2196/jmir.1770
5. Fülöp, M.: Happy and unhappy competitors: what makes the difference? Psychol. Top. **18**(2), 345–367 (2009)
6. Gal, R., May, A.M., van Overmeeren, E.J., Simons, M., Monninkhof, E.M.: The effect of physical activity interventions comprising wearables and smartphone applications on physical activity: a systematic review and meta-analysis. Sports Med. Open **4**(1), 42 (2018). https://doi.org/10.1186/s40798-018-0157-9
7. Gilson, L., Goldberg, C.: Editor's comment: so, what is a conceptual paper? Group Org. Manag. **40**(2), 127–130 (2015)
8. Hirschheim, R.: Some guidelines for the critical reviewing of conceptual papers. J. Assoc. Inf. Syst. **9**(8) (2008). https://doi.org/10.17705/1jais.00167
9. Jaakkola, E.: Designing conceptual articles: four approaches. AMS Rev **10**, 18–26 (2020). https://doi.org/10.1007/s13162-020-00161-0
10. Joseph, R., Ainsworth, B., Hollingshead, K., Todd, M., Keller, C.: Results of a culturally tailored smartphone-delivered physical activity intervention among midlife African American women: feasibility trial. JMIR mHealth uHealth **9**(4) (2021). https://doi.org/10.2196/27383
11. Kari, T., Piippo, J., Frank, L., Makkonen, M., Moilanen, P.: To gamify or not to gamify? Gamification in exercise applications and its role in impacting exercise motivation. In: Proceedings of the 29th Bled eConference "Digital economy". University of Maribor (2016)

12. Kolu, P., Vasankari, T., Luoto, R.: Liikkumattomuus ja terveydenhuollon kustannukset. Suomen lääkärilehti **12** (2014). https://docplayer.fi/6624785-Liikkumattomuus-ja-terveyden huollon-kustannukset.html
13. Leinonen, A., et al.: Feasibility of gamified mobile service aimed at physical activation in young men: population-based randomized controlled study (MOPO). JMIR mHealth uHealth **5**(10) (2017). https://doi.org/10.2196/mhealth.6675
14. Matthews, J., Win, K.T., Oinas-Kukkonen, H., Freeman, M.: Persuasive technology in mobile applications promoting physical activity: a systematic review. J. Med. Syst. **40**(3), 72 (2016). https://doi.org/10.1007/s10916-015-0425-x
15. Mollee, J., Middelweerd, A., Kurvers, R., Klein, M.: What technological features are used in smartphone apps that promote physical activity? A review and content analysis. Pers. Ubiquit. Comput. **21**, 633–643 (2017). https://doi.org/10.1007/s00779-017-1023-3
16. Nibbeling, N., Simons, M., Sporrel, K., Deutekom, M.: A focus group study among inactive adults regarding the perceptions of a theory-based physical activity app. Front. Publ. Health **9** (2021). https://doi.org/10.3389/fpubh.2021.528388. Article 528388
17. Oinas-Kukkonen, H., Harjumaa, M.: Persuasive systems design: key issues, process model, and system features. Commun. Assoc. Inf. **24**(1), 485–500 (2009)
18. Oinas-Kukkonen, H.: A foundation for the study of behavior change support systems. Pers. Ubiquit. Comput. **17** (2013). https://doi.org/10.1007/s00779-012-0591-5
19. Oinas-Kukkonen, H., Pohjalainen S., Agyei, E.: Mitigating issues with/of/for true personalization. Front. Artif. Intell. **5** (2022). https://doi.org/10.3389/frai.2022.844817
20. Orji, R., Nacke, L., Di Marco, C.: Towards personality-driven persuasive health games and gamified systems. In: Proceedings of the 2017 CHI Conference on Human Factors in Computing Systems (CHI 2017), pp. 1015–1027. Association for Computing Machinery, New York (2017). https://doi.org/10.1145/3025453.3025577
21. Orji, R., Vassileva, J., Mandryk, R.: Modeling the efficacy of persuasive strategies for different gamer types in serious games for health. User Model. User-Adap. Inter. (2014). https://doi.org/10.1007/s11257-014-9149-8
22. Orosz, G., Tóth-Király, I., Büki, N., Ivaskevics, K., Bőthe, B., Fülöp, M.: The four faces of competition: the development of the multidimensional competitive orientation inventory. Front. Psychol. **9**, 779 (2018). https://doi.org/10.3389/fpsyg.2018.00779
23. Oyebode, O., Ndulue, C., Mulchandani, D., Adib, A., Alhasani, M., Orji, R.: Tailoring persuasive and behaviour change systems based on stages of change and motivation. In: CHI Conference on Human Factors in Computing Systems (2021). https://doi.org/10.1145/341 1764.3445619
24. Romeo, A., et al.: Can smartphone apps increase physical activity? Systematic review and meta-analysis. J. Med. Internet Res. **21**(3), e12053 (2019). https://doi.org/10.2196/12053
25. Saunders, T., et al.: Sedentary behaviour and health in adults: an overview of systematic reviews. Appl. Physiol. Nutr. Metab. **45**(10(Suppl. 2)), 197–217 (2020). https://doi.org/10.1139/apnm-2020-0272
26. Schroé, H., Crombez, G., De Bourdeaudhuij, I., Van Dyck, D.: Investigating when, which, and why users stop using a digital health intervention to promote an active lifestyle: secondary analysis with A focus on health action process Approach–Based psychological determinants. JMIR mHealth uHealth **10**(1) (2022). https://doi.org/10.2196/30583
27. Shameli, A., Althoff, T., Saberi, A., Leskovec, J.: How gamification affects physical activity: large-scale analysis of walking challenges in a mobile application. In: Proceedings of the 26th International Conference on World Wide Web Companion, pp. 455–463, April 2017. https://doi.org/10.1145/3041021.3054172
28. Sporrel, K., Nibbeling, N., Wang, S., Ettema, D., Simons, M.: Unraveling mobile health exercise interventions for adults: scoping review on the implementations and designs of persuasive strategies. JMIR Mhealth Uhealth **9**(1), e16282 (2021). https://doi.org/10.2196/16282

29. Tikka, P., Oinas-Kukkonen, H.: Tailoring persuasive technology: a systematic review of literature of self-schema theory and transformative learning theory in persuasive technology context. Cyberpsychol. J. Psychosoc. Res. Cybersp. **13**(3) (2019). https://doi.org/10.5817/CP2019-3-6. Article 6
30. World Health Organization: Physical activity (2020). https://www.who.int/news-room/fact-sheets/detail/physical-activity

The Effect of Dark Patterns and User Knowledge on User Experience and Decision-Making

Tasneem Naheyan and Kiemute Oyibo(✉)

York University, Toronto, Canada
{tnaheyan,kiemute.oyibo}@yorku.ca

Abstract. Dark patterns, aka deceptive designs, have become prevalent in the online environment. In this paper, we examined how dark patterns and knowledge of them impact user experience, decision-making, and vendor reputation using the purchase of a subscription plan on a hypothetical streaming website as proof of concept. We conducted a between-subjects study to examine the effect of two common dark patterns (confirmshaming and trick-question) compared against a control condition. Overall, users perceived both patterns as manipulative. However, this negative perception did not negatively impact the website's perceived ease of use, trustworthiness and credibility. We found that users without knowledge of dark patterns were more likely to be persuaded by confirmshaming when making purchase decisions. In the confirmshaming condition, 68% of those without knowledge of dark patterns chose the expensive plan intended by the vendor over the cheap plan. The reverse is the case among those with knowledge of dark patterns: only 35% of them chose the expensive plan. This finding indicates that once users become aware of being manipulated, they are likely to go against the promoted choice, as 40% of knowledgeable users in the trick-question condition edited their initial choice, compared with 11% and 6% in the confirmshaming and control conditions, respectively. The findings highlight the need to raise awareness about dark patterns so that unsuspecting users are less likely to make decisions that are not in their best interest.

Keywords: Dark Pattern · Deceptive Design · Website · UX · Decision

1 Introduction

The design of a user interface (UI) influences how users perceive and interact with it [1,2], with choice architecture being able to nudge them in certain directions, including taking the designer's preferred actions [2]. Design techniques

N. Baghaei et al. (Eds.): PERSUASIVE 2024, LNCS 14636, pp. 190–206, 2024.
https://doi.org/10.1007/978-3-031-58226-4_15

such as nudging are typically applied with the intention of improving user experience (UX). For example, Naish et al. [25] and Bucinca et al. [26] found that nudging techniques can be used to reduce users' overdependence on artificial intelligence (AI) recommendations. However, they can also be deployed to benefit parties other than the user [3,4,8]. Due to the financial incentives that they offer, dark patterns (aka deceptive designs), aimed to manipulate, deceive, or coerce users into carrying out actions that are not in their best interest, have become prevalent in the online environment [5]. These unethical design patterns often appear in many e-commerce sites (e.g., Amazon [21]), social media sites (e.g., Facebook [22]), and online streaming platforms (e.g., Netflix [23]). They are so widespread that users are becoming accustomed to them to the extent that they are becoming "invisible." Studies have shown that they are a source of user frustration and privacy concerns, and pose a cognitive burden [6]. In online web interaction, cognitive burden causes users to spend unnecessary time, effort and attention on a task. As a result, users often opt for the promoted choice which benefits the service [6]. Despite the prevalence of dark patterns, there is little to no legislation as of yet protecting users from their use in many countries [6,8].

Research on the adverse impact of dark patterns on users is limited. As a result, critics often dismiss dark patterns as cases of aggressive marketing [6]. Although several studies have identified and defined dark patterns, few have examined their effect on user experience (UX) and vendor perception [6]. Consequently, we conducted a user study to assess the effect of commonly deployed dark patterns by online platforms on UX, decision-making, and website reputation. Although a few studies have explored the impact of dark patterns in e-commerce [7,9], our study focuses on account registration on a video streaming website - a common task required by users to access many online services.

The study investigates how aware users are of the prevalent use of dark patterns in online environments and whether dark patterns such as confirmshaming and trick-questions have a negative impact on the user experience, decision-making, and reputation of the service. Confirmshaming uses careful wording to guilt users into opting into something they normally would not [4]. Trick-question obscures the meaning of a question to make users opt for the service's promoted choice [4,7]. Both dark patterns are among the 15 types identified by Mathur et al. [7] in the analysis of product pages from 11K ecommerce websites. We chose to investigate confirmshaming and trick-question because they are frequently used by online platforms and can be very manipulative [9,15]. The dependent variables measured in this study include UX, website reputation and user choice. UX refers to "how people feel about a product and their pleasure and satisfaction when using it" (p. 13) [10]. It was operationalized as perceived ease of use and perceived persuasiveness. Perceived reputation is the belief that a website has a particular quality which can impact it positively or negatively [11,12]. It was operationalized as perceived non-manipulation, perceived trustworthiness, and perceived credibility. Finally, decision-making was operationalized as selected choice on the streaming website: standard (cheap) or premium (expensive) plan.

2 Related Work

The effect of dark patterns on UX and the reputation of online platforms among different populations is little examined. Most work on dark patterns focuses on defining, identifying and classifying dark patterns in existing websites and apps [2,3,13]. Mathur et al. [6] classified dark patterns into two broad types: information flow manipulation (IFM) and design space modification (DSM). IFM dark patterns are unethical designs aimed to hide information from or induce false beliefs in users through misleading statements, affirmative misstatements, or omissions. Examples of this type of dark patterns include bait and switch, sneak into basket, hidden costs, and disguised ads. On the other hand, DSM dark patterns are unethical designs that use covert, asymmetric or restrictive tactics to trick users to make decisions that benefit the vendor. Examples of this type of dark pattern include confirmshaming, forced action, trick-question, and bad default.

Mathur et al. [7] conducted an analysis of approximately 53K product pages from 11K e-commerce websites to uncover the types of dark patterns they contained. They found 1,818 dark pattern instances in 11% of the websites, with 183 of the websites exhibiting deceptive behaviors. They classified them into 15 types (e.g., hidden costs, sneak into basket, forced enrolment, confirmshaming and trick-questions) and 7 broader categories (e.g., Sneaking, Urgency, Misdirection, Social Proof, Scarcity). Moreover, Gunawan et al. [2] conducted a study in which they compared dark patterns in 105 popular services across different modalities (mobile apps, mobile browser and web browsers). They found 2320 instances of dark patterns across all of the services, which differed across the three modalities (mobile app - 35.94% , mobile browser - 32.59%, and desktop browser - 31.47%). In particular, they found that "no consent checkbox for Terms of Service/Privacy Policy" was the most prevalent, with two-third of the analyzed services using it across all three modalities. They also found that half of the services across all three modalities used forced action, preselection, roach motel, and aesthetic manipulation; and <5% used sneak into basket and bait and switch. [4] primarily provided taxonomies of dark patterns and discussed ethical concerns and responsibilities related to UX practice. Ahuja and Kumar [24] reviewed the literature on dark patterns taxonomies to investigate their impact on user autonomy. However, they did not conduct any user studies as a part of the investigation.

Few user studies have investigated knowledge about dark patterns and their effect on users. Di Geronimo et al. [13] examined whether users had developed blindness to dark patterns. Participants watched videos of usage of apps with dark patterns and answered usability questions afterwards. They found that users were mostly unaware of dark patterns in the explored services. In a similar study, Bhoot et al. [14] found that although a significant portion of users claimed they had never been deceived by websites, they were not able to identify all the dark patterns presented to them and thus were deceived by at least one. However, in Bongard-Blanchy et al.'s [18] study, they found users were aware of dark patterns' potential influence on their decisions and had the ability to recognize these patterns, but their awareness did not lead to significant resistance to manipulative design. Similarly, Maier [20] revealed that most study participants were somewhat aware of dark patterns, but unaware of how frequently they appeared. Moreover, Dunn et al. [19] found that users, irrespective of income, education or age, are potentially vulnerable to dark patterns, highlighting a need to raise awareness about this topic among users. Costello et al. [9] investigated the emotional and economic impact of dark patterns on users and vendors, respectively. They found that participants who encountered dark patterns experienced negative emotions and showed a bias towards maintaining their initial purchase decision or not making a purchase. Above all, they found that dark patterns not only have negative effects on users, they can potentially harm vendors' reputation in the long run. Luguri and Strahilevitz [15] investigated the effect of different degrees of dark patterns on users. They found that participants exposed to aggressive dark pattern conditions were four times as likely to subscribe to the plan as participants exposed to the control condition, whereas those exposed to mild dark patterns were twice as likely to subscribe.

Despite there being some research on dark patterns, few studies have been dedicated to how they impact UX and vendor reputation, and how prior findings generalize to other populations and domains. In this paper, we focused on the Canadian population and online streaming service. We examined how confirmshaming, trick-question, and knowledge of dark patterns influence user experience, decision-making and vendor reputation.

3 Method

The user study, which aimed to examine the effect of dark patterns and user knowledge on UX and decision-making, was approved by our university's research ethics board. The study simulated a website account registration process, followed by a questionnaire to assess user experience and website perception. Prior to conducting the actual study, a pilot run was carried out with 15 participants from a Canadian university community aged between 22 to 60 years to evaluate the reliability of the study's measures and improve them.

3.1 Participants

Two-hundred-and-eleven (211) participants, 18 years and older, were recruited within Canada using Amazon Mechanical Turk (AMT), a crowd-sourcing platform used for collecting relatively reliable data compared with in-person data. Participants were remunerated $4 CAD in appreciation of their time. After data cleaning, we were left with 203 participants for the final analysis.

3.2 Apparatus

The apparatus consists of an introductory survey, a mock-up account registration webpage, and a follow-up questionnaire. Three sets of the apparatus were created for two treatment conditions (confirmshaming and trick-question), and a

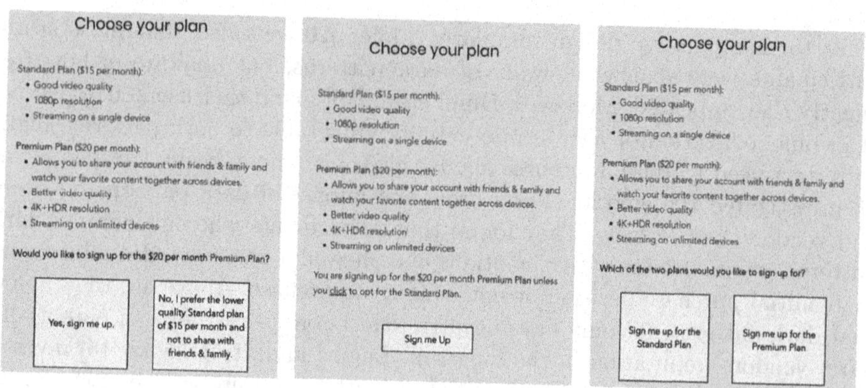

Fig. 1. *Wave* account registration website: confirmshaming condition (left), trick-question condition (middle), and control condition with no dark patterns (right).

control condition (Fig. 1). The introductory survey, created using Google Forms, first asked participants for their consent to participate in the study; then it presented a scenario introducing them to a fictional online streaming platform *Wave*, and explained the account registration task. The participants were then asked to register for an account on the website as though it were a real streaming service and assuming they had a monthly budget of $15 to $20. Afterwards, they were provided with a link to the account registration website created using a website builder (*Wix*). The format of the website followed loosely that of popular online services that require account creation, e.g., Netflix. Before reaching the page where they enter details (e.g. username, password) to create an account, they were intercepted by a registration page where the participant was given the choice between two plans: standard and premium. Figure 1 shows the 3 conditions of the website. After selecting a plan, participants were redirected to a confirmation page where they could confirm their selection or go back to the previous page and edit their choice before creating an account. After completing the task, they were given a link to the follow-up questionnaire.

The follow-up questionnaire included UX questions on perceived ease of use and perceived persuasiveness, and reputation-related questions on perceived credibility, perceived trustworthiness, and perceived non-manipulation (Table 1). Adapted from Oyibo and Morita [16], the questions were measured on a 7-point Likert scale ranging from "strongly disagree - 1" to "strongly agree - 7." Participants were also asked about their initial intention to sign up for the more expensive premium plan and whether they edited their initial choice or not. Finally, they were debriefed. After reading a brief description of dark patterns, participants were asked about their prior knowledge of such patterns. Depending on the treatment group, the dark pattern element used in the webpage was revealed to the participants, after which they were asked about the element's perceived persuasiveness and its impact on their account registration task. Demographic data including gender, age, language skills, and familiarity with existing streaming services were collected. Apart from users' survey responses, the website logged the time it took them to complete the task.

3.3 Design

The user study employed a mixed design. The independent variable is the dark pattern incorporated in the website. It has three levels: confirmshaming, trick-question, and control. The dependent variables are as follows:

Table 1. Measures. *Reversed to "perceived non-manipulation" in data analysis.

Construct	Items Operationalizing Construct
Perceived Ease of Use	1. The account registration website was easy to use. 2. I faced no difficulty creating an account on the Wave website. 3. No elements on the website led to confusion.
Perceived Trustworthiness	1. The account registration website was trustworthy. 2. I had no concerns while providing my personal data. 3. I trust the information provided on the website.
Perceived Credibility	1. The website reflects integrity. 2. The information provided by the website is reliable. 3. From my experience with the account registration task, I think Wave is a credible streaming platform.
Perceived Persuasiveness	1. The design of the account registration website persuaded me to sign up for Premium membership. 2. The account registration website presentation persuaded me to sign up for Premium membership. 3. I was convinced by the website's message that a Premium membership would benefit me.
Perceived Manipulation*	Wave contains some manipulative and/or deceptive interface designs, which are in the best interest of the online vendor or service.

- UX: measured using the participants' average rating of the perceived ease of use and perceived persuasiveness of the website.
- Reputation: measured using the participants' average rating of the perceived non-manipulation, perceived trustworthiness, and perceived credibility of the website. The variable "perceived manipulation, "operationalized in Table 1, was reversed to become "perceived non-manipulation" during data analysis.
- Selected choice: standard (cheap) or premium (expensive) plan.

Regarding UX, the experiment design was a 3×2 repeated measure with 3 between-group levels of dark pattern (confirmshaming, trick-question, and control) and two within-group levels of UX (perceived ease of use and perceived persuasiveness). Similarly, regarding reputation, the experiment design was 3×3 repeated measure with 3 between-group levels of dark pattern and 3 within-group levels of reputation (perceived non-manipulation, perceived trustworthiness, and perceived credibility). As earlier mentioned, participants were debriefed at the end of the survey. They were asked a binary question (yes/no) whether they had knowledge of the concept of dark patterns prior to taking the survey. During data analysis, they were classified into two groups: those with and those without knowledge of dark patterns. Additional data collected, such as whether participants edited their initial selected plan or not, provided more insights into whether the dark patterns successfully "tricked" participants into signing up for the vendor-intended choice (premium plan) and whether participants realized that they were being "manipulated" or not.

4 Results

Prior to the data analysis, we computed the reliability of each of the UX and reputation variables using McDonald's omega metric: a measure for non-normal data. The results indicated that the reliability requirement for each of the variables was satisfied ($\omega > 0.7$) [17]. Figure 2 shows the mean scores of the reputation and UX measures. Regarding perceived non-manipulation, the control condition was rated higher than the other two conditions. Regardless of condition, perceived ease of use was rated higher than perceived persuasiveness and the reputation variables. We conducted RM-ANOVA to uncover the main and interaction effects of knowledge of dark patterns.

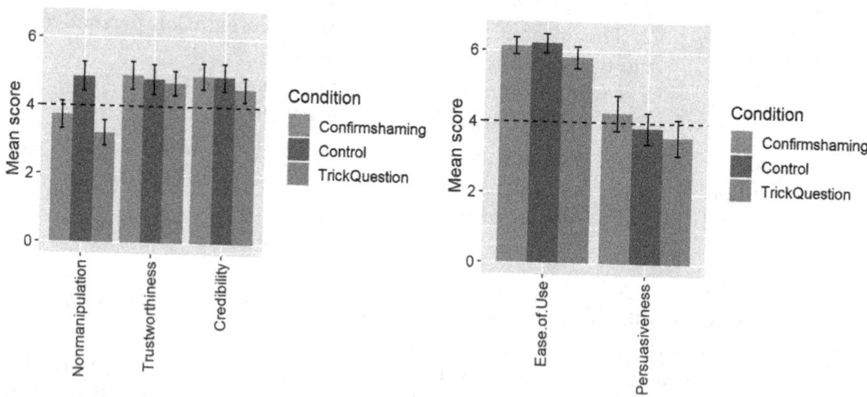

Fig. 2. Mean scores of reputation measures (left) and UX measures (right). Error bar: 95% confidence interval. Horizontal bar: neutral score on a 7-point scale.

4.1 RM-ANOVA with Regard to Reputation Variables

The results of a 3-way RM-ANOVA based on knowledge of dark patterns, condition and reputation measure showed that there are main effects of each variable and two interactions between condition and reputation ($F_{4,591} = 4.01, p < 0.01$), and between condition and knowledge ($F_{2,591} = 6.91, p < 0.01$). The interactions were explored further at each level of the interacting variables.

One-Way ANOVA at Each Level of Condition and Reputation Measure. We conducted a 1-way ANOVA based on reputation measure for each of the three conditions (Table 2). Regarding the control condition, the 1-way ANOVA showed that there is no main effect of reputation measure. However, regarding confirmshaming, there is a main effect of reputation measure ($F_{2,207} = 12.41, p = 0.000$). Similarly, regarding trick-question, the 1-way ANOVA showed that there is a main effect of reputation measure ($F_{2,207} = 23.27, p = 0.000$). Regarding confirmshaming and trick-question, posthoc pairwise analyses based on reputation measure showed that trustworthiness and credibility are significantly higher than perceived non-manipulation ($p < 0.001$) as indicated by the respective mean scores: >4.5 for trustworthiness and credibility and <3.8 for perceived non-manipulation. Due to the 2-way interaction between condition and reputation measure, we conducted a 1-way ANOVA based on condition for each of the 3 reputation measures (Table 2). Regarding perceived non-manipulation, the 1-way ANOVA shows that there is a main effect of condition ($F_{2,200} = 18.16, p < 0.001$), but this is not the case regarding trustworthiness and credibility. Kruskal-Wallis test based on condition (with the Bonferroni p-values adjustment) showed that the mean scores are significantly higher for the control condition than for confirmshaming ($p < 0.001$) and trick-question ($p < 0.001$).

Table 2. One-way ANOVA for each condition and reputation measure. CTR: Control: CSH: Confirmshaming, TQU: Trick-Question, NM: Perceived Non-Manipulation, TR: Trustworthiness, CR: Credibility, DP: Dark Pattern.

		One-way ANOVA for each reputation measure			
		NM	TR	CR	Measure Effect
One-way ANOVA for each condition	CTR	4.86	4.79	4.88	$F_{2,186} = 0.09$, $p = 0.991$
	CSH	3.73	4.90	4.90	$F_{2,207} = 12.41$, $p < 0.001$
	TQU	3.21	4.70	4.53	$F_{2,207} = 23.27$, $p < 0.001$
	DP Effect	$F_{2,200} = 18.16$, $p < 0.001$	$F_{2,200} = 0.86$, $p = 0.42$	$F_{2,200} = 2.26$, $p = 0.107$	

Table 3. One-way ANOVA for reputation at each level of knowledge and condition. CTR: Control: CSH: Confirmshaming, TQU: Trick-Question.

		One-way ANOVA for each level of knowledge		
		With	Without	Knowledge Effect
One-way ANOVA for each condition	CTR	4.69	4.91	$F_{1,187} = 0.10, p = 0.75$
	CSH	3.50	4.92	$F_{1,208} = 26.08, p < 0.001$
	TQU	3.96	4.28	$F_{1,208} = 2.94, p = 0.09$
	DP Effect	$F_{2,198} = 5.86$, $p < 0.01$	$F_{2,405} = 6.98$, $p < 0.001$	

One-Way ANOVA at Each Level of Condition and Knowledge. We conducted a 1-way ANOVA for each level of condition and knowledge. Table 3 shows that there is a main effect of knowledge regarding confirmshaming condition ($F_{1,208} = 26.08, p < 0.001$) and a main effect of condition among users with knowledge ($F_{2,198} = 5.86, p < 0.01$) and without knowledge ($F_{2,405} = 6.98, p < 0.01$). Among users with knowledge, a Kruskal-Wallis test $[X^2(2) = 11.18, p < 0.01]$ based on condition showed that the mean scores are significantly and marginally higher for the control condition than for confirmshaming ($p < 0.05$) and trick-question ($p = 0.07$), respectively. Among users without knowledge, the same test $[X^2(2) = 13.56, p < 0.01]$ based on condition showed that the mean scores are significantly higher ($p < 0.01$) for the control condition (M = 4.91) and confirmshaming (M = 4.92) than for trick-question (M = 4.28).

4.2 RM-ANOVA with Regard to UX Variables

We conducted a 4-way RM-ANOVA based on the knowledge, condition, selected plan, and UX measure. The results showed that there is a main effect of each variable and an interaction between condition and knowledge ($F_{2,360} = 5.28, p = 0.005$), and between selected plan and UX variable ($F_{1,360} = 62.84, p = 0.000$). The interactions were explored further at each level of the interacting variables.

One-Way ANOVA at Each Level of Condition and Knowledge. One-way ANOVA (Table 4) showed that, among users without knowledge, there is a main effect of condition ($F_{2,255} = 3.90, p < 0.05$). There is also a main effect of knowledge for confirmshaming ($F_{1,132} = 6.03, p < 0.05$). Due to the main effect of condition on UX among those without knowledge, we conducted a Kruskal-Wallis test $[X^2(2) = 7.00, p = 0.301]$ based on condition. The results showed that the overall mean score of UX for confirmshaming (M = 5.51) is significantly higher than that for trick-question (M = 4.69) at $p < 0.05$. However, confirmshaming (M = 5.51) or trick-question (M = 4.69) and the control condition (M = 5.00) do not significantly differ ($p > 0.05$).

Table 4. One-way ANOVA for UX for each level of knowledge and condition. CTR: Control: CSH: Confirmshaming, TQU: Trick-Question, DP: Dark Pattern.

		One-way ANOVA for each level of knowledge		
		With	Without	Knowledge Effect
One-way ANOVA for each condition	CTR	5.09	5.00	$F_{1,124} = 0.38, p = 0.54$
	CSH	4.56	5.51	$F_{1,132} = 6.03, p < 0.05$
	TQU	4.71	4.69	$F_{1,122} = 0.05, p = 0.82$
	DP Effect	$F_{2.123} = 0.84$, $p = 0.43$	$F_{2,255} = 3.90$, $p < 0.05$	

One-Way ANOVA at Each Level of Selected Plan and UX Measure. We conducted a 1-way ANOVA at each level of selected plan and UX measure (Table 5). The results regarding persuasiveness showed that there is a main effect of selected plan ($F_{1,190} = 87.92, p = 0.008$), but none regarding ease of use ($F_{1,190} = 1.038, p = 0.310$). There is also a main effect of UX regarding the standard plan ($F_{1,162} = 211.05, p = 0.000$) and premium plan ($F_{1,218} = 44.63, p = 0.000$), with ease of use (M = 6.02 and 6.14, respectively) significantly having a higher mean rating than persuasiveness (M = 2.56 and 4.88, respectively in both cases.

4.3 Relationship Between Condition/Knowledge and Selected Plan

Figure 3 shows the percentage of users in each condition or knowledge group that selected a given plan. Chi-square tests showed that there is no relationship between condition and selected plan [$X^2(2) = 1.05, p = 0.59$] for all of the valid participants (top-left), between knowledge and selected plan [$X^2(1) = 1.17, p = 0.28$] for the control group (top-right), and between knowledge and selected plan [$X^2(1) = 0.001, p = 0.97$] for the trick-question condition (bottom-right). However, there is a significant relationship between knowledge and selected plan [$X^2(1) = 6.31, p = 0.01$] for the confirmshaming condition (bottom-left), with a higher percentage of those without knowledge of dark patterns (68%) selecting the premium plan than of those with knowledge (35%).

Table 5. One-way ANOVA for each level of UX measure and selected plan. PEOU: Perceived Ease of Use, PP: Perceived Persuasiveness.

		One-way ANOVA for each UX measure		
		PEOU	PP	Measure Effect
One-way ANOVA for each plan	Standard	6.02	2.56	$F_{1,162} = 211.05, p < 0.001$
	Premium	6.14	4.88	$F_{1,218} = 44.63, p < 0.001$
	Plan Effect	$F_{1,190} = 1.04$, $p = 0.31$	$F_{1,190} = 87.92$, $p < 0.01$	

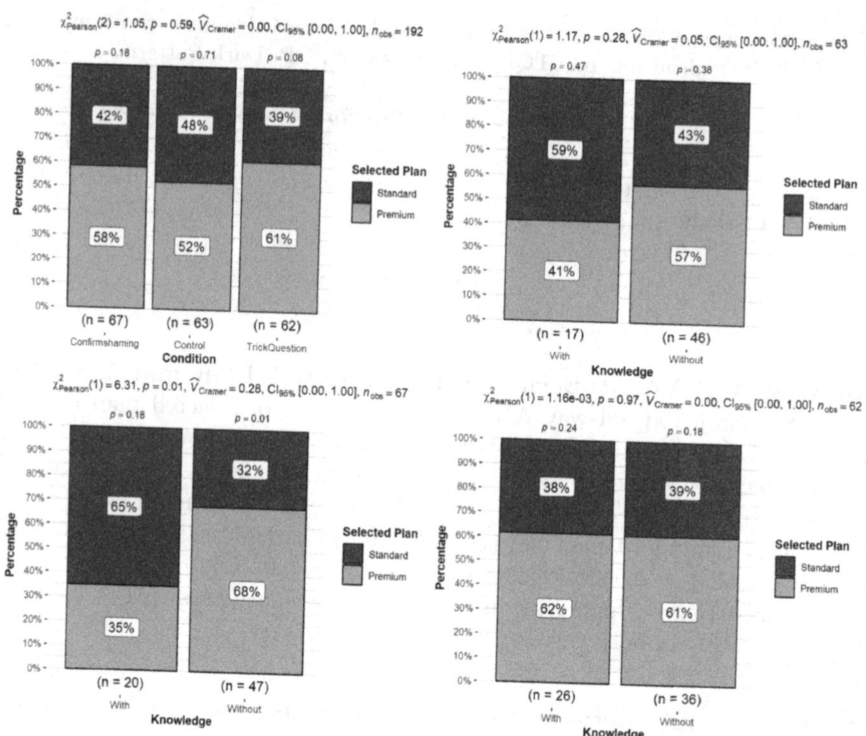

Fig. 3. Chi-square tests on the relationship between condition and selected plan (top-left); knowledge and selected plan for control condition (top-right), confirmshaming condition (bottom-left), trick-question condition (bottom-right).

4.4 Relationship Between Condition and Editing of Selected Plan

Figure 4 shows the percentage of participants in each condition or knowledge group that edited their selected plan for one reason or the other. A Chi-square test (top-left) showed that there is a relationship between edited plan and selected plan $[X^2(1) = 12.94, p < 0.001]$, with those that edited their plan (69%) more likely to select the standard plan than those the did not (37%).

Moreover, a Chi-square test (top-right) showed that there is a relationship between condition and editing of selected plan $[X^2(2) = 28.33, p = 0.000]$, with more participants in the trick-question condition editing their selected plan than the other two conditions. As shown in the top-right chart (Fig. 4), 4 out of 10 participants in the trick-question condition edited their selected plan compared with roughly 1 out of 10 participants in the confirmshaming or control condition. Finally, in both treatment conditions(bottom), there is no significant relationship between knowledge of dark patterns and editing of selected plan. However, in the trick-question condition (bottom-right chart), more users in the knowledgeable group (50%) edited their plan than in the non-knowledgeable group (33%). Specifically, 5 out of 10 participants with knowledge of dark patterns edited their

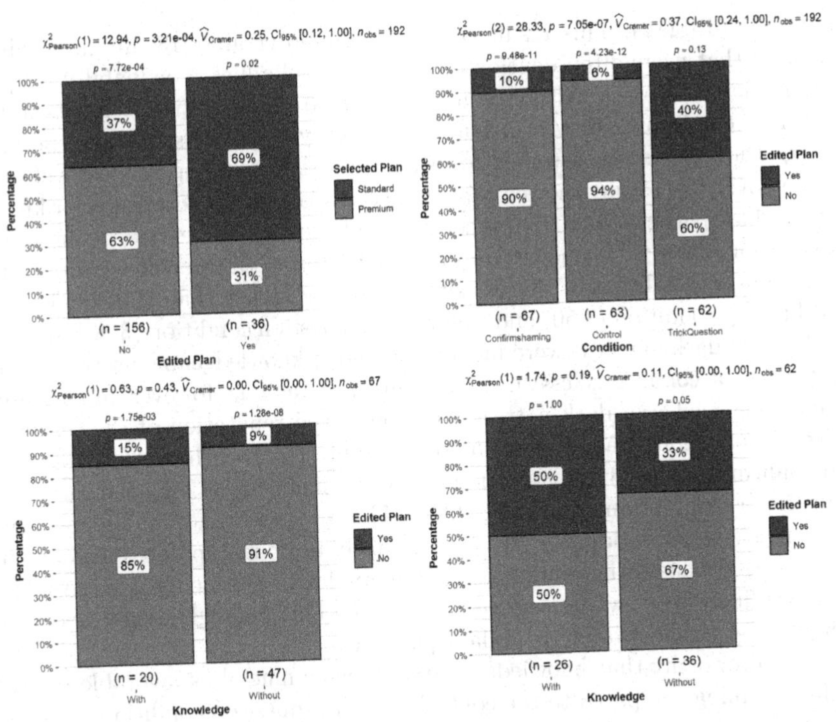

Fig. 4. Chi-square tests on the relationship between edited plan and selected plan (top-left), condition and edited plan (top-right); knowledge and edited plan for confirmshaming group (bottom-left) and for trick-question group (bottom-right).

choice compared with roughly 3 out of 10 participants without knowledge. In the non-knowledgeable group, the difference between those that edited their plan and those that did not is marginally significant ($p = 0.05$), but this is not the case in the knowledgeable group ($p > 0.05$)

5 Discussion

We have presented the analysis of the relationship between dark patterns and UX/reputation variables, on one hand, and selected choice, on the other hand. The results of the data analysis uncovered significant relationships between dark patterns and user experience, selected choice, and website reputation.

5.1 Reputation

The control condition received a higher rating in perceived non-manipulation (Fig. 2). In contrast, the confirmshaming and trick-question conditions were perceived to be manipulative. However, their perceived manipulation had no significant impact on the perceived trustworthiness and credibility of both treatment conditions (Table 2). This result echoes Geronimo et al.'s [13] findings, which indicated that users often develop "dark pattern-blindness" or inability to perceive malicious designs. Although users identified manipulative elements in the treatment conditions, they still trusted and viewed them as credible, perhaps because they were so accustomed to seeing these dark patterns in most websites.

Moreover, the results showed that there is a relationship between prior knowledge of dark patterns and the perceived reputation of the service. As shown in Table 3, for users with knowledge of dark patterns, the perceived reputation of the control condition of the website (4.69) was higher than that of the confirmshaming condition (3.50) and that of trick-question condition (3.96). In other words, both dark patterns were ineffective among knowledgeable users who rate the treatment conditions less than the neutral score of 4. However, among users without knowledge of dark patterns, the perceived reputation of the service in all three conditions was assessed more favorably (>4), with the control (4.91) and confirmshaming (4.92) conditions having a significantly higher mean rating than the trick-question condition (4.28). This suggests that users who do not have knowledge of dark patterns are more likely to be manipulated into making decisions that benefit the vendor since, compared with knowledgeable users, they are more likely to view the service as credible. This highlights the importance of increasing public awareness of dark patterns.

It is noteworthy that knowledgeable users were much less favorable towards confirmshaming compared to the control and trick-question conditions. The difference (1.42) in perceived reputation between those with and those without knowledge is statistically significant at $p < 0.001$ (Table 3). The study results suggest that the unfavorable disposition of users with knowledge of confirmshaming impacted their choice of plan. For example, among knowledgeable users (Fig. 3), 62% and 41% of those in the trick-question and control conditions, respectively, selected the premium plan (intended by the vendor). However, only 35% in the confirmshaming condition selected the premium plan. This is an indication that vendors and designers should be wary of confirmshaming dark pattern which has become prevalent in online platforms [7]. The results suggest that as more and more users become aware of dark patterns over time, they would be able to tell whether they are being manipulated or not.

5.2 User Experience

Overall, users found the website, regardless of condition, to be easy to use. Moreover, they found all three conditions easier to use than they found it persuasive (Fig. 2). However, the confirmshaming condition had a higher perceived UX than the trick-question condition among those without knowledge of dark patterns (Table 4). Of the 203 participants, 67% (136) had no prior knowledge of dark patterns. Among this group (Table 4), the confirmshaming condition was rated higher in UX (5.51) than the trick-question condition (4.69), but this is not the case among those with knowledge, where there is no significant difference between both conditions (4.56 and 4.71, respectively). As shown in Fig. 3, the higher vulnerability of those without knowledge to confirmshaming went as far as making them opt more for the premium plan (68%) compared with those in the trick-question condition (61%) or control condition (57%). However, this not the case among those with knowledge in the confirmshaming condition, who were less vulnerable to the premium plan (35%) than those in the trick-question (62%) and control (41%) conditions. Furthermore, regarding perceived persuasiveness, the 1-way ANOVA (Table 5) indicates that users who selected the premium plan were relatively persuaded by the design and content of the website (4.88), unlike those who selected the standard plan (2.56). This indicates that the design of a website, particularly, the use of confirmshaming, can nudge users, particularly those without prior knowledge of dark patterns, to make decisions that are in the best interest of the vendor. As shown in Fig. 3, 68% of those without knowledge selected the premium plan compared with 35% of those with knowledge that selected the premium plan. This finding (of 33% difference between the selected plans of the two knowledge groups) indicates that lack of knowledge of dark patterns can make users more vulnerable to the service-promoted choice.

5.3 Effectiveness of Dark Patterns

The results (Fig. 3) show that both dark patterns are effective in making the user take a decision in the best interest of the vendor, with trick-question effective for both knowledge groups and confirmshaming effective for those without knowledge only. The trick-question dark pattern led a higher percentage of users to select the expensive plan promoted by the vendor. Regardless of knowledge group, >60% of users in the trick-question condition selected the premium plan compared with 52% in the control group. The reason trick-question was most effective is that the default choice is the expensive plan. Opting out (i.e., for the standard plan instead) requires the user to click a text (Fig. 3), which might not be obvious to many users given the confusing nature of the question. Regarding confirmshaming, there is a relationship between knowledge and selected plan, with 68% of those without knowledge selecting the premium plan compared with 35% of those with knowledge. This indicates that once users become aware of the manipulative tactic of confirmshaming, they are likely to go against the vendor's promoted choice. It may also suggest that users with knowledge of dark patterns would be more likely to churn a service due to perceived manipulation. This hypothesis needs further investigation in future work.

5.4 Plan Selection and Editing

Regarding user certainty about selected plan, Fig. 4 indicates prior knowledge of dark patterns does impact the reconsideration and editing of the initial selected plan. As shown, the greatest percentage of users in the trick-question condition edited their initial choice of plan (40%, 28 out of 70 participants); the precentages were 11% (8 out of 70) and 6% (4 out of 63) for the confirmshaming and control conditions, respectively. This is an indication that a good number of the participants in the trick-question condition were confused by the deceptive statement they encountered: "*You are signing up for the $20 per month Premium plan* *unless you click to opt for the Standard plan.*" A few of the 28 trick-question participants (particularly knowledgeable users, half of whom edited their selected plan) also noted in their qualitative responses that they edited their response because they felt that the website was tricking them into signing up for the premium plan. We could conjecture that if not given the 'edit plan' option on the confirmation page, participants might have signed up for a premium plan mistakenly and the trick-question would have had more of an effect on their choice of plan. This observation is consistent with the findings of Luguri and Strahilevitz [15], in which the authors found that the trick-question technique was more effective compared to confirmshaming in getting participants to subscribe to the paid plan offered in the data privacy survey used in their experiments.

5.5 Additional Findings

In addition to the above findings, we found that the set of questions inquiring about the participants' use of streaming services showed that most participants were familiar with streaming services, using such services occasionally, frequently or daily, with only 5% (10 participants) indicating that they never used streaming services. Ninety-four percent of participants (190) selected English as their primary language so we can assume language barriers did not affect their perception of the account registration page and their choice of plan.

5.6 Limitations and Future Work

Only a subset of the data collected was analyzed in this paper. As such, we do not know the role unexplored variables such as task completion time and demographics other than knowledge of dark patterns play in the results. In future work, we plan to explore how completion time, age, gender, and personality influence the findings. We also plan to analyze the qualitative data to gain insights into the effect of each dark pattern on UX and website reputation.

6 Conclusion

In this paper, we examined the influence of confirmshaming and trick-question dark patterns on user experience, decision-making, and website perceived reputation using a video streaming service as proof of concept. The results showed that dark patterns and user knowledge of them influence users' purchase decisions to the benefit of the platforms that use them. The results also showed that users might change their purchase choices if aware of being manipulated. Particularly, users who are knowledgeable about dark patterns are more likely to reconsider their decision due to an inkling of being steered into making a decision that is not in their best interest. They are also more likely to react unfavorably towards dark patterns in general. Finally, the results revealed that the dark patterns achieved the platform's financial goal, as they were able to trick both those with and without knowledge of dark patterns and guilt shame non-knowledgeable users to choose the expensive plan over the cheap plan. The findings emphasize the need for user awareness, e.g., on how dark patterns can make them take decisions against their own interest. Given that users still considered the website trustworthy and credible despite recognizing that the treatment conditions were manipulative, public awareness cannot be over-emphasized. In future work, we plan to conduct further data analyses to uncover the moderating effect of age, gender, education, and personality on the current findings.

References

1. Vyas, D., Chisalita, C.M., Van Der Veer, G.C.: Affordance in interaction. In: Proceedings of the 13th European Conference on Cognitive Ergonomics: Trust and Control in Complex Socio-Technical Systems, pp. 92-99 (September 2006)
2. Gunawan, J., Pradeep, A., Choffnes, D., Hartzog, W., Wilson, C.: A comparative study of dark patterns across web and mobile modalities. Proc. ACM Hum.-Comput. Interact. **5**(CSCW2), 1–29 (2021)
3. Hanson, J.D., Kysar, D.A.: Taking behavioralism seriously: the problem of market manipulation. NYUL rev. **74**, 630 (1999)
4. Gray, C.M., Kou, Y., Battles, B., Hoggatt, J., Toombs, A.L.: The dark (patterns) side of UX design. In: Proceedings of the 2018 CHI Conference on Human Factors in Computing Systems, pp. 1-14 (April 2018)
5. Brignull, H.: What is dark pattern?, dark pattern (2022). https://www.deceptive.design (Accessed 09 Dec 2022)
6. Mathur, A., Kshirsagar, M., Mayer, J.: What makes a dark pattern... dark? design attributes, normative considerations, and measurement methods. In: Proceedings of the 2021 CHI Conference on Human Factors in Computing Systems, pp. 1-18 (2021)
7. Mathur, A., et al.: dark patterns at scale: findings from a crawl of 11K shopping websites. ACM Proc. Hum.-Comput. Interact. **3**(CSCW), 1-32 (2019)
8. Özdemir, Ş: Digital nudges and dark patterns: the angels and the archfiends of digital communication. Digital Scholarship Human. **35**(2), 417–428 (2020)
9. Costello, F.J., Yun, J., Lee, K.C.: Digital dark nudge: an exploration of when digital nudges unethically depart. In: Proceedings of the 55th Hawaii International Conference on System Sciences, pp. 4348-4357 (2022)
10. Sharp, H., et al.: Interaction Design: Beyond Human-Computer Interaction. John Wiley and Sons, Incorporated (2019)
11. Park, M., Yoo, J.: Social commerce: the effects of time pressure, product popularity, and website reputation on purchase intention. In: Global Marketing Conference, pp. 1131-1133 (July 2016)
12. Toth, M., Bielova, N., Roca, V.: On dark patterns and manipulation of website publishers by CMPs. In: PETS 2022-22nd Privacy Enhancing Technologies Symposium (July 2022)
13. Di Geronimo, L., Braz, L., Fregnan, E., Palomba, F., Bacchelli, A.: UI dark patterns and where to find them: a study on mobile applications and user perception. In: Proceedings of the 2020 CHI conference on Human Factors in Computing Systems, pp. 1-14 (April 2020)
14. Bhoot, A.M, Shinde, M.A, Mishra, W.P.: Towards the identification of dark patterns: an analysis based on end-user reactions. In: Proceedings of the 11th Indian Conference on Human-Computer Interaction, pp. 24-33 (November 2020)

15. Luguri, J., Strahilevitz, L.J.: Shining a light on dark patterns. J. Legal Anal. **13**(1), 43–109 (2021)
16. Oyibo, K., Morita, P.P.: The role UX design attributes play in the perceived persuasiveness of contact tracing apps. Multimodal Technol. Interact. **6**(10), 88 (2022)
17. Dunn, T.J., Baguley, T., Brunsden, V.: From alpha to omega: a practical solution to the pervasive problem of internal consistency estimation. Br. J. Psychol. **105**(3), 99–412 (2014)
18. Bongard-Blanchy, K., Rossi, A., Rivas, S., Doublet, S., Koenig, V., Lenzini, G.: I am definitely manipulated, even when i am aware of it. it's ridiculous!" - dark patterns from the end-user perspective. In: Designing Interactive Systems Conference 2021, pp. 763-776 (June 2021)
19. Zac, A., Huang, Y.C., von Moltke, A., Decker, C., Ezrachi, A.: Dark patterns and Online Consumer Vulnerability. Available at SSRN 4547964 (2023)
20. Maier, M., Harr, R.: Dark design patterns: an end-user perspective. Human Technol. **16**, 170-199 (2020). https://doi.org/10.17011/ht/urn.202008245641
21. Amazon.ca: Low prices - fast shipping - millions of items. Amazon.ca: Low Prices - Fast Shipping - Millions of Items. (n.d.-a). https://www.amazon.ca/
22. Log in or sign up. Facebook. (n.d.). https://www.facebook.com/
23. Unlimited movies, TV shows, and more. Netflix. (n.d.). https://www.netflix.com/ca/
24. Ahuja, S., Kumar, J.: Conceptualizations of user autonomy within the normative evaluation of dark patterns. Ethics Inf. Technol. **24**(4), 52 (2022)
25. Naiseh, M., Al-Mansoori, R. S., Al-Thani, D., Jiang, N., Ali, R.: Nudging through friction: an approach for calibrating trust in explainable AI. In: 2021 8th International Conference on Behavioral and Social Computing (BESC), pp. 1-5. IEEE (October 2021)
26. Buçinca, Z., Malaya, M.B., Gajos, K.Z.: To trust or to think: cognitive forcing functions can reduce overreliance on AI in AI-assisted decision-making. Proc. ACM on Hum.-Comput. Interact. **5**(CSCW1), 1–21 (2021)

Exploring the Influence of Game Framing and Gamer Types on the Effectiveness of Persuasive Games

Chinenye Ndulue(✉) and Rita Orji

Dalhousie University, Halifax, Canada
{cndulue,rita.orji}@dal.ca

Abstract. Although persuasive games are effective at promoting behaviour change, their effectiveness may be influenced by many factors, which include gamer personality type and game framing. This paper explores the relationship between game framing, gamer type and persuasive strategies, focusing on a persuasive game for Healthy Eating. In a between-study of 371 participants, our research revealed that, although the three game-framing versions (gain-framed, loss-framed, and gain-loss-framed) and four persuasive strategies implemented (reward, competition, praise, and suggestion) were perceived as effective, the effectiveness of the reward strategy was significantly different across the game-framing versions. It was more effective in the gain-loss framed version when compared to the other two versions. We also found that the reward strategy had the highest number of significant relationships with the gamer types across all the game framings, while the suggestion strategy showed no significant relationships with the gamer types across all framings. We conclude by discussing the insights from these results and how they affect persuasive game design for game framings and game types.

Keywords: Gain-framing · Loss-framing · Gain-Loss framing · Persuasive games · behaviour change · persuasive strategies · serious games

1 Introduction

Persuasive games are interactive systems strategically designed to promote behaviour and attitude changes through the implementation of various persuasive strategies [19, 24]. Research has shown that persuasive games are effective at promoting behaviour change across many domains [15, 21]. Consequently, there has been a growing investment in designing and developing persuasive gamified systems to address challenges in domains including environmental sustainability [8], promoting personal wellness, managing diseases [14], engaging in preventive behaviours, physical activity [16], healthy eating [23], avoiding risky behaviours, and substance abuse [9].

Previous research has highlighted the inadequacy of a one-size-fits-all approach in designing persuasive games for behaviour change [20]. Therefore, there is a growing focus on exploring how to tailor persuasive games based on user characteristics age

N. Baghaei et al. (Eds.): PERSUASIVE 2024, LNCS 14636, pp. 207–221, 2024.
https://doi.org/10.1007/978-3-031-58226-4_16

groups, gender groups [26], gamer types [20], gamification user type [22], and personality types [1, 18]. However, in the realm of game design, two pivotal factors significantly influencing the effectiveness of persuasive games are game framing and gamer type.

Game framing involves the intentional and strategic design of a game's context, mechanics, and objectives [33]. This concept encompasses three primary types of framing: gain-framing [12], loss-framing [38] and gain-loss-framing [13]. In the field of persuasive games, understanding the relationship between game framing and persuasive strategies is of paramount importance. Game framing not only lays the groundwork for the integration of persuasive game elements but also moulds players' perceptions of the game's purpose, context, and challenges. As a result, it can significantly impact the effectiveness of the embedded persuasive strategies aimed at motivating players toward specific behaviours or attitudes.

On the other hand, gamer type refers to the characteristics and preferences of game players [36]. Understanding different gamer types is essential for tailoring persuasive games to the diverse needs and motivations of the player base [20]. By recognizing the various player profiles and individual differences, game designers can strategies, and implement features and mechanics that resonate with specific gamer types, thereby enhancing the overall engagement and effectiveness of persuasive elements within the game [24]. In essence, the interplay between game framing and gamer type is a key consideration in the design and success of persuasive games. It is therefore important to explore the impact of game framing and gamer type together on the effectiveness of persuasive games and persuasive strategies.

To advance research in this area, firstly, we developed three versions of persuasive games for promoting healthy eating: gain-framing, loss-framing, and gain-loss framing. Secondly, we conducted a large-scale study with 371 participants, exploring how various gamer types, based on the HEXAD Model [36], responded to four persuasive strategies (reward, competition, praise, and suggestion [19]). These strategies were implemented in three different game-framing versions of a Space-Invader-styled persuasive game focused on healthy eating – gain-framing, loss-framing, and gain-loss framing. Next, we developed models showing how these gamer types respond to the individual strategies in each game framing type using the Partial Least Square Structural Equation Modeling (PLS-SEM) [28]. Our result revealed that, despite the overall perceived effectiveness of all game versions and persuasive strategies, the reward strategy exhibited a significant overall difference across the three game-framing types. Specifically, it was more effective in the gain-loss framed version when compared to the other two versions We also found that the reward strategy had the highest number of significant relationships with the gamer types across all the game framings, while the suggestion strategy showed no significant relationships with the gamer types across all framings. We conclude by discussing the insights from these results and how they affect persuasive game design, especially tailoring them based on the game framings and game types. Our research addresses the following specific research questions:

RQ1: What is the perceived effectiveness of the persuasive game overall and the individual persuasive strategies implemented in the game across the three game framings?

RQ2: Are there any differences in the effectiveness of the persuasive game versions and the persuasive strategies across the three game framings?

RQ3: What are the relationships between gamer types and the effectiveness of persuasive strategies across the three game framing versions?

2 Literature Review

In this section, we will review persuasive strategies used in health-focused persuasive games and explore framing in persuasive design.

2.1 Persuasive Game and Strategies

Research indicates a growing trend in the development of persuasive games across diverse domains of health. For instance, COVID Dodge [4] is a persuasive game promoting awareness of COVID-19 precautions. The game employs strategies such as Rewards (points for lasting in the game), Reminders (push notifications on safety measures), Suggestions (random safety tips during gameplay), Competition (global leaderboard), and Punishment (losing a life for proximity to characters) [17]. Furthermore, 'SmokeScreen' [27] is a persuasive game for high school students, promoting avoidance of tobacco abuse. It employs Simulation, Rehearsal, Reward, and Similarity strategies. Players navigate virtual characters through a school, making decisions affecting their avatar's health – Similarity and Rehearsal. Healthy decisions yield progress and points – Reward, while wrong choices result in health point loss. The game concludes after a series of decisions, allowing players to observe their avatars' overall health – Simulation.

Some other persuasive games include 'LunchTime' [23], a persuasive game for motivating healthy eating which employs the Reward, Competition, and Comparison strategies, 'Nourish Your Tree' [25], a persuasive game for physical activity that employs various persuasive strategies including Self-monitoring, Simulation, Praise, Suggestion, Reminders, Rewards, Competition, and Recognition.

2.2 Framings

Framing plays a pivotal role in enhancing user engagement across applications, and games, influencing emotional connections, immersion, and identification with system elements. Carefully framed system features can heighten motivation for interaction and learning. However, research outcomes on gain and loss framing's impact on behaviour change vary.

Lim et al. [12] examined gain-framed performance feedback in relation to users' intentions to adopt fitness apps, finding it more effective than loss-framed messages. This positive framing significantly influenced user intentions for fitness app adoption, as supported by Yadav et al.'s [37] work in exercise apps and Schlottmann's [32] work on how children and adults view gains and losses.

On the other hand, Ye et al. [38] discovered that loss-framed messages were more effective in promoting vaccination intentions during a public health crisis. Roby [29] demonstrated the effectiveness of loss framing in improving coordination in a minimum-effort game.

Despite evidence of the effectiveness of gain and loss framing in specific contexts, there is a lack of comprehensive research on the overall impact of gain framing, loss framing, and gain-loss framing on persuasive game effectiveness and the interaction of persuasive strategies with gamer types. Our research addresses this gap.

3 Method

In this section, we describe the game design, study design, measurement instrument, participant demography, and the data analysis methods employed in our study.

3.1 Game Design

To investigate the impact of game framing on the effectiveness of persuasive games, we designed three versions of a space-invader-style game for healthy eating. Each version corresponds to the three different persuasive game framing types. We present each of these framings and their implementation in detail in the following sections.

Persuasive Gain Game Framing (GF). This game version emphasizes the positive effects (benefits) of healthy eating. specifically, it integrates elements of game design and gameplay mechanics, emphasizing potential benefits or gains associated with taking specific actions within the game.

In this version, players are incentivized to consume healthy food items. Specifically, they gain points and enhance their in-game performance. The primary objective is to actively engage with and target the nutritious food items within the game environment. Additionally, players must also efficiently gather these healthy food items as they drop down from the top of the screen within a time limit, adding a layer of challenge, skill and timing to the gameplay. The more successfully the player collects and consumes healthy foods, the higher their score, contributing to a positive and rewarding gaming experience with a focus on gaining points and emphasizing the benefits of healthy eating in the game. (see Fig. 1B).

Persuasive Loss Game Framing (LF). This game version emphasizes the consequences of unhealthy eating. specifically, it integrates elements of game design and gameplay mechanics, emphasizing potential losses or negative consequences associated with not engaging in desired behaviours or actions within the game.

In this version, the objective is to eliminate unhealthy food items positioned at the top of the screen. They also must avoid these unhealthy foods as they drop from the top of the same screen. When an unhealthy food item hits the player the player loses some in-game life. This version introduces a risk-reward dynamic, where players must strategically eliminate threats (unhealthy foods) to maintain their in-game vitality, creating a sense of urgency and potential consequences for failing to address the looming "loss" condition (see Fig. 1A).

Persuasive Gain-Loss Game Framing (GLF). This game version emphasizes both the benefits and consequences of unhealthy eating. specifically, it integrates elements of game design and gameplay mechanics that strategically highlight both the potential gains and losses associated with specific behaviours or choices within the game.

In this version, players encounter a dynamic mix of challenges as both healthy and unhealthy food items populate the game environment. The primary objective is to collect all healthy food items while eliminating and avoiding all unhealthy food items at the top of the screen. Simultaneously, players must navigate their spaceship to avoid unhealthy foods as they drop from the top while actively collecting healthy ones for points. This version introduces a strategic balance between offensive actions, where players seek to gain points by shooting all food items, and defensive manoeuvres, as they strive to avoid the negative consequences associated with unhealthy foods. The complexity arises from the need to make quick decisions, weighing the potential gains against the risks and consequences of encountering detrimental elements. The gain-loss framing creates a compelling gameplay experience that challenges players to effectively manage both offensive and defensive aspects to succeed in the game, allowing the players to weigh both the benefits of healthy eating and the consequences of unhealthy eating.

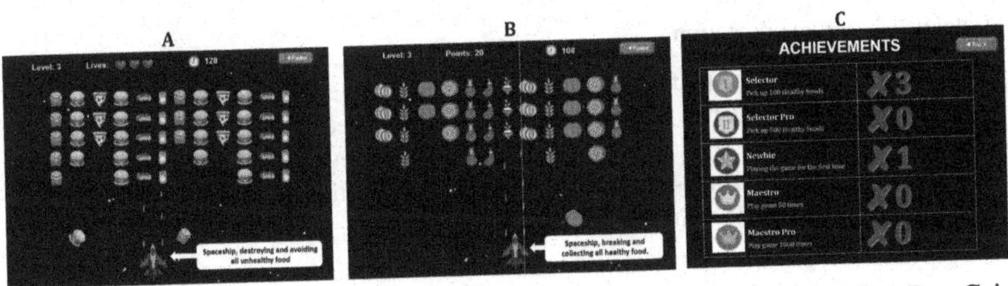

Fig. 1. Screenshot of gameplay for the game framing versions (A = Loss-Framing, B = Gain-Framing, C = Reward Strategy in the Gain-Framed version).

3.2 Measurement Instrument and Demographics

As indicated in the previous section, we created three versions of a persuasive game for promoting healthy eating, implementing four persuasive system design (PSD) model strategies: Reward, Competition, Suggestion, and Praise [19]. Figure 1C shows screenshots of the competition strategy in the gain-framed version, while Table 1 shows a description of all the persuasive strategies and their implementations.

After the game design phase, the games underwent assessment by two game design experts to identify and address potential design issues. These experts also ensured that all the persuasive strategies were consistently and similarly implemented across the three game framings versions. To evaluate the effectiveness of game versions and the implemented strategies, we recruited 409 participants, who installed the game and played it game daily for at least 15 min over three days. Post-gameplay, participants provided survey feedback on effectiveness and strategies. Specifically, we designed a survey prompting users to rate the perceived effectiveness of the game versions and associated strategies. Using a between-study design, participants were allocated to framings: 136 gain-framing, 136 loss-framing, and 137 gain-loss-framing. Table 2 shows the demographic distribution of the participants. To minimize potential bias resulting from question order, we created four survey versions, each containing the same questions but arranged in a randomized sequence. The survey aimed to assess the perceived effectiveness of both the overall game and the four implemented persuasive strategies. To achieve this, we utilized a scale adapted from Thomas et al. [35] and Drodz et al. [6]. This scale, a well-established measure for evaluating the perceived persuasiveness of system features, has been employed in various Human-Computer Interaction (HCI) and persuasive technology-related research studies [2, 14]. We also collected the participants' gamer type, using the HEXAD scale [36]. We measured these questions on a 7-point Likert scale ranging from "1 = Strongly disagree" to "7 = Strongly agree" for each strategy and the overall game. After excluding incomplete responses, our analysis included 371 responses – 125 gain-framing, 122 loss-framing, and 124 gain-loss-framing.

Table 1. Persuasive strategies and their implementations

Strategy	Implementation
Reward	Badges and points for completing in-game achievements Badges aligned with framing types: Gain-framed achieved by shooting and collecting 100 healthy foods; loss-framed achieved by avoiding 100 unhealthy foods, and gain-loss-framed obtained by collecting 50 healthy foods and avoiding 50 unhealthy foods
Competition	In-game leaderboard, tailored to the game framings, ranks players based on accumulated points. (See Fig. 1)
Suggestion	Random pop-up tips on healthy and unhealthy eating, tailored to framing types. Gain-framed encourages nutritious choices, loss-framed dissuades unhealthy foods with negative aspects, and gain-loss combines positive and negative reinforcement
Praise	Image and textual positive feedback for completing in-game achievements

Table 2. Demographic distribution of the participants

Demographics	Participants
Gender	Female = 112 (30%), Male = 259 (70%)
Age Distribution	18–25 = 106 (29%), 26–35 = 189 (51%), 36–45 = 76 (20%)
Educational Background	Bachelor's = 255 (69%), Master's = 85 (23%), High school = 19 (5%), College diploma = 12 (3%)

3.3 Data Analysis

Our primary research objective was to examine the game's effectiveness across three framing types and understand the relationships between gamer types and implemented persuasive strategies. To achieve this, we conducted the following analysis:

i. We used Cronbach's alpha to check the reliability of the responses. The reliability analysis showed that all the scales were internally consistent, with a Cronbach's alpha value of 0.86 which is an acceptable level of reliability [3].
ii. We conducted a one-sample t-test on the overall rating of each version of the game, to verify the perceived effectiveness of each version.
iii. We conducted a repeated measure ANOVA on the mean ratings of each game version and each persuasive strategy to identify the significant difference in their effectiveness. The analysis was conducted after validating the ANOVA assumptions, followed by pairwise comparison (using the Bonferroni method for adjusting degrees of freedom for multiple comparisons)
iv. Furthermore, we investigated gamer type relationships with persuasive strategies. We developed structural models depicting relationships between gamer type and strategies persuasiveness (Fig. 2), with gamer type as exogenous constructs, using Partial Least Square Structural Equation Modeling (PLS-SEM) [10]. PLS-SEM is a popular method for estimating complex relationships between observed and latent variables [31]. We used SmartPLS 4 [34] to design the model.

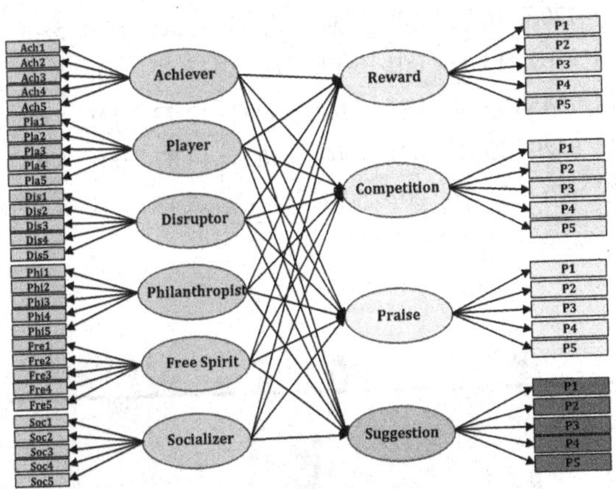

Fig. 2. PLS-SEM model structure for each game framing version. (P1–P5 = Rating responses of the five persuasiveness scale questions; Ach1, Achi2 … Soc1, Soc2 = Rating responses to the HEXAD scale questions for each gamer type).

4 Results

In this section, we present the result of the analysis of the data collected in our study.

To answer R1 *(What is the perceived effectiveness of the persuasive game overall and the individual persuasive strategies implemented in the game across the three game framings?)*, we verified the effectiveness of the game versions and the persuasive strategies implemented, using a one-sample t-test. This t-test was performed on the mean score of the user ratings of each game version and persuasive strategies, with a reference to the neutral point of 4 on a 7-point persuasiveness scale.

The findings indicated that all versions of the game and all the persuasive strategies implemented were perceived to be significantly effective – gain framing ($t(124) = 25.171, p < .001$), loss framing ($t(121) = 26.483, p < .001$), gain-loss framing ($t(122) = 24.779, p < .001$). Furthermore, all the persuasive strategies deployed within the game were perceived as significantly effective across all framing types, as illustrated in Table 3 (Fig. 3).

Table 3. T-Test of the mean values of the three-game versions and the persuasive strategies implemented. (All means were significant at $p < .0001$, test value = 4).

	Gain Framing				Loss Framing				Gain-Loss Framing			
	df = 124				df = 121				df = 123			
Strategies	M	SD	t	p	M	SD	t	p	M	SD	t	p
Reward	5.15	.7706	16.71	.001	5.349	.7600	19.61	.001	5.48	.9396	17.41	.001
Competition	5.14	.9369	13.65	.001	5.170	.8122	15.92	.001	5.40	.9511	16.31	.001
Praise	4.95	.7945	13.31	.001	5.026	.8903	12.73	.001	5.05	.7976	14.65	.001
Suggestion	5.04	.8429	13.82	.001	5.161	.8623	14.87	.001	5.05	.8356	13.96	.001
Overall	5.07	.476	25.17	.001	5.18	.491	26.48	.001	5.25	.557	24.78	.001

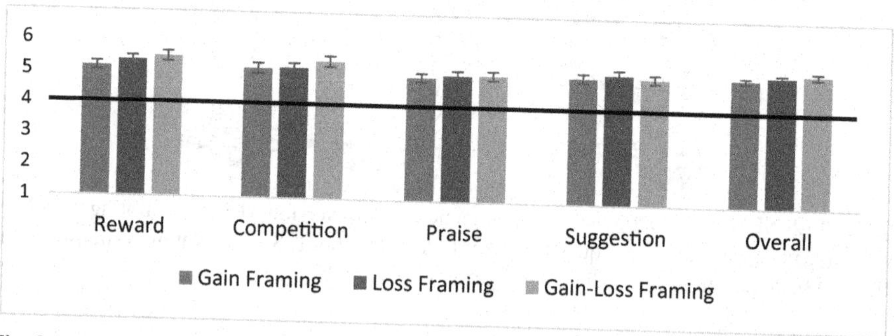

Fig. 3. A bar chart showing the perceived effectiveness of the game overall and its persuasive strategies, across the three game framings.

To answer RQ2 *(Are there any differences in the effectiveness of the persuasive game versions and the persuasive strategies across the three game framings?)*, we conducted a repeated measure ANOVA on the mean ratings of the persuasiveness of the game across the three framing types versions with framing types as the between-subject factor and the strategies as the within-subject. Our results showed that there was a significant main effect of the framing type on the effectiveness of the games overall: $F(2,242) = 3.334$, $p = 0.037$, $\eta 2 \geq 0.027$). Furthermore, a post-hoc pairwise comparison revealed that there was a significant difference in effectiveness between the gain-framed version and the gain-loss-framed version, indicating that the gain-loss-framed version was perceived as significantly more effective than the gain-framed version ($p < .035$). However, there was no statistically significant difference between the loss-framed and the gain-loss-framed version and between the loss-framed version and the gain-loss-framed version.

Similarly, we explored the differences in the effectiveness of the individual persuasive strategies implemented in the games, across the game versions. We conducted a repeated measure ANOVA on the mean ratings of the four persuasive strategies (Reward, Competition, Praise, and Suggestion) across the three framing types, with framing types as the between-subject factor and the strategies as the within-subject. The analysis demonstrated that only the Reward strategy showed a significant main effect across the three game framing versions: ($F(2,242) = 4.414$, $p = 0.013$, $\eta 2 \geq 0.035$). Furthermore, a post-hoc pairwise comparison of the Reward strategy also revealed that there was a significant difference in the effectiveness of the strategy between the gain-framed version and the gain-loss-framed version. This result reveals that the gain-loss-framed version was perceived as significantly more effective than the gain-framed version ($p < .013$). Surprisingly, no significant difference emerged between the loss-framed and gain-framed versions and between the loss-framed and gain-loss-framed versions.

The non-significant outcomes from our comparative analysis for the competition, praise and suggestion strategies across the three framings imply that these strategies are equally effective irrespective of the framing type; the persuasive strategies were generally effective. In other words, the impact of these strategies remained generally consistent and unaffected by the specific framing employed in the game design.

4.1 Relationship Between the Gamer Types and Persuasive Strategies

To answer RQ3 *(What are the relationships between gamer types and the effectiveness of persuasive strategies in three game versions?)*, we analyzed the relationships between the gamer types and the four persuasive strategies across the three game framing versions. We achieved this using structural models [31]. These structural models determined the relationship between the six gamer types and the persuasiveness of the strategies (see Fig. 2). An important criterion to measure the strength of relationships between variables in structural models is to calculate the level of the path coefficient β (which measures the influence of one variable on another), and the significance of the path coefficient, p [10]. The values of the significant path coefficients across the three game framing versions can be seen in Table 4.

For the gain-framed version, the results from the structural model showed that the reward strategy significantly influences people belonging to all gamer types. However, the other strategies showed no significant relationships with any gamer type in this game-framed version.

Table 4. Standardized path coefficients and significance of the models for the game versions. Bolded coefficients are p < .001, non-bolded are p < .05 and '-' represents non-significant coefficients, where negative values represent demotivation and positive values represent motivation.

	Gain framing						Loss framing						Gain-Loss framing					
	Ach	Dis	Fre	Phi	Pla	Soc	Ach	Dis	Fre	Phi	Pla	Soc	Ach	Dis	Fre	Phi	Pla	Soc
REWD	0.36	0.24	0.31	0.34	0.28	0.32	0.22	–	–	–	–	–	0.31	–	–	0.08	–	0.18
COMP	–	–	–	–	–	–	0.26	–	0.17	–	–	0.16	0.27	–	–	–	–	–
PRAS	–	–	–	–	–	–	–	–	–	–	–	–	–	0.04	–	–	0.16	0.04
SUGG	–	–	–	–	–	–	–	–	–	–	–	–	–	–	–	–	–	–

REWD = Reward, COMP = Competition, PRAS = Praise, SUGG = Suggestion

For the loss-framed version, the results show that the reward strategy significantly motivated the people high in the achiever gamer type. Furthermore, the competition strategy positively influences people high in the achiever, free spirit, and socializer gamer type. The other strategies showed no significant relationships with the gamer types in this loss-framed version.

Interestingly, for the gain-loss framing, the reward strategy significantly influenced people high in the achiever, philanthropist, and socializer gamer types. However, the competition strategy significantly influenced people high in the achiever gamer type, while the praise strategy significantly influenced people high in the disruptor, player and socializer gamer type.

5 Discussion

In this section, we discuss some interesting insights from the results pertaining to game types and persuasive strategies within game-framing types.

5.1 Gamer Types and Persuasive Strategies

An interesting aspect of our results revealed that the reward strategy had a strong positive relationship with the achiever gamer type in all the framing versions. This implies that people high in the achiever gamer type are strongly positively motivated by rewards regardless of the game framing type. This is no surprise since achievers are often motivated by a sense of accomplishment and mastery [36]. Rewards can act as acknowledgements of their achievements, providing a tangible representation of their gaming skills and progress. When designing rewards for achievers, **we strongly recommend that persuasive game designers implement badges that show gradual mastery of game elements**. This would incrementally increase the level of engagement for this gamer type while maintaining their interest.

Interestingly, the praise strategy only showed a significant relationship with participants high in the disruptor, player, and socializer gamer types. This is likely because positive reinforcement, such as praise, has been identified as a powerful motivator by reinforcing positive behaviours and accomplishments [5]. Whether it's recognizing a disruptor's creative approach, a player's competitive success, or a socializer's achievements in the gaming community, praise fosters a sense of achievement.

Similarly, the free-spirit gamer type showed a significant relationship with competition strategy in the loss-framed version. Free spirits, identical to explorers, are known for their love of exploration, variety, and new experiences in gaming [11]. In loss-framed games, which emphasize challenges and obstacles, individuals with a high free spirit gamer type may find the competitive elements more engaging and stimulating. The competitive strategy, which introduces challenges and rivalries, aligns with the free spirit's desire for variety and excitement. We recommend that persuasive game developers **integrate dynamic challenges tied to leaderboards** to enhance engagement for free spirits.

Another interesting result is that the philanthropists only showed a significant relationship with the reward strategy in the gain-framed and the gain-loss-framed versions. This may be because philanthropists are driven by a sense of purpose and meaning [36]. Using rewards in games gives players clear goals, making the game feel purposeful and meaningful. This connection encourages players to stay engaged, potentially leading to positive outcomes. Persuasive game designers can leverage this understanding when creating games for philanthropists. By implementing rewards that carry **personalized meanings to the player**, designers can forge a deeper connection to the player's sense of purpose and meaning. Additionally, incorporating **rewards with incrementally staged goals** can sustain the philanthropist player's interest, keeping them motivated and eager for more purposeful experiences within the game. This tailored approach enhances player engagement and aligns with the intrinsic motivations of philanthropist gamers.

The socializer gamer type showed a significant positive relationship with reward strategy in the gain-framed version, competition in the loss-framed version and reward and praise in the gain-loss-framed version. A reason why socializers may be influenced by competition strategies such as leaderboards is that they often thrive on social interactions and comparisons [36]. Leaderboards provide clear platforms for comparing one's performance with that of others, fostering a sense of status and accomplishment. Socializers may be motivated to engage more actively in the game to improve their leaderboard standings and showcase their achievements to their social circle. To enhance the persuasiveness of games designed for socializers, we **propose incorporating game goals and elements that are closely linked to interactions with other gamers**. This strategic integration aligns with the motivational preferences of socializers, leveraging the potent influences of social interaction, such as comparisons and recognitions, to foster a more persuasive gaming experience. By emphasizing these aspects, persuasive games can tap into the inherent social nature of socializers, making the gameplay more engaging and compelling for this gamer type.

5.2 Other Discussions

The absence of significant negative path coefficients in any of the versions indicates that there were no discernible demotivational factors for any of the gamer types across the different framings. Consequently, none of the four strategies employed can be identified as a strong demotivating factor for any specific gamer type. This absence of negative consequences suggests that these strategies can be implemented without concern, underscoring their potential for positively influencing gamer types.

Also, the suggestion strategy showed no significant relationships with any of the game types across all framing types. This is understandable due to the nature of the suggestion strategy. This strategy generally targets behaviour change by recommending small, easily attainable actions. Whether employing loss, gain or gain-loss framing, these recommendations tend to harmonize effortlessly with individuals' pre-existing beliefs and behaviours, thereby promoting cognitive consistency [7]. Additionally, as suggestions often empower individuals to make independent choices, thereby enhancing their perceived autonomy, this becomes a critical motivator [30]. Despite the framing employed, the autonomy afforded by suggestion strategies could result in comparable outcomes, fostering a sense of control over their actions among individuals.

Interestingly the reward persuasive strategy had the highest number of significant relationships with the gamer types across the three framing versions. This shows the versatility of the reward strategy as a very strong strategy in promoting behaviour change, especially in the healthy eating domain. Persuasive game designers should endeavour to employ rewards as often as possible when creating persuasive games. The fact that the reward strategy resonates with various gamer types suggests a broad appeal. Different gamers may have diverse preferences, motivations, and playstyles, but the common thread of responding positively to rewards highlights the generalizability of this strategy. This versatility is crucial for persuasive game designers, as it allows them to craft experiences that cater to a wide audience. Also, research has shown that the use of rewards aligns with well-established psychological principles, such as reinforcement and positive reinforcement, which can significantly impact player behaviour. The relationship between reward strategies and the gamer types further underscores the broad appeal and effectiveness of this approach across diverse player preferences.

6 Conclusion

In conclusion, this paper explored the relationship of gamer types, game framing, and persuasive strategies within the context of a healthy eating persuasive game. While persuasive games have demonstrated efficacy in behaviour change, our study sheds light on some factors influencing their effectiveness. The examination of three game-framing versions and four persuasive strategies revealed that all strategies were perceived as effective, with the reward strategy standing out as significantly different across framing types. Notably, the reward strategy had the most consistent and significant relationships with all gamer types across various game framings, emphasizing its broad appeal and potential to motivate diverse player preferences. Conversely, suggestions showed no significant relationships with gamer types across all framings.

These findings offer valuable insights for persuasive game designers, suggesting that an understanding of gamer types and their responsiveness to specific strategies is paramount. Moving forward, these results highlight the importance of reevaluating persuasive game design principles. We urge persuasive game designers to consider tailoring their games based on gamer characteristics such as gamer types and considering the choice of framing game content. By leveraging the strengths inherent in this tailored design approach, persuasive games can become more effective in their potential to promote positive behaviour change in players.

References

1. Anagnostopoulou, E., Magoutas, B., Bothos, E., Schrammel, J., Orji, R., Mentzas, G.: Exploring the links between persuasion, personality and mobility types in personalized mobility applications. In: de Vries, P.W., Oinas-Kukkonen, H., Siemons, L., Beerlage-de Jong, N., van Gemert-Pijnen, L. (eds.) PERSUASIVE 2017. LNCS, vol. 10171, pp. 107–118. Springer, Cham (2017). https://doi.org/10.1007/978-3-319-55134-0_9
2. Busch, M., Mattheiss, E., Reisinger, M., Orji, R., Fröhlich, P., Tscheligi, M.: More than sex: the role of femininity and masculinity in the design of personalized persuasive games. In: Meschtscherjakov, A., De Ruyter, B., Fuchsberger, V., Murer, M., Tscheligi, M. (eds.) PERSUASIVE 2016. LNCS, vol. 9638, pp. 219–229. Springer, Cham (2016). https://doi.org/10.1007/978-3-319-31510-2_19
3. Chin, W.W.: The partial least squares approach for structural equation modeling. Modern Methods Bus. Res. **295**, 295–336 (1998)
4. Ndulue, C., Orji, R.: Heuristic evaluation of an African-centric mobile persuasive game for promoting safety measures against COVID-19. In: AfriCHI 2021 (2021). https://doi.org/10.1145/3448696.3448706
5. Deci, E.L., Vallerand, R.J., Pelletier, L.G., Ryan, R.M.: Motivation and education: the self-determination perspective. Educ. Psychol. **26**, 325–346 (1991). https://doi.org/10.1080/00461520.1991.9653137
6. Drozd, F., Lehto, T., Oinas-Kukkonen, H.: Exploring perceived persuasiveness of a behavior change support system: a structural model. In: Bang, M., Ragnemalm, E.L. (eds.) Persuasive 2012. LNCS, vol. 7284, pp. 157–168. Springer, Heidelberg (2012). https://doi.org/10.1007/978-3-642-31037-9_14
7. Festinger, L.: A Theory of Cognitive Dissonance [1957]. Standford University, Standford (1997). 291
8. Gamberini, L., et al.: Saving is fun: designing a persuasive game for power conservation. In: ACE 2011 (2011). https://doi.org/10.1145/2071423.2071443
9. Gamberini, L., Breda, L., Grassi, A.: VIDEODOPE: applying persuasive technology to improve awareness of drugs abuse effects. In: Shumaker, R. (ed.) ICVR 2007. LNCS, vol. 4563, pp. 633–641. Springer, Heidelberg (2007). https://doi.org/10.1007/978-3-540-73335-5_68
10. Hair, J.F., Ringle, C.M., Sarstedt, M.: PLS-SEM: indeed a silver bullet. J. Mark. Theory Pract. **19**, 139–152 (2011). https://doi.org/10.2753/MTP1069-6679190202
11. Hamari, J., Tuunanen, J.: Player types: a meta-synthesis. Trans. Digit. Games Res. Assoc. **1**(2) (2014). https://doi.org/10.26503/todigra.v1i2.13
12. Lim, J.S., Noh, G.Y.: Effects of gain-versus loss-framed performance feedback on the use of fitness apps: mediating role of exercise self-efficacy and outcome expectations of exercise. Comput. Hum. Behav. **77**, 249–257 (2017). https://doi.org/10.1016/J.CHB.2017.09.006
13. Mandel, D.R.: Gain-loss framing and choice: separating outcome formulations from descriptor formulations. Organ. Behav. Hum. Decis. Process. **85**, 56–76 (2001). https://doi.org/10.1006/OBHD.2000.2932
14. Ndulue, C., Orji, R.: STD PONG 2.0: field evaluation of a mobile persuasive game for discouraging risky sexual behaviours among Africans youths. In: SeGAH 2021 - 2021 IEEE SEGAH (2021). https://doi.org/10.1109/SEGAH52098.2021.9551912

15. Ndulue, C., Orji, R.: Games for change - a comparative systematic review of persuasive strategies in games for behaviour change. IEEE Trans. Games, 1 (2022). https://doi.org/10.1109/TG.2022.3159090
16. Ndulue, C., Orji, R.: Persuasive games for physical activity in app stores: a systematic review. In: 2022 IEEE (SeGAH), pp. 1–6. IEEE (2022). https://doi.org/10.1109/SEGAH54908.2022.9978574
17. Ndulue, C., Orji, R.: Player personality traits and the effectiveness of a persuasive game for disease awareness among the african population. In: Baghaei, N., Vassileva, J., Ali, R., Oyibo, K. (eds.) Persuasive Technology: 17th International Conference, PERSUASIVE 2022, Virtual Event, March 29–31, 2022, Proceedings, pp. 134–144. Springer, Cham (2022). https://doi.org/10.1007/978-3-030-98438-0_11
18. Ndulue, C., Oyebode, O., Iyer, R.S., Ganesh, A., Ahmed, S.I., Orji, R.: Personality-targeted persuasive gamified systems: exploring the impact of application domain on the effectiveness of behaviour change strategies. UMUAI **32**, 165–214 (2022). https://doi.org/10.1007/S11257-022-09319-W
19. Oinas-Kukkonen, H., Harjumaa, M.: Persuasive systems design: key issues, process model, and system features. Commun. Assoc. Inf. Syst. **24**, 485–500 (2009)
20. Orji, R., Mandryk, R.L., Vassileva, J., Gerling, K.M.: Tailoring persuasive health games to gamer type. In: CHI 2013, p. 2467. ACM Press, New York (2013)
21. Orji, R., Moffatt, K.: Persuasive technology for health and wellness: state-of-the-art and emerging trends. Health Inform. J. (2018). https://doi.org/10.1177/1460458216650979
22. Orji, R., Tondello, G.F., Nacke, L.E.: Personalizing persuasive strategies in gameful systems to gamification user types. In: CHI 2018 (2018). https://doi.org/10.1145/3173574.3174009
23. Orji, R., Vassileva, J., Mandryk, R.L.: LunchTime: a slow-casual game for long-term dietary behavior change. Pers. Ubiquit. Comput. (2013). https://doi.org/10.1007/s00779-012-0590-6
24. Orji, R., Vassileva, J., Mandryk, R.L.: Modeling the efficacy of persuasive strategies for different gamer types in serious games for health. User Model User-Adapt Interact. **24**, 453–498 (2014). https://doi.org/10.1007/s11257-014-9149-8
25. Oyebode, O., Maurya, D., Orji, R.: Nourish your tree! Developing a persuasive exergame for promoting physical activity among adults. In: SeGAH 2020 (2020). https://doi.org/10.1109/SeGAH49190.2020.9201637
26. Oyibo, K., Orji, R., Vassileva, J.: Investigation of the persuasiveness of social influence in persuasive technology and the effect of age and gender. In: PPT Workshop 2017 (2017)
27. Pentz, M.A., et al.: A videogame intervention for tobacco product use prevention in adolescents. Addict. Behav. (2019). https://doi.org/10.1016/j.addbeh.2018.11.016
28. Ring, C.M., Wende, S., Will, A.: Smart PLS, Hamburg, Germany (2005)
29. Roby, C.: Can loss framing improve coordination in the minimum effort game? J. Econ. Interact. Coord. **16**, 557–588 (2021). https://doi.org/10.1007/s11403-021-00318-5
30. Ryan, R.M., Deci, E.L.: Self-determination theory and the facilitation of intrinsic motivation, social development, and well-being. Am. Psychol. **55**, 68–78 (2000). https://doi.org/10.1037/0003-066X.55.1.68
31. Sarstedt, M., Cheah, J.-H.: Partial least squares structural equation modeling using SmartPLS: a software review. J. Mark. Anal. **7**, 196–202 (2019). https://doi.org/10.1057/s41270-019-00058-3
32. Schlottmann, A., Tring, J.: How children reason about gains and losses: framing effects in judgement and choice **64**, 153–171 (2006). https://doi.org/10.1024/1421-0185.64.3.153
33. Sicart, M.: Beyond Choices: The Design of Ethical Gameplay. Beyond Choices (2013). https://doi.org/10.7551/MITPRESS/9052.001.0001
34. SmartPLS GmbH Product | SmartPLS

35. Thomas, R.J., Masthoff, J., Oren, N.: Can i influence you? Development of a scale to measure perceived persuasiveness and two studies showing the use of the scale. Front. Artif. Intell. (2019). https://doi.org/10.3389/frai.2019.00024
36. Tondello, G.F., Wehbe, R.R., Diamond, L., Busch, M., Marczewski, A., Nacke, L.E.: The gamification user types Hexad scale. In: CHI PLAY 2016 (2016). https://doi.org/10.1145/2967934.2968082
37. Yadav, R., Yadav, M., Mittal, A.: Effects of gain-loss-framed messages on virtual reality intervened fitness exercise. Inf. Discov. Deliv. **50**, 374–386 (2022). https://doi.org/10.1108/IDD-04-2021-0051
38. Ye, W., Li, Q., Yu, S.: Persuasive effects of message framing and narrative format on promoting COVID-19 vaccination: a study on Chinese college students. Int. J. Environ. Res. Public Health **18**, 9485 (2021). https://doi.org/10.3390/ijerph18189485

Exploring the Influence of Persuasive Strategies on Student Motivation: Self-determination Theory Perspective

Fidelia A. Orji[1](✉), Francisco J. Gutierrez[2], and Julita Vassileva[1]

[1] Department of Computer Science, University of Saskatchewan, Saskatoon, Canada
fidelia.orji@usask.ca, jiv@cs.usask.ca

[2] Department of Computer Science, University of Chile, Santiago, Chile
frgutier@dcc.uchile.cl

Abstract. The role of persuasive strategies is crucial in designing systems to influence behaviour. Understanding how students are affected by these strategies is critical to creating customized motivational interventions and educational methods that boost student motivation, engagement, and, ultimately, academic success. In the realm of persuasive technology in education, more research that leverages the Self-Determination Theory (SDT) of motivation is needed to understand the impact of persuasive strategies, such as Self-monitoring, Commitment and Consistency, Social Comparison, and Competition on student learning. Our study sought to investigate the responsiveness of undergraduate students (N = 185) to these persuasive strategies and how they correlate with the principles of SDT. The findings indicate that strategies such as commitment & consistency, and self-monitoring are more effective in motivating students toward specific educational objectives than competition and social comparison. Our research also uncovered diverse connections between student persuadability and the SDT constructs. Based on our results, we propose guidelines for designing more motivational education systems. These insights may help to develop and personalize persuasive educational systems and interventions.

Keywords: Persuasive Technology · Education · Personalization · Tailoring · Persuasive Strategies · Self-monitoring · Commitment and Consistency · Social Comparison · Competition · Self-Determination Theory · Intrinsic Motivation · Extrinsic Motivation · Autonomy · Competence · Relatedness

1 Introduction

The integration of persuasive strategies in educational settings is primarily aimed at fostering student engagement, motivation, and guiding them toward favorable achievements. There has been a notable increase in employing these strategies to shape students' attitudes, behaviours, and decision-making [1, 2]. Educational practitioners and online system designers frequently use a variety of approaches, ranging from motivational speeches and goal-setting exercises to reward systems, competitive elements, and gamification [3]. However, the impact of these persuasive strategies varies across different

N. Baghaei et al. (Eds.): PERSUASIVE 2024, LNCS 14636, pp. 222–236, 2024.
https://doi.org/10.1007/978-3-031-58226-4_17

educational contexts, raising crucial questions about students' responsiveness to these approaches and the effects on their motivation and well-being.

The prevailing belief is that persuasive strategies can benefit education by boosting student engagement and fostering a desire for learning. Indeed, many educators and institutions leverage these strategies in their pedagogical approaches, hoping to kindle the flames of motivation in their students. As a result, various persuasive technologies (PTs) targeting specific educational goals have been developed. This includes the application of socially oriented strategies of PT to improve student engagement [4], enhancing learning behaviour using PTs in higher education [5], and the application of PTs in the teaching and learning process [1].

Understanding how these strategies influence students is critical, as it has significant implications for educational practices and policy-making. However, the efficacy of persuasive strategies depends on the specific domain and context. For example, scarcity, reciprocity, and liking might not effectively motivate students toward some learning objectives. Moreover, different user groups respond differently to different persuasive strategies. While some students may respond positively and become more driven toward their goals, others might perceive these strategies as coercive, negatively impacting their motivation. This observation has led to a growing interest in adapting and tailoring persuasive strategies to align with the susceptibility of the target users. Studies reveal that tailoring enhances the effectiveness of persuasive systems in diverse domains [6–8]. Persuasive strategies, such as Self-monitoring, Commitment and Consistency, Social Comparison, and Competition, are frequently used to design personalized persuasive systems in various domains. However, there is not enough research on how they can be adapted to boost the effectiveness of persuasive *educational* systems. Therefore, examining strategies that can be effectively implemented and personalized within persuasive educational systems is crucial.

Motivation plays a vital role in education, influencing students' learning experiences, engagement, and academic achievements. Educational theorists and practitioners have developed various models and frameworks to understand the determinants of motivation. The Self-Determination Theory (SDT) [9] is currently one of the dominant frameworks, suggesting that individuals are driven by innate psychological needs for autonomy, competence, and relatedness and that fulfilling these needs leads to more self-determined and enduring motivation. While SDT offers valuable insights into understanding motivation, the educational landscape continuously evolves, posing new challenges and opportunities. The relation between students' susceptibility to persuasion and the key constructs of self-determination requires further exploration.

Our study seeks to bridge two significant but distinct areas of educational research: student susceptibility to persuasive strategies and their motivation constructs according to SDT. While PTs are known to influence behavioural motivation, the specific impacts of various persuasive strategies on student motivation remain unclear. To shed light on enhancing persuasiveness in educational and learning systems, we conducted a study involving 185 students exploring how they respond to four common persuasive strategies and their association with the SDT motivation constructs. Specifically, in this paper, we address the following questions:

RQ1: *How susceptible are students to four common persuasive strategies – Self-monitoring, Commitment & Consistency, Social Comparison, and Competition persuasive strategies – in the context of designing educational systems?*

RQ2: *What is the relationship between students' susceptibility to persuasive strategies and the motivation constructs of SDT, namely intrinsic and extrinsic motivation, autonomy, competence, and relatedness?*

This research makes the following contributions: Firstly, we show that the four strategies explored in this study are effective and applicable in an educational context. Secondly, we evaluate the effectiveness of the strategies and show that their overall persuasiveness in stimulating student learning varies, emphasizing the importance of tailoring these strategies to align with student preferences for improved effectiveness. Additionally, we offer an in-depth understanding of the relationship between the four persuasive strategies and the SDT constructs, providing valuable insights for designers of persuasive systems, educators, policymakers, and researchers in education. Finally, we discuss the implications of our findings in advancing and improving PT application in education and learning and present design guidelines for persuasive systems.

2 Related Work

This section overviews the theoretical frameworks relevant to investigating students' susceptibility to persuasive strategies and their relation to the SDT motivation constructs. It also lays the foundation for understanding the key constructs, concepts, and empirical findings that inform the current study.

2.1 Persuasive Strategies

The persuasive strategies of self-monitoring, social comparison, and competition, central to this research, were selected from Oinas-Kukkonen's twenty-eight persuasive design principles [10]. *Self-monitoring* helps people observe and assess their actions and achievements using logs, sensors, messages, dashboards, and graphs for data presentation. *Social comparison* enables users to observe the performance of others to encourage similar or improved efforts. *Competition* offers a framework for users to engage in tasks in a competitive environment. *Commitment & consistency* were selected from Cialdini's [11] principles of influence; it is a persuasive strategy that fosters a sense of responsibility towards specific activities.

These four strategies have been employed and evaluated in various domains to determine their capacity to drive desired behaviours. Anagnostopoulou et al. [12] adapted persuasive messages implementing the strategies of Self-monitoring, Social Comparison, and Suggestion to the persuadability profiles of users, aiming to change their mobility choices towards more sustainable alternatives, and observed notable behaviour modifications. Research explored the relation between the persuasiveness of ten persuasive strategies, including Competition, Self-monitoring, and Social Comparison with ARCS' model of motivation, and found that the model's constructs have strong associations with persuasiveness [13]. In the health and physical activity sectors, mobile applications often utilize Self-monitoring, leveraging wearable tracking devices for steps, heart rate, sleep quality, and other vital data, thus helping users manage their health and fitness. For instance, research on pedometer use has demonstrated increased physical activity and lowered blood pressure and body mass index [14]. Katzev et al. [15] and Lokhorst et al. [16] explored the effectiveness of commitment & consistency in environmental behaviour modification and found the strategy beneficial for both short- and long-term behaviour changes. Furthermore, previous research [17] has employed Competition, Social Comparison, and Reward in a game encouraging healthy eating, with players comparing their scores with others, resulting in positive shifts in dietary attitudes. Overall, extensive research on behaviour change across health and environmental sustainability domains confirms the efficacy of self-monitoring, social comparison, and competition, along with commitment & consistency in promoting desirable behaviours.

Furthermore, research on applying persuasive strategies to education has shown promising results in encouraging students to achieve specific learning goals. For example, social comparison and competition applied in a large university class motivated students to improve their engagement [4]. Social comparison and competition could be personalized to students in higher education to promote their education and learning [18]. Gesser-Edelsburg and Singhal [19] presented a framework for creating educational narratives with a high potential for persuasive influence. A study reviewed the application of persuasive technology (PT) in education and indicated that PT offers interesting opportunities to obtain new pedagogical methods and practices that will inspire and support students to acquire new knowledge and skills [20].

2.2 Constructs of Self-determination Theory of Motivation

The Self-Determination theory is a widely recognized psychological framework that seeks to understand human motivation and behaviour [21]. SDT posits that individuals have innate psychological needs for autonomy, competence, and relatedness, and satisfying these needs is crucial for fostering motivation, performance, and well-being. Self-determination constructs encompass a rich body of literature surrounding intrinsic motivation, extrinsic motivation, autonomy, competence, and relatedness [9]. These constructs have been pivotal in understanding human motivation and behaviour across various domains. On the one hand, *intrinsic motivation* as an internal drive to engage in an activity for its inherent satisfaction, interest, or curiosity has been extensively explored in literature. According to Ryan and Deci [22], intrinsic motivation is essential for high-quality learning and creativity. On the other hand, *extrinsic motivation* involves engaging in an activity for external rewards or to avoid punishments. Likewise, *autonomy* refers to having control over one's actions, decisions, and behaviours; *competence* refers to the perceived ability to perform tasks effectively; and *relatedness*, i.e., the sense of connection and belongingness, emphasizes the significance of social relationships in human motivation.

The constructs of SDT have been applied to inform the design and evaluation of many education and persuasive interventions [23, 24]. For instance, a study that investigated motivation and experience in a virtual learning environment applied the SDT and the hedonic theory to understand how 3D virtual reality technology contexts foster or undermine psychological needs and their impact on behavioural intentions and sustained engagement [24]. Similarly, Haque et al. [25] reported in an eight-week evaluation that a persuasive application incorporating SDT motivated users to improve their physical activity in the workplace. Furthermore, a study investigating the relationship between users' types of motivation and feature preferences in persuasive apps for mental and emotional well-being revealed that perceived persuasiveness of different features was significantly influenced by users' motivation types [26].

In summary, persuasive strategies have been widely studied and applied in designing persuasive and behaviour change systems in various domains, such as health and marketing. However, little is known in the education domain about the motivational support provided by commonly used strategies, such as self-monitoring, commitment & consistency, social comparison, and competition. Addressing this gap, we conducted an empirical study with university students to investigate the suitability of the above-mentioned persuasive strategies in the education domain.

3 Study Design and Method

Our study was designed to offer insights regarding the effectiveness of persuasive systems or interventions that utilize four common persuasive strategies in motivating student engagement, thereby assisting them in attaining desired learning goals. Additionally, it explored the relationships between the strategies and constructs of the SDT.

Complying with ethical standards when conducting research involving human subjects, the students provided explicit, free, and informed consent. Our study was approved on ethical grounds by the Institutional Review Board at the University of Chile and the University of Saskatchewan. The participants were recruited from undergraduate students taking an introductory programming course at the University of Chile. A total of 185 responses were included in the analysis, after filtering out incomplete and incorrect responses. Students did not receive compensation. Our participants were at least 18 years old at the time of data collection; 58 were female (31%), and 127 were male (69%).

To measure students' susceptibility to *social comparison* and *competition* with respect to learning, we adapted the persuasive inventory (PI) developed by Busch et al. [27], which was applied as a self-reported questionnaire of 11 items in a 9-point Likert scale. Likewise, to measure susceptibility to *self-monitoring and commitment & consistency,* we reviewed existing literature and constructed questions measured on a 5-point Likert scale. We assessed the reliability and validity of our questions using Factor analysis. The Kaiser-Meyer-Olkin (KMO) test value was 0.73, and Bartlett's test of sphericity was significant at $p < .001$, indicating that the sample was suitable for factor analysis. After removing variables with loading less than 0.5 and those that did not load correctly, we identified six factors for self-monitoring and four factors for commitment & consistency. The Cronbach's Alpha for self-monitoring and commitment & consistency are 0.78 and 0.74, respectively.

Students' responses to questions that assess motivation constructs of SDT were also collected to determine students' motivation. Intrinsic and extrinsic motivation were assessed on a 7-point Likert scale using a short version of the academic motivation scale [28]. The scale comprises seven subscales which aim to evaluate three types of intrinsic motivation (motivation to acquire knowledge, to accomplish tasks, and to experience stimulation), three forms of extrinsic motivation (external, introjected, and identified regulation), and amotivation. The subscales for intrinsic and extrinsic motivation were each averaged to get their respective scores. The SDT constructs *autonomy*, *competence*, and *relatedness* were measured on a 5-point scale using the Basic Psychological Needs Satisfaction scale [29]. The Academic Motivation Scale [30] and the Basic Psychological Needs Satisfaction Scale [29] are widely used valid and reliable scales.

4 Data Analysis

Our work has two objectives: (1) to assess the susceptibility of students to four commonly used PT strategies concerning their ability to motivate students in their education and learning, and (2) to explore the relations between the four PT strategies and the constructs from the SDT theory of motivation.

An overview of the steps undertaken to analyze our data is as follows: (1) Data was collected using 9-point, 7-point, and 5-point Likert scales. We transformed the 9-point and 7-point Likert scales into a 5-point scale following standard procedures [31]. (2) We performed the Kaiser–Meyer–Olkin (KMO) sampling adequacies and the Bartlett test of sphericity to check the validity of our data. Cronbach's Alpha was applied to test the reliability of our data. (3) To assess and compare the effectiveness of the strategies, we computed the average score for each strategy and then performed a repeated-measures analysis of variance (RM-ANOVA), followed by pairwise comparisons using Bonferroni correction for multiple comparisons. We conducted the analysis after validating the ANOVA assumptions about normality and sphericity. (4) To determine the relationship between the motivation constructs of SDT and the four persuasive strategies, we used SmartPLS 4. Partial Least Square Structural Equation Modelling (PLS-SEM) is recommended for modelling relationships between variables [32]. We performed PLS-SEM to investigate the relation between Intrinsic Motivation, Extrinsic Motivation, Autonomy, Competence, and Relatedness from SDT and the four persuasive strategies. As shown in Fig. 1, we modelled the strategies individually.

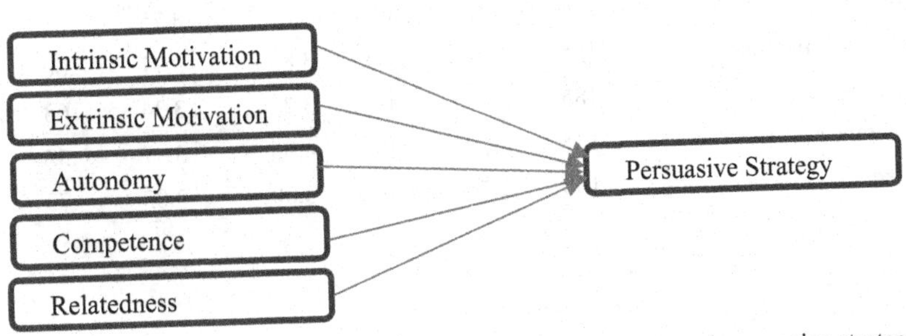

Fig. 1. PLS-SEM model structure for the motivation constructs and persuasive strategy

Many researchers (e.g., [6, 33]) have used PLS-SEM to estimate relationships between variables. Our PLS-SEM model shows the relations between the SDT constructs and the individual strategy. As recommended in literature [34, 35], we checked the composite reliability, AVE (i.e., the average variance extracted by the variables from its indicator items), and the discriminate validity of our data. The required criteria for PLS-SEM validity and reliability were satisfied; all heterotrait-monotrait (HTMT) ratios of correlations were below the recommended limit of 0.9, and AVEs were above the recommended threshold of 0.5. In determining the strength of the relationships in the structural models, we calculated the path coefficient (β) and its significance (p) [34]. Path coefficients measure the influence of one variable on another.

5 Results

We present the measurement validation and descriptive statistics, followed by the results of the overall persuasiveness of the strategies, and then our SEM analysis results.

5.1 Measurement Validation

Our results showed that the KMO value of data was 0.632, which is above the recommended value of 0.6. The Bartlett test of sphericity was statistically significant ($\chi^2(990) = 4056.379, p < 0.0001$). Cronbach's alpha (α) was 0.801, well above the recommended 0.7. These results demonstrate that our data was appropriate for further analysis. The descriptive statistics of the data are presented in Table 1.

Table 1. Descriptive Statistics (mean age of participants = 19.2 years)

	N	Min	Max	Median	Mean	Std. Dev
Self-monitoring	185	3.00	5.00	3.83	3.95	.42
Commitment & Consistency	185	2.75	5.00	4.00	4.06	.49
Social comparison	185	1.08	4.75	3.67	3.48	.78
Competition	185	1.80	5.00	3.80	3.75	.66
Intrinsic Motivation	185	2.11	5.00	3.83	3.75	.58
Extrinsic Motivation	185	1.67	5.00	3.83	3.71	.60
Autonomy	185	1.75	5.00	3.25	3.34	.63
Competence	185	2.50	5.00	4.00	3.97	.53
Relatedness	185	1.50	5.00	3.00	3.05	.72

5.2 Comparing the Persuasiveness of the Strategies

Figure 2 shows the overall mean rating of the persuasive strategies. Based on the result of one-sample t-test, all the strategies were perceived as persuasive, as each strategy has a mean rating which is significantly higher ($p < .001$) than the neutral score of 2.5, representing the midpoint on the scale, illustrated by a dotted line in Fig. 2. Table 2 shows the number of participants that can be persuaded by different strategies. More than half of the participants (65%) could be motivated by the four strategies. The majority (100%) could be persuaded using self-monitoring and commitment & consistency. The results demonstrate that all four strategies are effective and can positively influence students' learning. The difference in students' susceptibility to social comparison and competition highlights the need to tailor persuasive educational interventions based on students' susceptibility to persuasive strategies to improve efficacy.

For our ANOVA analysis, Mauchly's test indicated that the assumption of sphericity was violated, $\chi^2(5) = 65.33$, $p = .001$; therefore, the degrees of freedom were corrected using Huynh-Feldt estimates of sphericity ($\varepsilon = 0.849$). The results of the ANOVA show significant main effects of strategy type ($F_{(2.55,\ 468.68)} = 82.06$, $p < .001$, $\eta^2 = 0.308$) for overall persuasiveness. This means there is an overall effect for the four strategies with respect to their persuasiveness. The results of a post-hoc test using Bonferroni correction for multiple comparisons revealed that the mean of *Self-monitoring* is significantly higher than those of *Social Comparison* ($p < .0001$) and *Competition* ($p < .001$). The difference between *Self-monitoring* and *Commitment & Consistency* is not significant ($p = .061$). Also, the mean of *Commitment & Consistency* is significantly higher than those of Social *Comparison* ($p < .001$) and *Competition* ($p < .001$), and the mean of *Competition* is significantly higher than *Social Comparison* ($p < .005$). *Self-monitoring* and *Commitment & Consistency* emerged as the most persuasive among the four strategies.

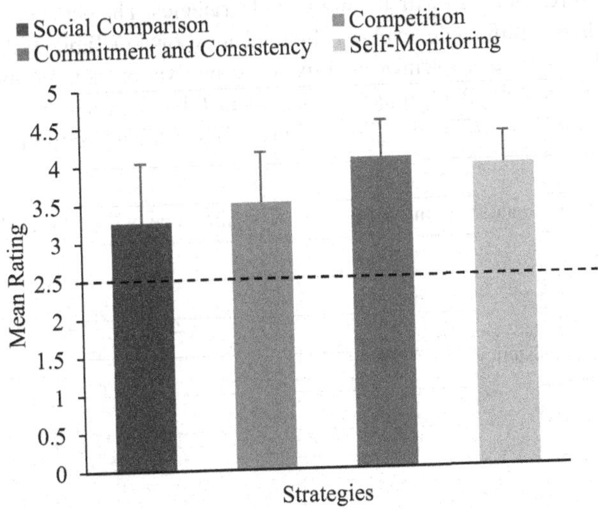

Fig. 2. Mean rating of the four strategies

Table 2. Number of participants that could be motivated by the strategies ("Commitment and Consistency" is abbreviated to "Commitment" for compactness)

Strategies	Number of Students Susceptible	Percentage of Students (%)
Self-monitoring - Commitment -Social comparison - Competition	122	65
Self-monitoring - Commitment -Social comparison	134	72
Self-monitoring - Commitment - Competition	160	87
Self-monitoring - Commitment	185	100
Self-monitoring - Social comparison	134	72
Commitment -Social comparison	134	72
Social comparison - Competition	121	65

5.3 Relationships Between SDT Constructs and Susceptibility to the Persuasive Strategies Based on PLS-SEM Models

The results yielded by the structural model show differences in the SDT constructs concerning their relationship with the individual strategies. The path coefficients (β) and the corresponding significance level (p) obtained are shown in Table 3. INT, EXT, AUT, COM, and REL represent intrinsic and extrinsic motivation, autonomy, competence, and relatedness, respectively. Bolded coefficients in Table 3 are significant at $p < .0001$, non-bolded ones at $p < .05$, and "–" represents non-significant coefficients.

Table 3. Standard path coefficients and significance of the relationships

Strategy	INT	EXT	AUT	COM	REL
Self-monitoring	**.27**	**–.31**	.25	–	–
Commitment & Consistency	**.29**	–	.19	.23	–
Social Comparison	–	–	–	–	–.25
Competition	**.23**	–	.23	.19	**.23**

Self-monitoring

A system can motivate students by providing tools that allow them to track their learning behaviour and progress. Our results reveal that *self-monitoring* is significantly associated with *intrinsic motivation* ($\beta = .27, p < .0001$) and *autonomy* ($\beta = .25, p < .018$), whereas it is negatively related to *extrinsic motivation* ($\beta = -.31, p < .0001$). This means that the *self-monitoring strategy* motivates students because it fosters intrinsic motivation and autonomy and makes a persuasive system relevant.

Commitment and Consistency
The strategy focuses on the idea that once individuals commit or take a small action in a particular direction, they are more likely to remain consistent with that commitment. Applying this strategy to a learning system can enhance engagement and persistence. Our results show that the *commitment & consistency* strategy is significantly related to *intrinsic motivation* ($\beta = .29, p < .0001$), *autonomy* ($\beta = .19, p < .008$), and *competence* ($\beta = .23$, $p < .001$). This means that the *commitment & consistency* strategy interacts positively with *intrinsic motivation, autonomy*, and *competence* to create a dynamic and reinforcing relationship that supports students' learning. When students commit to their learning goals or tasks, they are likelier to feel a sense of personal responsibility and accountability. This commitment serves as a motivational factor. As students consistently engage in learning activities, their ongoing commitment contributes to a positive cycle of motivation, reinforcing the enjoyment and satisfaction derived from the learning process.

A commitment to learning often involves setting personal goals and choosing how to approach one's education. This aligns with autonomy and empowers students to make choices that align with their interests and preferences. As students persist in their efforts to learn and achieve their goals, they gain knowledge and skills, which, in turn, boost their confidence and competence in the subject matter.

Social Comparison
A system that allows students to compare their learning activities progress and outcome with others will motivate them in their learning. Our results indicate that the *social comparison* strategy does not relate to most of the constructs except that it negatively relates to *relatedness* ($\beta = -.25$, $p < .004$).

Competition
This strategy refers to allowing people to compete with others or with other computer systems to inspire them to carry out specific tasks. Our results reveal that *competition* is significantly related to *intrinsic motivation* ($\beta = .23$, $p < .0001$), *autonomy* ($\beta = .23$, $p < .001$), *competence* ($\beta = .19$, $p < .005$), and *relatedness*: ($\beta = .23$, $p < .0001$). This implies that well-structured competitive tasks that provide students with challenging tasks aligning with their capabilities foster a sense of competence. The inherent challenge can also contribute to intrinsic motivation as students find the competition intellectually stimulating. So, when students are genuinely interested in competitive tasks, they are more likely to be motivated to participate and excel. Structuring competitive tasks in a way that allows students some choice in their approach promotes autonomy because they will have a degree of control over how they engage with the competitive tasks and that can enhance their sense of autonomy. Competition provides a platform for students to develop and showcase their skills. They can enhance their competence and mastery in a particular area as they engage in the competitive process. The feedback competitors receive from peers, instructors, or the results of the competition itself supports competence by helping students understand their strengths and areas for improvement.

6 Discussion

The findings of this research can be used to inform the design of persuasive systems for education and learning. To answer our first research question (RQ1) our findings revealed that the four strategies (self-monitoring, commitment & consistency, social comparison, and competition) could be used to promote desired learning behaviour among students and that self-monitoring and commitment & consistency strategies were effective in motivating all participants. Thus, in personalization of PTs in the education domain, the two strategies should be given preference.

For our RQ2, the results of our SEM model revealed relationships between SDT constructs and susceptibility to the four persuasive strategies. Based on our findings we propose the following guidelines for designing more motivational education systems.

Guideline 1: *When applying PTs in education, the Self-monitoring and Commitment & Consistency strategies should be given preference.* Students who are motivated by a genuine interest in learning and have the autonomy to guide their educational journey are likely to experience lower levels of stress and higher levels of satisfaction. This can lead to continuous pursuit of knowledge and personal development beyond the formal educational setting. Persuasive system designers should provide a mechanism that allows students to track and monitor their learning behaviour and progress, defining and committing to specific personal learning goals and time frames to achieve them. The mechanism should allow students to choose target learning behaviours to monitor (such as time spent on reading, progress made on a task, frequencies, etc.). Then, checklists, graphs or other common understandable visualizations could be used in presenting tracked data. The two strategies make people aware and more prone to assume responsibility for their behaviour.

The competition strategy emerged as the third most persuasive strategy of the four. However, 64 of the 185 participants (35%) were not motivated by both competition and social comparison (see Table 2), a combination of strategies often applied in gamified educational environments. Also, 25 participants (15%) were not motivated when adding competition to self-monitoring and commitment & consistency. This finding agrees with the educational literature [36]: while some students may thrive in competitive settings, others find them stressful and demotivating.

Guideline 2: *Competition should be applied selectively, recognizing, and accommodating individual differences in students' preferences for competition.* Competition should be applied preferably in combination with self-monitoring and commitment & consistency because a high proportion (87%) of the participants would be motivated by this combination. To implement competition, persuasive system designers can provide a mechanism that allows students to compete in performing a specific task, such as gamification. Options should be provided for competitive and non-competitive students to cater to a diversified learning environment. The social comparison strategy was also perceived as persuasive but should also be applied selectively because 51 students (28%) would not respond to this strategy.

Guideline 3: *Persuasive educational systems that allow students to view and compare their progress and performance with that of others must be personalized based on* *students' preferences/susceptibility to social comparison to improve efficacy and mitigate undesirable effects.* Visualizations and learning analytics could be applied to show students how they are doing relative to others.

Intrinsic motivation and autonomy have significant positive relationships with three (self-monitoring, commitment, and competition) out of the four strategies investigated. Intrinsic motivation and autonomy are crucial in promoting positive student outcomes in academic and personal development.

Guideline 4: *Persuasive educational systems should attract and sustain the interest and curiosity of students and foster their freedom to choose tasks, contents, or projects that align with their interest or need to promote persuasiveness and greater willingness of students to use the system.*

Furthermore, competence has significant positive relationships with competition and commitment & consistency strategies. Engaging in competitive activities challenges students to refine their knowledge and abilities – they are motivated to master the content or skills required for success in the competition, contributing to increased competence. Consistency in practice, study, or application of knowledge is a key aspect of commitment & consistency strategies. It supports the retention and application of skills, ultimately contributing to students' competence. Success and competence in learning activities reinforce the commitment to continue.

Guideline 5: *The combination of competition and commitment can create a positive feedback loop, leading to improved competence. Aligning competition goals with broader educational objectives ensures that the competitive aspect enhances student competence.* Therefore, the positive relationship between commitment & consistency and competition strategies with students' competence lies in the strategic alignment of these elements. When competitions in persuasive education systems are designed to motivate, challenge, and foster commitment while maintaining a positive learning environment, they can contribute to developing students' competence.

Finally, our findings can be used to design and adapt persuasive interventions by informing the choice of appropriate strategies for motivating students to learn depending on whether promoting intrinsic motivation, autonomy, competence, or relatedness is the targeted behaviour.

7 Conclusion, Limitations, and Future Work

Before implementing a persuasive system/intervention design, it is crucial to assess the suitability of the PT strategies for a specific user group. Incorporating the right strategies into PT design enhances its effectiveness in achieving its intended goals. To address the scarcity of research on how persuasive strategies influence learners' motivation, our study with 185 students explored their susceptibility to four commonly used persuasive strategies (self-monitoring, commitment & consistency, social comparison, and competition) and their relationship with the constructs of SDT (intrinsic and extrinsic motivation, autonomy, competence, and relatedness). The results allow us to propose five design guidelines about what persuasive strategies to employ depending on the targeted motivational outcome by promoting autonomy, competence, and relatedness.

The main limitation of our study is the use of self-reporting to measure susceptibility and motivation constructs. Although self-reporting is a commonly applied method for assessing persuasiveness and motivation, we acknowledge that the results of the actual implementation of the strategies may differ. Therefore, as part of future work, we plan to examine the persuasiveness and motivational appeal of the strategies in the context of a persuasive education intervention/system. Future research will also explore opportunities for adapting the constructs and strategies. Furthermore, this study was carried out on a specific population of students in a country's elite academic institution, which may have higher motivation and competitiveness than other student populations. The replication of this study, particularly analyzing how the findings reported in this paper resonate with or contrast to a broader population and the influence of socio-cultural factors in the design of PT systems for education are also a direction for future work.

Acknowledgments. This work was supported by NSERC through the Vanier Canada Graduate Scholarship CGV-175722 and Michael Smith Foreign Study Supplement of the first author, Vicerrectoría de Investigación y Desarrollo (VID), Universidad de Chile, grant: Ayuda de Viaje VID 2023 of the second author and the Discovery Grant program RGPIN-2021-03521 of the third author.

Disclosure of Interests. The authors have no competing interests to declare that are relevant to the content of this article.

References

1. Alvarez, A.G., Dal Sasso, G.T.M., Iyengar, M.S.: Persuasive technology in teaching acute pain assessment in nursing: results in learning based on pre and post-testing. Nurse Educ. Today **50**, 109–114 (2017)
2. Mustafa, M.Q., Hussein, S.K., Ali Raad, A., Yussalita, M.Y.: Design and development of an interactive persuasive mathematics game for primary school children. Int. J. Eng. Technol. **7**, 272–276 (2018)
3. Denny, P., McDonald, F., Empson, R., Kelly, P., Petersen, A.: Empirical support for a causal relationship between gamification and learning outcomes. In: Proceedings of the 2018 CHI Conference on Human Factors in Computing Systems - CHI 2018, pp. 1–13. ACM Press, New York (2018)
4. Orji, F.A., Vassileva, J., Greer, J.: Evaluating a persuasive intervention for engagement in a large university class. Int. J. Artif. Intell. Educ. **31**, 700–725 (2021). 2021 314
5. Widyasari, Y.D.L., Nugroho, L.E., Permanasari, A.E.: Persuasive technology for enhanced learning behavior in higher education. Int. J. Educ. Technol. High. Educ. **16**, 1–16 (2019)
6. Orji, R., Nacke, L.E., Di Marco, C.: Towards personality-driven persuasive health games and gamified systems. In: Conference on Human Factors in Computing Systems – Proceedings, pp. 1015–1027. ACM Press, New York (2017)
7. Orji, F.A., Greer, J., Vassileva, J.: Exploring the effectiveness of socially-oriented persuasive strategies in education. In: Oinas-Kukkonen, H., Win, K.T., Karapanos, E., Karppinen, P., Kyza, E. (eds.) PERSUASIVE 2019. LNCS, vol. 11433, pp. 297–309. Springer, Cham (2019). https://doi.org/10.1007/978-3-030-17287-9_24
8. Kaptein, M., De Ruyter, B., Markopoulos, P., Aarts, E.: Adaptive persuasive systems: a study of tailored persuasive text messages to reduce snacking. ACM Trans. Interact. Intell. Syst. **2**(2), 1–25 (2012)

9. Ryan, R.M., Deci, E.L.: Self-determination theory and the facilitation of intrinsic motivation, social development, and well-being. Am. Psychol. **55**, 68–78 (2000)
10. Oinas-Kukkonen, H., Harjumaa, M.: Persuasive systems design: key issues, process model and system features. Commun. Assoc. Inf. Syst. **24**, 485–500 (2009)
11. Cialdini, R.: Influence: The Psychology of Persuasion. William Morrow e Company, New York (1984)
12. Anagnostopoulou, E., et al.: From Mobility Patterns to Behavioural Change: leveraging travel behaviour and personality profiles to nudge for sustainable transportation. J. Intell. Inf. Syst. **54**, 157–178 (2020)
13. Orji, R., Reilly, D., Oyibo, K., Orji, F.A.: Deconstructing persuasiveness of strategies in behaviour change systems using the ARCS model of motivation. Behav. Inf. Technol. **38**, 319–335 (2019)
14. Bravata, D., et al.: Using pedometers to increase physical activity and improve health: a systematic review. Jama **298**, 2296–2304 (2007)
15. Katzev, R., Wang, T.: Can commitment change behavior? A case study of environmental actions. J. Soc. Behav. Personal. **9**, 13–26 (1994)
16. Lokhorst, A.M., Werner, C., Staats, H., van Dijk, E., Gale, J.L.: Commitment and behavior change: a meta-analysis and critical review of commitment-making strategies in environmental research. Environ. Behav. **45**, 3–34 (2013)
17. Orji, R., Vassileva, J., Mandryk, R.L.: LunchTime: a slow-casual game for long-term dietary behavior change. Pers. Ubiquitous Comput. **17**, 1211–1221 (2013)
18. Orji, F.A., Oyibo, K., Orji, R., Greer, J., Vassileva, J.: Personalization of persuasive technology in higher education. In: ACM UMAP 2019 - Proceedings of the 27th ACM Conference on User Modeling, Adaptation and Personalization, pp. 336–340 (2019)
19. Gesser-Edelsburg, A., Singhal, A.: Enhancing the persuasive influence of entertainment-education events: rhetorical and aesthetic strategies for constructing narratives. Crit. Arts. **27**, 56–74 (2013)
20. Devincenzi, S., Kwecko, V., De Toledo, F.P., Mota, F.P., Casarin, J., Da Costa Botelho, S.S.: Persuasive technology: applications in education. In: Proceedings - Frontiers in Education Conference, FIE, pp. 1–7. IEEE (2017)
21. Deci, E.L., Ryan, R.M.: Self-determination theory: a macrotheory of human motivation, development, and health. In: Canadian Psychology, pp. 182–185 (2008)
22. Ryan, R.M., Deci, E.L.: Intrinsic and extrinsic motivations: classic definitions and new directions. Contemp. Educ. Psychol. **25**, 54–67 (2000)
23. Guay, F.: Applying self-determination theory to education: regulations types, psychological needs, and autonomy supporting behaviors. Can. J. Sch. Psychol. **37**, 75–92 (2022)
24. Huang, Y.C., Backman, S.J., Backman, K.F., McGuire, F.A., Moore, D.W.: An investigation of motivation and experience in virtual learning environments: a self-determination theory. Educ. Inf. Technol. **24**, 591–611 (2019)
25. Haque, M.S., Isomursu, M., Kangas, M., Jämsä, T.: Measuring the influence of a persuasive application to promote physical activity. In: Personalized Persuasive Technology Workshop Proceedings, pp. 43–57 (2018)
26. Alqahtani, F., Orji, R., Riper, H., McCleary, N., Witteman, H., McGrath, P.: Motivation-based approach for tailoring persuasive mental health applications. Behav. Inf. Technol. **42**, 569–595 (2022)
27. Busch, M., Schrammel, J., Tscheligi, M.: Personalized persuasive technology – development and validation of scales for measuring persuadability. In: Berkovsky, S., Freyne, J. (eds.) PERSUASIVE 2013. LNCS, vol. 7822, pp. 33–38. Springer, Heidelberg (2013). https://doi.org/10.1007/978-3-642-37157-8_6
28. Kotera, Y., Conway, E., Green, P.: Construction and factorial validation of a short version of the Academic Motivation Scale. Br. J. Guid. Couns. **51**, 274–283 (2021)

29. Betoret, F.D., Artiga, A.G.: The relationship among student basic need satisfaction, approaches to learning, reporting of avoidance strategies and achievement. Electron. J. Res. Educ. Psychol. **9**, 463–496 (2011)
30. Vallerand, R.J., Pelletier, L.G., Blais, M.R., Briere, N.M., Senecal, C., Vallieres, E.F.: The academic motivation scale: a measure of intrinsic, extrinsic, and amotivation in education. Educ. Psychol. Meas. **52**, 1003–1017 (1992)
31. IBM: Transforming different Likert scales to a common scale. https://www.ibm.com/support/pages/transforming-different-likert-scales-common-scale
32. Kupek, E.: Beyond logistic regression: Structural equations modelling for binary variables and its application to investigating unobserved confounders. BMC Med. Res. Methodol. **6**, 13 (2006)
33. Drozd, F., Lehto, T., Oinas-Kukkonen, H.: Exploring perceived persuasiveness of a behavior change support system: a structural model. In: Bang, M., Ragnemalm, E.L. (eds.) PERSUASIVE 2012. LNCS, vol. 7284, pp. 157–168. Springer, Heidelberg (2012). https://doi.org/10.1007/978-3-642-31037-9_14
34. Hair, J.F., Ringle, C.M., Sarstedt, M.: PLS-SEM: indeed a silver bullet. J. Mark. Theory Pract. **19**, 139–152 (2011)
35. Anderson, J.C., Gerbing, D.W.: Structural equation modeling in practice: a review and recommended two-step approach. Psychol. Bull. **103**, 411–423 (1988)
36. Verhoeff, T.: The Role of Competitions in Education. Futur. World Educ. 21st Century, pp. 1–10 (1997)

SmileApp: The Design and Evaluation of an mHealth App for Stress Reduction Through Artificial Intelligence and Persuasive Technology

Joseph Orji, Gerry Chan(✉), Chinenye Ndulue, and Rita Orji

Faculty of Computer Science, Dalhousie University, Halifax, NS, Canada
gerry.chan@dal.ca

Abstract. Mobile health apps are becoming popular and capable of addressing a wide range of health-related issues including stress. In this study, we designed, developed, and evaluated an mHealth application called *SmileApp* to promote positive mood as a means of reducing stress. The design of *SmileApp* is grounded in psychological theories and integrates artificial intelligence (AI) and persuasive technology (PT). To evaluate *SmileApp*, we conducted a two-week in-the-wild study involving 72 participants. This was followed by an optional semi-structured interview with 23 participants. Quantitative results suggest that *SmileApp* is usable, and the use of the features can convince users to smile more frequently, as well as feel a sense of companionship and connectedness. Furthermore, qualitative results suggest that *SmileApp* was a unique design to help users alleviate stress. These results offer valuable insights into innovative approaches for designing mHealth applications that promote positive mood. Moreover, the findings underscore the importance of utilizing technology to support emotional wellbeing. We present a novel approach to promote desired behaviors by motivating users to read supportive messages and play mobile games by smiling.

Keywords: Artificial Intelligence · Mobile Health · Persuasive Technology · Emotional Wellbeing

1 Introduction

Early-life stressors or chronic stress throughout adulthood can significantly impact emotional wellbeing and increase susceptibility to depression [1]. Moreover, stress has been classified as an epidemic by the World Health Organization (WHO) and is a significant contributor to mortality rates [2]. While there is existing research evidence indicating that frequent smiling can contribute to stress reduction [3], the evidence that mobile apps can improve health outcomes is weak [4]. Furthermore, there remains a limited number of evidence-based research on technological solutions designed to encourage individuals to smile more frequently and very few apps designed to promote emotion regulation [5]. For example, Moore et al. [6] proposed an application that solely served as a reminder for users to smile, without implementing the proposed study or exploring its potential efficacy.

N. Baghaei et al. (Eds.): PERSUASIVE 2024, LNCS 14636, pp. 237–251, 2024.
https://doi.org/10.1007/978-3-031-58226-4_18

In this paper, we present the design, development, and evaluation of the effectiveness of a persuasive mHealth app called *SmileApp* that was purposefully designed to promote smiling and elicit a positive mood. The development of *SmileApp* is based on prior studies that have highlighted the potential of positive psychology strategies as preventive and therapeutic measures for treating depression [7]. Research shows that the act of mimicking a smile through facial muscle movement can delude the brain into experiencing a more positive mood [8]. Research also shows that smiling can mitigate the intensity of the body's stress response [9], and the use of mobile applications are effective for promoting happiness [6]. However, there is little research on mHealth apps that combine artificial intelligence (AI) and persuasive technology for promoting emotional wellbeing. As such the goal of this research is to evaluate *SmileApp*, a persuasive intervention app developed to promote users to smile more often and experience more positive moods. We conducted a two-week study involving 72 participants in-the-wild, followed by a semi-structured interview with 23 participants to answer the research question: "To what extent can *SmileApp* encourage people to smile, and in turn, elicit positive moods?".

Our results show that *SmileApp* is usable, and use of the features can convince users to smile more frequently, as well as feel a sense of companionship and connectedness. Our results also show that *SmileApp* can help users alleviate stress. These findings suggest that *SmileApp* positively impacts users' emotional wellbeing by fostering positive moods. These results offer valuable insights into innovative approaches for designing mHealth applications that promote positive moods. We contribute to the field of Human-Computer Interaction (HCI) and persuasive system design in three ways. Firstly, an innovative approach aimed at fostering positive emotional states, particularly the enhancement of smiles, is comprehensively explored and evaluated. Secondly, the user study elucidates the influence of anonymous one-way messaging on users' perceptions of social connectedness. Thirdly, the research introduces a novel approach to the design of mHealth applications with a focus on promoting emotional wellbeing rooted in the principles of positive psychology.

2 Background and Related Work

2.1 Persuasive Technology and Design

Persuasion can be defined as an attempt by a human being or organizational authority to motivate a target audience (human being) manually [10]. The advent of modern interactive devices such as smartphones and wearables have created many opportunities to integrate the power of persuasion into technology, called Persuasive Technology (PT). PT can be defined as the use of technology to influence the behavior and the attitude of users without coercion [11]. Relatedly, persuasive design aims to enhance motivation, simplify tasks to improve ability, and effectively trigger behavior change. Oinas-Kukkonen and Harjumaa [12] categorizes persuasive design principles for developing system contents and functionalities into four main groups: (1) primary task support, (2) dialogue support, (3) system credibility support, and (4) social support. Principles such as self-monitoring (keeping track of one's own status supports the user in achieving goals [13]), belonging to the "primary task support" category, and rewards (systems that reward target behaviors may have great persuasive powers [13]) in the "dialogue support" category, can provide insights into their respective prevalence and potential effectiveness in influencing behavior change.

2.2 Inducing Positive Feelings Using mHealth Apps

Research in the area of persuasive design intending to promote positive emotions and mental wellbeing is growing [14, 15]. Many researchers have examined the potential of mHealth apps for stress and emotion management [16, 17], as well as inducing positive feelings [18]. In this section, we highlight various approaches that have been employed to promote positive feelings.

One approach that is often employed to promote positive feelings is to identify the sources of stress [19]. In the context of mental health, researchers have utilized technology to detect the possibility or presence of stress and depression [20]. Previous interventions primarily detected stress, lacking a focus on emotion regulation, which is the central objective of our work. Our emphasis is on alleviating negative emotions. For instance, Jungmann et al.'s [21] chatbot (Ada) can identify mental disorders but cannot provide interventions for addressing these challenges. Another approach that can be used to promote positive feelings is educating users about the benefits of cultivating positive emotions and identifying activities that evoke positive feelings. Some researchers have taken the approach of training users on simple techniques aimed at enhancing their emotional wellbeing as a means of promoting mental health. This involves providing users with knowledge and recommendations for activities that can regulate their emotions, decrease the intensity of negative moods, and increase the intensity of positive moods [22]. The outcome of these studies showed that educating users on techniques to improve their emotional wellbeing was effective, but adherence is not guaranteed, in our intervention we guided users to actions which guarantees adherence. While digital technology-based training and psychology education effectively enhance wellbeing, there is limited research on integrating these solutions seamlessly into users' daily routines without causing disruption. Gamification, the use of game mechanics in non-game contexts [23], has also been widely used by many researchers to motivate behavior change and support individuals in their journey towards better mental health [24]. For example, Farve [25] used point elements by giving users a score of the number of smiles captured within a period, while Moltrecht et al. [26] used challenge elements by engaging the user to solve picture riddles and tap on happy faces as fast as possible.

Although informative, the potential of using both persuasive design and AI to promote positive emotions remains relatively under-researched.

3 SmileApp System Design

3.1 System Architecture

SmileApp was developed using Dart programming language [27], Flutter framework [28], Java programming language [29] and the Spring Boot framework [30]. We placed a strong emphasis on optimizing the performance of *SmileApp* to ensure its use on a wide range of devices, including low-performance devices. This consideration was essential as our target audience spans various regions, from developed nations to developing countries. To address the challenge that users may face in running the app on low-performance devices, we adopted a client-server architecture [31] for the entire system. In this architecture, we separated most of the computationally intensive processes from the mobile application. This separation of responsibilities allowed us to offload the computational burden from the mobile app and leverage the processing power of the backend infrastructure. To minimize the impact on the user's device and reduce network bandwidth usage, we implemented a local temporary memory within the mobile app. This temporary memory stored data locally on the device and was only sent to the backend after a user stopped using a feature instead of sending data as the user used the feature, thereby reducing frequent API calls. By employing this approach, we not only improved the overall efficiency of the system but also mitigated potential bandwidth constraints. The high-level system architecture of *SmileApp* is depicted in Fig. 1, illustrating the different components of the entire system and their interactions.

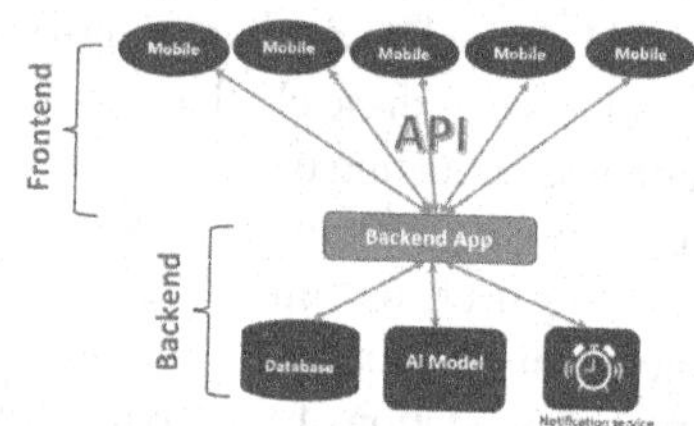

Fig. 1. System architecture of *SmileApp* (mobile app and backend interactions).

3.2 Features and User Interface

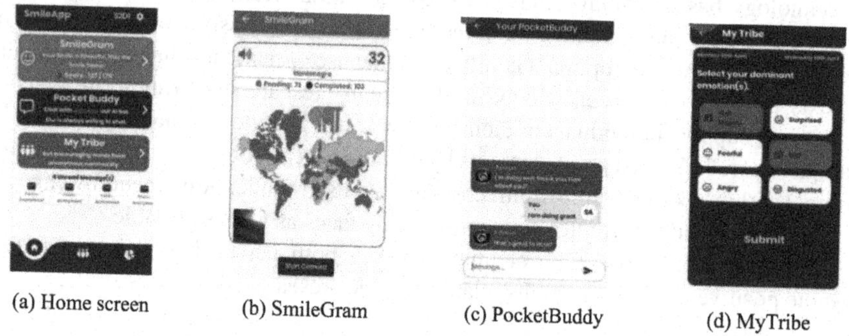

(a) Home screen (b) SmileGram (c) PocketBuddy (d) MyTribe

Fig. 2. *SmileApp* user interface and features.

The design of *SmileApp* is grounded in three well-established psychological constructs: (1) the flow theory [32], (2) the PSD Model [11], and (3) the PERMA model of wellbeing [33]. These constructs provided the conceptual basis for our persuasive system [21], and consequently, *SmileApp* (Fig. 2) consists of three main features: (1) SmileGram (Fig. 2b), (2) PocketBuddy (Fig. 2c), and (3) MyTribe (Fig. 2d).

SmileGram. This feature attempts to encourage users to focus and energize them to smile which aligns with the concept of flow [34] leading to genuine satisfaction [35]. Studies have shown that a smile helps the body to release neuropeptides which fight off stress [3]. As the overall purpose of our intervention is to elicit positive moods, we used this feature to persuade users to smile to fight off stress and improve users' moods which will lead to positive emotions. According to Conner et al. [36], one can build positive emotions by doing creative activities they enjoy. As such, we designed SmileGram with gaming elements to captivate users' interest and give them pride in accomplishing goals with their smiles compared to other users in the system. The core of this feature is to motivate a user to smile, irrespective of the present situation around them.

The SmileGram feature (Fig. 3) presents users with a mission to transform the world from grey to green through the power of the user's smile as an innovative way to give the user target goal in line with the persuasive system design model. The feature encompasses a map representing 175 countries (F), that initially appears in grey. The user is tasked with painting the entire map green by aligning two icons (E) with their smile. Each time the icons overlap perfectly with a specific country, indicated by the country name appearing (C), that country will be painted green. The number of countries painted green is numerically displayed (D) and a camera preview of the user as they smile is presented on the bottom left corner to provide feedback (G).

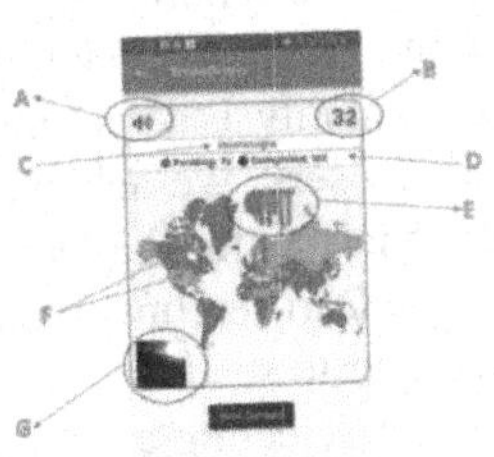

Fig. 3. SmileGram features (letters A-G represent components of this feature).

To accomplish this task, users must maintain a smile until the two icons overlap. Precision is crucial, as the user needs to promptly pause their smile once the icons align, preventing them from moving past each other. To track the user's smile, the SmileGram feature utilizes the Google Machine Learning Kit (ML) (Flutter package) [37] The ML Kit has high accuracy which has been likened to that of humans [38]. This technology detects the user's smile and ensures that they actively participate in the game and engage with the feature. If the smile is not detected for 3 s, a voice note is played, reminding the user to "Keep smiling." Users have the option to mute this sound by using the sound control button (A). Additionally, a countdown timer (B) is implemented to provide users with an indication of the time required to align the moving icons, adding a sense of challenge and urgency to the experience to give users a sense of accomplishment is also in line with the PERMA model [33].

PocketBuddy. PocketBuddy is a conversational chatbot with the persona of a friend called Adaeze, who interacts with users as a friend would to keep them company. Chatbot as defined by Shevat is a kind of interface [39] which stands between the abstract computing process of the computer and the user. Studies have shown the efficacy and feasibility of using an AI chatbot to address mental health-related issues [40]. Although chatbots have been used for several purposes like customer service inquiry, here we implemented the conversational agent as a companion. Hence, the name "PocketBuddy", is like giving users a "friend" to converse with. Unlike other chatbot implementations that focused on delivering information, we used a chatbot to deliver a sense of companionship to users. The chatbot can engage in any type of discussion on any topic making it a worthy companion. Companionship has been shown to improve mood [41]. To achieve this, we used tone transformation prompt techniques over ChatGPT API to generate empathic and supportive response to the user. There are no keywords required to initiate a conversation between the user and the chatbot. To interact with the chatbot, the user clicks on the feature and can start any form of conversation with a key phrase or anything as shown in Fig. 2c. It is important to note that the chatbot does not replace the need of a professional and does not provide professional services. It only engages in an informal conversation anyone can have with their friend.

MyTribe. This feature simulates a community of users who share supportive messages anonymously. This feature was designed to build a sense of support, connectedness, and relationship amongst users as it reflects flourishing wellbeing according to the PERMA model [33]. The MyTribe feature is aimed at building a community where everyone feels loved, supported and valued – in the PERMA model, it is referred to as "relationship" [42]. Every interaction in the community is kept safe, supportive, and empathic by censoring every message shared by users. We achieved this by using Dart sentiment 0.0.9, an AFINN-based sentiment analysis for the Dart programming language [43] as the first point of the check. When the Dart sentiment flags the content of the message as positive, the system will allow the user to send it.

This feature is initiated by a user selecting an emotion that closely relates to how they feel from the emotion palate adapted from Ekman et al.'s [44] six basic emotions: (1) not happy, (2) surprised, (3) fearful, (4) sad, (5) angry, and (6) disgusted. When the user clicks on the "submit" button, the app notifies all users about the emotion of the anonymous user. The notification generated by the system to inform other users of the user's emotion is subjected to a persuasive rephrasing process aimed at increasing its impact on users. For instance, when a user indicates their emotional state as "Not Happy" within *SmileApp*, the system encapsulates this information in an alert message that reads, "An individual is in an unhappy state. Would you be willing to offer words of kindness and encouragement by replying?" The intention behind such formulation is to motivate users to actively engage in supporting and uplifting others through their responses in the MyTribe feature. When other users receive the alert, they will compose a supportive and empathetic message for this user. If the message is not positive the app will alert the user to edit it or else, it will not be sent. When the user receives an empathic message from other community members anonymously, they can only unlock the message with a smile. They click on the message envelope icon that appears and wait for the 2-s countdown then smile to the camera.

4 User Study Design

To evaluate the perceived persuasiveness of the features and usability of *SmileApp*, we used a mixed-methods user study approach. Both quantitative and qualitative data were collected for analysis. The evaluation consisted of four steps: (1) complete a pre-study questionnaire, (2) use *SmileApp* for 14 days, (3) complete a post-study questionnaire and (4) participate in an optional interview.

4.1 Recruitment and Procedures

After receiving ethics clearance from our university ethics board, the recruitment of participants commenced. Participants were recruited using social media campaigns on platforms such as Twitter and LinkedIn, as well as email notices. To participate in the study, participants must be over 18 years old, proficient in English, and have access to a smart phone with the ability to connect to the internet. Participants were asked to complete a screening questionnaire and those who met the inclusion criteria, were invited to proceed with the following four-step procedure:

- **Step 1**: After reading the consent form and agreeing to the terms and conditions, participants completed a demographics questionnaire asking them to provide information such as age, gender, and level of education.
- **Step 2**: After completing step 1, participants were provided with a link to download *SmileApp* and were asked to use it for a period of 14 days.
- **Step 3**: After 14 days, participants completed a post-study questionnaire that evaluated their experience with using the app. The questionnaire statements were composed of validated measurement instruments that have been commonly used in HCI research to assess user preferences. In particular, usability was evaluated using the System Usability Scale (SUS) developed by Lewis and Sauro [45]. The SUS consists of 10 items and has been used to evaluate a wide range of products and applications, including mHealth apps [46]. In addition to usability, persuasiveness of the features was also measured using a modified version of the perceived persuasiveness scale (4-items) developed by Drozd et al. [47] and has been validated and employed in many studies including Orji et al. [48]. Participants indicated their level of agreement on a 7-point Likert scale (1 = strongly disagree to 7 = strongly agree).
- **Step 4**: Participants who wished to offer more thoughts about their experience with *SmileApp* were invited to participate in an optional one-on-one interview. Interviews were conducted virtually and took approximately 30 min.

4.2 Data Analysis

Before performing the data analysis, the data was screened for missing values, outliers, and any out-of-range values to ensure the data quality. Results were analyzed using both quantitative and qualitative data analysis techniques. Quantitative data collected in the questionnaire were analyzed using descriptive statistics to first explore the data, followed by a one-sample t-test to determine whether the subjective ratings are above the mid-point (neutral score), and significance. Although 101 participants were recruited, only 72 participants completed the post-study questionnaire after using the app for 14 days.

Thus, an analysis was performed on a data set of 72 responses. Qualitative interview data were analyzed using a thematic analysis.

5 Results

5.1 Participant Demographics

As shown in Table 1 most participants fall in the age bracket of 18–25 years old (47%), most of the participants were women (63%) while for academic qualification, the majority held a bachelor's degree (51%).

Table 1. Participants' demographic information (N = 72).

Characteristics	Frequency (%)
Age (years)	18–25 (47%), 26–35 (38%), 36–45 (15%), prefer not to answer (1%)
Gender	Man (36%), woman (63%), prefer not to answer (1%)
Level of Education	High school (24%), bachelor's degree (51%), college diploma (11%), master's degree (8%), prefer not to answer (6%)

5.2 Quantitative Results

Overall, SUS scores were reported to provide an overview of the usability of *SmileApp*. The SUS revealed an average score of 79.51 ($SD = 15.00$), suggesting that the overall usability of the app is "good" [49]. Next, we analyzed the persuasiveness of each feature and the overall persuasiveness of *SmileApp* by performing a one-sample t-test on the perceived persuasive scale data against a neutral rating of 4. Results (Fig. 4 and Table 2) show that all three features (SmileGram, PocketBuddy and MyTribe) and the app overall, was perceived to be persuasive suggesting that features can convince users to smile more frequently, as well as feel a sense of companionship and connectedness.

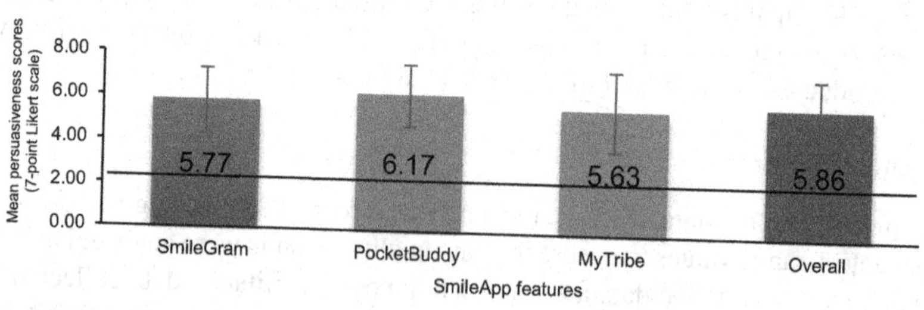

Fig. 4. A bar chart showing the mean results for perceived persuasiveness of *SmileApp* features and overall, on a 7-point Likert scale. The black horizontal line indicates the neutral rating of 4.

Table 2. Descriptive statistics and one-sample t-test for perceived persuasiveness ($N = 72$).

	Descriptive statistics		One-sample t-test			
Features	*M*	*SD*	*t*	*df*	*p*	Cohen's *d*
SmileGram	5.77	1.49	10.10	71	< .001	1.19
PocketBuddy	6.17	1.40	13.18	71	< .001	1.55
MyTribe	5.63	1.81	7.62	71	< .001	0.90
Overall	5.86	1.38	11.45	71	< .001	1.35

5.3 Qualitative Results

To obtain additional feedback and a broader perspective of participants' experiences, we conducted semi-structured interviews to better understand the users' views about *SmileApp*. Of the 72 participants who used the app and completed the post-study questionnaire, 23 participants (45% males and 55% females) opted to participate in the optional interview. Interview recordings were transcribed and a thematic analysis following Braun and Clarke's [50] six phase approach was used to analyze the qualitative interview data. This analysis aimed to identify and explore key themes related to participants' interest in using *SmileApp*, as well as the impact and general perception of *SmileApp*. In general, our analysis revealed a consistent optimistic response, with many participants expressing their admiration for the app's innovative features and the positive impact it had on them which resulted in four themes as follows. The extracts are presented with minor spelling and grammatical corrections.

Theme 1: This is an innovative and interesting way to make me smile. Most participants found *SmileApp* to be unique and innovative, especially the SmileGram feature which allows them to play games with their smile. Many participants commented on how they had never seen something like this before and thought that it was an interesting way to make them smile. For example, one participant said "*Interesting. I've never had to do something like that before and having a piece of technology to encourage me to do something. I thought was a* ***very interesting and new experience for me****. I was using it so that that was kind of interesting*" [P1], while another participant thought that "*…my first time using that kind of app that will require one to smile.* ***When I am not in a good mood, I just open the app and Smile***" [P13]. One more participant said that "***The moving image alone is captivating****. Because it's not just your smile, but the fact that it is* ***tied to moving objects***" [P16]. Overall, this suggests that the app was well perceived as a novel way to encourage people to smile more often. Participants were interested in the experience and the game like experience of moving objects to collect points was an effective method for increasing the level of engagement.

Theme 2: This is a useful tool for stress relief. We observed a common consensus among participants on how the app was useful for them to relieve stress. Many participants talked about how using the app helped them reduce stress. For example, one participant said "*My experience with this app has been so amazing. It helps me to* ***achieve my aim in terms of trying to live up to reduce stress***" [P8], while a different participant thought that "*It's a* ***brilliant way to ease stress as you forget about some things happening to you*** *while using the app*" [P20]. One more participant believed that using the app "*was really stress-relieving because at some point when you get stressed up, you just go look at the app. Since it connects with your smile, your smile is all you need to do and* ***in the process all the facial muscles get relaxed***" [P16]. Another participant described relieved after using the app when they "*I never knew that smiling can have something correlating to feeling good. I remember there was a day I was feeling anxious.* ***Like I had a lot of pain and I tried using the app. I just used the app not as a remedy to my anxiety; I just wanted to use it suddenly I realized when I started using the app, I started feeling much better****. So, after that day, I realized that, OK, this smiling of a thing can, you know help me even when you're faking it. So, it's a good idea and to be honest I play with the smiling app more than the chat. I use the chat slightly but overall; I love the smile and I love the app in general*" [P2]. Furthermore, some participants explained how using the app was a way to take a break while at work and help with managing their emotional stress. For example, one participant said "*It's very useful, especially for me, that juggles between my career and entrepreneurship. I work, and I do business. You know,* ***most times I don't even get time to go out with friends and relax****. So, during the period, we were reviewing this app, I think one of the things that helped me is that* ***I could be in the office, and when I see that I'm stressed, I can just open it and smile***" [P9], while a different participant said "*Sometimes emotional stress can pop up anytime, but* ***work stress is the most****. So,* ***I use this app to rest***" [P19]. Collectively, this suggests that using the app can alleviate stress, and help users forget about or cope with their negative experiences, such as anxiety.

Theme 3: Using the app improves my mood and makes me laugh. We noticed a trend in participants' responses which provides valuable insight into how participants perceive *SmileApp* as an effective tool for improving their mood and motivating them to smile more often. For example, one participant said that "*Using the app, mostly the SmileGram, it* ***relieves me of headaches and enhances my mood and distracts me from whatever was bothering me*** *at the moment*" [P74], while another participant felt that "*You know to* ***wind down and try distracting myself from everything that is frustrating*** *me in the day. So, I found it highly useful*" [P2]. Some participants thought that the app was fun and entertaining when it made them laugh, even when they did not want to. For example, one participant said "*I find the SmileGram very,* ***very funny****, especially when I must* ***open my teeth. Even when I don't feel like smiling. I just must open because I want to really color the world***" [P12], while a different participant said "*If I don't have reason to smile again, the app now comes to mind, and* ***I'll just take up SmileApp and then I will start smiling***" [P16]. Based on these observations, *SmileApp* can improve one's mood and make people laugh. This further supports the quantitative findings that the SmileGram feature was perceived to be persuasive because users were motivated by purposeful actions (i.e., coloring the world) using their smile. The app also served as a good reminder to smile more often as participants were thinking about it giving them a reason to smile, and practice activities that can improve their wellbeing.

Theme 4: This app is useful, and I want to continue using it. We found that many participants indicated a strong interest in using the app beyond the study. The benefits and positive feelings were key components for continuing to use the app. For example, one participant said "***I've gotten a lot out of this****. I will not stop using it. I will not at all, because* ***the app brings out so many good things***" [P11]. However, usage depends on whether they will need to pay to use the app when one participant said "*If there is no intention to monetize it,* ***if it will like free stuff where I can go to and release stress, I don't mind continuing using it****. It's something* ***I can recommend to my mom*** *for her to use*" [P19]. Furthermore, a participant said they would continue to use the app because "*it* ***helps me relieve stress****. So,* ***on days when I have hectic work and I need to rest, I just lie on my bed, and bring the app****. I'm smiling and I've already recommended it to my husband. So,* ***I'm smiling as if the whole family is smiling with the app****.*" [P23]. One more participant said that they "*will keep using it after the study. Especially* ***PocketBuddy. Because like I said, it informs****. And yeah,* ***I keep chatting with it****. I chat with it*" [P4]. In general, this suggests that users are likely to continue using the app over the long term because it they found it beneficial to their wellbeing such as reducing stress, feeling a sense of presence and belongingness with the whole family, as well as engaging in social conversations.

6 Discussion

This study investigated the effectiveness of *SmileApp* which was specifically designed to promote smiling and elicit positive moods. In general, our results showed that the app was usable and perceived to be persuasive as use of the features can convince users to smile more frequently, as well as feel a sense of companionship and connectedness. Furthermore, qualitative results suggest that *SmileApp* was a unique design to help users alleviate stress and users will continue to use it, as they found it beneficial for improving their mood, as well as motivating them to smile and laugh more often.

6.1 Implications for Design

Based on our results, we offer the following three recommendations that will help both researchers and mHealth application developers who wish to design an app that elicits positive emotions and better wellbeing.

Design Recommendation 1: Engage users by using points, colors, and animation. Our results showed that the SmileGram feature was persuasive, and many participants commented on how the novelty and interactive nature motivated them to keep smiling. In particular, our qualitative results showed that even when users did not feel like smiling, they were encouraged to keep smiling because they wanted to color the world. As such, we recommend that apps can increase the level of interactivity and engagement by employing similar techniques we used to design the SmileGram feature such as points or rewards system, colors, and animation. Offering these elements is likely to not only make engaging in activities that promote wellbeing fun and entertaining but will also add a sense of purpose to performing the activity.

Design Recommendation 2: Adapt features (persuasive principles) into the lives, habits, and activities of the user. Many participants used the app as a source of stress relieve in their daily lives, particularly at work. We found that participants used it to not only to enhance their mood and distract them from what was bothersome, but also used the app to make themselves laugh and experience feelings of social connectedness with their family members. As such, we recommend that apps can adapt to people's life situations and habits. For example, when the app detects that the user is alone at home or at work and has not been in contact with anyone all day, the system can encourage the user to engage in social interactions and conversations.

Design Recommendation 3: Remind and give reasons for the user to practice activities that benefit their wellbeing. It is important to anchor the activities that people engage in with some kind of purpose and remind them that it is beneficial for improving and sustaining their wellbeing. Our results showed that when participants did not find any specific reason to smile, they thought of the *SimleApp*. Participants found that the app offered a purpose for them to smile and keep on smiling. Thus, we recommend that apps should occasionally remind users of the benefits of smiling and give reasons through different means (e.g., playing a game or reading supportive messages) to smile more often.

6.2 Limitations and Directions for Future Work

Although the study presented some interesting findings, there are several limitations. One limitation is that we used subjective questionnaires and interviews as our data collection methods. As such, there could be potential biases associated with subjective reports. A future study could aim to collect more objective data to further verify these results. Another limitation is the study was conducted in-the-wild, and although this has high ecological validity, it also poses uncertainty as it could have been possible that users may have allowed their friends to use the app rather than themselves. There is no way we could monitor or verify who used the app as such monitoring has the potential to violate participant's privacy. One more limitation is the short duration of the study of two weeks and the small to moderate sample size of the quantitative data. A future study can collect data for a longer period and evaluate the long-term effectiveness of the features with a larger sample as many participants indicated that they would continue to use the app after two weeks. Furthermore, as this is an mHealth app, we also acknowledge potential scenarios (e.g., during personal tragedies or in response to distressing news) where smiling may not be feasible.

7 Conclusion

In closing, we sought to leverage the power of PT to improve wellbeing. As such, we designed and developed *SmileApp*, and evaluated its effectiveness for experiencing wellbeing which included features to encourage people to smile more often, as well as feel a greater sense of companionship and social connectedness. To the best of our knowledge, this is one of the first designs to integrate game elements, conversational AI, and a simulation of a social community within an mHealth application for encouraging people to practice activities that are beneficial to their wellbeing through smiling. Our findings provide valuable insights into the role of persuasive technology and how it can be creatively employed to promote emotional wellbeing and have important implications for the design and development of future mHealth applications.

References

1. Gold, P.W.: The organization of the stress system and its dysregulation in depressive illness. Mol. Psychiatry **20**, 32–47 (2014)
2. Prior, A., Fenger-Grøn, M., Kjaer Larsen, K.: Original Contribution The Association Between Perceived Stress and Mortality Among People With Multimorbidity: A Prospective Population-Based Cohort Study (2016)
3. There's Magic in Your Smile I Psychology Today
4. Iribarren, S.J.: Effectiveness of mobile apps to promote health and manage disease: systematic review and meta-analysis of randomized controlled trials. JMIR mHealth uHealth **9**, e21563 (2021)
5. Eisenstadt, M., Liverpool, S., Infanti, E.: Mobile Apps That Promote Emotion Regulation, Positive Mental Health, and Well-Being in the General Population: Systematic Review and Meta-analysis (2021)
6. Moore, G., Galway, L., Donnelly, M.: Remember to smile design of a mobile affective technology to help promote individual happiness through smiling. PervasiveHealth Pervasive Comput. Technol. Healthc. 348–354 (2017)
7. Santos, V., Paes, F., Pereira, V.: The role of positive emotion and contributions of positive psychology in depression treatment: systematic review. Clin. Pract. Epidemiol. Ment. Heal. **9**, 221–237 (2013)
8. Marmolejo-Ramos, F., Murata, A., Sasaki, K., Yamada, Y., Ikeda, A., Hinojosa, J.A.: Your Face and Moves Seem Happier When I Smile. **67**, 14–22 (2020)
9. Grin and Bear It! Smiling Facilitates Stress Recovery – Association for Psychological Science – APS
10. Nkwo, M., Orji, R., Ugah, J.: Persuasion for promoting clean and sustainable environment. In: AfriCHI '18: Thriving Communities, pp. 1–5. ACM, New York, NY, USA (2018)
11. Oinas-Kukkonen, H., Harjumaa, M.: A systematic framework for designing and evaluating persuasive systems. In: Oinas-Kukkonen, H., Hasle, P., Harjumaa, M., Segerståhl, K., Øhrstrøm, P. (eds.) PERSUASIVE 2008. LNCS, vol. 5033, pp. 164–176. Springer, Heidelberg (2008). https://doi.org/10.1007/978-3-540-68504-3_15
12. Oinas-Kukkonen, H., Harjumaa, M.: Persuasive systems design: key issues, process model, and system features. Commun. Assoc. Inf. Syst. **24**, 485–500 (2009)
13. Oinas-Kukkonen, H., Harjumaa, M.: Persuasive systems design: key issues, process model, and system features. Commun. Assoc. Inf. Syst. **24** (2009)
14. Brindal, E., Hendrie, G.A., Freyne, J., Noakes, M.: A mobile phone app designed to support weight loss maintenance and well-being (MotiMate): randomized controlled trial. JMIR mHealth uHealth **7**, e12882 (2019)
15. Ahtinen, A., Andrejeff, E., Väänänen, K.: Brainwolk - a mobile technology mediated walking meeting concept for wellbeing and creativity at work (2016)
16. Lau, N., O'Daffer, A., Colt, S.: Android and iPhone mobile apps for psychosocial wellness and stress management: systematic search in app stores and literature review. JMIR mHealth uHealth **8** (2020)
17. Christmann, C.A., Hoffmann, A., Bleser, G.: Stress management apps with regard to emotion-focused coping and behavior change techniques: a content analysis. JMIR mHealth uHealth **5** (2017)

18. Wang, T.: The impact of gamification-induced users' feelings on the continued use of mhealth apps: a structural equation model with the self-determination theory approach. J. Med. Internet Res. **23** (2021)
19. Folkman, S.: The case for positive emotions in the stress process. Anxiety Stress Coping **21**, 3–14 (2008)
20. Denecke, K., Vaaheesan, S., Arulnathan, A.: A mental health chatbot for regulating emotions (SERMO) - concept and usability test. IEEE Trans. Emerg. Top. Comput. **9**, 1170–1182 (2021)
21. Jungmann, S.M., Klan, T., Kuhn, S., Jungmann, F.: Accuracy of a chatbot (Ada) in the diagnosis of mental disorders: comparative case study with lay and expert users. JMIR Form. Res. **3**, e13863 (2019)
22. van Emmerik, A.A.P., Berings, F., Lancee, J.: Efficacy of a mindfulness-based mobile application: a randomized waiting-list controlled trial. Mindfulness (N. Y) **9**, 187–198 (2018)
23. Deterding, S., Dixon, D., Khaled, R., Nacke, L.: from game design elements to gamefulness: defining "gamification." In: MindTrek '11 Proceedings of 15th International Acadamic and MindTrek Converence Envisioning Future Media Environment, pp. 9–15 (2011)
24. Lockwood, J., Williams, L., Martin, J.L., Rathee, M., Hill, C.: Effectiveness, user engagement and experience, and safety of a mobile app (Lumi Nova) delivering exposure-based cognitive behavioral therapy strategies to manage anxiety in children via immersive gaming technology: preliminary evaluation study. JMIR Ment. Heal. **9**, e29008 (2022)
25. Farve, N.: Smile Catcher - A Gamified Approach to Smiles
26. Moltrecht, B., Patalay, P., Deighton, J.: A school-based mobile app intervention for enhancing emotion regulation in children: exploratory trial. JMIR mHealth uHealth **9**, e21837 (2021)
27. Dart | Google Developers
28. Flutter - Build apps for any screen
29. What is Java used for? 6 practical Java uses - FutureLearn
30. Spring Boot Reference Documentation
31. Client Server Architecture - CIO Wiki
32. Csikszentmihalyi, M.: Toward a psychology of optimal experience. Flow Found. Posit. Psychol. Collect. Work. Mihaly Csikszentmihalyi. 209–226 (2014)
33. Seligman, M.E.P.: Flourish: a visionary new understanding of happiness and well-being (2011)
34. Mirvis, P.H., Csikszentmihalyi, M.: Flow: The Psychology of Optimal Experience (1991)
35. Csikszentmihalyi and Happiness
36. Conner, T.S., DeYoung, C.G., Silvia, P.J.: Everyday creative activity as a path to flourishing. J. Posit. Psychol. **13**, 181–189 (2018)
37. google_ml_kit | Flutter Package
38. Smile, You're on WebRTC — Using MLKit for Smile Detection | by Houseparty | Good Audience
39. Cameron, G., et al.: Assessing the usability of a chatbot for mental health care. In: Bodrunova, S.S., et al. (eds.) INSCI 2018. LNCS, vol. 11551, pp. 121–132. Springer, Cham (2019). https://doi.org/10.1007/978-3-030-17705-8_11
40. Fitzpatrick, K.K., Darcy, A., Vierhile, M.: Delivering cognitive behavior therapy to young adults with symptoms of depression and anxiety using a fully automated conversational agent (Woebot): a randomized controlled trial. JMIR Ment. Heal. **4**, e19 (2017)
41. Keyvanfar, S., Sadeghnia, A., Namnabati, M.: The effects of a neonatal critical care nurse companionship with parents during hospital–home transfer of preterm infants on mothers' mood status. Nurs. Midwifery Stud. **9**, 16 (2020)
42. The PERMA Model: Your Scientific Theory of Happiness
43. dart_sentiment | Flutter Package

44. Ekman, P., et al.: Are There Basic Emotions? (1992)
45. Lewis, J.R., Sauro, J.: The factor structure of the system usability scale. In: Kurosu, M. (ed.) HCD 2009. LNCS, vol. 5619, pp. 94–103. Springer, Heidelberg (2009). https://doi.org/10.1007/978-3-642-02806-9_12
46. Santoso, I.S., Ferdinansyah, A., Sensuse, D.I., Suryono, R.R., Kautsarina, Hidayanto, A.N.: Effectiveness of gamification in mHealth apps designed for mental illness. In: Proceeding - 2021 2nd International Conference on ICT Rural Development, IC-ICTRuDev 2021 (2021)
47. Drozd, F., Lehto, T., Oinas-Kukkonen, H.: Exploring perceived persuasiveness of a behavior change support system: A structural model. In: Bang, M., Ragnemalm, E.L. (eds.) PERSUASIVE 2012. LNCS, vol. 7284, pp. 157–168. Springer, Heidelberg (2012). https://doi.org/10.1007/978-3-642-31037-9_14
48. Orji, R., Vassileva, J., Mandryk, R.L.: Modeling the efficacy of persuasive strategies for different gamer types in serious games for health. User Model. User-Adap. Inter. **24**, 453–498 (2014)
49. Bangor, A., Kortum, P., Miller, J.: Determining what individual SUS scores mean: adding an adjective rating scale. J. usability Stud. **4**, 114–123 (2009)
50. Braun, V., Clarke, V.: Using thematic analysis in psychology. Qual. Res. Psychol. **3**, 77–101 (2006)

How the Role of a Persuasive Robot Impacts One's Attitude Towards It

Peter A. M. Ruijten(✉), Jin Smeding, and Jaap Ham

Eindhoven University of Technology, Eindhoven, The Netherlands
p.a.m.ruijten@tue.nl

Abstract. Recent years have seen a development of social robots in all kinds of different roles. For social robots to be tailored to the needs of the user and become more accepted, we need to understand how people perceive and interact with robots in these different roles. This study investigates people's attitudes toward robots in two different roles (utilitarian: practically oriented vs hedonic: socially oriented) after interacting with them at home for several days. Results show that people's attitudes towards the same robot differ between the roles that were applied to the robot. People also described their interactions with the robot in different terms depending on its role. Implications of these findings are discussed in light of tailored approaches in the design of interactions between humans and social robots.

Keywords: Attitude change · Tailored HRI · Roles of social robots

1 Introduction

Social robots embody aspects of all three canonical categories of humans, animals and artifacts (i.e., objects made by humans, e.g., tools), and they cannot merely be placed within one of those categories [15]. People will see social robots as a new ontological category in addition to humans, animals and artifacts. This indicates that a social robot can have different roles, in which more human- or animal-like interactions and conceptualizations overlap more with the social aspects of the robot and the more artifact-like interactions and conceptualizations more with the practical aspects.

This is in line with the distinction between utilitarian and hedonic product aspects within the field of human-computer interaction [11,12]. Utilitarian aspects are much more practical, providing instrumental value to the user. This implies that there is an objective external to the interaction with the product, such as increasing task performance. Hedonic aspects do not focus on such external objectives. Instead, the mere interaction with the hedonic product aspects can be considered an end in itself, providing self-fulfilling value to the user.

Based on this, a social robot can be perceived as a utilitarian system - focusing on the tasks that it can perform – or a hedonic system - focusing on the opportunity for social interaction and relationship building [5]. [3] makes a similar distinction, dividing the role of a robot into machines or tools on one end, and assistants, companions and partners on the other end.

N. Baghaei et al. (Eds.): PERSUASIVE 2024, LNCS 14636, pp. 252–261, 2024.
https://doi.org/10.1007/978-3-031-58226-4_19

[5] found that utilitarian aspects are crucial in determining whether people use a social robot or not, but once they do choose to use the robot, the hedonic social interactions seem to become much more important. [24] found a similar importance of hedonic social interactions. When studying a vacuum robot, they found that some – but not all – users named it, played with it, gave it a personality and gender, in addition to using it for its intended purpose of cleaning. This shows that people can assign different roles to a robot in their home. Indeed, earlier research suggested that the role a robot uses influences the robot's effectiveness [23]. That is, when a robot used an evaluative role (as compared to a non-evaluative role), it was more effective in stimulating learning behavior of its user [23]. Moreover, [24] found that social activities led to a significantly higher satisfaction with the robot. Furthermore, a social robot with low social interaction skills is evaluated more negatively in terms of sociability and competence compared to a robot with high social interaction skills [14]. This suggests that the perceived social aspects of a robot could lead to a more positive evaluation of the robot.

In contrast, some studies have shown that a robot in a utilitarian role is preferred over a robot in a social role. Indeed, the idea of having an electronic assistant that makes life easier by carrying out tasks for you might be very appealing to most people [13]. The utility of a robot (e.g., usefulness and ease of use) has been shown to be an important factor in people's acceptance of that robot [4,7]. Furthermore, [8] found the social impact of functional robots to be overestimated. The social activities with the robot that the participants engaged with - such as talking and playing with it - wore off when people became familiar with the robot, possibly due to a novelty effect. Moreover, [10] found that social and companionship possibilities of domestic robots were not appreciated and evaluated negatively.

1.1 Types of Attitudes Towards Social Robots

Based on these findings, we argue that people's evaluations of a robot might depend on the role of the robot. Such evaluations are captured in people's attitude. Rooted in the work of Allport [1], an attitude is now often defined as "a psychological tendency that is expressed by evaluating a particular entity with some degree of favor or disfavor" [6, p. 1]. Attitudes can be divided into affective, behavioral, and cognitive levels [20]. Regarding a social robot, a person's affective attitude reflects their feelings or emotions toward the robot, their behavioral attitude reflects their observable behavior toward the robot, and their cognitive attitude reflects their thoughts about the robot.

The distinction between affective, behavioral, and cognitive attitude is not always explicitly made or made between all three components. However, this distinction is useful as it can provide a more in-depth view of a person's attitude. For example, people might believe a social robot to be worthwhile (positive cognitive attitude), while feeling uneasy when interacting with the robot (negative affective attitude). Furthermore, it can potentially account for some of the mixed findings identified in previous research [18].

While previous work does indicate an influence of the role of a robot on people's attitude toward that robot, no previous research has yet been found that empirically compares attitudes across different roles of the same robot. As described before, a social robot can have a utilitarian or hedonic role, but the impact of those roles on how people evaluate that robot is still unclear.

[16] did look at differences in attitude across utilitarian and hedonic robots, but they used two different types of robots (the zoomorphic Pleo robot and the Roomba vacuum robot). They found a higher enjoyment with the hedonic robot, while the utilitarian robot was perceived more useful and easier to use.

1.2 Research Aims

In this study our aim was to investigate to what extent people's attitudes towards a social robot would change between a utilitarian and a hedonic role. This role was manipulated solely by changing the description of the robot. The attitudes that people had towards the robot were measured on three levels: affective, behavioral, and cognitive. Based on earlier work on people's evaluations of utilitarian aspects of robots [5,7,8,13], we expected that overall, people's attitudes towards the utilitarian robot would be more positive than those towards the hedonic robot.

2 Method

2.1 Participants and Design

The sample size was mainly determined by more practical restrictions; there were five robots available with four weeks of data collection, enabling the experiment to be conducted with 20 participants in total (five participants per week). A total of 20 participants (3 males, 16 females, 1 unknown; age $M = 23.35$, $SD = 1.790$, Range = 20 to 28) participated in a field experiment about attitudes towards social robots. The experiment had two conditions: utilitarian vs hedonic role. Attitudes toward the robot (divided into three levels: affective, behavioral, and cognitive) were the dependent variables. All participants used the robot in both a utilitarian role and a hedonic role (order was counterbalanced). In both conditions, attitudes were measured through an online survey, behavior statistics and qualitative interviews.

2.2 Materials

The robot used in this experiment is the Anki Vector robot, which is a small programmable robot. Vector is made to explore and react to its surroundings. The Vector robot has a variety of sensors, including a camera, touch sensors, an accelerometer and several microphones. In order to initiate an interaction with Vector, the user must say "hey Vector". The robot will indicate that it is listening, after which the desired command can be given. If no command is given, Vector automatically reverts back to exploring its environment. Vector can communicate with vocal sounds and lights, as well as through expressions with its eyes and movements with its arm. If the robot is low on battery, it will go to its charger automatically.

In order to manipulate the role of the robot, participants were given an information sheet about each of the two robots. In the information sheets, first some basic information about the robot is explained. This includes information about the Wi-Fi, the cube, the button on the robot, the meaning of different lights on the robot, volume settings and charging. This information was provided in both conditions. The second part of the sheet differed between the two conditions. In the utilitarian condition, it contained elements such as setting a timer, asking the weather, unit conversions, general knowledge questions. In the hedonic condition, elements such as playing a game, dancing, and fist-bumping were included. The number of items between the two types of information sheets were similar. The conditions were counterbalanced, and the order of the conditions was assigned randomly.

Since the exact same robot was going to be used in both conditions, it was important to make people believe these were different. Therefore, the robot for the second condition was introduced as a new robot with a different eye color and differently colored tracks. Furthermore, the robot was taken back at the end of the first condition, then the participants had a rest day and after that the second robot was introduced.

2.3 Measurements

People's attitudes toward the Vector robot were measured on three levels: affective, behavioral, and cognitive. Affective attitude was measured through the Negative Attitudes toward Robots Scale (NARS) [19]. The scale was adapted to be applicable to the Vector robot. This scale had 14 items that were rated on a 5-point Likert scale ranging from strongly disagree (1) to strongly agree (5). Answers to the 14 questions were summed into an Affective Attitude score ($\alpha = 0.66$). As this scale measures negative attitudes, the lower the score, the more positive the participant's affective attitude towards the robot was.

Behavioral attitude was measured through behavioral statistics that were automatically collected with the robot. They include the number of wakewords ("hey vector"), the total distance driven (in cm) and the number of utilities used.

Cognitive attitude was measured through the Robot Attitude Scale (RAS) [2]. This scale is a semantic differential scale with 11 items that were rated on an 8-point scale. Answers to the 14 questions were summed into a Cognitive Attitude score ($\alpha = 0.78$). As this scale measures negative attitudes, the lower the score, the more positive the participant's Cognitive Attitude towards the robot was.

Due to the low number of participants, we decided to also include qualitative data to be able to shed more light on the quantitative results. A short semi-structured interview was conducted at the end of the experiment to gain more meaningful insights. During this interview, the participants were asked about their experiences with Vector, how they used the robot (e.g., placement, frequency, duration), and their experiences with the different conditions.

2.4 Procedure

Before the experiment started, participants read an information sheet and gave consent for participating in this study. Then, the robot was introduced together with an information sheet (for either the utilitarian or hedonic condition), participants completed the first attitude measurement, and they were told that they could use the robot freely for the next two days. After these two days, the experimenter picked up the robot and the attitude measurements were conducted again. After one day without the robot, the experimenter went back to introduce the second robot, as well as the second information sheet. Again the attitude measures were performed, participants used the robot for two days, and the robot was retrieved again. The behavior statistics were taken from the robot upon retrieval after each of the two conditions. During the retrieval, participants completed the final attitude measures and were interviewed about their experiences. Finally, participants were thanked for their participation, debriefed about the main goal of the experiment, and compensated with €20.

3 Results

Due to violations of normality, data on the behavioral measures were transformed by taking the square root of the raw data. After transformation, assumptions of normality were met for all transformed variables, except for the number of utilities used in the utilitarian condition. As this was only a very slight violation (Shapiro-Wilk test: $p = .052$, Skewness-Kurtosis test: $p = .049$) and all other behavioral statistics variables passed this test, analyses were performed on the transformed data.

3.1 Affective Attitude

A significant main effect of the role of the robot on Affective Attitude toward that robot was found, $F(1,19) = 8.10$, $p = .010$, $\eta^2_{\text{partial}} = .30$. Participants' affective attitude was more negative towards the utilitarian robot ($M = 35.50$, $SD = 6.27$) compared to the hedonic robot ($M = 33.65$, $SD = 4.92$).

The outcomes of the statistical analyses showed a more negative Affective Attitude in the utilitarian condition compared to the hedonic condition. As participants perceived the robot in the hedonic role much more as a social being compared to the robot in the utilitarian role, this gave rise to feelings of pride (e.g., when the robot correctly executed a command), guilt (e.g., when turning the robot off), loss (after the robot was retrieved from their home) or companionship (e.g., having something to come home to). These feelings indicate that participants formed a bond/attachment to the robot, which might explain their preference for the hedonic role over the robot in the utilitarian role to which they did not feel strongly attached.

3.2 Behavioral Attitude

The wakeword and distance statistics are an indication of the frequency/duration of use of the robot. Neither the number of wakewords used ($t(18) = -0.93$, $p = .365$) nor the distance driven ($t(18) = -0.14$, $p = .892$) differed significantly between the two roles of the robot. However, participants did pet the robot longer in the hedonic condition ($M = 140\,\text{s}$, $SD = 159$) compared to the utilitarian condition ($M = 55\,\text{s}$, $SD = 72$), $t(18) = -2.37$, $p = .029$, $d = -.46$. In addition, participants used significantly more utilities when the robot had a utilitarian role ($M = 15$, $SD = 10.95$) compared to a hedonic role ($M = 3.7$, $SD = 4.14$), $t(18) = 5.84$, $p < .001$, $d = .97$.

The differences in behavioral attitude towards the robot between the conditions were clearly visible in the quantitative behavior statistics measured. The qualitative data showed that participants did not notice many behavioral differences or changes themselves. Not many noteworthy aspects of the behavioral attitude were mentioned, other than participants trying out different types of functionalities that the robot was explained to have in each of the conditions.

3.3 Cognitive Attitude

No significant difference on cognitive attitude was found between the utilitarian ($M = 40.53$, $SD = 8.51$) and hedonic ($M = 41.53$, $SD = 9.20$) roles of the robot, $F(1,19) = 0.57$, $p = .461$.

The qualitative data showed that participants were overall impressed by the robot's intelligence. As one participant put it, when trying something new they thought "oh this is *also* something it can do", which may have positively influenced their cognitive attitude toward the utilitarian role of the robot. Some participants mentioned that the social connection provided by the hedonic role of the robot was unnecessary. Their need for social interactions was already satisfied by seeing their friends and family regularly, so having the robot was not necessary for them. This suggests that the hedonic aspects of the robot were less important to them, perhaps influencing their cognitive attitude toward the hedonic role negatively.

Finally, when participants were asked specifically about their attitudes towards both types of robots, it seemed that short-term attitude change is more related to utilitarian aspects and novelty effects, while hedonic aspects seemed more relevant for attitude changes in the long-term.

4 Discussion

The aim of this study was to investigate the influence of the role of a social robot (utilitarian or hedonic) on people's attitude toward that robot. Both the quantitative and the qualitative results indicated that there were differences in people's attitude toward a robot across the roles of that robot. Results showed that hedonic aspects seemed to be more important - as opposed to utilitarian aspects - for people's Affective Attitude. The role of the robot also influenced specific behaviors that people showed towards the robot, as petting duration was higher with the hedonic role of the robot and number of utilities used was higher in the utilitarian condition. No differences between the two roles were found on people's Cognitive Attitude.

Participants' affective attitude was significantly more positive when the robot had a hedonic role compared to a utilitarian role. This finding contrasts our expectations. Through the interviews it became apparent that the majority of participants liked the social aspects of the robot the most and that those aspects elicited feelings of companionship, pride, guilt and loss. As previously emphasized [14,24], this suggests that hedonic aspects of social robots are very important to people's evaluation of (the interaction with) a robot.

The behavioral statistics revealed that participants did use the robot differently between the roles of the robot. As utilitarian aspects are related to more extrinsic objective in the interaction with the robot, and hedonic aspects more to intrinsic value [11,12], people's motivation to interact with the robot might also play a role in their behavior toward the robot. It must be noted however, that the petting instruction was only provided on the information sheet for the hedonic condition and not for the utilitarian condition, which could have led to this difference.

No significant differences were found in participants' cognitive attitude between the conditions, even though the descriptions of the robot given in the interviews do show that the robot in the utilitarian condition was thought of differently than the robot in the hedonic condition. A possible explanation for this could be that different items of the RAS might appeal more to different roles of the robot (e.g., "useful" relating more to utilitarian aspects and "friendly" more to hedonic aspects). Furthermore, the explicit measurement of the cognitive attitude led participants to think about their attitude toward the robot, allowing them to rationalize their answers. In this cognitive effort, overall negative aspects of the robot (e.g., slow responses of the robot, the robot often not understanding the voice commands) might have been weighed against the benefits of the utility (in the utilitarian condition) or the companionship (in the hedonic condition) of the robot, leading to a similar cognitive attitude in both conditions.

Overall, the robot in the utilitarian role and the robot in the hedonic role were regarded as two different robots, indicating that people do view robots differently if they have a different role. The robot in the utilitarian role was often compared to assistants and described as a small machine, computer or tool, while the robot in the hedonic role was mostly compared to a pet and described as a companion. This is in line with the distinction between utilitarian and hedonic aspects of a robot as described in previous literature [3,5,11,12], and it underlines the success of the manipulation of the role of the robot.

4.1 Limitations and Future Research

We used self-report measures to measure attitude. This means that only the explicit attitude – and not the implicit attitude – was investigated, making the results more vulnerable to several biases [9]. While explicit responses need cognitive resources and are made more consciously, implicit responses relate more to subconscious affective reactions [21,22]. A person's implicit attitude can differ from their explicit attitude, for example due to not being aware of or understanding their attitude, or due to concealing their attitude (e.g., self-presentation or social desirability biases) [17]. Especially as implicit measures are related to the affective attitude, it would be very insightful to investigate the implicit attitude toward social robots - both in general and across the roles of a robot - in more depth.

The home setting of the experiment enabled ecologically valid results, allowing the participants to respond to and interact with the robot as they find comfortable and how they naturally would. This also meant that it was difficult to control for all variables compared to a lab study. However, the distinction between the utilitarian and hedonic roles of a social robot was very pronounced in the qualitative data, highlighting this distinction as a very interesting topic for further research. A more controlled setting allows for a much more focus on the role of the robot, through which more insights into the exact influence of the role of the robot - on perceptions of and interactions with the robot - and the underlying processes can be gained.

4.2 Conclusion

The utilitarian and hedonic roles of the robot seem to be a useful distinction in human-robot interactions, as people described, perceived and interacted with the robot in these two roles differently. While valuable insights into the interplay between the roles of the robot and people's attitude toward the robot were provided, further research is necessary to gain a better understanding of people's complex attitudes toward robots and dive deeper into the underlying processes. An exploratory investigation into attitude change due to interaction with the robot indicated a positive effect and suggested short-term attitude change to be more dependent on utilitarian aspects and novelty effects, while hedonic aspects seemed more important in the long-term. This provided interesting insights into more long-term interaction with a social robot.

Insights from this study enrich our understanding of robots as persuasive technology, and reveal opportunities for further research: utilitarian and hedonic roles of a social robot and attitudes toward robots over time. These topics for further research can hopefully contribute to the development of future social robots and improve the fit between robots and the users' needs.

References

1. Allport, G.W.: 1. Attitudes. Terminology **219** (1933)
2. Broadbent, E., Tamagawa, R., Kerse, N., Knock, B., Patience, A., MacDonald, B.: Retirement home staff and residents' preferences for healthcare robots. In: RO-MAN 2009-The 18th IEEE International Symposium on Robot and Human Interactive Communication, pp. 645–650. IEEE (2009)
3. Dautenhahn, K.: Methodology & themes of human-robot interaction: a growing research field. Int. J. Adv. Rob. Syst. **4**(1), 15 (2007)
4. Davis, F.D.: Perceived usefulness, perceived ease of use, and user acceptance of information technology. MIS Q. **13**, 319–340 (1989)
5. De Graaf, M.M., Allouch, S.B., Klamer, T.: Sharing a life with Harvey: exploring the acceptance of and relationship-building with a social robot. Comput. Hum. Behav. **43**, 1–14 (2015)
6. Eagly, A.H., Chaiken, S.: The Psychology of Attitudes. Harcourt Brace Jovanovich College Publishers, New York (1993)
7. Ezer, N., Fisk, A.D., Rogers, W.A.: Attitudinal and intentional acceptance of domestic robots by younger and older adults. In: Stephanidis, C. (ed.) UAHCI 2009. LNCS, vol. 5615, pp. 39–48. Springer, Heidelberg (2009). https://doi.org/10.1007/978-3-642-02710-95
8. Fink, J., Bauwens, V., Kaplan, F., Dillenbourg, P.: Living with a vacuum cleaning robot: a 6-month ethnographic study. Int. J. Soc. Robot. **5**, 389–408 (2013)
9. Fisher, R.J., Katz, J.E.: Social-desirability bias and the validity of self-reported values. Psychol. Mark. **17**(2), 105–120 (2000)
10. de Graaf, M.M., Ben Allouch, S., Van Dijk, J.A.: Why would i use this in my home? A model of domestic social robot acceptance. Hum.-Comput. Interact. **34**(2), 115–173 (2019)
11. Hassenzahl, M., Tractinsky, N.: User experience-a research agenda. Behav. Inf. Technol. **25**(2), 91–97 (2006)
12. Van der Heijden, H.: User acceptance of hedonic information systems. MIS Q. **28**, 695–704 (2004)
13. Horstmann, A.C., Krämer, N.C.: Great expectations? Relation of previous experiences with social robots in real life or in the media and expectancies based on qualitative and quantitative assessment. Front. Psychol. **10**, 939 (2019)
14. Horstmann, A.C., Krämer, N.C.: Expectations vs. actual behavior of a social robot: an experimental investigation of the effects of a social robot's interaction skill level and its expected future role on people's evaluations. PLoS ONE **15**(8), e0238133 (2020)
15. Kahn, P.H., Jr., Gary, H.E., Shen, S.: Children's social relationships with current and near-future robots. Child Dev. Perspect. **7**(1), 32–37 (2013)
16. Lee, N., Shin, H., Sundar, S.S.: Utilitarian vs. hedonic robots: role of parasocial tendency and anthropomorphism in shaping user attitudes. In: Proceedings of the 6th International Conference on Human-Robot Interaction, pp. 183–184 (2011)
17. MacDorman, K.F., Vasudevan, S.K., Ho, C.C.: Does Japan really have robot mania? Comparing attitudes by implicit and explicit measures. AI Soc. **23**, 485–510 (2009)
18. Naneva, S., Sarda Gou, M., Webb, T.L., Prescott, T.J.: A systematic review of attitudes, anxiety, acceptance, and trust towards social robots. Int. J. Soc. Robot. **12**(6), 1179–1201 (2020)

19. Nomura, T., Kanda, T., Suzuki, T.: Experimental investigation into influence of negative attitudes toward robots on human-robot interaction. AI Soc. **20**, 138–150 (2006)
20. Rosenberg, M.J.: Cognitive, affective, and behavioral components of attitudes. In: Attitude Organization and Change, pp. 1–14 (1960)
21. Sanders, T.L., Schafer, K.E., Volante, W., Reardon, A., Hancock, P.A.: Implicit attitudes toward robots. In: Proceedings of the Human Factors and Ergonomics Society Annual Meeting, vol. 60, pp. 1746–1749. SAGE Publications Sage, Los Angeles (2016)
22. Smith, C.T., Nosek, B.A.: Affective focus increases the concordance between implicit and explicit attitudes. Soc. Psychol. **42**, 300–313 (2011)
23. Song, H., Barakova, E.I., Markopoulos, P., Ham, J.: Personalizing HRI in musical instrument practicing: the influence of robot roles (evaluative versus nonevaluative) on the child's motivation for children in different learning stages. Front. Robot. AI **8**, 699524 (2021)
24. Sung, J.Y., Grinter, R.E., Christensen, H.I., Guo, L.: Housewives or technophiles? Understanding domestic robot owners. In: Proceedings of the 3rd ACM/IEEE International Conference on Human Robot Interaction, pp. 129–136 (2008)

Experiential Learning or Direct Training: Fostering Ethical Cybersecurity Decision-Making via Serious Games

Bakhtiar Sadeghi[1(✉)], Deborah Richards[1], Paul Formosa[2], and Michael Hitchens[1]

[1] School of Computing, Macquarie University, Sydney, Australia
bakhtiar.sadeghi@hdr.mq.edu.au, {deborah.richards, michael.hitchens}@mq.edu.au

[2] Department of Philosophy, Macquarie University, Sydney, Australia
paul.formosa@mq.edu.au

Abstract. Achieving secure cybersecurity systems requires a dual focus on technological aspects and human factors, both of which raise questions around ethical decision-making. While the objective is to ensure the comprehensive security of cybersecurity solutions, overlooking the ethical implications of decisions can lead to unexpected as well as unethical outcomes, giving rise to concerns aligned with basic ethical principles such as achieving *benefits*, avoiding *harm*, respecting *choice*, *fairness*, and *transparency*. To tackle this challenge, we have developed a serious game to educate cybersecurity participants to be mindful of the consequences of their decisions. All participants in our study engaged in experiential learning by discussing ethical dilemmas with non-player characters (NPCs) in this game. Additionally, half of our participants (training group) received explicit training in five ethical principles and undertook reflective activities. The control group did not receive this explicit training. We aimed to investigate whether experiential learning is adequate or whether additional explicit training in ethics is needed in this context. Analysis of pre- and post-tests revealed that both the training and control groups significantly improved their ability to recognise the importance of ethics after playing the game. The control group, receiving no direct training, performed equally as well as the training group in ethical decision-making. In analysing what made the ethical training effective, participants reported that virtual team discussions and choice/decision events were the most influential. The game will be further enhanced and evaluated in a future study.

Keywords: Ethical decision-making · Cybersecurity · Experiential learning · Ethical serious game

1 Introduction

Recently, it has been recognised [1, 2] that a well-structured cybersecurity system relies not only on technological components. Specifically, we are concerned with the ethical values and priorities that shape decision-making within this cybersecurity system. There

N. Baghaei et al. (Eds.): PERSUASIVE 2024, LNCS 14636, pp. 262–272, 2024.
https://doi.org/10.1007/978-3-031-58226-4_20

is an urgent need to educate a wide spectrum of users, including system architects, administrators, and privileged users, as well as non-expert users who are the primary focus of the present study, about the potential ethical conflicts and dilemmas that may surface in cybersecurity scenarios [3]. This educational effort plays an essential role in fostering improved moral judgment [4].

Serious games can be used as educational tools by establishing a secure and immersive virtual environment that facilitates the simulation of ethically relevant scenarios [5–7]. Serious games can provide a technological avenue for imparting knowledge and persuading individuals to consider the ethical ramifications of their choices within the realm of cybersecurity. They are also effective and engaging educational tools that are comparatively easy to deploy and scale [8]. To explore their value for helping cybersecurity practitioners to grasp the ethical implications inherent in various cybersecurity scenarios, this study narrows its focus to end-users. To provide safe exposure and practice for end-users, we have created a serious game that simulates common cybersecurity related scenarios in which players are engaged in conversations with our non-player characters (NPCs) who provide different viewpoints. Players are also required to make a decision to resolve a plausible cybersecurity ethical dilemma. The key objective of this study is to evaluate whether players improve their ethical awareness and reasoning through the experiential learning of playing the game alone, or whether it is also necessary to include explicit training on the ethical framework that underpins our game by instructing players about the five ethical principles and by having them engage in reflective activities.

2 Literature Review

Understanding the shortcomings between the present and an ideal ethical climate is crucial for both business ethics practices and overall business viability. A study involving 817 participants, including MBA students and working professionals, aimed to explore this relationship, and concluded that exposure to ethics significantly shaped students' views on the ideal relationship between organizational ethics and business outcomes [9]. Considerable research has highlighted that ethical education holds significant promise in enhancing ethical decision-making and reminding people about moral behavior [9–12]. Kozhuharova, et al. [13] offer some recommendations concerning how to deal with ethical issues in modern data management and processing domains, such as cloud computing. However, they do not provide recommendations on how to effectively increase ethical awareness or how to provide training to assist individuals to recognise ethical concerns. Treviño, et al. [14] suggest that addressing ethical challenges directly can help us learn more about individual ethical behavior in organizations. This aligns with our approach to create real-world cybersecurity scenarios that allow trainees to learn through exploration of different learning and teaching strategies.

Learning by doing, also known as experiential learning in the context of learning via serious games, has been shown to be a successful approach for knowledge transfer in a range of contexts [15–17]. Experiential learning draws upon Kolb's experiential learning cycle [18], which describes effective learning through four stages of concrete experience, reflective observation, abstract conceptualization, and active experimentation. Experiential learning has been effectively used in many fields, including for STEM education (e.g. [19]). Relevant specifically to cybersecurity breaches, Rege, et al. [20] aimed to determine the impact of experiential learning on undergraduate students' understanding of social engineering. They also emphasised the applicability of academic-industry dialogue in shaping experiential learning projects. Also relevant to our design is the work of Roshni and Rahim [21] who highlight the effectiveness of small group discussions as a teaching-learning methodology for understanding the principles of family medicine compared to traditional lectures. Finally, we acknowledge the importance of reflection in the learning process, particularly in applied and practical contexts [22]. Bringing together learning by doing, group discussion, reflection, and exploration of cybersecurity scenarios, we propose the creation of a serious ethical game to raise players' awareness of ethical issues and to allow them to engage in realistic but safe ethical decision-making. According to a study conducted by Sansare, et al. [23], moral engagement holds a crucial role in the design of ethical games. This implies that a disconnect between the overarching perspective encompassing social and moral aspects and the more technical aspects of serious game design for cybersecurity training could lead to moral disengagement, i.e., the failure of players to recognise ethical issues. For our ethical framework we used a principlist approach because it allows us to both connect cybersecurity situations to basic ethical concerns and move beyond a simplistic focus solely on privacy, which is common in cybersecurity, by situating privacy within the context of other ethical principles. For this reason we have adopted the ethical framework developed by Formosa, et al. [24] for the cybersecurity domain that includes the five ethical principles of beneficence, non-maleficence, autonomy, justice, and explicability. We applied these principles to design scenarios, dialogues, training, and evaluation materials. Additionally, we use this framework to explore how individuals prioritise ethical principles in cybersecurity and how these principles shape their decision-making.

3 Methodology

The aim of this study is to provide cyberethics training via a serious game and to understand what features of the training game are effective in improving participants' awareness of ethics within the context of cybersecurity. Knowing what parts of the game are most effective and for whom will help us to develop tailored versions of the game in the future as well as to extend the models we have previously developed [25]. We thus explore the following research questions here:

RQ1. To what extent do team conversations with NPCs within the game influence players' understanding and application of various ethical principles in the context of cybersecurity?

RQ2. Does the inclusion of explicit ethics education, comprising sensitisation to and reflection on our five ethical principles, impact players' knowledge of the ethical principles and their application in the context of cybersecurity?

We conducted a 45-min online study approved by Macquarie University Human Ethics Research Subcommittee 52021623528300. We chose to focus our study on the education of end users of cybersecurity since they are more likely to perform a breach [26]. To receive course credits, students studying a first-year psychology unit in the second half of 2023 could select our study from a pool of studies.

3.1 Study Design: Materials

To achieve the aim of this study, we have designed four versions of a cybersecurity game, two with and two without additional explicit training (see Sect. 3.2), containing one of two different scenarios. Mimicking ethical situations that arise in real-world cybersecurity contexts [27], we created two in-game scenarios. One (AppScenario) revolves around ethical discussions and decision-making regarding the installation of a free app designed to streamline daily work tasks for a player. The app exhibits all the characteristics of a legitimate application, including an official website and positive user reviews. The other in-game scenario (MobileScenario) delves into a situation where an individual uses their personal phone for work-related applications, such as MS Outlook and Slack.

We conducted a 2 (scenario 1 or scenario 2) × 2 (training or no training) between subjects' experiment in which participants were randomly assigned to one of four groups: Group 1 - scenario 1 (AppScenario), training; Group 2 - scenario 1 (AppScenario), no-training; Group 3 - scenario 2 (MobileScenario), training; Group 4 - scenario 2 (MobileScenario), no-training. We extensively modified the original game [6, 28, 29] designed for cybersecurity students/professionals with new scenarios suitable for cybersecurity end users.

In our game, players are assigned the role of a human resources psychologist (to fit with participant cohort) named Alex within the simulated organization. The game facilitated player interaction with NPCs through direct messages, emails, or group chats. Players were presented with a range of pre-written options for responding to these communications. For example, Fig. 1 (left) shows the player, as Alex, discussing the ethical concerns with installing a free app with several virtual colleagues via team chat. The NPCs offer different viewpoints to help players consider different aspects before making any decision.

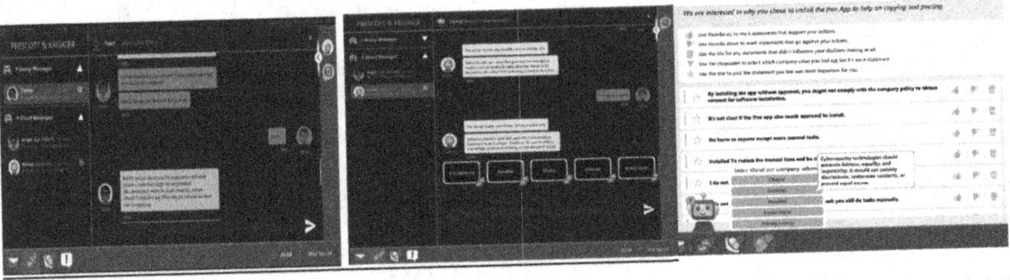

Fig. 1. NPCs interactions (left), Ethbot Training snippet (middle), Reflection Statement (right)

3.2 Procedure and Data Collection

The study procedure and data captured are shown in Table 1. We also recorded players' in-game choices. Pre- and post-test text-based scenarios assessed changes in ethical awareness. For the training group, their in-game decision and reason in response to the scenario were captured twice, before and after direct training using the reflection statement to determine if the training impacted their ethical decisions after the reflection statement. 5-point scale data were converted into continuous data. We used paired T-test as well as repeated measures ANOVA in IBM SPSS Statistics V28 for the data analysis assuming a normal data distribution based on the dataset's size, and following Norman [30]: "*Parametric statistics can be used with Likert data..with non-normal distributions, with no fear of 'coming to the wrong conclusion'. These findings are consistent with empirical literature dating back nearly 80 years* [30, p. 626–7]." Table 2 shows qualitative coding schema for open responses developed after team discussion.

Table 1. Study Procedure

Step	Activity
1.	Read study information and obtain consent.
2.	Enter demographic data (age, gender, cultural identity, personality (using the Ten-Item Personality Inventory (TIPI)[31])*, and self-assessed knowledge of ethics (asked "How good is your knowledge about the ethics in IT?", from Terrible (1) to Excellent (5)).
3.	Asked "How important is it to consider ethical issues when making cybersecurity decisions?" (1-not at all important– 5-extremely important), plus free-text justification.
4.	Pre-game text-based scenario followed by a prompt to capture the players' choice, and a free-text field for them to justify their decisions.
5.	Game onboarding (outline player's role, game functions, and navigation)
6.	Ethbot's ethical principle training and quiz (training groups only)
7.	Play in-game scenario 1 (AppScenario) or scenario 2 (MobileScenario)
8.	After making decisions, asked Q1- "How relevant are ethical issues in this scenario?", and Q2- "How important were the ethical issues on the decision you made?" (1-not at all -5-extremely).
9.	Complete ethical reflection statement (training groups only)
10.	Post-game text-based scenario followed by a prompt to capture the players' choice, and a free-text field for them to justify their decisions.
11.	Free texts questions: See Table 2 heading.
12.	Capture game experience with the Player Experience of Need Satisfaction (PENS) [32]* - [Optional] – complete Schwartz's theory of basic human values*.

White rows = in-game; Grey rows = pre- and post-gam survey *Not reported in this paper

Table 2. Coding Scheme

	Q1: What concepts, ideas, or principles influenced your decisions in this game?"	Q2: Where/when did you become aware of these concepts
1	Referred to 1 of our 5 principles by a related name	When interacting with NPCs
2	Relevant ethical issues not part of our 5 principles	When interacting with Ethbot
3	Referred to company policy or culture compliance	When making choices
4	Referred to a relevant non-ethical issue	When completing the reflection
5	No relevant response or no response provided	At other moments in the game
6	N/A	No relevant response

4 Results

A total of 246 students signed up for the study, 205 (163 females, 40 males, two non-binary; average age of 20.63 (SD = 5.52)) of whom played the full game and provided valid responses, characterized by the absence of uniformity in their replies to the survey inquiries. Self-reported ethics knowledge was 2.57. The majority (72.68%) studied psychology, followed by 17.56% in other studies, and 5.83% in business. Participants identified culturally as: Oceania (51.70%), South-East Asian (12.19%), North-African and Middle East (6.82%), North-East Asian (4.87%), and others in smaller proportions.

4.1 Measuring Importance of Ethical Considerations

Table 3 shows significant changes (<0.001) for all groups after playing the game. The results of two-way repeated measures analysis of variance (RM-ANOVA) prompted an additional one-way between-group analysis for each measurement (pre and post) between the four scenarios, that showed no significant results: pre-test: $F(3, 201) = 0.094$ ($p = 0.964$); post-test: $F(3, 201) = 1.120$ ($p = 0.211$). We also did the same ANOVA on the difference between pre- and post-test, diff: $F(3, 201) = 1.141$ ($p = 0.514$). Table 4 reports qualitative coding results. Paired T-Tests measuring change in ethical reasoning after the training group did the reflection revealed no significant differences (Table 5).

Table 3. Pre and post-game response to (see the question in Table 1 step 3)

Outside of the game	Pre-game			Post-game			P-value
Ethical considerations	N	Mean	SD	N	Mean	SD	
Training Group (1)	43	5.58	1.277	43	6.74	0.581	<0.001
Training Group (3)	49	5.71	1.429	49	6.67	0.628	<0.001
Control Group (2)	57	5.61	1.320	57	6.40	1.233	<0.001
Control Group (4)	56	5.61	1.275	56	6.57	0.735	<0.001

Table 4. Open-ended qualitative analysis. *see Table 2 heading for Q1 & Q2

Outside game	Size	Codes					
Q1 *	N	1 (%)	2 (%)	3 (%)	4 (%)	5 (%)	N/A
Training Group 1	43	21(48.83)	10(23.25)	4(9.30)	5(11.62)	3(6.97)	
Training Group 3	49	25(51.02)	13(26.53)	1(2.04)	3(6.12)	7(14.28)	
Control Group 2	57	11(19.29)	17(29.82)	1(1.75)	15(26.31)	13(22.80)	
Control Group 4	56	18(32.14)	22(39.63)	0	9(16.07)	7(12.5)	
Q2 *	N	1 (%)	2 (%)	3 (%)	4 (%)	5 (%)	6 (%)
Training Group 1	43	12(27.91)	5(11.63)	16(37)	3(6.98)	3(6.98)	4(9.30)
Training Group 3	49	18(36.73)	7(14.29)	9(18.3)	5(10.20)	2(4.08)	8(16.3)
Control Group 2	57	28(49.12)	0	14(24.5)	0	4(7.02)	11(19.3)
Control Group4	56	26(46.43)	0	13(23.21)	0	5(8.93)	12(21.4)

Table 5. In-game Pre- and Post-Reflection Analysis *see Table 1 step 8 for Q1 & Q2

In-game		Pre-reflection			Post-reflection			T-test
	Questions	N	Mean	SD	N	Mean	SD	P-value
Training Group (1)	Q1*	43	3.95	0.815	43	3.86	1.203	0.317
	Q2*	43	3.93	0.828	43	3.98	1.457	0.395
Control Group (2)	Q1	57	3.49	1.297	N/A	N/A	N/A	N/A
	Q2	57	3.54	1.402	N/A	N/A	N/A	N/A
Training Group (3)	Q1	49	3.53	1.002	49	3.37	1.648	0.221
	Q2	49	3.69	0.769	49	3.39	1.441	0.063
Control Group (4)	Q1	56	3.57	0.838	N/A	N/A	N/A	N/A
	Q2	56	3.69	0.829	N/A	N/A	N/A	N/A

5 Discussion

We analysed participant responses to ethical dilemmas before, during, and after gameplay. All groups dealt with cybersecurity-related decisions before and after playing the game, such as locking a friend's university-issued laptop without consent and installing antivirus software on a borrowed laptop. Participants also engaged in team discussions with NPCs and answered questions about the ethical aspects of their in-game choices. Training groups revisited these questions after completing ethical reflection statements to assess any shifts in perspectives. The players in the training group submitted an in-game reflection report after each decision to elucidate the primary ethical factors underpinning their decision, drawing upon our five ethical principles. To offer participants a deeper understanding of the potential consequences of their choices, prior to making their in-game decisions, they were exposed to considerations raised by NPCs about potential impacts in terms of our five ethical principles. The self-reported importance of ethical considerations for all groups significantly improved after engaging in the game. Furthermore, no significant differences emerged in the ANOVA for the pre- and post-game, suggesting that, despite not receiving the specific training (offered by Ethbot involving the definition of ethical principles a quiz to reinforce comprehension, and ethical reflection statements), the control group also showed a significant improvement in their ability to recognise an ethical issue after playing the game. This potentially confirms the effectiveness of experiential learning for ethical decision-making in cybersecurity domains and extends literature into a different context [7, 19, 20]. An alternative explanation is that our training was too short or poor to aid learning and further review of our materials is warranted.

The qualitative analysis suggests that the experiential learning components of team conversation with NPCs and the decision-making option at the end of the NPC interactions had a high impact on players' ethical awareness were influential for them. Direct training appeared to have little influence; reinforced by the relatively small contribution for both training groups mentions by players: (Ethbot (12 out of 92) or reflection statement (8 out of 92)), which referred to the explicit training components of the game. As presented in Table 3, ethical awareness improved after playing the game for all four groups. In summary, as presented in Table 4, the cumulative contributions of codes 1 and 2 from the four groups selecting ethics topics outweigh the contributions of codes 3 and 4, which relate to subjects such as company policy and other issues that are relevant but not explicitly ethical. Hence, the control group, lacking direct ethical training, still managed to attain comparable results with the training group. A noteworthy observation is that the control group (2) had 15 out of 57 instances of code 4 (mentioned non-ethical issues), which contrasts with the other three groups. This discrepancy could be attributed to the scenario that the group encountered in the game. Similarly, Table 5 shows no significant change after the training groups completed the reflection statements, implying the reflection part of the direct training had no significant influence on their ethical decisions, probably because they had already been influenced by the experiential learning of engaging with the NPCs.

Answering RQ1, team conversations played a crucial role in enhancing ethical awareness aligned with the five ethical principles. Firstly, both training and control groups benefited from team conversations with NPCs and all groups showed a significant boost in self-reported ethical understanding. Secondly, qualitative analysis highlighted the pivotal role of team discussions and decision-making in enhancing players' ethical engagement with the game. In response to RQ2, the in-game analysis suggests that completing the ethical reflection statement had no significant impact on players' reports about how relevant/important the ethical issues were in the scenario/decisions. Qualitative analysis also confirmed players gave minimal attention to Ethbot training and reflection, making a modest impact on their decision-making in the game. We acknowledge the limitations of using of non-identical pre and post-test scenarios to avoid training effects.

6 Conclusions and Future Work

This study compared the impact of experiential learning (team discussions with NPCs) and direct training (experiential learning plus Ethbot Training and Reflection Statements) to enhance ethical awareness in cybersecurity. Team conversations with NPCs significantly improved ethical understanding in both training and control groups, while direct training did not significantly increase understanding. Qualitative insights revealed that team discussions and decision-making influenced players to consider ethical issues. The study underscores the effectiveness of experiential learning for cybersecurity ethical education and use of dynamic, engaging methods in serious games.

Acknowledgments. This study was supported by Australian Research Council DP20010213.

References

1. Park, S., Lim, J., Kim, D.: The human factor of cybersecurity and the prevention and counter measures against cybercrime in South Korea. Webology (ISSN 1735-188X) 19 (2022)
2. Langner, G., Furnell, S., Quirchmayr, G., Skopik, F.: A comprehensive design framework for multi-disciplinary cyber security education. In: Furnell, S., Clarke, N. (eds.) HAISA 2023. IFIP (AICT), vol. 674, pp. 105–115. Springer, Cham (2023). https://doi.org/10.1007/978-3-031-38530-8_9
3. Blanken-Webb, J., Palmer, I., Deshaies, S.-E., Burbules, N.C., Campbell, R.H., Bashir, M.: A case study-based cybersecurity ethics curriculum. In: 2018 USENIX Workshop on Advances in Security Education (ASE 18) (2018)
4. Jamal, A., Ferdoos, A., Zaman, M., Hussain, M.: Cyber-ethics and the perceptions of Internet users: a case study of university students of Islamabad. Pakistan J. Inf. Manag. Libr. **16** (2015)
5. Hodhod, R., Kudenko, D., Cairns, P.: Serious games to teach ethics. In: The Society for the Study of Artificial Intelligence and Simulation of Behaviour Convention, pp. 43–52 (Adaptive and Emergent Behaviour and Complex Systems 2009)
6. Ryan, M., Staines, D., Formosa, P.: Focus, sensitivity, judgement, action: four lenses for designing morally engaging games. Trans. Digit. Games Res. Assoc. **2** (2017)
7. Aura, I., Hassan, L., Hamari, J.: Gameful civic education: a systematic literature review of empirical research. In: Proceedings of the 6th International GamiFIN Conference 2022 (GamiFIN 2022) (2022)
8. Westera, W.: Why and how serious games can become far more effective: accommodating productive learning experiences, learner motivation and the monitoring of learning gains. J. Educ. Technol. Soc. **22**, 59–69 (2019)

9. Luthar, H.K., Karri, R.: Exposure to ethics education and the perception of linkage between organizational ethical behavior and business outcomes. J. Bus. Ethics **61**, 353–368 (2005). https://doi.org/10.1007/s10551-005-1548-7
10. Cagle, J.A.B., Baucus, M.S.: Case studies of ethics scandals: effects on ethical perceptions of finance students. J. Bus. Ethics **64**, 213–229 (2006). https://doi.org/10.1007/s10551-005-8503-5
11. Gino, F., Ayal, S., Ariely, D.: Contagion and differentiation in unethical behavior: the effect of one bad apple on the barrel. Psychol. Sci. **20**, 393–398 (2009). https://doi.org/10.1111/j.1467-9280.2009.02306.x
12. Whitty, M., Doodson, J., Creese, S., Hodges, D.: Individual differences in cyber security behaviors: an examination of who is sharing passwords. Cyberpsychol. Behav. Soc. Netw. **18**, 3–7 (2015). https://doi.org/10.1089/cyber.2014.0179
13. Kozhuharova, D., Kirov, A., Al-Shargabi, Z.: Ethics in cybersecurity. what are the challenges we need to be aware of and how to handle them? In: Cybersecurity of Digital Service Chains: Challenges, Methodologies, and Tools, pp. 202–221 (2022)
14. Treviño, L.K., Weaver, G.R., Reynolds, S.J.: Behavioral ethics in organizations: a review. J. Manag. **32**, 951–990 (2006). https://doi.org/10.1177/0149206306294258
15. Gee, J.P.: What video games have to teach us about learning and literacy. Comput. Entertain. (CIE) **1** (2003)
16. Gee, J.P.: Learning by design: good video games as learning machines. E-Learn. Digit. Media **2**, 5–16 (2005). https://doi.org/10.2304/elea.2005.2.1.5
17. Hauge, J.M.B., Pourabdollahian, B., Riedel, J.C.K.H.: The use of serious games in the education of engineers. In: Emmanouilidis, C., Taisch, M., Kiritsis, D. (eds.) APMS 2012. IAICT, vol. 397, pp. 622–629. Springer, Heidelberg (2013). https://doi.org/10.1007/978-3-642-40352-1_78
18. Kolbe, D.A.: Experiential learning. New Jersey, Eaglewood Cliffs (1984)
19. Remington, T.F., Chou, P., Topa, B.: Experiential learning through STEM: recent initiatives in the United States. Int. J. Train. Dev. (2023)
20. Rege, A., Williams, K., Mendlein, A.: An experiential learning cybersecurity project for multiple STEM undergraduates. In: 2019 IEEE Integrated STEM Education Conference (ISEC), pp. 169–176 (2019). https://doi.org/10.1109/ISECon.2019.8882112
21. Roshni, M., Rahim, A.: Small group discussions as an effective teaching-learning methodology for learning the principles of family medicine among 2(nd)-year MBBS students. J Family Med. Prim. Care **9**, 2248–2252 (2020). https://doi.org/10.4103/jfmpc.jfmpc_1228_19
22. Maudsley, G., Strivens, J.: Promoting professional knowledge, experiential learning and critical thinking for medical students. Med. Educ. **34**, 535–544 (2000)
23. Sansare, V., Ryan, M., McEwan, M.: Oscillatory Design to Develop Moral Engagement Through Systemic Play (2023)
24. Formosa, P., Wilson, M., Richards, D.: A principlist framework for cybersecurity ethics. Comput. Secur. **109** (2021). https://doi.org/10.1016/j.cose.2021.102382
25. Sadeghi, B., et al.: Modelling the ethical priorities influencing decision-making in cybersecurity contexts. Organ. Cybersecur. J.: Pract. Process People **3**, 127–149 (2023). https://doi.org/10.1108/OCJ-09-2022-0015
26. Stanton, J.M., Stam, K.R., Mastrangelo, P., Jolton, J.: Analysis of end user security behaviors. Comput. Secur. **24**, 124–133 (2005). https://doi.org/10.1016/j.cose.2004.07.001
27. Jones, T.M.: Ethical decision making by individuals in organizations: an issue-contingent model. Acad. Manag. Rev. **16**, 366–395 (1991). https://doi.org/10.5465/amr.1991.4278958
28. Sadeghi, B., Richards, D., Formosa, P., McEwan, M., Hitchens, M.: How to increase ethical awareness in cybersecurity decision making. In: ACIS 2022, pp. 1–11 (2022)

29. Ryan, M., McEwan, M., Sansare, V., Formosa, P., Richards, D., Hitchens, M.: Design of a serious game for cybersecurity ethics training. In: DiGRA 22, pp. 1–18. Digital Games Research Association (2022)
30. Norman, G.: Likert scales, levels of measurement and the "laws" of statistics. Adv. Health Sci. Educ. **15**, 625–632 (2010). https://doi.org/10.1007/s10459-010-9222-y
31. Gosling, S.D., Rentfrow, P.J., Swann, W.B.: A very brief measure of the Big-Five personality domains. J. Res. Pers. **37**, 504–528 (2003). https://doi.org/10.1016/s0092-6566(03)00046-1
32. Ryan, R.M., Rigby, C.S., Przybylski, A.: The motivational pull of video games: a self-determination theory approach. Motiv. Emot. **30**, 344–360 (2006). https://doi.org/10.1007/s11031-006-9051-8

Estimating Sense of Agency from Behavioral Logs: Toward a Just-in-Time Adaptive Intervention System

Ryunosuke Togawa[1](✉), Roberto Legaspi[1], Yasutaka Nishimura[1], Akihiro Miyamamoto[2], Bo Yang[1], Eriko Sugisaki[1], Kazushi Ikeda[1], Nao Kobayashi[1], and Yasushi Naruse[2]

[1] KDDI Research, Inc., 2-1-15 Ohara, Fujimino-Shi, Saitama 3568502, Japan
ry-togawa@kddi.com

[2] National Institute of Information and Communications Technology, 558-2 Iwaokacho Iwaoka Nishi-Ku, Kobe-Shi 651-2401, Hyogo-Ken, Japan

Abstract. Sense of agency (SoA) is the subjective experience that one's volitional action caused an event. It has been widely investigated that SoA plays a significant role in shaping and moderating human cognition, emotion, and behavior. Thus far, there is no method that accounts for recognizing SoA in real-time in complex natural settings. To this end, we estimated SoA from logs of human behavior phenotypes, which include heart rate readings, physical activities, smartphone-usage time, application usage and GPS. Using smartphone app and wearable device, we collected user behavioral logs and SoA ground truths ($n = 25$, over 4,000 data points), and built and compared multiple models to estimate the SoA. Our results showed that models with daily behavioral logs as independent variables significantly outperformed the baseline model that contains demographic and personality information, confirming the predictive utility of daily behavioral logs for SoA estimation. We then discussed the viability of this model in developing just-in-time adaptive interventions.

Keywords: Sense of agency · Smartphone and wearable log · Just-in-time adaptive intervention (JITAI)

1 Introduction

Sense of agency (SoA) is the perception that we are responsible for and in charge of our own actions, which consequently influences the world around us [1–4]. For instance, SoA is experienced when driving if the operation of the steering wheel and pedal results in the car's movement as intended by the one driving. However, when the car moves independent of the driver's control, as in autonomous driving, SoA diminishes because one's intentional actions are disconnected from the outcome [5]. Inspired by learnings that have emerged from the life sciences on the compelling nature of SoA, theoretical research on intelligent system behavior, as well as applied research on, inter alia, automated vehicles, HCI, and robotics have adopted the SoA construct and its underlying

N. Baghaei et al. (Eds.): PERSUASIVE 2024, LNCS 14636, pp. 273–286, 2024.
https://doi.org/10.1007/978-3-031-58226-4_21

principles (see [6] for deep survey and analyses). In the case of persuasive technologies, however, investigations on SoA remains scarce (see [4, 7]).

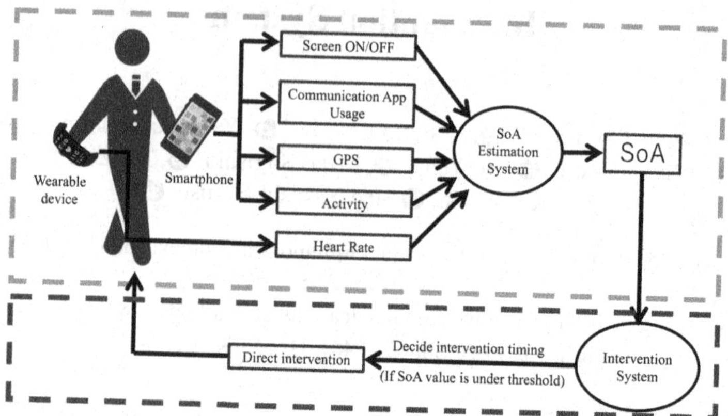

Fig. 1. Proposed system for an SoA-JITAI that consists of SoA-centered estimation and intervention components. We investigated, designed and validated the SoA estimation component, and expounded at the end the intervention component in light of our target persuasive system.

When and how an AI agent can provide an SoA-aware support is also non-trivial. The just-in-time adaptive intervention (JITAI) has been conceived for the purpose of providing timely and ample amount of support by adapting to an individual's changing mental, which in our case is SoA, and contextual states [8, 9]. The accessibility to increasingly potent mobile and sensing technologies is at the foundation of the use of JITAI wherein a person's state can be monitored and regulated in the natural, albeit complex, environment where the individual dwells. This is the end in mind of this research – we envision an SoA-cognizant JITAI (SoA-JITAI for brevity; in Fig. 1).

We posit that a predictive model that can estimate SoA from behavioral log data can be used to realize timely persuasive interventions, i.e., it is when user SoA deteriorates that persuasive intervention by the system can be effective [4, 7]. Based on Damen et al.'s theory [10], Legaspi and colleagues [7] proposed an SoA-cognizant persuasive AI (Fig. 2) that would sense the moment the user's SoA declines, which consequently renders the user's self-persuasion ineffective. At that point, the user's self-motivation deteriorates since he feels powerless (low SoA) to account for any consequence and change in his situation. When this occurs, the AI may employ persuasion to boost the user's SoA and bring back or enhance the user's ability to achieve self-initiated behavior change. It has been suggested that self-persuaded change can impact one's perception and reaction to a circumstance even with a slight or transient boost of experienced control [10]. This is relevant for creating persuasive technologies that can modify user behavior. We reckon our SoA-JITAI system can be a core component of Legaspi et al.'s SoA-cognizant AI.

In light of the above, we pursued the following research question: *Does behavioral log data that can be acquired through smartphones and wearable devices contribute to an accurate estimation of SoA?* To address this research question, we collected real-world data that consists of both daily behavioral logs and SoA ground truths. We created

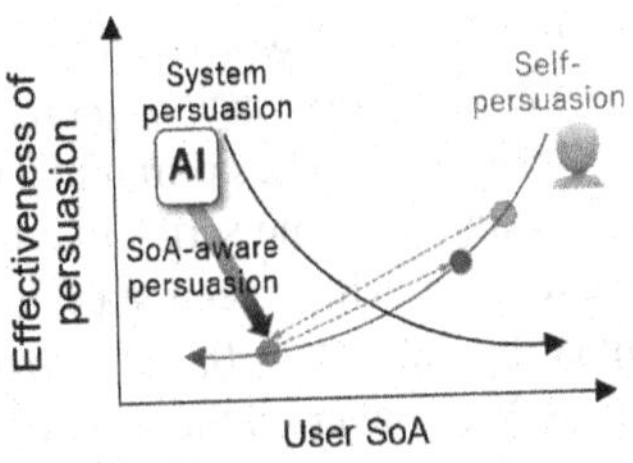

Fig. 2. Interplay of user SoA and the effectiveness of user and system persuasions per [4].

multiple models that combine the features obtained from the behavioral log data to detect a decline in SoA. Our results will show that models using not only demographic and personality traits but also behavioral log data as features significantly outperformed models constructed using only the traits. We can confirm that behavioral log data had predictive utility in detecting changes in SoA. From these motivating results, we then elucidate how such models can be viable in an SoA-JITAI system.

2 Method

Our proposed SoA-JITAI system (Fig. 1) consists of SoA estimation and SoA-base intervention components. The first component estimates SoA in real-time from behavioral log data obtained from smartphones and wearable devices. The aim is to use a trained model for real-time SoA estimation in daily living in order to carry out JITAI. While we employed user self-reporting in order to obtain the SoA ground truth needed to train and validate our model, once our model is generalized, it can then be used in normal living settings in which SoA can be estimated without any more interrupting the users to report their SoA while they are engaged in their daily tasks. The intervention component would determine the intervention policy based on whether the SoA level fell below the threshold, which could be indicative of a diminished SoA.

2.1 Time Series Data for Estimating the SoA

The tasks in which SoA had been assessed were straightforward and under very controlled experimental settings. Equally detrimental to measuring SoA is that self-reporting by the participants required interrupting their actions. These make the current methods less viable when dynamic changes in SoA need to be assessed naturally [4]. We hypothesize, however, that changes in SoA level may reveal themselves as changes in human physiology, and the state of the environment can strongly influence SoA. Such changes can be reflected by the log data recorded by smartphones and wearable devices, which we consider viable in determining user behavior (thus, behavioral log data) and realizing JITAI. These kinds of data have been used effectively to infer affective (emotion or mood) states [11]. Research in cognitive neuroscience shows that agency and affect interact in our daily life in diverse ways [12, 13], which suggests that SoA can be modulated by affective factors [14]. From these we posit that devices of this nature that have been used to quantify affect can be used to effectively quantify SoA.

Table 1 summarizes the features we used to estimate SoA. We collected via a smartphone the user's communication application usage, screen state, GPS data, and activity, all of which we treated as time series data. The communication application (e.g., SMS, Gmail, Discord, Facebook etc.) usage is a time series that is assigned a value 1 if these applications are used, and 0 otherwise. The screen state represents whether the user's monitor is on or off and assigns the value 1 or 0, respectively. We use the GPS information to represent user location. We converted the user's GPS information to a 100-m mesh. From this, we estimated the mesh where the user stayed the longest during the preparation period as "first place", second longest as "second place", and third longest as "third place". For each of these locations, we assigned the value 1 when the user stayed in that place, and 0 otherwise. Lastly, we collected activity data from the smartphone's built-in 3-axis accelerometer. Following the study of Fukazawa et al. [15] that estimated psychological indices from smartphone log data, we calculated the activity time series data (in m/s^2 unit) as follows:

$$Activity = \sqrt{a_x^2 + a_y^2 + a_z^2}, \quad (1)$$

where a_x, a_y, and a_z are the tri-axial accelerations, respectively, that were sampled every second. Identifying body position and movement in free-living environments can provide user -specific activity data, and accelerometer-based activity monitors have proved to provide objective measurements of human activities during free-living [16].

Table 1. List of behavioral log data

Category of behavioral log data		Collected Data			How to calculate feature from Log data
		Value	Sampling rate	Device	
Application Usage		0 or 1	1 Hz	Smartphone	$\sum$ last T sec
Screen State		0 or 1	1 Hz	Smartphone	$\sum$ last T sec
GPS	First place	0 or 1	1 Hz	Smartphone	$\sum$ last T sec
	Second place	0 or 1	1 Hz	Smartphone	$\sum$ last T sec
	Third place	0 or 1	1 Hz	Smartphone	$\sum$ last T sec
Activity		0–1	1 Hz	Smartphone	Mean in last T seconds
Heart Rate		0–1	1/60 Hz	Wearable	Mean, Max, stdev in last T second

The heart rate feature indicates the number of times each minute that the heart beats. It has been shown in lab experiments that interoception, i.e., the central processing and representation of internal bodily signals, including heartbeats and respiration, has been shown to play an important role in mechanisms underlying the emergence of SoA [17,

18]. Since the sampling interval for the heart rate is different from the sampling interval of the other features, the heart rate was upsampled to every 60 s.

For activity, we used as feature values the mean of the period of T seconds before and until the actual time the subject started to answer the SoA questionnaire. The value of T depends on the model used (described in Sect. 2.4). For the heart rate, we used as feature values the statistics (max, mean, and standard deviation) of the period of T seconds before. On the other hand, for the smartphone features: apps used, screen state, and GPS, we summed their individual values within every T-second period.

2.2 Measuring the Sense of Agency

The subjective experience of agency has been characterized into the judgment and feeling of agency (JoA and FoA, respectively). JoA is argued to be interpretative and conceptual as it stems from one's agency-related cognitions (e.g., situational and social cues, as well as intentions and thoughts). This is in contrast to the pre-reflective and non-conceptual FoA that stems largely from sensorimotor processes [19]. Studies have commonly observed and analyzed both JoA and FoA following localized events [4, 20]. There was not a legitimate and reliable instrument to measure decontextualized and cross-situational cognitions until the emergence of the Sense of Agency Scale (SoAS) that describes the cognitive and meta-cognitive experience of SoA [20]. Rather than the items of SoAS relating to specific actions or outcomes, the SoAS captures the aggregate of one's multiple aspects of the agency experience, which allows it to consistently quantify individual or contextual variations in a global experience of agency [20]. But we also note that our model is not entirely void of contextual observations as it accounts for the user's mobile app usage, location, and activities. Thus, employing the SoAS fits our research purposes well since we want to create a model of SoA that generalizes across individual and contextual variations.

We collected SoA ground truths using the SoAS, whose questionnaire items distinguish between the positive and negative senses of agency (SoPA and SoNA, respectively; Table 2). The SoPA and SoNA allowed for the separation of the general SoA spectrum into two distinct conscious judgments: respectively, having control of one's mind, body and environment, and being existentially powerless.

We presented the Japanese version of the SoAS questionnaire [4] to our participants using a smartphone app, called ULogger, developed by our organization. Using the notification function of their smartphones, the subjects SoA were probed three times a day at designated times in the morning, lunch time, and at night. The participants responded from among seven options: 7 (very applicable), 6 (fairly applicable), 5 (somewhat applicable), 4 (undecided), 3 (not very applicable), 2 (mostly not applicable), and 1 (not applicable at all). We obtained 4,156 SoA values (Mean: 68.0, SD: 13.2). In order to estimate the SoA using a regression model in our proposed system, we normalized to (0,1) the self-reported SoA values (Mean: 0.65, SD = 0.20).

Table 2. SoAS. Items 1, 4, 8, 9, 12 and 13 measures SoPA; the rest quantifies SoNA.

1. I am in full control of what I do
2. I am just an instrument in the hands of somebody or something else
3. My actions just happen without my intention
4. I am the author of my actions
5. The consequences of my actions feel like they don't logically follow my actions
6. My movements are automatic—my body simply makes them
7. The outcomes of my actions generally surprise me
8. Things I do are subject only to my free will
9. The decision whether and when to act is within my hands
10. Nothing I do is actually voluntary
11. While I am in action, I feel like I am a remote-controlled robot
12. My behavior is planned by me from the very beginning to the very end
13. I am completely responsible for everything that results from my actions

Table 3. List of SoA estimation models, their feature sets and T value

Feature	M_{base}	MM					
		10 m	30 m	1 h	2 h	6 h	24 h
Big Five	✓	✓	✓	✓	✓	✓	✓
Age and gender	✓	✓	✓	✓	✓	✓	✓
Screen	–	↑	↑	↑	↑	↑	↑
App usage	–						
GPS	–	10 m	30 m	1 h	2 h	6 h	24h
Activity	–	↓	↓	↓	↓	↓	↓
Heart Rate	–						

2.3 Data Collection

We recruited 52 Japanese subjects, and all were briefed on the content of this experiment prior to data collection, and permissions to use their data were obtained. They were made aware in advance of the many types of data that would be collected, the procedures for doing so, the measures taken to protect their privacy, and the means of rewarding them. Their gratuity basically depended on the number of survey items they answered. We asked them to install the ULogger to measure their individual SoA at designated times during the day. We collected their behavioral log data using the commercially available wearable device MiBand6 (Xiaomi), which they were asked to wear as much as possible during the experiment period. A questionnaire was also used to measure their Big Five

(29 questions, 7-point Likert scale [22]) prior to the experiments. All collected data were hashed for the subjects not be identified, thereby protecting their privacy while still allowing their data to be analyzed.

We conducted the data collection for three months starting December 2022. Because some subjects answered the SoA measurement questionnaire invariably (their answers mostly did not change), we excluded the data of subjects whose standard deviation for SoPA in all periods is below 1.5. At the end, we used data from 25 subjects (9 females; age mean: 39.9, min: 31, max: 49, SD: 5.3) for analysis.

2.4 Estimating the Sense of Agency

We prepared several regression models, each using different feature sets and T values (Table 3), with SoA as dependent variable. We first created a baseline model, M_{base}, using only the Big Five, as well as age and gender, which have been shown to correlate with SoA [22, 23]. We then created multi-device models (MMs) using behavioral log data together with the baseline features. Each MM depends on T (in seconds), which indicates how far back in time an MM was employed until the actual time the subjects started responding to the questionnaire, specifically: 10, 30 min ago; or 1, 2, 6, 24 h ago (per Table 3) in their actual T seconds equivalent, i.e., t mins $\times$ 60, or t hours $\times$ 3,600. We used the Light Gradient Boosting Machine (LightGBM) [24] to train each regression model. The main advantage with LightGBM is its short training time and higher accuracy than most boosting methods (e.g., XGBoost [25]).

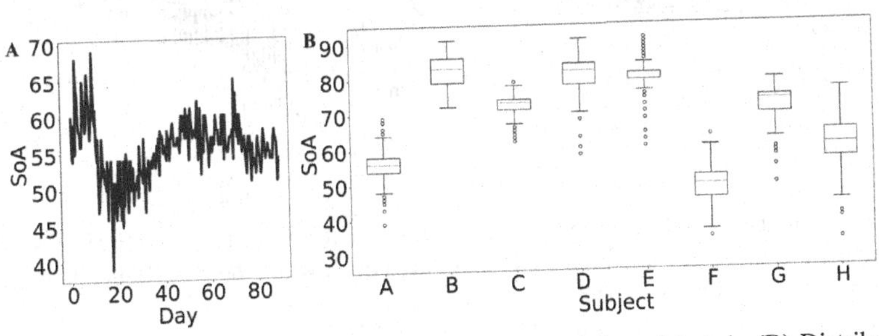

Fig. 3. Actual measures of SoA. (A) Time variation of SoA for subject A. (B) Distribution of SoA across eight subjects.

3 Result

We have observed that the behavior of SoA is not uniform. For instance, the variation in subject A's SoA (Fig. 3A) was somewhat high immediately after the start of the experiment. However, about 10 days later, the A's SoA decreased rapidly. Thereafter, the SoA level slowly increased around the 20th day. Finally, the SoA recovered to a state similar to that at the beginning of the experiment. This confirms that SoA is not uniform and indicates that SoA can fluctuate from day to day. Figure 3B shows the distribution of SoA across eight subjects, which confirms that the distribution of SoA varies widely among subjects. This suggests that estimating SoA in real-time is non-trivial.

Furthermore, SoA can exhibit both commonalities and unique tendencies across different individuals. As such, a regression model built solely on data derived from existing users cannot accurately predict a new user's SoA. To enhance the accuracy of our estimations, we applied a few-shot learning method. This approach improved the model's accuracy by adding a small amount of new user data to an already trained model, and then re-training it. We incrementally increased the number of data samples added through few-shot learning until we achieved a satisfactory level of accuracy. As a result, we found a significant improvement in the model's estimation accuracy when we incorporated data spanning five days (equivalent to 15 samples). Beyond this point, adding more data did not result in substantial performance improvement. Therefore, we decided to confine our model's learning to the data collected up to the fifth day. This optimized model was then used for validation purposes.

We measured the prediction performance of our system using leave-one-out cross validation, i.e., we treated one subject as a new user and the others as existing data. We evaluated the model from two perspectives, data fit and prediction accuracy. For the former, the coefficient of determination (R^2) and root mean squared error (RMSE) were used. For the latter, we used accuracy, recall, precision rates, as well as ROC-AUC.

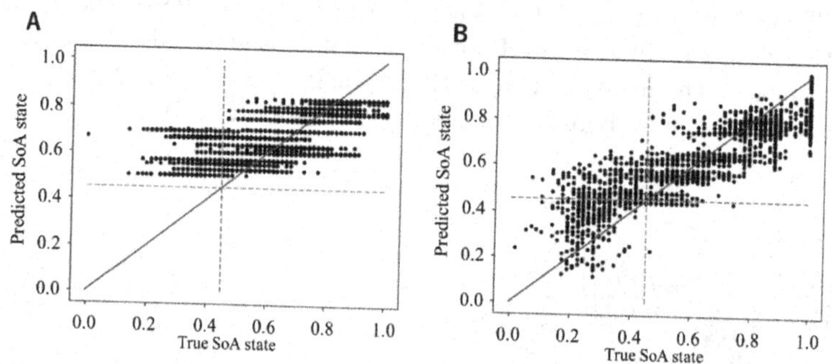

Fig. 4. The scatter plot of the true and predicted value where (A) is M_{base} and (B) is *MM-6h*. The red line indicates if the true and predicted values are equal; while the blue dashed line indicates the threshold for detecting SoA decline.

To predict the states in which the user's SoA has significantly decreased, we defined an *aberrant* state, i.e., the state when the SoA is more than one standard deviation below the mean. The threshold value was determined using the difference between the mean and standard deviation of the SoA values of all subjects. SoA values that fell below the threshold were labeled as 1, and 0 for all other values. The task was to accurately predict whether the SoA is aberrant or not. We measured the prediction performance of this model using accuracy, recall and precision rates.

A scatterplot of the actual and predicted values of SoA that were estimated by the baseline model and MM-6h are shown in Fig. 4. The estimation results of the baseline model (Fig. 4A) were constant for each subject. For example, the estimated value for subject A was always 0.7 regardless of time. In addition, no SoA was determined to be in a reduced state in the baseline model. On the other hand, compared to the baseline model, the MM-6h results (Fig. 4B) show a distribution centered at the intersection of blue dashed lines, i.e., the point where the true and the predicted values coincide. This means that MM-6h is a more accurate estimation model than the baseline model.

Furthermore, there were only few samples that were false negative. The evaluation results for each model are shown in Table 4. The baseline model was not able to detect the state of reduced SoA, so the recall value was 0, and the precision value could not be calculated. The baseline model uses only parameters that do not change from day to day and are constant per individual when estimating the SoA, hence, the results show that SoA is uniform for each user. On the other hand, all models with additional behavioral log data improved the various evaluation indicators over the baseline. Previous studies on emotional and psychological characteristics have shown that behavioral log data have predictive power for those indicators, suggesting that SoA has similar predictive power.

Table 4 also shows that the estimation accuracy improved as the period T increased. The fact that the features capturing the long-term dependencies contributed to improving the estimation accuracy may represent the long-term and dynamic way in which the SoA fluctuates as shown in Fig. 3A. Our results suggest that behavioral log data has strong predictive utility for recognizing abnormal declines in SoA. Further, it was able to detect the state of low SoA, thus, recognized the SoA-decreasing conditions.

Table 4. SoA estimation results for each model

Model	RMSE	R^2	Acc	Recall	Precision	ROC-AUC
M_{base}	0.159	0.38	0.81	0	–	0.74
MM-10m	0.127	0.71	0.84	0.54	0.83	0.92
MM-30m	0.130	0.69	0.82	0.51	0.79	0.92
MM-1h	0.128	0.70	0.84	0.44	0.98	0.93
MM-2h	0.132	0.68	0.84	0.54	0.84	0.92
MM-6h	0.125	0.71	0.84	0.49	0.88	0.93
MM-24h	0.109	0.72	0.87	0.37	0.96	0.94

Finally, we performed a partial correlation analysis between the features of each model and SoA. As an example, the MM-6h results are shown in Table 5. In these models, partial correlation coefficient values were low except for Age, Openness and Neuroticism. Other models have similar result. However, we reckon that the correlation between SoA and some of the behavior log data maybe weak but important considering the complexity of the setting by which SoA was obtained and the size of the dataset.

4 Discussion

4.1 Implications to a Timely-Intervention Policy

Based on the SoA estimation results in Table 4, if M_{base} is implemented in SoA-JITAI it can result to a uniform intervention policy for all users since it cannot accurately detect the decline in SoA. This is highly counter-intuitive to SoA-JITAI's purpose: it would become oblivious to providing direct (or indirect) persuasion at the time when it is needed. Hence, M_{base} is unsuitable to use as SoA measurement method for SoA-JITAI. On the other hand, in the models with behavioral log data, precision remains as high as about 0.9 and recall is about 0.4. The JITAI study [26] reported that random timing interventions have little effect. Low precision (<0.5) is synonymous to a randomly timed intervention. Thus, a high precision of about 0.9 is important to prevent erroneous interventions. In an actual scenario, it would be annoying for users to be intervened by the system so many times a day. This implies that it is unnecessary for the system to intervene each time the SoA drops, which means a recall of around 0.4 would be sufficient. Our results therefore suggest that the SoA estimation performance with behavioral log data is promising for the realization of SoA-JITAI.

As of the current, the feature set of the behavioral logs used in this paper is limited. Indeed, there is room for improving the accuracy of our SoA estimation. As future work, we plan to examine the predictive power of utilizing SoA using a wider feature set (e.g., wake-sleep state, body temperature, web search history via a mobile phone) in order to improve the SoA estimation accuracy. We also plan to verify the effect of SoA-JITAI in field experiments on behavior change using the trained SoA model and to investigate which features are strongly indicative of SoA than others and why.

Table 5. Partial correlation coefficient between SoA and each feature (left table show invariant features and right one show log-data features) in *MM-6h*. If a p-value is less than 0.05, it is flagged with one star (*). If p-value is less than 0.01, flag with (**). If less than 0.001, flag with (***).

feature		Partial correlation
gender		-0.28***
Age		-0.17***
Big Five	Openness	0.33***
	Conscientiousness	0.08***
	Extraversion	0.14***
	Agreeableness	0.19***
	Neuroticism	-0.50***

feature		Partial correlation
Activity		0.00
HR	Max	-0.04
	SD	0.09***
	Mean	0.08***
Screen-on time		-0.18***
Communication App Usage		0.03
GPS	First place	-0.05***
	Second place	-0.04*
	Third place	0.08

4.2 SoA-JITAI in a Real-World Application

Our team's mission is to develop applications to help users improve their daily behavior toward a desired state, i.e., a positive behavior change. We envision our SoA-JITAI to monitor users' behavior patterns in daily life and the SoA levels that emerge from such patterns in real-time. It would promote more effective behavior change by intervening at the time when persuasion would achieve optimal positive behavior change (Fig. 2). For our target real-world application, we shall adapt the application of Legaspi et al. in [4], which they used to conduct a multi-dimensional analysis of SoA in a com-plex, natural setting where participants performed daily their goal-directed tasks. They designed and deployed their own mobile application to assess their subjects' SoA, while at the same time assessing their healthy (or unhealthy) eating behavior. Their app is called "Shokuji Kiroku" ("meal record" in English). For easy recall, they named it MLogger ("M" for meal). The subjects took photos of what they were about to eat and made voice recordings of their perception of their meal (healthy or otherwise). The subjects also reported their perceptions of their own SoA using the SoAS installed in MLogger. The empirical results they obtained show the strength of SoA varied inter-individually and therefore demonstrates the need to personalize the user model. They posit that this will have viable results and analyses towards implementing adaptive system persuasions. They imagined for instance MLogger's persuasive actions may begin with something simple, e.g., "Keep on keeping on with your goal! You can do it!", to boost the user's SoA if diminished, and consequently, activate the user's self-driven persuasion to change their unhealthy diet [10]. In contrast to MLogger's current use of generic messages, our system would instead provide action-cognizant persuasive messages, such as "Best not go outside now and smoke, only to ruin your stride. You can do this!", for users to be able to observe their action's causal consequence clearly, raising their SoA as the expected and actual outcomes only to ruin your stride. You can do this!", for users to be able to observe their action's causal consequence clearly, raising their SoA as the expected and actual outcomes line up. Such kind of message, albeit simple, not only provides means for observing the link between the cause and consequence when it comes to the user's behavior, but also reminds the user of the target behavior during the use of MLogger and the behavior change necessary by providing means for action that would get them an inch closer to the goal while in pursuit of it. We reckon that this adheres in some extent to the simulation, reminder, and tunneling design principles, respectively, in persuasive system development (PSD in [27]). Legaspi et al. suggest that such upgrade to MLogger would entail machine learning capabilities for the system to be SoA-cognizant, which we have accomplished here. Hence, we aim to incorporate SoA-JITAI in MLogger (Fig. 5), which would therefore allow MLogger to automatically estimate SoA without requiring (disturbing) the user to self-report.

SoA-JITAI's intervention system will figure out the best time to intervene with the messages it generates. It would use sensor data and the estimated SoA as inputs and monitor the effects of interventions on user SoA in real time to detect the timing at which the intervention effects are maximized. The interventional message generation will send system feedback according to the SoA level. For example, if the SoA is low, SoA-JITAI may employ praising and monitoring as persuasion strategies per PSD and generate the message "Don't stop now, you've been doing great for the past six days remember?" Perhaps, even follow it up with personalization and liking per PSD, such as "Don't forget, your diet today should be mainly vegetables :=)", as the user may be more susceptible to the influence of his surroundings (e.g., lots of good food around).

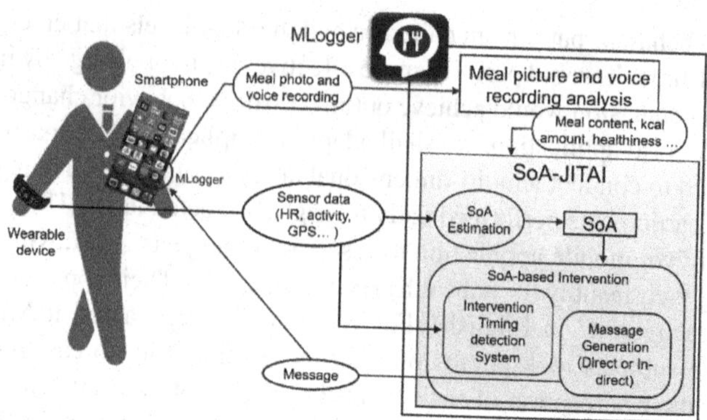

Fig. 5. Our target application, MLogger, with the SoA-JITAI system.

On the other hand, if the SoA is high, SoA-JITAI may display expertise through indirect persuasion, such as explaining in understandable terms the impact of high fat diet on life expectancy, as the user is less susceptible to be influenced (per [4, 9]). In other words, alternative system actions may be provided to achieve the desired outcome. It has been shown that SoA increases when several alternative actions that can lead to the same outcome are made available [28]. Conventional JITAI systems can only adjust either the intervention content or the intervention timing, but we envision SoA-JITAI to adaptively adjust both, making it more effective than conventional JITAI systems. Finally, per Legaspi et al., it would also entail machine learning capabilities to recognize the kinds of food included in the meal and some measure (e.g., in kcal) of user diet from the photo and voice recording the users upload in MLogger.

4.3 Ethical Considerations

Conducting ethically our experiments was paramount to us. Mobile device-sensing studies like ours is by nature unobtrusive but observational as it collects large volumes of continuous user data, which therefor require ethics approval from organizational review boards and consent from subjects and potential users. As in other psychological studies, the participants in our study enrolled voluntarily, and we were transparent through our informed-consent process that explains to them in three different occasions the details of the experiment, the kinds of data that will be collected, and how the data will be used. We obtained consent both on the web and on paper. When installing the ULogger, the terms of use were displayed and only those who clicked the "I agree" button could install and thereby use this application to collect their data. We purposely preserve the privacy and dignity of all our subjects and our experiments passed ethical review. We expect the same transparency before our system starts collecting consumers' personal information when deployed. This can be achieved, for instance, through a comprehensive and clearly written privacy policy, which would include among other essential information how personal data will be collected, what we intend to do with the data, and what we do with the information emerging from any analyses of the data.

5 Conclusion and Future Work

We focused on the impact of SoA on behavior change and proposed a system, SoA-JITAI, which could measure SoA in real time and provide appropriate, timely interventions according to the SoA state. Conventional measurement methods, such as the use of questionnaires while subjects are engaged in controlled cognitive tasks, makes it hardly possible to constantly monitor users' SoA in daily living while engaged in various (hence, non-localized) natural tasks. In this paper, we have verified through experiments using real-world data that behavioral log data obtained from commercially available smartphones and wearable devices have predictive power for monitoring human SoA levels. Our results, to the best of our knowledge, demonstrate for the first time the feasibility of actually overcoming this constraint.

There are many verification items in order to realize SoA-JITAI in the real world. For instance, we mentioned in Sect. 4.2 how the system can send via the MLogger messages that remind, suggest, personalize, or tunnel alternative actions as persuasion techniques, but depending on the situation and SoA level, other strategies may need to be considered. In addition, it is necessary to adjust how model learning could be carried out continuously and how often will model re-training be done. In the future, we will verify and resolve these issues through simulations and field tests to realize SoA-JITAI.

References

1. Gallagher, S.: Multiple aspects in the sense of agency. New Ideas Psychol. **30**(1), 15–31 (2012)
2. Moore, J.W.: What is the sense of agency and why does it matter? Front. Psychol. **7** (2016)
3. Haggard, P.: Sense of agency in the human brain. Nat. Rev. Neurosci. **18**(4), 196–207 (2017)
4. Legaspi, R., Xu, W., Konishi, T., Wada, S., Ishikawa, Y.: Multidimensional analysis of sense of agency during goal pursuit. In: Proceedings of the 30th ACM Conference on User Modeling, Adaptation and Personalization, pp. 34–47 (2022)
5. Victor, T.W., Tivesten, E., Gustavsson, P., Johansson, J., Sangberg, F., Ljung Aust, M.: Automation expectation mismatch: incorrect prediction despite eyes on threat and hands on wheel. Hum. Factors **60**(8), 1095–1116 (2018)
6. Legaspi, R., et al.: The sense of agency in human–AI interactions. Knowl.-Based Syst. **286** (2024)
7. Legaspi, R., Xu, W., Konishi, T., Wada, S.: Positing a sense of agency-aware persuasive AI: its theoretical and computational frameworks. In: Ali, R., Lugrin, B., Charles, F. (eds.) PERSUASIVE 2021. LNCS, vol. 12684, pp. 3–18. Springer, Cham (2021). https://doi.org/10.1007/978-3-030-79460-6_1
8. Hardeman, W., Houghton, J., Lane, K., Jones, A., Naughton, F.: A systematic review of just-in-time adaptive interventions (JITAIs) to promote physical activity. Int. J. Behav. Nutr. Phys. Activity **16**(1) (2019)
9. Nahum-Shani, I., et al.: Just-in-time adaptive interventions (JITAIs) in mobile health: Key components and design principles for ongoing health behavior support. Ann. Behav. Med. **52**(6) (2018)
10. Damen, T.G.E., Müller, B.C.N., Baaren, R.B., Van, Dijksterhuis, A.: Re-examining the agentic shift: the sense of agency influences the effectiveness of (self) persuasion. PLoS ONE **10**(6) (2015)

11. Legaspi, R., Fukui, K.I., Moriyama, K., Kurihara, S., Numao, M., Suarez, M.: Ad-dressing the problems of data-centric physiology-affect relations modeling. In: International Conference on Intelligent User Interfaces, Proceedings IUI, pp. 21–30 (2010)
12. Synofzik, M., Vosgerau, G., Voss, M.: The experience of agency: an interplay between prediction and postdiction. Front. Psychol. **4**(127) (2013)
13. Gentsch, A., Synofzik, M.: Affective coding: the emotional dimension of agency. Front. Hum. Neurosci. **8** (2014)
14. Christensen, J.F., Costa, S.D., Beck, B., Haggard, P.: I just lost it! Fear and anger reduce the sense of agency: a study using intentional binding. Exp. Brain Res. **237**(5), 1205–1212 (2019)
15. Fukazawa, Y., Ito, T., Okimura, T., Yamashita, Y., Maeda, T., Ota, J.: Predicting anxiety state using smartphone-based passive sensing. J. Biomed. Inform. **93** (2019)
16. Javed, A.R., Sarwar, M.U., Khan, S., Iwendi, C., Mittal, M., Kumar, N.: Analyzing the effectiveness and contribution of each axis of tri-axial accelerometer sensor for accurate activity recognition. Sensors (Switzerland) **20**(8) (2020)
17. Garfinkel, S.N., Seth, A.K., Barrett, A.B., Suzuki, K., Critchley, H.D.: Knowing your own heart: distinguishing interoceptive accuracy from interoceptive awareness. Biol. Psychol. **104**, 65–74 (2015)
18. Koreki, A., et al.: The relationship between interoception and agency and its modulation by heartbeats: an exploratory study. Sci. Rep. **12**(1) (2022)
19. Synofzik, M., Vosgerau, G., Newen, A.: Beyond the comparator model: a multifactorial two-step account of agency. Conscious. Cogn. **17**(1), 219–239 (2008)
20. Tapal, A., Oren, E., Dar, R., Eitam, B.: The sense of agency scale: a measure of consciously perceived control over one's mind, body, and the immediate environment. Front. Psychol. **8** (2017)
21. Namikawa, T., Tani, I., Wakita, T., Kumagai, R., Nakane, A., Noguchi, H.: Development of a short form of the Japanese Big- Five scale, and a test of its reliability and validity. Japan. J. Psychol. **83**(2), 91–99 (2012)
22. Cioffi, M.C., Cocchini, G., Banissy, M.J., Moore, J.W.: Ageing and agency: age-related changes in susceptibility to illusory experiences of control. Roy. Soc. Open Sci. **4**(5) (2017)
23. Schwarz, K.A., Klaffehn, A.L., Hauke-Forman, N., Muth, F.V., Pfister, R.: Never run a changing system: action-effect contingency shapes prospective agency. Cognition **229**, 1–9 (2022)
24. Ke, G., et al.: LightGBM: a highly efficient gradient boosting decision tree. In: Advances in Neural Information Processing Systems, vol. 2017-December (2017)
25. Mienye, I.D., Sun, Y.: A survey of ensemble learning: concepts, algorithms, applications, and prospects. IEEE Access **10** (2022)
26. Naughton, F., et al.: A context-sensing mobile phone app (Q sense) for smoking cessation: a mixed-methods study. JMIR mHealth uHealth **4**(3) (2016)
27. Oinas-Kukkonen, H., Harjumaa, M.: Persuasive systems design: key issues, process model, and system features. Commun. Assoc. Inf. Syst. **24**(28), 485–500 (2009)
28. David, N., Newen, A., Vogeley, K.: The "sense of agency" and its underlying cognitive and neural mechanisms. Conscious. Cogn. **17**(2), 523–534 (2008)

Counterfactual Reasoning Using Predicted Latent Personality Dimensions for Optimizing Persuasion Outcome

Donghuo Zeng[1(✉)], Roberto S. Legaspi[1(✉)], Yuewen Sun[2], Xinshuai Dong[2], Kazushi Ikeda[1(✉)], Peter Spirtes[2], and Kun Zhang[2]

[1] KDDI Research, Inc., Saitama, Japan
{do-zeng,ro-legaspi,kz-ikeda}@kddi-research.jp
[2] Carnegie Mellon University, Forbes Avenue, Pittsburgh, PA 15213, USA
{xinshuad,ps7z,kunz1}@andrew.cmu.edu

Abstract. Customizing persuasive conversations related to the outcome of interest for specific users achieves better persuasion results. However, existing persuasive conversation systems rely on persuasive strategies and encounter challenges in dynamically adjusting dialogues to suit the evolving states of individual users during interactions. This limitation restricts the system's ability to deliver flexible or dynamic conversations and achieve suboptimal persuasion outcomes. In this paper, we present a novel approach that tracks a user's latent personality dimensions (LPDs) during ongoing persuasion conversation and generates tailored counterfactual utterances based on these LPDs to optimize the overall persuasion outcome. In particular, our proposed method leverages a Bi-directional Generative Adversarial Network (BiCoGAN) in tandem with a Dialogue-based Personality Prediction Regression (DPPR) model to generate counterfactual data $\tilde{D}$. This enables the system to formulate alternative persuasive utterances that are more suited to the user. Subsequently, we utilize the D3QN model to learn policies for optimized selection of system utterances on $\tilde{D}$. Experimental results we obtained from using the PersuasionForGood dataset demonstrate the superiority of our approach over the existing method, BiCoGAN. The cumulative rewards and Q-values produced by our method surpass ground truth benchmarks, showcasing the efficacy of employing counterfactual reasoning and LPDs to optimize reinforcement learning policy in online interactions.

Keywords: Counterfactual reasoning · Latent personality dimensions · Policy learning

1 Introduction

Persuasive conversations [12,18,22,25] aim to change users' opinions, attitudes, or behaviors by employing effective communication strategies, utilizing techniques such as reasoning and emotional appeals. They involve deliberate communication with the specific goal of convincing or persuading the user to adopt

N. Baghaei et al. (Eds.): PERSUASIVE 2024, LNCS 14636, pp. 287–300, 2024.
https://doi.org/10.1007/978-3-031-58226-4_22

a particular viewpoint or take action. In individual conversations, effective persuasion hinges on identifying unique, often hidden factors, or latent variables, such as personality (BigFive), beliefs, motivations, and experiences. Tailoring persuasive approaches to these individual nuances increases the likelihood of influencing opinions, attitudes, or behaviors.

Existing works on persuasive conversation systems have explored the impact of persuasive strategies, such as inquiry [16,19], on the outcome of persuasion tasks, emphasizing strategy learning over personalized approaches. For instance, the work in [3] argues that when targeting demographics, the sequence of persuasive strategies might be immaterial and suggests using a fixed order of persuasive appeals. However, these approaches lack flexibility and dynamics, as it relies solely on pre-defined strategy sequences while overlooking the nuanced differences in natural language. Natural language presents a challenge for persuasive conversation systems in dynamically adapting their conversations to align with individual user personalities. The complexities involved in tracking user states hinder these systems' ability to deliver adaptive and flexible dialogues.

In this work, we introduce an approach designed for a system to dynamically track and leverage the latent personality dimensions (LPDs) of the users during ongoing persuasive conversations. Our proposed method employs a Bidirectional Generative Adversarial Networks (BiCoGAN) [4,7] partnered with a Dialogue-based Personality Prediction Regression (DPPR) model to generate counterfactual data $\tilde{D}$. This enables our system to generate alternative responses fit to the user's current state, as predicted by the DPPR model. Subsequently, we optimize the system response selection using D3QN model, adapting the conversation flow to the inferred user traits.

The contribution of this work is three-fold: (1) we trained a DPPR model to uncover the hidden aspects of their personalities over time, facilitating the tracking of user states during persuasive conversations. (2) Leveraging the BiCoGAN model with estimated individual LPDs derived from the trained DPPR model, we constructed counterfactual data $\tilde{D}$. This dataset provides alternative system utterances based on LPDs, extending the original dialogues of PersuasionForGood [21] dataset. (3) Employing the D3QN [13] model to learn policies on the counterfactual data $\tilde{D}$, which improves the quality of persuasive conversations, particularly in terms of enhancing persuasion outcomes.

2 Related Work

Persuasive strategies identified from data gathered in persuasive online discussions and social media are frequently utilized to refine argument mining methodologies [1,20,23,24] in the construction of dialogue systems. While these works have introduced several valuable persuasion strategies, none of them have explored an efficient and automated method for applying these strategies effectively. Contrasting these approaches, [21] introduced the PersuasionForGood dataset through crowd-sourcing, simulating donation-related persuasive scenarios in conversational formats. [16] extended on this dataset to develop an agenda-based persuasion conversation system. However, their strategy maintained a rigid

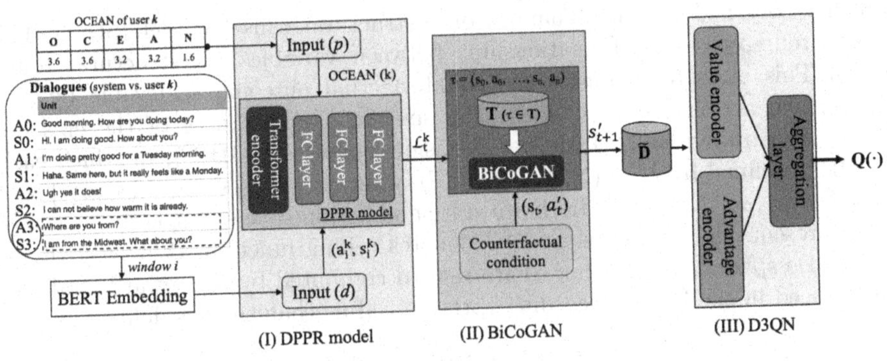

Fig. 1. The overview of our architecture.

sequence of persuasive appeal strategies and lacked user modeling. To address this issue, [19] adopts reinforcement learning with dynamic user modeling to optimize the sequence of persuasive appeals based on dialogue history and the user's inclination towards donation. Persuasive systems lack fluent communication and flexibility due to strategy reliance and absence of counterfactual cases. Leveraging GANs' success in persuasive dialogue [17], we generate counterfactual data to enhance adaptability.

Personalization in persuasion [3,5,8,10,14] is important for the persuasive system to adapt to individual scenarios. Tailoring persuasive messages to align with the interests and concerns of the users is a way to enhance system effectiveness. For instance, [5] explores the customization of persuasive technologies to individual users through persuasion profiling, utilizing both explicit measures from standardized questionnaires and implicit, behavioral measures of user traits. However, employing truthful personalization to enhance the persuasion dialogue may not be the optimal solution as it could impact responses over multiple steps and overlook the changing, hidden personality-related factors. Our research focuses on dynamically leveraging LPDs to capture the evolving, hidden personality-related factors during persuasive conversation. Subsequently, we employ counterfactual reasoning with LPDs to construct counterfactual data, thereby improving the persuasion outcomes.

3 Our Architecture

In this section, we introduce problem setting and three parts of our architecture: 1) estimation of individual latent personality dimensions, 2) counterfactual data $\tilde{D}$ establishment, and 3) policy learning.

3.1 Problem Setting

Let's assume that all the dialogues are padded to the same length, and $D = \{(s_t, a_t, s_{t+1})\}_{t=0}^{T-1}$ represents an observed episode within a decision-making process governed by the dynamics of a structural causal model (SCM) [11], which represents causal relationships between variables via structural equations. This aims to delineate the counterfactual outcome achievable by any alternative action sequence under the specific circumstances of the episode. We explore Individualized Markov Decision Pocesses (IMDPs), in which each IMDP is defined by $M = (S, A, \mathcal{L}, f, R, T)$, where $S = \{s_0, s_1, s_2, ..., s_{\lceil T/2 \rceil}\}$ and $A = \{a_0, a_1, a_2, ..., a_{\lfloor T/2 \rfloor}\}$ are finite state and action spaces, respectively, where $\lfloor \cdot \rfloor$ represents floor function and $\lceil \cdot \rceil$ denotes ceiling function. $\mathcal{L}$ is the individual LPDs space. R is the immediate reward computed by the reward model as introduced in the Eq. 5. Accordingly, the causal mechanism f is defined as

$$s_{t+1} = f(s_t, a_t, \mathcal{L}_t, \varepsilon_{t+1}) \tag{1}$$

where s_t, a_t, and $\mathcal{L}_t$ are the state, action, and estimated LPDs at time t, respectively, and ε_{t+1} is the noise term independent of (s_t, a_t). A graphical representation of the individual state transition process is depicted in Fig. 2.

Suppose D is the real-world data, BiCoGAN by using estimated LPDs creates a set of N counterfactual datasets $\tilde{D} = \{\tilde{D}_0, \tilde{D}_1, ..., \tilde{D}_N\} = \{(s_t^{'}, a_t^{'})\}_{t=0}^{T-1}$. Our target is to learn policies to optimize the persuasion outcome on counterfactual data $\tilde{D}$.

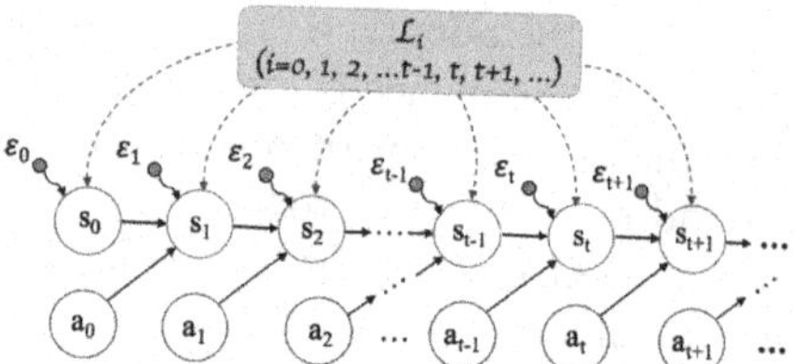

Fig. 2. The individualized transition dynamics model.

3.2 Estimation of Individual Latent Personality Dimensions

The OCEAN model[1] is widely recognized in psychology and social sciences for its reliability in assessing and understanding personality traits, which is validated across different cultures, age groups, and demographic backgrounds. However, critics argue that it falls short in representing the nuanced dynamics of personalities such as in ongoing dialogues. In addressing this, we endeavor to estimate individual LPDs in real-time to foster adaptability during conversations. It helps in dynamically adjusting persuasive approaches, such as system utterances, based on the inferred user traits for individualized conversation. For this purpose, we developed a dialogue-based personality prediction regression (DPPR) model that consists of a transformer encoder followed by three fully connected layers (refer to (I) in Fig. 1). During model training, the inputs comprise utterances between system and user, alongside the annotated 5-dimensional personalities OCEAN values [15] attributed to the users. Each input is a one-turn utterance constituting a one-time exchange within a dialogue between the system and user. When a new user engages, the model progressively infers the user's LPDs over time to better understand them during the conversation. This enables the system to dynamically adapt the new utterances in the persuasion dialogue, optimizing the outcome based on the inferred individual LPDs.

[1] The "Big Five" includes Openness, Conscientiousness, Extroversion, Agreeableness, and Neuroticism.

3.3 Counterfactual Data $\tilde{D}$

Persuasive systems heavily rely on past online interactions, often leading to sub-optimal outcomes due to the absence of sufficient actual observed results. Counterfactual reasoning enables the assessment of unobserved scenarios, encompassing various conditions and user-diverse reactions. Constructing counterfactual data facilitates enhanced policy learning, optimizing the decision-making process to achieve better outcomes.

We assume that the state s_{t+1} satisfies the SCM: $s_{t+1} = f(s_t, a_t, \mathcal{L}_t, \varepsilon_{t+1})$, then, we employ BiCoGAN (refer to (II) in Fig. 1) to learn the function f by minimizing the disparity between the input real data and the generated data, maintaining realistic counterfactual states aligned with observed scenarios for practical relevance. Simultaneously, it estimates the value of noise term ε_{t+1}, representing disturbances arising from unobserved factors, seen in Fig. 3. Specifically, the BiCoGAN proceeds in two directions: 1) mapping from (s_t, a_t, $\mathcal{L}_t$, ε_{t+1}) to s_{t+1} in the generator G, and 2) estimating (s_t, a_t, $\mathcal{L}_t$, ε_{t+1}) from s_{t+1} via the encoder E. The discriminator D is trained to distinguish between real and inferred data. The decoder and encoder distributions are formulated as follows, respectively.

$$\begin{aligned} P(\hat{s}_{t+1}, s_t, a_t, \mathcal{L}_t, \varepsilon_{t+1}) &= P(s_t, a_t, \mathcal{L}_t, \varepsilon_{t+1}) P(\hat{s}_{t+1} | s_t, a_t, \mathcal{L}_t, \varepsilon_{t+1}), \\ P(s_{t+1}, \hat{s}_t, \hat{a}_t, \hat{\mathcal{L}}_t, \hat{\varepsilon}_{t+1}) &= P(s_{t+1}) P(\hat{s}_t, \hat{a}_t, \hat{\mathcal{L}}_t, \hat{\varepsilon}_{t+1} | s_{t+1}) \end{aligned} \quad (2)$$

where $\hat{s}_t$, $\hat{s}_{t+1}$, $\hat{a}_t$, $\hat{\mathcal{L}}_t$, and $\hat{\varepsilon}_t$ are estimations of s_t, s_{t+1}, a_t, $\mathcal{L}_t$, and ε_{t+1}, respectively. The $P(\hat{s}_{t+1} | s_t, a_t, \mathcal{L}_t, \varepsilon_{t+1})$ and $P(\hat{s}_t, \hat{a}_t, \hat{\mathcal{L}}_t, \hat{\varepsilon}_t | s_{t+1})$ are respectively the conditional distributions of the decoder and encoder. To deceive the discriminator model, the objective function is optimized as a minimax game defined as

$$\begin{aligned} \min_G \max_D V(D, G, E) = \min_G \max_D \{ & \mathbb{E}_{s_{t+1} \sim p_{\text{data}}(s_{t+1})} [\log D(E(s_{t+1}), s_{t+1})] \\ & + \mathbb{E}_{z_t \sim p(z_t)} [\log(1 - D(G(z_t), z_t))] \\ & + \lambda E_{(s_t, a_t, s_{t+1}) \sim p_{\text{data}}(s_t, a_t, s_{t+1})} [R((s_t, a_t), E(s_{t+1}))] \} \end{aligned} \quad (3)$$

where $z_t = (s_t, a_t, \mathcal{L}_t, \varepsilon_{t+1})$, R is a regularizer with its hyperparameter λ to avoid overfitting issues.

After learning the SCM, counterfactual reasoning can be carried out to build the counterfactual data $\tilde{D}$. Suppose at time t, we have the tuple (s_t, a_t, $\mathcal{L}_t$, s_{t+1}), we want to know what would the state s'_{t+1} be if we take an alternative action a'_t. To determine this, we take (s_t, a'_t, $\mathcal{L}_t$), as input for the trained generator model G_T, which consequently outputs the counterfactual state s'_{t+1}. Additionally, to achieve this process, we first need to build the set of counterfactual actions $\{a'_t\}$. We derived the counterfactual actions $\{a'_t\}$ from the real-world actions $\{a_t\}$ through random selection.

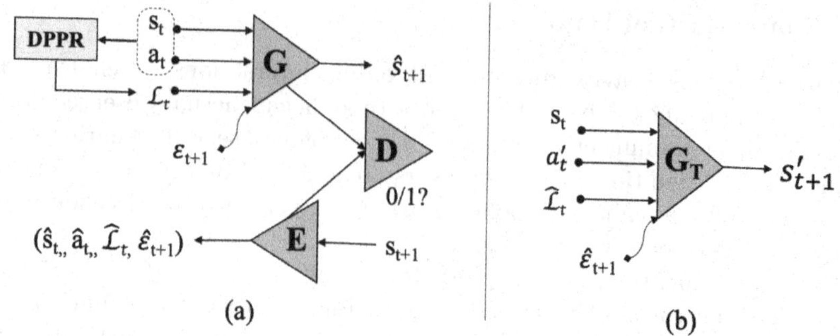

Fig. 3. (a) Trained DPPR model, Generator G, Encoder E, and Discriminator D in the training. (b) Trained Generator G_T in counterfactual states generating.

3.4 Policy Learning

Following the generation of counterfactual data $\tilde{D}$, our approach involves learning policies on $\tilde{D}$ to maximize future rewards. We employ the Dueling Double-Deep Q-Network (D3QN) [13] as an enhanced variant of the standard Deep Q-Networks (DQNs) [9] to address Q-value overestimation (refer to (III) in Fig. 1). D3QN mitigates this issue by segregating the value function into state-dependent advantage function $A(s, a)$ and value function $V(s)$, where $A(s, a)$ capitalizes on how much better one action is than the other actions, and $V(s)$ indicates how much reward will be achieved from state s. The Q-values can be calculated on $\tilde{D}$ as follows:

$$Q(s', a'; \theta) = \mathbb{E}\left[r(s', a') + \gamma \max_{a'} Q(s', a'; \theta^-) \mid s^{'}, a^{'}\right], \tag{4}$$

where $r(s^{'}, a^{'})$ is the reward of taking action $a^{'}$ at the state $s^{'}$, the γ is the discount factor of the max q value among all possible actions from the next state. The $r(\cdot)$ is a reward function that is used for the calculation of reward value for a given action input. The reward function is an LSTM-based architecture trained using dialogues and their corresponding donation values, the reward value of (s'_t, a'_t) is calculated as

$$r(s', a') = \begin{cases} 0, & \text{if } t < T-1, \\ LSTM(BERT_{embedding}(\{s'_t, a'_t\}_{t=0}^{T-1})), & \text{otherwise,} \end{cases} \tag{5}$$

where T is the length of one dialogue in time unit. The target Q-values are derived from actions obtained through a feed-forward pass on the main network, diverging from direct estimation from the target network. During policy learning, the state transition starts with state $s_0^{'}$, and computing $argmax_{a_{0i}^{'}}$ $Q(s_0^{'}, a_{0i}^{'}; \theta, \alpha, \beta)$ leads to selecting the optimal action a_0^* for state s'_0 in $\tilde{D}$, where $i = 0, 1, 2, .., N-1$. In the end, we apply the Mean Squared Error (MSE) as a loss function to update the weights of D3QN neural networks.

4 Experiment

4.1 Dataset

ER:	Good Evening
EE:	Hello there. how are you?
ER:	I am doing well! How are doing today?
EE:	I am doing pretty well. thanks for asking!
ER:	I'd like to tell you about a great program I am working on! Have you ever heard of Save the Children?
EE:	I may have in passing, but could you tell me more information about it?
ER:	Save the Children is a non-governmental organization that operates worldwide wide raising funds through partners and donations to fight for children's rights and provide relief and support for children in developing countries.
EE:	Sounds interesting and something worth donating towards a good cause. Would you donate to this fund?
ER:	I would and I have! 9 out of every 10 dollars goes directly to a child in need.
EE:	That is great to know. Any additional information you could tell me about the Save the Children program?
ER:	Absolutely! There are a variety of ways to be a part of the program outside of donations. They have a program to sponsor a child in need, you can throw a fundraising event or participate in events such as triatholons to raise funds, or help advocate for children.
EE:	Thank you for the information. What is the best way I could get involved with this charity?
ER:	You are more than welcome to donate today and your donation will be sent to Save the Children to go towards programs that help the children directly.
EE:	Great. How much are the donations?
ER:	You can donate up to two dollars of your payment, but more is always appreciated!
EE:	Alright. $2 sounds good enough. Could I get a web address to the fund if I have any more questions?
ER:	Thank you so much for you generous donation! To answer any more questions the link is URL
EE:	Thanks you. I will be more than glad to donate.

Fig. 4. An example (ID: 20180904154250_98_*live*, donation: $2.0, OCEAN values: 3, 3.2, 3, 3.6, 3) persuasive dialogue between persuader (ER) and persuadee (EE) from PersuasionForGood dataset. Dynamic modeling of the dialogue, utterances of ER as actions (grey), utterance of EE as states (white).

To verify our method, we use the *PersuasionForGood*[2] dataset of human-human dialogues. This dataset aims to facilitate the development of intelligent persuasive conversational agents and focuses on altering users' opinions and actions regarding donations to a specific charity. Through the online persuasion task, one participant as *persuader* (ER) was asked to persuade the other as *persuadee* (EE) to donate to a charity, Save the Children[3]. This large dataset comprises 1,017 dialogues, including annotated emerging persuasion strategies

[2] https://convokit.cornell.edu/documentation/persuasionforgood.html.
[3] https://www.savethechildren.org/.

in a subset. Notably, the recorded participants' demographic backgrounds, such as the Big-Five personality traits (OCEAN), offer an opportunity to estimate the LPDs of users (*persuadees*). Additionally, each dialogue includes donation records for both *persuader* and *persuadee*. Our focus in this work is primarily on the donation behavior of the *persuadee*, with 545 (54%) recorded as donors and 472 (46%) as non-donors. The dialogue data utilized in this study is represented by BERT embeddings extracted by a pre-trained BERT model [2] from Hugging Face[4]. Each natural language utterance of EE or ER in the dialogue is represented by a 768-dimensional BERT feature vector. The OCEAN are the real values sourced from the original dataset. For instance, in Fig. 4, the OCEAN of a specific *persuadee* (ID=180904154250_98_*live*) is presented as a 5-dimensional vector.

4.2 Experimental Setup

All implementations were executed using PyTorch and models were trained on a GeForce RTX 3080 GPU (10G). Our method is a teamwork of three models, which are trained separately by using different formats of the input data. Hyperparameters shared by the models are listed in Table 1. A five-fold cross-validation is employed to ensure the reliability of the DPPR model, which allows us to assess its generalizability to unseen data. For BiCoGAN, we set the dimension of the noise item to be the same as BERT's embedding, which is 768. In the end, we generated a total of 100 counterfactual data by using different sets of counterfactual actions. To guarantee the robustness of the reward model training, dialogues featuring donation amounts surpassing $20.0 were intentionally removed. The aim behind removing these dialogues is to reduce potential bias and ensure a more balanced training for the model. The final number of dialogues is 997, featuring 25 exchanges of utterances between EE and ER, alternating between the two roles in each dialogue. We split the data into training and testing sets using a 80/20 split. All the model is optimized using Adam [6] with a learning rate of 0.0001. In addition, we set the discount factor γ in the D3QN to 0.9.

Table 1. The hyperparameters across various models.

Model	hidden units	batch size	lr	epochs
DPPR	1024	64	0.0001	100
BiCoGAN	100	100	0.0001	10
RM	256	64	0.0001	1,000
D3QN	256	60	0.001	20

4.3 Results

To facilitate the creation of the counterfactual world data $\tilde{D}$, we introduce the counterfactual actions $\{a_t'\}$ as inputs into the trained BiCoGAN for $\tilde{D}$ generation. An initial step in this process involves establishing the counterfactual actions set $\{a_t'\}$, which is derived through random selection from real-world action set $\{a_t\}$. However, when randomly selected as counterfactual actions,

[4] https://huggingface.co/bert-base-uncased.

some greeting utterances will appear in the middle or end of a conversation, which is inappropriate.

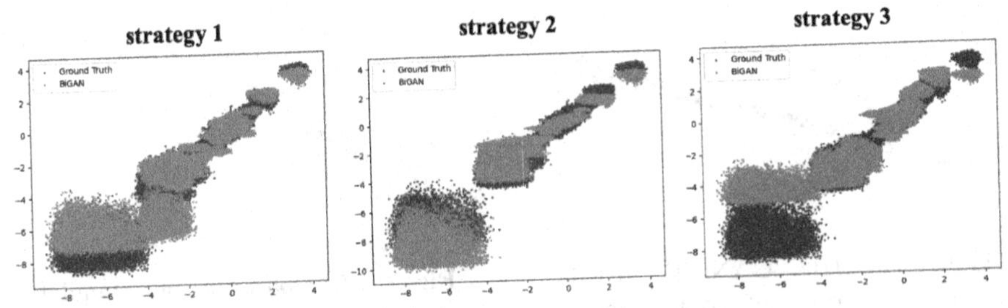

Fig. 5. The relationship between the counterfactual action a_t' and the next state: counterfactual case s_{t+1}' generated by BiCoGAN or ground truth s_{t+1}

To address this issue, we define three strategies of counterfactual action selection based on whether or not the greetings are selected: In strategy 1, all the greetings are selected, we shuffle all the real-world actions as $\{a_t'\}$; in strategy 2, the first greeting is not selected, we remove the first utterance of persuader $\{a_0\}$ per dialogue, then sample from the rest actions $\{a_t\}$ - $\{a_0\}$ as $\{a_t'\}$; in strategy 3, all the greetings are not selected, we remove the first three utterances $\{a_0, a_1, a_2\}$ per dialogue, then sample from the rest actions $\{a_t\}$ - $\{a_0, a_1, a_2\}$ as $\{a_t'\}$. To leverage the quality of the counterfactual data across the three strategies of counterfactual action sets, we conducted a comparison between the generated counterfactual states by the trained BiCoGAN generator and the ground truth states, seen in Fig. 5. We can observe that strategy 2 yields superior results as it better aligns the real world's next state, s_{t+1}, and counterfactual next state, s_{t+1}', compared to the other two strategies. Finally, counterfactual data $\tilde{D}$ can be represented as

$$\begin{aligned}\tilde{D} &= \{\tilde{D}_0, \tilde{D}_1, ..., \tilde{D}_i, ..., \tilde{D}_{N-1}\} \\ &= \{(s_0', a_0', s_1', a_1', ..., s_t', a_t', ..., s_{T-1}')_{j=0}^{\Sigma-1}\}_{i=0}^{N-1},\end{aligned} \tag{6}$$

where T typically represents the total number of steps or time points in the sequence, Σ is the number of dialogues, and N is the number of counterfactual databases.

Following the estimation of the dynamics model and the creation of an augmented dataset $\tilde{D}$ through counterfactual reasoning, the subsequent step involves training policies on the counterfactual data $\tilde{D}$ to optimize the Q values and improve the future predicted cumulative rewards. To ensure fairness in policy learning, we aim for balanced predicted cumulative rewards of $\tilde{D}$, with 50 counterfactual databases exceeding and 50 counterfactual databases falling short of the ground truth, thus forming our final counterfactual data $\tilde{D}$. (cf: Sect. 3.3).

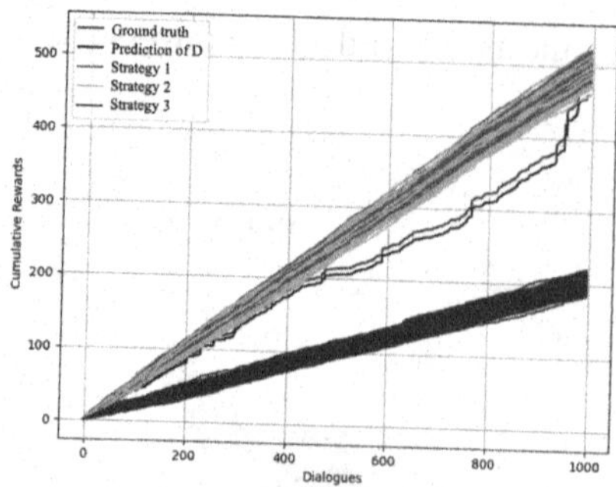

Fig. 6. The (BiCoGAN + DPPR) reward predictions of counterfactual data on three strategies and real data D (black), compared with ground-truth (blue). (Color figure online)

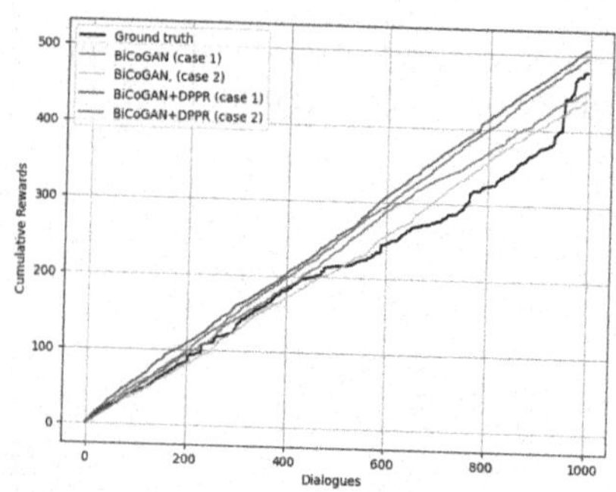

Fig. 7. Comparison of cumulative rewards in dialogues between ground truth and counterfactual cases utilizing BiCoGAN or BiCoGAN+DPPR.

For cumulative reward computation, we first input the dialogue into the reward model (Equation (5)), then perform a cumulative sum operation on the predicted reward of the trained reward model. Figure 6 shows the cumulative reward prediction for the three strategies, where strategies 1 and 2 are mostly higher than the ground truth's, while strategy 3 is lower than the ground truth.

During policy learning with the D3QN model, the process involves computing Q values for 100 action candidates from 100 counterfactual databases at each state. The model selects the action with maximum Q value for each time step. As a result, this process generates a counterfactual dialogue and then utilizes the trained reward model (cf: Equation (5)) to predict the reward. Determining whether the counterfactual dialogue in natural language signifies a donation or not will be our focus for future work. For the optimization of D3QN, we established two distinct cases based on the optimization time for the loss function. In **Case 1**, where the loss function is optimized once per dialogue. For example, the sequence of j-th dialogue starts from state $s^{'}_{j,0}$. It proceeds with a series of action-state pairs $a^{'}_{j,0}$, $s^{'}_{j,1}$, ..., $a^{'}_{j,i}$, $s^{'}_{j,i}$, ..., $a^{'}_{j,12}$, $s^{'}_{j,12}$, for each state $s^{'}_{j,i}$, based on $k = argmax(Q(s^{'}_{j,i}, a^{'}_{j})_{i=0}^{N})$ (N=99) to select the next action $a^{'}_{j,k}$ from the j-th dialogue of $\tilde{D}_k$. In contrast, **Case 2** differs as the loss function optimization takes place once per state. The action selection process is illustrated in Fig. 8

After the policy learning, we obtain a corresponding counterfactual dialogue for donation prediction, aligning with each real-world dialogue. The sequences of real-world dialogues begin from s_0, while the counterfactual dialogues starts from $s^{'}_0$, where maintaining the equivalence of $s_0 = s^{'}_0$. In Fig. 7, the cumulative rewards of both BiCoGAN and BiCoGAN+DPPR models in two cases are higher than the ground truth overall. It can be observed that the BiCoGAN+DPPR (case 1) gets the best cumulative rewards and BiCoGAN+DPPR (case 2) obtains the second results over dialogues. The final cumulative rewards/donation

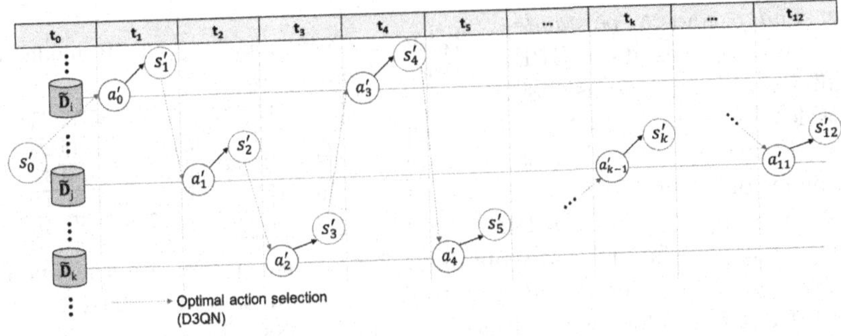

Fig. 8. The process of counterfactual dialogue produced for reward prediction during the policy learning.

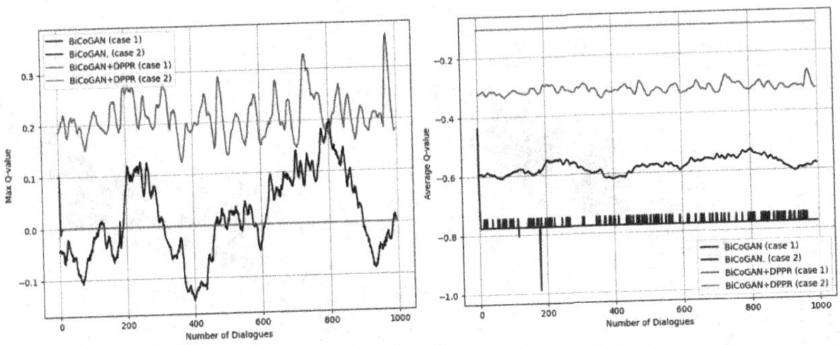

Fig. 9. Comparison of maximum and average Q values in dialogues between ground truth and counterfactual cases utilizing BiCoGAN or BiCoGAN+DPPR.

amounts are \$506.82 (+\$29.2) and \$496.15 (+\$18.53) respectively, higher than ground truth cumulative rewards \$477.62 and the BiCoGAN in case 1 and case 2, achieved \$453.02 (-\$24.6) and \$441.11 (-\$36.51), respectively.

Furthermore, when estimating the Q-values of the learned optimal policy (Fig. 9), the optimal policy derived from BiCoGAN with LPDs exhibits higher estimated Q-values, both in maximum and average, compared to the single BiCoGAN model. In Case 1 of BiCoGAN+DPPR, the maximum Q-values surpass Case 2, while the average Q-values are lower in Case 1 than in Case 2. This discrepancy arises from weight optimization in D3QN primarily at the dialogue's end, potentially leading to actions with exceptionally high Q-values.

4.4 Ablation Study

Impact of window size plays an essential role in the DPPR model, it will influence the accuracy of prediction and determine how much information is meaningful for the individual LPDs estimation. We separately set the window size as 1, 2, 3, and 4 turns, each turn includes exchange utterances between a *persuader* and a *persuadee*. The evaluation[5] results of DPPR on different window size is shown in Table 2, we can observe that when the window sizes decrease, the precision increase, so we choose one-turn to train DPPR model for counterfactual data building. To further investigate the one-turn trained model, we leverage the first top two canonical components, shown in Fig. 10, the CCA values for each are 0.894 and 0.888, respectively, which indicate there exist relatively high correlations between the one-turn utterance and personality.

Table 2. Performance of DPPR model with varied window sizes.

Win size	MSE	RMSE	MAPE	R2	MAE
1 turn	0.166	0.407	0.092	0.830	0.254
2 turns	0.258	0.508	0.119	0.641	0.323
4 turns	0.441	0.664	0.178	0.387	0.474
8 turns	0.488	0.698	0.195	0.319	0.518

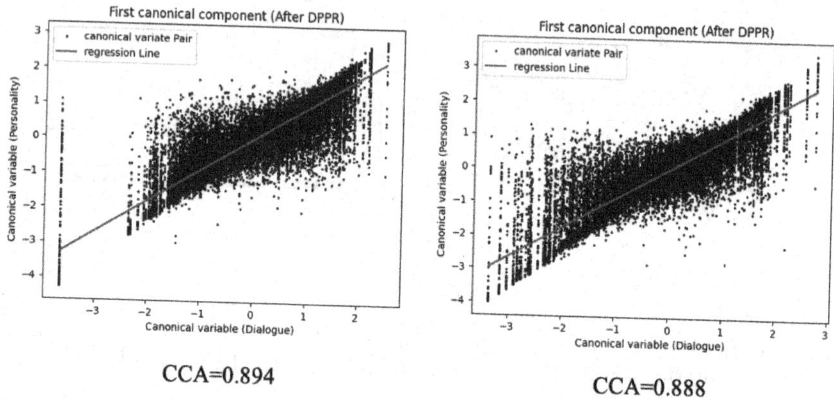

Fig. 10. The canonical coefficient of the top two CCA components.

5 Conclusion

In this paper, we highlight the limitations of existing persuasive conversation systems, particularly in adapting to individual user traits. We augmented the BiCoGAN model, which creates counterfactual data that simulates an alternative world, with our DPPR models to enable awareness of latent user dimensions during persuasive interactions. This facilitated an optimized conversation flow using the D3QN model. In the experiments conducted on the PersuasionForGood dataset, our approach showcased superiority over existing method, BiCoGAN, and ground truth, demonstrating the efficacy of leveraging latent traits to enhance persuasion outcomes.

[5] MSE - Mean Squared Error; RMSE - Root Mean Squared Error; MAPE - Mean Absolute Percentage Error; R2 - R-squared (Coefficient of Determination); MAE - Mean Absolute Error.

References

1. Chakrabarty, T., Hidey, C., Muresan, S., McKeown, K., Hwang, A.: AMPERSAND: Argument mining for PERSuAsive oNline discussions. In: EMNLP-IJCNLP, pp. 2933–2943. ACL, Hong Kong, China (Nov 2019)
2. Devlin, J., Chang, M.W., Lee, K., Toutanova, K.: Bert: Pre-training of deep bidirectional transformers for language understanding. arXiv preprint arXiv:1810.04805 (2018)
3. Hirsh, J.B., Kang, S.K., Bodenhausen, G.V.: Personalized persuasion: tailoring persuasive appeals to recipients' personality traits. Psychol. Sci. **23**(6), 578–581 (2012)
4. Jaiswal, A., AbdAlmageed, W., Wu, Y., Natarajan, P.: Bidirectional conditional generative adversarial networks. In: Jawahar, C.V., Li, H., Mori, G., Schindler, K. (eds.) Computer Vision – ACCV 2018: 14th Asian Conference on Computer Vision, Perth, Australia, December 2–6, 2018, Revised Selected Papers, Part III, pp. 216–232. Springer International Publishing, Cham (2019). https://doi.org/10.1007/978-3-030-20893-6_14
5. Kaptein, M., Markopoulos, P., De Ruyter, B., Aarts, E.: Personalizing persuasive technologies: explicit and implicit personalization using persuasion profiles. Int. J. Hum Comput Stud. **77**, 38–51 (2015)
6. Kingma, D.P., Ba, J.: Adam: A method for stochastic optimization. arXiv preprint arXiv:1412.6980 (2014)
7. Lu, C., Huang, B., Wang, K., Hernández-Lobato, J.M., Zhang, K., Schölkopf, B.: Sample-efficient reinforcement learning via counterfactual-based data augmentation. arXiv preprint arXiv:2012.09092 (2020)
8. Matz, S., Teeny, J., Vaid, S.S., Harari, G.M., Cerf, M.: The potential of generative ai for personalized persuasion at scale (2023)
9. Mnih, V., et al.: Human-level control through deep reinforcement learning. Nature **518**(7540), 529–533 (2015)
10. Orji, R., Tondello, G.F., Nacke, L.E.: Personalizing persuasive strategies in gameful systems to gamification user types. In: Proceedings of the 2018 CHI Conference On Human Factors in Computing Systems, pp. 1–14 (2018)
11. Pearl, J., et al.: Models, reasoning and inference. Cambridge, UK: CambridgeUniversityPress **19**(2), 3 (2000)
12. Prakken, H.: Formal systems for persuasion dialogue. Knowl. Eng. Rev. **21**(2), 163–188 (2006)
13. Raghu, A., Komorowski, M., Ahmed, I., Celi, L., Szolovits, P., Ghassemi, M.: Deep reinforcement learning for sepsis treatment. arXiv preprint arXiv:1711.09602 (2017)
14. Rieger, A., Shaheen, Q.U.A., Sierra, C., Theune, M., Tintarev, N.: Towards healthy engagement with online debates: An investigation of debate summaries and personalized persuasive suggestions. In: Adjunct Proceedings of the 30th ACM Conference on User Modeling, Adaptation and Personalization, pp. 192–199 (2022)
15. Roccas, S., Sagiv, L., Schwartz, S.H., Knafo, A.: The big five personality factors and personal values. Pers. Soc. Psychol. Bull. **28**(6), 789–801 (2002)
16. Shi, W., Wang, X., Oh, Y.J., Zhang, J., Sahay, S., Yu, Z.: Effects of persuasive dialogues: testing bot identities and inquiry strategies. In: Proceedings of the 2020 CHI Conference on Human Factors in Computing Systems, pp. 1–13 (2020)
17. Su, H., Shen, X., Hu, P., Li, W., Chen, Y.: Dialogue generation with gan. In: Proceedings of the AAAI Conference on Artificial Intelligence, vol. 32 (2018)

18. Torning, K., Oinas-Kukkonen, H.: Persuasive system design: state of the art and future directions. In: Proceedings of the 4th International Conference on Persuasive Technology, pp. 1–8 (2009)
19. Tran, N., Alikhani, M., Litman, D.: How to ask for donations? learning user-specific persuasive dialogue policies through online interactions. In: Proceedings of the 30th ACM Conference on User Modeling, Adaptation and Personalization, pp. 12–22 (2022)
20. Wachsmuth, H., et al.: Computational argumentation quality assessment in natural language. In: Proceedings of the 15th Conference of the European Chapter of the Association for Computational Linguistics: Volume 1, Long Papers, pp. 176–187 (2017)
21. Wang, X., et al.: Persuasion for good: Towards a personalized persuasive dialogue system for social good. In: Korhonen, A., Traum, D.R., Màrquez, L. (eds.) ACL 2019, pp. 5635–5649. ACL (2019)
22. Wei, Z., Liu, Y., Li, Y.: Is this post persuasive? ranking argumentative comments in online forum. In: Erk, K., Smith, N.A. (eds.) Proceedings of the 54th Annual Meeting of the Association for Computational Linguistics (Volume 2: Short Papers), pp. 195–200. ACL, Berlin, Germany (Aug 2016)
23. Wei, Z., Liu, Y., Li, Y.: Is this post persuasive? ranking argumentative comments in online forum. In: Proceedings of the 54th Annual Meeting of the Association for Computational Linguistics (Volume 2: Short Papers), pp. 195–200 (2016)
24. Yang, D., Chen, J., Yang, Z., Jurafsky, D., Hovy, E.: Let's make your request more persuasive: Modeling persuasive strategies via semi-supervised neural nets on crowdfunding platforms. In: Proceedings of the 2019 Conference of the North American Chapter of the Association for Computational Linguistics: Human Language Technologies, Volume 1 (Long and Short Papers), pp. 3620–3630 (2019)
25. Yoshino, K., Ishikawa, Y., Mizukami, M., Suzuki, Y., Sakti, S., Nakamura, S.: Dialogue scenario collection of persuasive dialogue with emotional expressions via crowdsourcing. In: Proceedings of the Eleventh International Conference on Language Resources and Evaluation (LREC 2018) (2018)

Author Index

N. Baghaei et al. (Eds.): PERSUASIVE 2024, LNCS 14636, pp. 301–302, 2024.
https://doi.org/10.1007/978-3-031-58226-4

S

T

V

W

Y

Z

Printed in the United States
by Baker & Taylor Publisher Services